The Appian Way
Adolphe Appia and the Scenography of Modern Architecture

The Appian Way
Adolphe Appia and the Scenography of Modern Architecture

Ross Anderson

edited by Thomas Weaver

PARK BOOKS

to Hannah

PRELUDE

One of the few surviving photographs of Adolphe Appia shows the ageing scenographer seated at his drawing board, captured in a moment of repose. Wearing a striped nautical *pull marin* and a canvas jacket, he gazes past lightly patterned curtains towards the distant horizon. Most of the room is lost in shadow as the light from the window falls on him. Heavily bearded and greying at the temples, there is something of the solitary prophet or ancient mariner about his bearing.

Appia's drawing board is tilted gently towards him, away from the camera, so it is not possible to tell what he was working on at the time, but since the photograph was taken in the summer of 1909, it was very likely one of his austere yet atmospheric *Espaces rythmiques*, all of which are abstract compositions of stairs, landings, platforms and terraces, staged before a distant horizon under a luminous sky.

If people know of Appia, it tends to be through this set of drawings, or rather a small sample of them, typically reproduced as irresolute black and white images serving as a complement to narratives concerning other stage designers or modern architects. While others performed heroically upon the stage that Appia prepared for them, he himself has gone largely unacknowledged, due partly to the underrated role of theatre in the development of the modern aesthetic, and partly to his own character – always reticent and distant yet also always enigmatically present. Shortly before he died, Appia wrote to a friend – whether in resignation or indignation – 'anonymity is the essence of my whole existence'.[1]

One of the reasons for writing this book has been to relieve Appia of his anonymity. Aligned with the writing of micro-history – an approach that in the most basic of terms attempts to 'restore personal dignity to the losers of history'[2] – it traces the contours of Appia's life: his personal circumstances, convictions, aesthetic preferences, motivations, desires and vices, successes and multiple setbacks. However, occasionally the narrative steps back from Appia in order to situate him within the life of his times. That is, it operates at two different scales: the micro and the macro. In his final work, *History: The Last Things Before the Last*, the German journalist and historian Siegfried Kracauer described these two different kinds of historical gaze as having two different focal lengths.[3] Following him, we might say that the micro-history dimension of the book is akin to a portrait, while the macro view takes in the cultural landscape of Central Europe over the final quarter of the nineteenth century and the first half of the twentieth.

Individual characters and events are generally introduced and developed in the order in which they appeared, and the whole is structured as a dramatic story, making it a work of narrative history that acknowledges the world of human actions as 'both real and mysterious, that is to say, mysteriously real'.[4] As a work of historiography, it is firmly grounded in archival research, drawing on a wide range of primary sources including Appia's drawings, photographs and official records, plus the many letters, postcards and calling cards that he sent and received – all aimed at constructing a comprehensive portrayal of his life and his work within the horizons of his time.[5]

While Appia undoubtedly commands centre stage, he is surrounded by a remarkable ensemble that includes fellow scenographers, composers and musicians, directors and actors, choreographers and dancers, writers and

facing and following spread
Giovanni Battista Piranesi, Via Appia, *c* 1756.

publishers, political philosophers and dictators, painters and architects, photographers and archaeologists, surgeons, psychologists and even a hypnotist. Although some of these characters play fleeting roles, many reappear time and again as Appia's story unfolds in a European drama beginning and ending in Switzerland, with interludes in France, Germany and Italy, where he was identified by different names – *Adolphe*, *Adolf* or *Adolfo*.

Partly in sympathy with Appia's own inclination to remain in the background, the narrative largely develops through foreshadowing, recollection and analogy rather than through an overarching thematic principle or theoretical framework. In the process, some of the responsibility for making sense of the drama, composed as four acts and a coda, is devolved to the reader.

While the title of this book – *The Appian Way* – refers to the way of Adolphe Appia, it of course also brings to mind the Via Appia, one of ancient Rome's most important consular roads, tethering the capital to the port of Brindisi in the south.[6] Known as *regina longarum viarum*, the queen of the long roads,[7] the Via Appia was in fact a kind of necropolis – a memorial avenue lined with tombs and mausolea, monuments and altars, shrines and cinerary urns. The scene awaiting the traveller was a mingling of 'the grand, the grim, the holy and the sordid'.[8] Long after the empire had crumbled, the German polymath Johann Wolfgang von Goethe embarked on his famed *Italian Journey* and recorded the following in his 1786 travel diary: 'Today I visited the ruined tombs along the Via Appia ... The Romans built for eternity; they omitted nothing from their calculations except the foolishness of the vandals, for whom nothing is sacred.'[9]

The impressions the Via Appia made that day on Goethe were coupled with those he collected for his library, including an etching made by Giovanni Battista Piranesi, which the famously inventive printmaker, architect and antiquarian used as the second frontispiece to volume two of his *Le antichità romane*.[10] In Piranesi's visually arresting version of the Via Appia, which owes as much to his graphic imagination as it does to archaeological reality, a remarkable assortment of memorials to the dead vie for attention, fronting onto the 'queen of the long roads' that issues towards a point on the horizon, straight as a line in one of Appia's *Espaces rythmiques*.

Piranesi invites an analogy between the Via Appia, with its jostling sepulchral monuments set amidst regularly paced milestones, and the eventful life of an individual set against the constant rhythm of the years. His scene quite literally centres on the second milestone, meaning that when the etching was printed as a double-page spread the stout freestanding column on which 'II VIA APPIA' is inscribed descends into the gutter between the pages and disappears out of sight. Appia himself might be thought of in the same terms – central to the drama of modern scenography and architecture and yet withdrawn from view, overwhelmed by the dominant personalities who surrounded him during his lifetime, and by the dominant narratives that developed in their wake.

ALAN
RAMSAY
SCOTI
PICTORI
ET IN
OMNI
LIBERAL
ARTIV
FACVLTATE
CELEBER
D.M.
VIA
APPIA

SEPVLCHRVM
SERVILIORVM

II. Tom.
DIS·MAN
TVLLIAE
M·T·CICE
F·CARISS
CASTISSI
VIXIT·AN
XXXII·P
QVOS·EIV
ANIMVS
AD·SVPE
EVOLAVIT
ANTIQVVS·BIVII
VIARVM·APPIAE
ET·ARDEATINAE
PROSPECTVS
AB·III·LAPIDEM·EXTRA
PORTAM·CAPENAM

5"
(FIG 26 · pp 125)

EARLY

preceding left page
Appia seated at his drawing board in the Château de Glérolles at age forty-seven in 1909.

Just as the sound of the name suggests, the roots of the Appia family tree are Italian, and they can be traced to the northwest region of Piedmont in the fifteenth century. A rough sketch of the family's coat of arms made by their unofficial historian shows three silver magpies standing proudly in formation above two crossed hatchets; Appia probably derives from *happia*, an old Gallo-Romance word for hatchet. Though the full account is lost to history, Appia's ancestors were apparently Waldensians, members of a fundamentalist religious movement that based its faith entirely on the teachings of the Bible. Like other families in the Piedmont region that lies just to the south of the Alps, they found the new doctrines of Jean Calvin appealing and travelled north in the 1540s to Geneva to hear him speak at St Pierre Cathedral – he would preach twice on Sundays and three times during the week.

below
The Appia Family coat of arms, drawn by Béatrice Appia Blacher.

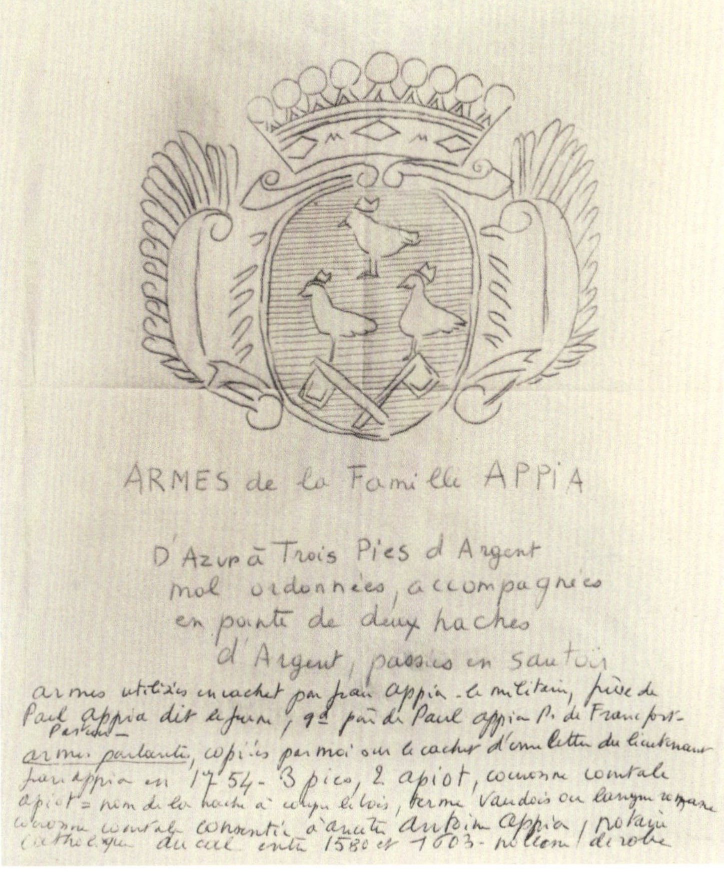

Three centuries and countless sermons later, Adolphe Appia was born in the city of Calvin on Monday, 1 September 1862, in the street in which the theologian himself had lived, possibly even in the very same house – the address was 5 rue Calvin. A photograph taken from just outside the Appia family's front door shows the cathedral dominating that part of the city; not only its urban setting but also the moral orientation, and even aesthetic disposition, of the citizens living below it.[1] On the whole, Genevans lived quiet and well-regulated lives. The Appia family was no exception. Appia's parents, Louis Paul Amédée Appia and Anne Caroline Lasserre, had three children – Paul, Hélène and Marie – before the arrival of their fourth, Adolphe.

Appia's father, Louis, was born in 1818, the son of an evangelical pastor in Frankfurt. After attending secondary school in that city and Geneva, he began his medical studies in Heidelberg in 1838, which he concluded with his doctorate in 1843. Louis returned to Frankfurt, which is where he met Caroline. After marrying in 1853, the newlyweds moved to Geneva. Louis quickly gained renown as a surgeon. He would be elected president of the Société médicale de Genève in 1861, but it was in 1863 – the year after his son Adolphe was born – that he banded together with four comrades to create the Commission de Cinq (Committee of Five), precursor to the International Committee of the Red Cross.

The Commission de Cinq believed that wounded soldiers, no matter which side they happened to be fighting on, should receive appropriate medical treatment after being conveyed to safety by brave stretcher-bearers whose only concern was for the immediate well-being of their prone charges. This was a radical idea, certainly, and one that to his great credit Appia's father pursued with extreme conviction, going so far as to volunteer to be the very first to test the idea in the midst of a war. He travelled north to the contested

following page
Armband worn by doctor Louis Paul Amédée Appia in 1864 as a neutral observer during the war between Prussia and Denmark; an extract from Appia's birth certificate, 1 September 1862.

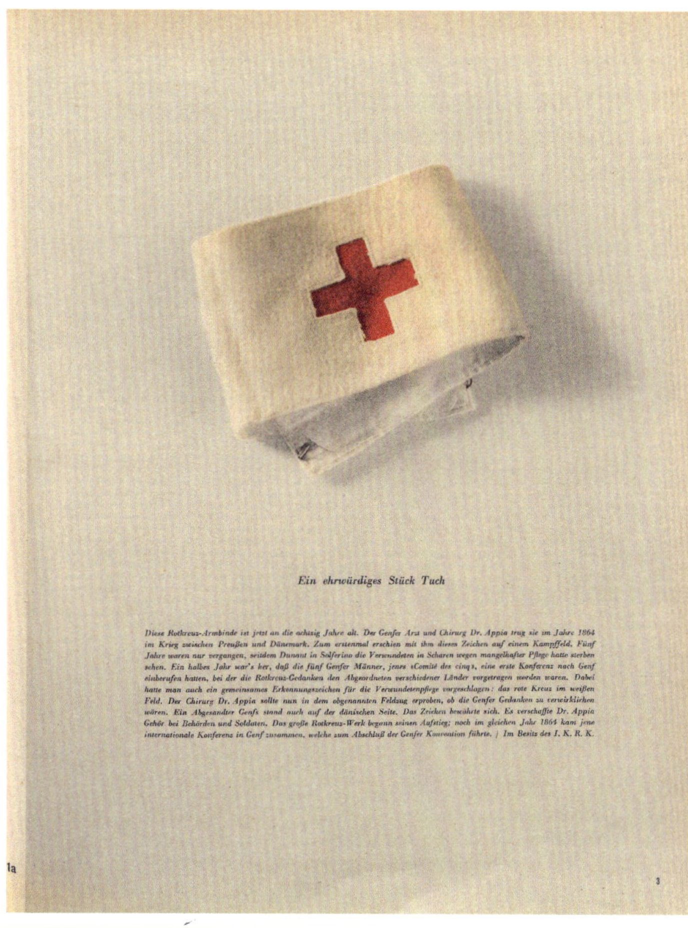

Ein ehrwürdiges Stück Tuch

Diese Rotkreuz-Armbinde ist jetzt an die achtzig Jahre alt. Der Genfer Arzt und Chirurg Dr. Appia trug sie im Jahre 1864 im Krieg zwischen Preußen und Dänemark. Zum erstenmal erschien mit ihm dieses Zeichen auf einem Kampffeld. Fünf Jahre waren nur vergangen, seitdem Dunant in Solferino die Verwundeten in Scharen wegen mangelhafter Pflege hatte sterben sehen. Ein halbes Jahr war's her, daß die fünf Genfer Männer, jenes «Comité des cinq», eine erste Konferenz nach Genf einberufen hatten, bei der die Rotkreuz-Gedanken den Abgeordneten verschiedener Länder vorgetragen worden waren. Dabei hatte man auch ein gemeinsames Erkennungszeichen für die Verwundetenpflege vorgeschlagen: das rote Kreuz im weißen Feld. Der Chirurg Dr. Appia sollte nun in dem obgenannten Feldzug erproben, ob die Genfer Gedanken zu verwirklichen wären. Ein Abgesandter Genfs stand auch auf der dänischen Seite. Das Zeichen bewährte sich. Es verschaffte Dr. Appia Gehör bei Behörden und Soldaten. Das große Rotkreuz-Werk begann seinen Aufstieg; noch im gleichen Jahr 1864 kam jene internationale Konferenz in Genf zusammen, welche zum Abschluß der Genfer Konvention führte. / Im Besitz des I. K. R. K.

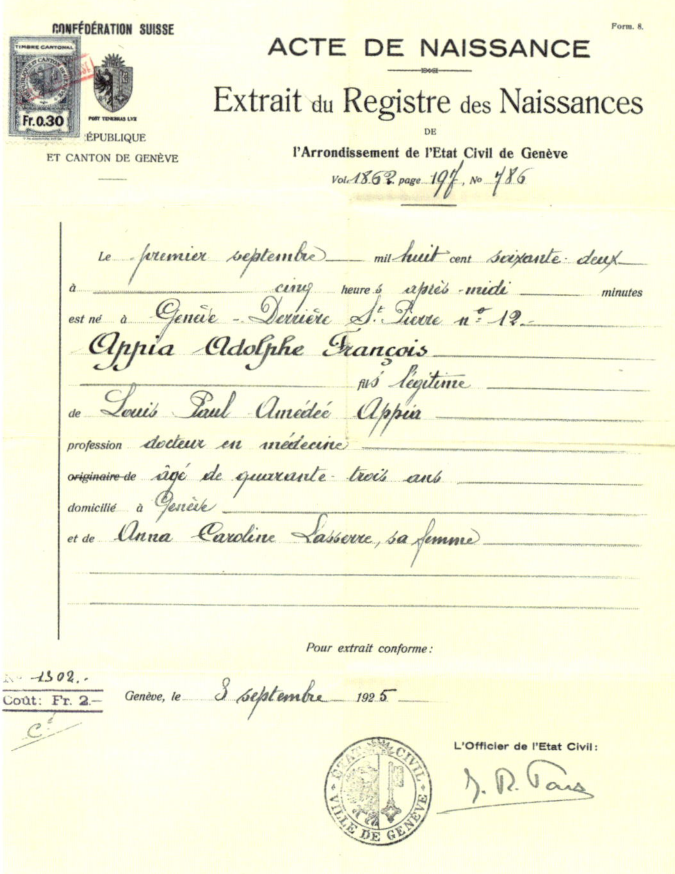

CONFÉDÉRATION SUISSE

Fr. 0.30

RÉPUBLIQUE ET CANTON DE GENÈVE

Form. 8.

ACTE DE NAISSANCE

Extrait du Registre des Naissances de l'Arrondissement de l'Etat Civil de Genève

Vol. 1862 page 197, No 486

Le premier septembre mil huit cent soixante-deux à cinq heures après-midi minutes est né à Genève - Derrière St Pierre no 12 Appia Adolphe François fils légitime de Louis Paul Amédée Appia profession docteur en médecine âgé de quarante-trois ans domicilié à Genève et de Anna Caroline Lasserre, sa femme

Pour extrait conforme:

No 1302.
Coût: Fr. 2.–

Genève, le 3 septembre 1925

L'Officier de l'Etat Civil:

Danish-Prussian border in April 1864, and at the Battle of Dybbøl pulled on the now-famous white armband emblazoned with a red cross – the very first time the symbol had appeared on a battlefield, according to the author of 'Ein ehrwürdiges Stück Tuch' (A Venerable Piece of Cloth). The idea of the Red Cross had been presented to representatives of various countries just six months before, at the first conference convened by the Commission de Cinq in Geneva: 'They proposed that there should be some common identifier worn by those who were taking care of the wounded – the Red Cross in a field of white. Now the time had come for the surgeon Dr Appia to test the idea, in the heat of battle. An emissary from Geneva also stood on the side of the Danish. The symbol proved itself – Dr Appia was acknowledged by commanders and soldiers alike.'[2]

Though recognised at the moment of the battle, Louis Appia was less well acknowledged by history, as Adolphe wrote in a downcast letter to a friend, conflating his father's fate with his own: 'Anonymity is the essence of my whole existence, as it was for my father, Dr Louis Appia. According to the evidence (letters and other documents) it was he – Appia – who gave Dunant the idea for the Red Cross. But it is Dunant who is given the credit, and it is he who has a street named after him in Geneva! And does anybody know that it was my father's idea to invert the Swiss flag (a white cross on a red background) to create a symbol for the new association? No. So, Appia and anonymity, they belong together.'[3]

Though they shared their anonymity, Adolphe and his father had little else in common. 'The notion of the theatre – even its name – was banned in our family', Appia wrote. But rather than deterring the future scenographer, his parents' prohibition charged his interest in the theatrical milieu: 'There is no doubt in my mind that this abstention had the contrary effect – it only served to stimulate my imagination.'[4]

Just why his parents decided to send Adolphe to boarding school is unknown, but in 1873, at the age of eleven, he was enrolled in the Collège de la ville de Vevey. Academically, young Appia was a middling student, and part way through his studies he asked to be moved from the classical stream that focused on languages and literature to the more vocationally oriented industrial stream, as recorded in a letter sent by the head of the school to Appia's father on 19 June 1877: 'Your son asked that I move him out of the *latine* class into *industrielle*, and I was pleased to approve his request. Whatever advantages classical studies may indeed have, I am convinced that there is nothing to be gained by fighting against a student's inclinations and convictions. And besides, your son is already fifteen years old, so postponing a decision would be a mistake so far as the remainder of his education goes – merely antagonising him out of a sense of institutional obligation could have the most unfortunate effect upon him. Finally, the lessons that he is now undertaking correspond to his natural leanings, he is applying himself, and he enjoys them – that is the most important thing. He is currently in the third term of *industrielle* and will be able to continue his studies here – if you deem it is suitable – for another two and half years, and then go on to study in Zurich at the ETH (Eidgenössische Technische Hochschule) or in some other similar place of higher education. To summarise, if my point of view carries some weight in the matter, I am convinced that bearing in mind the natural aptitudes that your son Adolphe possesses, and also the condition of his health, it will be better to relinquish classical languages rather than impose them upon him. Thank you, moreover, for asking me for my opinion on this matter.'[5]

Photograph taken from the front step of the Appia family home at 5 rue Calvin in Geneva, looking toward St Pierre Cathedral, 1885.

Appia's grades duly improved in the *industrielle* stream; the range of subjects suited him better, and the skills that he learned in *dessin industriel* (technical drawing) in particular would be decisive for his later achievements as a scenographer. This must have been where Appia learned how to set up and execute a perspective drawing, gaining the drafting skills to complement his natural ability in *dessin artistique*. Unsurprisingly, music was the other subject in the curriculum that Appia enjoyed and performed well in.[6]

There were few opportunities for Appia to indulge in the theatrical world that so 'stimulated his imagination' at school in Vevey. But years later, he would recount a decisive episode that took place while working with a classmate on a cardboard model for a stage. When it came to the question of scenery, his friend wanted to crowd the small stage with conventional painted flats. Appia, however, insisted on making three-dimensional pieces. An argument broke out and, as Appia recalled, 'in order to restore the peace, we solemnly burnt the whole thing down'.[7]

St Pierre Cathedral in Geneva, *c* 1888; two photographs from 1888 of the sculpture of Jean Calvin in Geneva.

With the kindling of that little blaze, Appia made himself the lead character in his own *Bildungsroman*, a literary form in which a simple-minded hero – one example of the type is Parsifal – 'ranges heaven and hell, makes terms with them and strikes a pact with the unknown'.[8] The hero's character develops 'in conflict between bourgeois decorum and adventure', as Thomas Mann wrote.[9] Those words hold true for Appia himself, but also for the conflicted times he was living in – a late-nineteenth century dominated, not only in the world of music but in many other fields besides, by Richard Wagner.

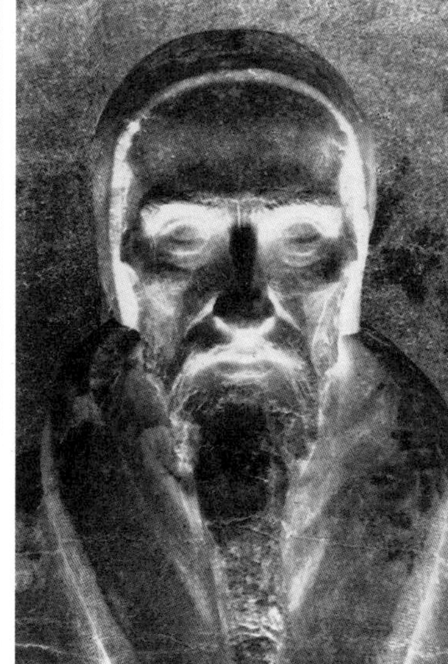

A recent Wagner scholar has asserted: 'There is no path into the twentieth century – for good or evil – that bypasses Wagner'.[10] The imperious German composer, conductor and polemicist became the single unwavering presence in Appia's life, inspiring his first theoretical musings and – most importantly – his first drawings, which, with their spare moodiness and architectural forms, laid the foundation for all that would follow. The drawings he made for Wagner's majestic *Wort-Tondrama* (word-tone drama), *Der Ring des Nibelungen*, project a modern aesthetic that would at first seem *contra* Wagner, but what Appia was in fact attempting to do was deliver into the visual realm what he recognised and admired most in the music – its *newness*. Friedrich Nietzsche likewise paid tribute to Wagner as a paragon of modernity, writing that it is 'through Wagner that modernity speaks most intimately, concealing neither its good nor its evil … and conversely: one has almost completed an account of the value of what is modern once one has gained clarity about what is good and evil in Wagner'.[11]

The language through which Wagner's modernity spoke was German. Unlike most opera composers, he penned both the libretto and the music, and had a keen ear for both, as Nietzsche noted: 'Wagner's poetry is all about revelling in the German language, the warmth and candour in his communion with it, something that cannot be felt in any other German writer except perhaps Goethe. Earthiness of expression, reckless terseness, control and rhythmic diversity, an extraordinary richness of powerful and significant words, the simplification of syntactical constructions, an almost unique inventiveness in the language of surging feeling and presentiment, and every now and then a totally pure bubbling forth of colloquialisms and proverbs – we ought to make a list of such characteristics, and even then, we would forget the most powerful and admirable of them … the forging of a distinctive new language for each work and the giving of a *new* body and a *new* sound to each *new* interior world.'[12]

Wagner's distinctively new modern world was in fact forged in the crucible of the past. He was inspired not only by Germanic myths but also by the real geographical features that often feature in them; mountain ranges, forests and rivers, such as the mighty Rhine, which in the German Middle Ages was simply referred to as *der Fluß* – the river. In his *Autobiographische Skizze* (Autobiographical Sketch), Wagner recalled his emotions on returning to Dresden after a sojourn in Paris: 'For the first time I saw the Rhine – with hot tears in my eyes, I, poor artist, swore eternal fidelity to my German fatherland.'[13]

The reason Wagner moved back to Dresden was to oversee the premiere production of his opera *Rienzi* at the Königliches Hoftheater (Royal Court Theatre). Its success led to other staging invitations in the city, culminating in his full-time appointment as the Royal Saxon Court Conductor. All the while, Wagner mixed the cultural with the political and became an active figure in left-wing politics, an involvement that eventually spelled the end of his time in the city. Wagner's discontent and that of his socialist German nationalist comrades came to a head in 1849 with the May Uprising in Dresden, in which the composer played a supporting role – he apparently made hand grenades and stood as a lookout atop the Church of the Holy Cross – whereas his friend, the architect Gottfried Semper, played a greater role as a member of the Kommunalgarde (Civic Guard), erecting barricades and fighting in the streets. When the rebellion collapsed, both Wagner and Semper were declared 'Staatsverbrecher und Hochverräter' (traitors and enemies of the State) and went on the run, though in different directions – Semper to France and Wagner to Switzerland. This is how the composer was described in the warrant issued for his arrest: 'Wagner, Richard, Conductor in Dresden; Age: 38, Stature: Medium, Hair: Brown, wears glasses'; the architect was described as 'Semper, Gottfried, Professor of Architecture in Dresden; Age: Around 40, Stature: Medium, Hair: Brown with flecks of white, Complexion: Pale, moustache and beard.'[14] Neither was caught, but the State long maintained its enmity; Semper later wrote to his fellow architect Heinrich Hübsch: 'What must I have done in '48, that one persecutes me forever? One single barricade did I construct – it held because it was practical and since it was practical, it was beautiful.'[15]

Richard Wagner at age forty-seven in 1860.

Settled in Switzerland but without any income or opportunity to perform, Wagner set about writing a set of polemical essays, the motivation for which he revealed in a letter to fellow composer Franz Liszt in 1849: 'I must make people afraid of me. Well, I have no money, but what I do have is an enormous desire to commit acts of artistic terrorism.'[16] In *Die Kunst und*

following page
Hand grenade allegedly made by Richard Wagner in 1849; conductor's baton designed by Gottfried Semper for Richard Wagner in 1858.

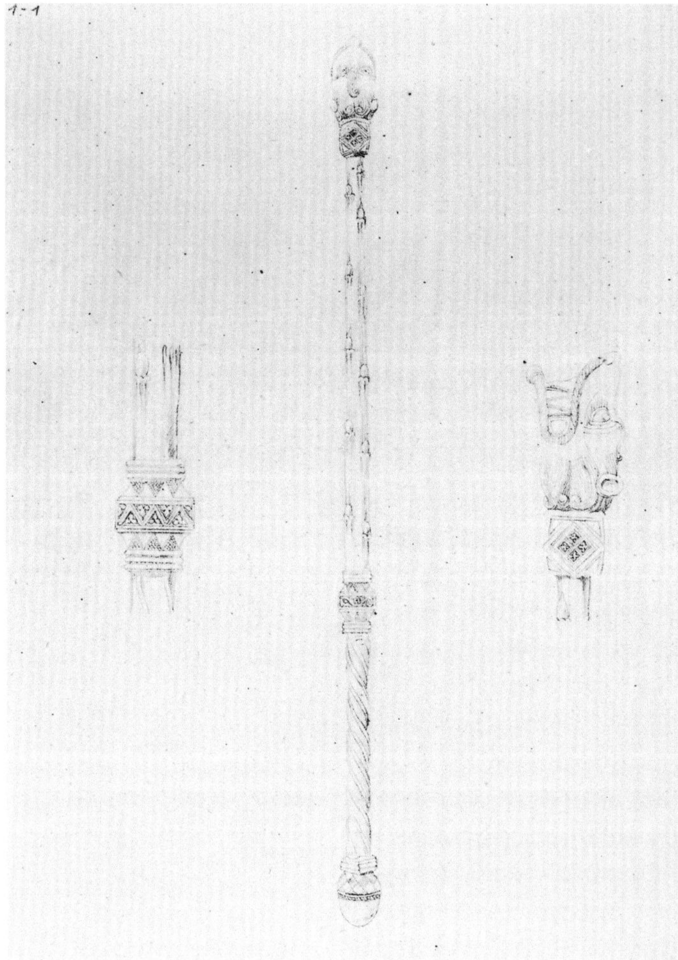

die Revolution (Art and Revolution) and *Das Kunstwerk der Zukunft* (The Artwork of the Future), Wagner formalised his now famous vision of the *Gesamtkunstwerk* (total work of art) – the unison of music, theatre, dance, poetry, painting, sculpture and architecture.[17] He promoted art as a means to a higher culture through the orchestration of a self-referential aesthetic order of total concordance, all controlled by the artist-conductor (himself).[18] In *The Artwork of the Future* he wrote of the unifying task of architecture: 'Architecture can set before itself no higher task than to frame for a fellowship of artists, who in their own persons portray the life of man, the special surroundings necessary for the display of the human *Kunstwerk*. Only that edifice built according to necessity answers most befittingly an aim of humanity: the highest aim of man is the artistic aim; the highest artistic aim – the *Drama*. In buildings erected for daily use, the builder has only to answer to the lowest aim of humanity: beauty is therein a luxury. In buildings reared for luxury, he must satisfy an unnecessary and unnatural need: his fashioning therefore is capricious, unproductive and without beauty. On the other hand, in the construction of that edifice whose every part shall answer to a common and artistic aim alone, in the building of the theatre, the *Baumeister* needs only to comport himself as a *Künstler*, to keep a single eye upon the *Kunstwerk* ... Everything that breathes and moves upon the *Bühne* (stage) thus breathes and moves alone from an eloquent desire to impart, to be seen and heard within those walls which, however circumscribed their space, seem to the actor from his scenic standpoint to embrace the whole of humanity; whereas the *Publikum*, that representative of daily life, forgets the confines of the auditorium, and lives and breathes now only in the *Kunstwerk*, which seems to it as life itself, and on the stage, which seems the wide expanse of the entire universe.'[19]

Still ruminating in 1851 on the practical application of his theoretical ideas in the creation of artworks of the future, Wagner wrote an autobiographical essay that amounted to a manifesto, and which he sent out to his circle of friends: 'I shall never write an Opera more.

Bayreuth, Festspielhaus

16

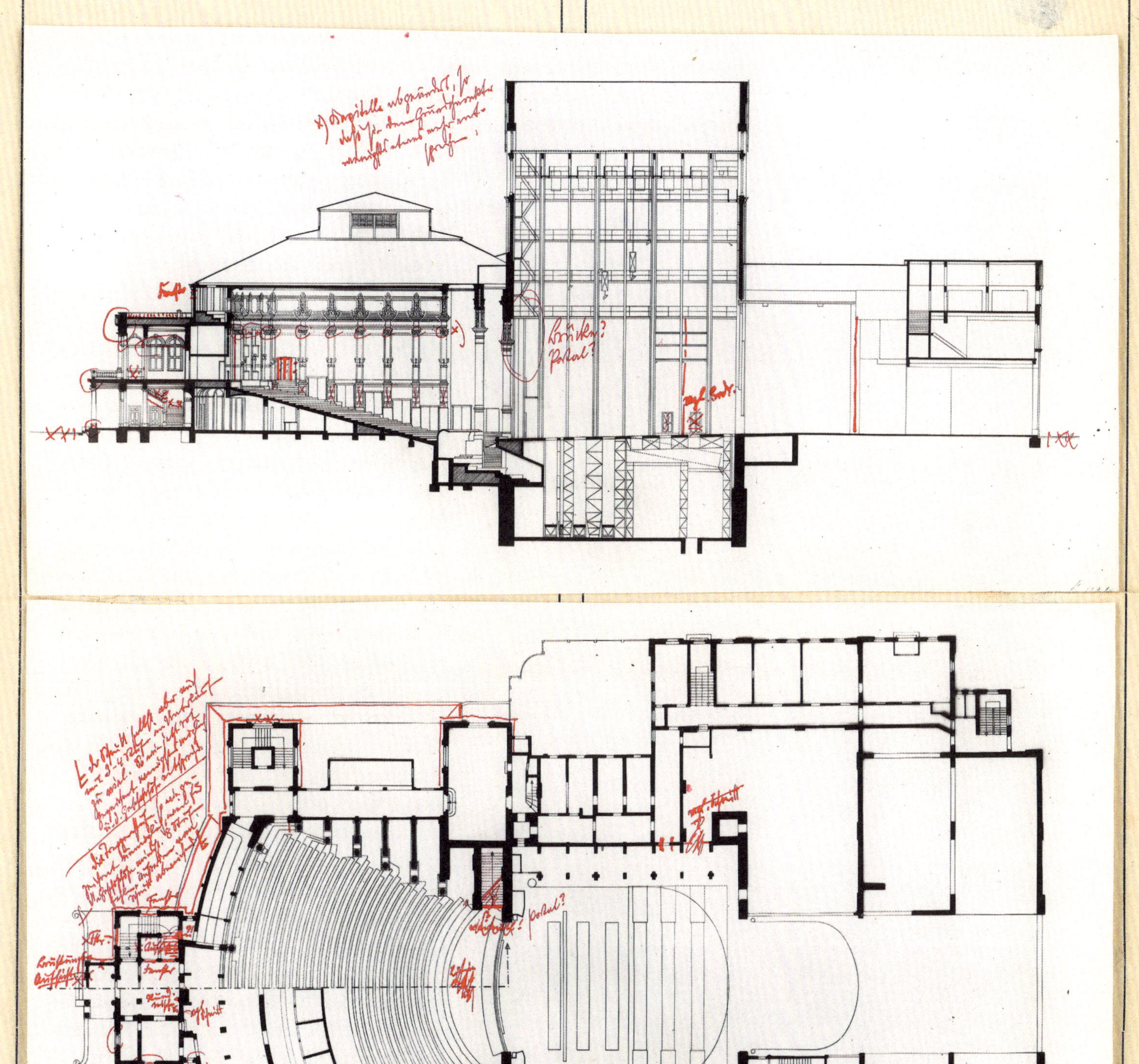

preceding page
Otto Brückwald, Bayreuth Festspielhaus, 1876 (plan and section drawn in 1940).

As I have no wish to invent an arbitrary title for my works, I will call them *Dramen* (dramas) ... I propose to produce my myth in three complete dramas, preceded by a lengthy *Vorspiel* (prelude). ... At a specially appointed *Festspiel*, I propose, in some future time, to produce those three Dramas with their Prelude, *in the course of three days and a fore-evening*' (emphasis in the original).[20]

It was in fact to the draft of a scenario begun back in pre-uprising Dresden that the composer turned. At that time, Wagner had written the libretto for a single opera – *Siegfrieds Tod* (Siegfried's Death) – but now in exile in Switzerland he filled out the story that would become *Der Ring des Nibelungen*, a four-opera cycle that would be produced 'in the course of three days and a fore-evening'.

above
Otto Brückwald, auditorium of the Bayreuth Festspielhaus, 1876.

Right from the outset, Wagner's inspiration was Jacob Grimm's *Deutsche Mythologie*, which had struck him with the force of a revelation that he later used an architectural metaphor to describe: 'Formed from the scanty remains of a vanished world ... I found here the outline of a chaotic building ... Nothing in it was complete, nor was there anything resembling an architectural line, and I was often tempted to abandon the bleak task of building something from it at all. And yet, I was firmly in the power of its marvellous magic ... There arose in my soul a whole world of shapes, which proved to be unexpectedly graphic and related to one another in some fundamental way ... The effect they produced on my innermost being I can only describe as a complete rebirth.'[21]

The modern *Meister* first wrote the four libretti – *Das Rheingold, Die Walküre, Siegfried* and *Götterdämmerung* – before turning his attention to the music, and also to the creation of a unique Festspielhaus (festival theatre) in which the cycle was exclusively to be performed. With his former comrade-in-arms, Gottfried Semper, he contrived an audacious plan for a Festspielhaus in Munich that was to be a radical revaluation of everything that an opera house up to that time was thought to involve. However, Wagner and Semper parted ways when the composer decided that the proper location for his Festspielhaus was not the Bavarian metropolis – with its mocking urban intellectuals and critics – but rather somewhere quieter, out in the German *Landschaft*, the nourishing soil of the *deutsche Volk*. His Festspielhaus was to be a holy place of pilgrimage, a site for national communion. Wagner settled on the Bavarian town of Bayreuth, which donated a large plot of land – *Der Grüne Hügel* (Green Hill) – and in 1871 he handed the little-known architect Otto Brückwald the plans that Semper had prepared, which were crystal-clear in their intentions and merely required a modest, competent architect to execute.

Within a year, the foundation stone of the Festspielhaus was ready to be laid, and Wagner used that occasion on a late spring day in 1872[22] to gather his thoughts in regard to the meaning of the Festspielhaus for his art and to reflect on the architectural composition of his theatre, which was to be as modern, as a work of architecture, as the stories performed inside it were archaic.

But before Wagner delivered his speech, he treated the crowd of patrons who had travelled all the way to Bayreuth to a performance of Beethoven's Ninth Symphony. Wagner's motivations behind this choice of music were not as straightforward as they might seem to have been. While it is true that he was indeed honouring the (German) genius of Beethoven by performing the

Siegfried Wagner directing the Bayreuth Festspielhaus Orchestra.

mighty, uplifting music, he was also reiterating the belief he had expressed in *The Artwork of the Future* that 'the *last* symphony had *already been written*'.[23] That is, the Ninth Symphony was the final work of any real historical consequence in a now supposedly exhausted genre, one that would be superseded by Wagner's *Gesamtkunstwerke*, which were only ever to be performed inside his own unique Festspielhaus.

It was in fact to the architecture of his Festspielhaus that Wagner devoted most of his speech. He began by describing the compulsion that first gripped him, which was to 'find a way to render invisible the technical furnace of the music – the orchestra. For this one constraint led step by step to the total redesign of the auditorium of our neo-European theatre.'[24] For Wagner, 'the constant and, indeed, insistent sight of the technical apparatus required to produce the music constitutes a most tiresome distraction', so he decided to banish the orchestra from sight by sinking it down to such a depth that the audience would look right over the top of it, gaining an unimpeded view of the events unfolding on the stage. This first radical decision precipitated those that followed. The seating had therefore to 'consist of gradually ascending rows whose ultimate height would be determined only by the need for a clear view of the stage setting'. The priority of a 'clear view' for every member of the audience also meant that the rows of seats assumed the shape of a classical amphitheatre, although as Wagner pointed out there could be no question of actually executing the traditional form of an amphitheatre that 'would have projected so far on either side as to produce, or even exceed, a full half-circle, for the object of which the audience requires a clear overview is no longer the Greek chorus in the classical orchestra, which was largely surrounded by the amphitheatre, but rather the Greek *skene*, which was presented to Greek audiences merely in the form of a projecting surface but which in our particular case was to be used in all its depth'.[25] And then – in a statement as matter of fact in expression as it was profound in consequence – Wagner said: 'We thus found ourselves strictly at the mercy of the laws of perspective, according to which the rows of seats might widen as they rose up from the stage that they must always face.'

These two fundamental decisions – firstly to render the orchestra invisible, and secondly to submit to the laws of perspective – posed two related architectural problems that were solved in one fell aesthetic swoop, though it took two architectural minds to come up with it. The proscenium was the answer, though it was worked harder architecturally than it had ever been before, insofar as it was transformed from a picture frame into something properly spatial, in fact, all-encompassing. This is what Wagner said in his speech to the gathered crowd: 'The proscenium exerted a decisive influence on the remainder of the design – the actual frame of the *Bühnenbildes* (scenic picture) necessarily triggered this arrangement. My demand that the orchestra be made invisible proved an inspiration to the famous architect (Semper) whom I was initially privileged to consult on this matter.' In his own words, Wagner had encouraged 'this man of genius to find a purpose for the void that arose between the stage and the rows of seats in the auditorium', which he then referred to as the *mystischer Abgrund* (mystical abyss) because its function was to 'separate reality from ideality'.[26]

Semper came up with the idea of closing off this abyss at the front with a second, wider proscenium, the effect of which Wagner described as follows: 'Thanks to the relation between this second proscenium and the narrower one behind it, the architect was immediately able to promise the most wonderful illusion that makes the actual events onstage appear to be further away than they are, persuading the spectator to think that the action is very remote, while allowing him to observe events with the clarity of actual proximity. In turn, this gives rise to a second illusion, allowing the figures onstage to appear to be of larger, superhuman size.'[27] So, that was one problem solved. But there was another: what to do with the two unsightly wedge-shaped spaces (Wagner's words) left over to either side of the auditorium, between the fan arrangement of the seats and the parallel side walls of the building?

Wagner recounted the solution that Brückwald (not a man of genius, just the composer's 'present adviser') came up with: 'In order to render as innocuous as possible this area that was opened up on either side of the proscenium and that ruined the overall impression, my present adviser had, with his customary inventiveness, already hit upon the idea of adding a third proscenium – even wider and further forward than the other two. Much taken by the excellence of this idea, we soon went even a step further and found that – in order to do full justice to the idea of an auditorium narrowing in true perspective towards the stage – we should extend the process to the *whole* interior, adding proscenium after proscenium until they culminated in the gallery that crowns the whole design, thereby enclosing every member of the audience, no matter where they are sitting, within this *proscenic perspective.*' Ending on a practical note, Wagner pointed out that the requisite entrances and stairs were concealed within these multiple proscenia, and with this 'we ultimately settled all our interior spatial arrangements, as depicted in the accompanying architectural drawings'.[28]

These architectural drawings comprised two floor plans (one at lower-ground level and the other at the level of the stage), a perspective of the auditorium (oddly without seats, or an audience for that matter, though a proud gentleman with a cane wanders aimlessly about), a front and a side elevation, a transverse section and also a longitudinal one that is the most interesting of the set, insofar as it clearly depicts the radical modernity of the building. 'Form follows function' would later become a mantra for architectural modernism, but here it is a simple fact stated most emphatically; we are dealing with two distinct buildings that have two distinct purposes, held together–apart by the 'mystical abyss'.

Having devoted the first half of his speech to the first of these two buildings – the auditorium – Wagner now turned his attention to the second of them – the stage and all the myriad contrivances required above, below and behind it. Wagner was very clear about what inspired the bulky form, stating that his 'sole concern' had been to provide 'the greatest volume required to install the most perfect scenery'.[29] He calculated the height as being 'three times the height viewed by the audience', since the sets that rest upon the stage need to be both lowered beneath it as well as raised above it: that is, the setting would need to rise to twice its height above the actual stalls. Wagner then announced, in wholly modern terms: 'If this simple functional fact is honestly expressed, then the architectural result must be a composite of two buildings of the most disparate shape and size.' He went on: 'Most architects who have recently designed theatres have sought to conceal this disparity as far as possible by significantly raising the auditorium and then adding non-defined spaces above it that are generally used as scenery-painting workshops or as administrative offices, but which on account of their extreme inconvenience are in fact seldom used at all.' They also added tiers of excessively high boxes 'meant only for the poorer classes, on whom architects think nothing of inflicting the inconvenience of a hazy bird's-eye view of the performance taking place in the stalls far beneath them'.[30]

Sounding more and more like a modern architect, Wagner announced: 'I believe that by refusing to act disingenuously and by responding to the dictates of sheer need, the task that we set ourselves of building an outwardly artless provisional theatre has in fact brought us closer to a clearer statement of the architectural problem. It now lies before us, naked and well defined.'

He continued: 'In order to meet the altogether ideal expression of purpose, in our theatre we had to discard – one by one – all of the traditional arrangements of the interior, dismissing them as inappropriate and therefore useless, replacing them with our new arrangement in which there is no place for any traditional ornamentation, whether on the interior or exterior.' His self-congratulation now at a crescendo, Wagner concluded: 'We have ventured on the path to discovery of a German architectural style that would certainly not prove unworthy of a building consecrated to German art in its most popular national manifestation – on the stage; a unique architectural style noticeably distinct from others.'[31]

Otto Brückwald was the emissary of this new architectural style, and he also penned an account of the Festspielhaus, though his was couched in terms less lofty than those of Wagner, oriented rather to the concerns of the readership of the *Deutsche Bauzeitung* (organ of the German architect and engineering associations). Brückwald wrote first about the means of access and egress in the building: 'The entrances to the auditorium are situated under covered halls, and they are provided in ample numbers on all sides. Additionally, provision has been made to enter and exit amidst the broad rows of seats'; then about ventilation: 'Since the performances in this Festspielhaus will only be staged in the final months of summer (during the recess of the Hoftheater), particular care has been given to the circulation of cool, clean air, vented from underneath the seats'; then about the lighting: 'In most theatres, the auditorium is brilliantly lit, but we have refrained from doing that here; illumination has only been provided at a level that is essential for safe egress and also to facilitate reading. But all the more attention has therefore been given to the stage lighting, which attains the most extraordinary effects.' After that, he enumerated the complex machinery and stage devices designed to the specifications of Carl Brandt from Darmstadt: 'The stage is 27.74 metres wide and including the back of the stage it is 35.62 metres deep. It rises to a height of 29.20 metres above the surface of the stage, and if the floor level of the lower machinery is taken into account, this dimension extends to 39.42 metres. The building is half-timbered, but four masonry towers provide reinforcement at the corners. Their arrangement is not very favourable as far as the external appearance of the building is concerned, but unfortunately, due to reasons of expediency, there was no alternative.' And then, finally, he provided an update on progress: 'At this present time, the exterior of the building has been completed, and the interior is also nearing completion. Attention has now turned to preparing the stage so that rehearsals will be able to commence in the new year. The Brückner brothers from Coburg will be responsible for the execution of the scenery, based on the drawings made by the painter Josef Hoffmann from Vienna.'[32]

The search that led to Hoffmann, the painter from Vienna, had been an arduous one, since in his own words, Wagner was not willing to entrust the *Ring* to a 'routine *Theaterdekorationsmaler* (stage scenery painter)'. He was looking for 'a *true artist*',[33] one capable of 'genuine artistic innovations – a brand-new style', as he wrote in a letter to his future benefactor, King Ludwig II.[34] The artist at the top of his list was Arnold Böcklin – famed now for his remarkable *Die Toteninsel* (Isle of the Dead). It was 'a fine task for Böcklin', wrote Wagner, 'he has just the right imagination for it',[35] but the Swiss Symbolist painter turned down the offer.[36] And so Wagner contacted Hoffmann, writing to him on 28 July 1872 to enquire whether he would be interested in designing the sets for the *Ring*.[37] The composer had never set eyes on a single one of the landscape painter's works, but was going on reputation alone. He remained adamant that a professional scenic painter was never going to be able to achieve anything worthy of the epithet *deutsch*, at least not in the noblest sense of the word.

Otto Brückwald, Bayreuth Festspielhaus, 1876.

Hoffmann's response arrived by post a fortnight later: 'Honourable Sir, your enterprise cannot be praised highly enough – time will prove to the *deutsche Volk* just how much they have profited from the founding of an institution devoted entirely to pure art. It is only when all our energies are focused on the one, the highest goal – without subsidiary aims – that art itself will flourish. We are well on the way to achieving a theatre that will become

a *Bildungsinstitut* (educational institution) in the truest sense of the word, one where the best that a nation can hope to accomplish will be realised.'[38]

Bearing in mind the stale conditions of stage production at the time, Wagner was well justified in his choice of the outsider Hoffmann, who did have some theatrical experience but was first and foremost a painter of landscapes – an important prerequisite for the *Ring*, whose dramatic confrontations between gods, giants and humans take place mostly out of doors. Furthermore, Hoffmann was welcoming of new stagecraft technologies, a definite plus given the extreme technical challenges of the *Ring* that Wagner's stage technician, Carl Brandt, was already grappling with at the time.

Following their promising written exchange, Wagner invited Hoffmann to Bayreuth for a three-way meeting with himself and Brandt. The composer's first in-person impression of the painter from Vienna was of a man who

Josef Hoffmann, *Das Rheingold*, Prelude and Scene 1: In the Depths of the Rhine, 1876.

'rambled a bit' and had a 'self-confident air bordering on arrogance', but who also seemed understanding.[39] He commented to Brandt after the meeting that Hoffmann 'did not displease me, despite his awkwardness that made for boring moments every now and then. If he comprehends the seriousness of the task – and he paints really well – then is there not hope for us?'[40]

While the topics of conversation at that first meeting in Bayreuth were at times lofty, practical matters also came up for consideration, such as how the stage sets would actually be executed – that is, how Hoffmann's paintings made on an easel would be blown up to the giant proportions of the Bayreuth

stage. This question was pressing, since at the time there was no *Malersaal* (painting hall) in the city large enough to accommodate the 12×13 metre background scenes laid out flat for painting. The only viable option was to build a capacious new painting hall, which is what Wagner committed himself to doing. Just ten days after the meeting with Hoffmann and Brandt, the composer wrote simultaneously to his architect Brückwald and to Brandt: 'I have decided that it is necessary for us to custom build a *Malersaal* and I will give it high priority, diverting funds to its construction so that hopefully by summer it will be possible to begin painting in it.'[41] On the very same day, he wrote to Hoffmann, assuring him that he would commission Brückwald to design the hall in the near future, and expressing the conviction that 'everything will turn out to your satisfaction'.[42]

The painting hall that Brückwald designed for Hoffmann was a simple half-timbered building located directly behind the Festspielhaus and dimensioned in exact accord with the 12×13 metre background scenes that it was specially built to accommodate, and that, as the architect reported, would make it 'of a size never seen before'.[43]

Hoffmann was to present his first sketches for the *Ring* to Wagner and Brandt at a second conference in Bayreuth, scheduled to take place just over a year after the first one. He arrived at the agreed time of 3pm, but had somehow managed to leave his sketches behind – an 'annoying coincidence, and to make matters worse the weather was terrible' – wrote Wagner's wife Cosima in her diary. She found Hoffmann to be 'peculiarly obstinate', and wondered whether he was indeed the gifted painter they had held him up to be, or whether perhaps he was just full of hot air – 'the sketches will answer this question'.[44] The following morning, Wagner himself gave Hoffmann and Brandt a tour of the Festspielhaus, which was by then under construction, and in the afternoon the sketches finally arrived – 'two days lost due to clumsiness', noted Cosima. These drawings apparently made a 'beautiful, powerful' first impression, but the closer Wagner looked, the more he realised that Hoffmann's historicist-realist accuracy in fact obscured some of the composer's dramatic intentions for the *Ring*, especially in the architecture of Hunding's Hut and the landscape it was set within.[45] Hoffmann held firm in the face of Wagner's critique, and the two of them wrangled late into the night over what at first seemed to be a question of stylistic preference, but which actually hinged on Wagner's move away from history to myth in his *Wort-Tondramen*. 'The incomparable thing about myth', he once wrote, 'is that it is always true'.[46]

Wagner slept on it and reconvened with Hoffmann the following morning for another look over the painter's sketches, and the impression they made in the light of day was a much more positive one – 'really beautiful, particularly Valhalla, which has been rendered complete'.[47]

They agreed upon a schedule that involved Hoffmann first travelling to Darmstadt in January to work together with Brandt in his workshop to translate his two-dimensional paintings into three-dimensional models, and then moving to Bayreuth in March or April to begin with the actual task of painting the gigantic stage sets in the *Malersaal*. There was no way that Hoffmann was going to be able to complete all these paintings by himself by the strict deadline that was now only one and a half years away, so, in consultation with Brandt, it was agreed that the artist himself would paint five to seven of the stage sets in Bayreuth, while the remainder would be executed by the stage design workshop of the Brückner brothers in Coburg. Brandt knew Max and Gotthold Brückner well, and it was he who recommended them to Hoffmann, who then travelled to Coburg to meet with the brothers in early December 1873. The negotiations must have proceeded smoothly, since a fortnight later the Brückners confirmed that they would be pleased to complete the share of the sets that had been offered to them. However, they pointed out that given their 'large – colossal in fact – dimensions, we are going to have to build a new *Malersaal* to paint them in, since our workshop cannot accommodate them. This expense will not be insignificant.'[48] Given the outlay, the brothers demanded they be guaranteed at least six full stage sets, payment for which would be made upon delivery.

So now the main actors in the staging of the *Ring* in Bayreuth – the *Komponist* Richard Wagner, the *Landschaftsmaler* Josef Hoffmann, the two *Bühnenbildner* brothers, the Brückners, and the *Theater-Machinisten* Carl Brandt – had been cast, and the drama would soon begin. Hoffmann and Brandt clashed most often, though the mood amongst the others became strained as well. Concerned by the tense atmosphere that was starting to develop between his chief collaborators, Wagner decided to invite them all, together with his architect Brückwald, to a house-warming party on Tuesday, 28 April 1874, the day that he, Cosima, and their children Isolde, Eva and Siegfried moved into their villa in the centre of Bayreuth, for which Wagner had invented the name Wahnfried – a compound of *Wahn* (delusion, madness) and *Fried(e)* (peace, freedom).[49] And the evening get-together went very well, as Cosima recorded in her diary: 'The mood was joyous; everybody was filled to the brim with devotion to our cause – the house simply could not have been inaugurated more beautifully.'[50] Contracts were signed the following morning, and then everybody bid each other a warm farewell.

Soon afterwards, Hoffmann temporarily settled himself in Darmstadt so that he and Brandt could work together on the models for the *Ring*, and by the end of July those for *Das Rheingold* and *Die Walküre* were complete. By mid-August, all the models were ready to be sent off to Bayreuth, accompanied by a letter from Hoffmann in which he noted that 'the crates must be stored in a secure, dry location' and then, more pertinently, that they 'must remain unopened until I arrive'.[51] But now the story becomes strange. Brandt arrived in Bayreuth on Monday, 24 August and though the meeting with Hoffmann, the Brückner brothers and Wagner was set for the following morning, the landscape painter from Vienna was nowhere to be seen. An urgent enquiry was fired off to Frau Brandt in Darmstadt, who reported that after Hoffmann had packed up the models, he and his wife set off on a journey on the Rhine, leaving no forwarding address; Hoffmann provided only the verbal assurance that he 'would make his way to Bayreuth on the 5th of September'. '*Großer Ärger* (great annoyance) in Haus Wahnfried', wrote Cosima, 'since the models have been sitting around in their crates, useless, for weeks now'.[52]

Though opening the crates went against Hoffmann's express instructions, Wagner did so anyway, 'with the help of Brandt and Brückner from Coburg'. Given the circumstances, that was surely the only sensible thing to do; time was running short, and nobody knew when Hoffmann would arrive in Bayreuth – or even whether he would show up at all. The Brückner brothers needed to see the models to know how much work stood before them and how long it would take them to complete. Wagner reviewed the models with Brückner from morning until late afternoon, and then had them repacked and shipped back to Coburg.[53] All this trouble, together with his precarious financial situation, upset him so much that he ceased work on his score for *Götterdämmerung*, which was the final act of the *Ring*, and the only score that he had left to write.

Hoffmann failed to appear in Bayreuth on 5 September, only arriving five days later. He reported to Wahnfried and was 'turned away', as Cosima noted in her diary. On 13 September, Wagner received a letter from Hoffmann:

'If you, in fact, still attach some importance to my further participation in your work, please do enlighten me as to the reasoning behind your actions'.[54] Wagner and Cosima decided to invite Hoffmann and his young wife Nina to dinner that very evening, in an attempt to smooth the waters. Nina had keen powers of observation and she provides a vivid picture of the private life of the Wagners, recalling the 'evening spent in the salon that, given its scale and its vaulted ceiling, might just as well have been a church or temple'.[55] 'In that immense room that is covered entirely with a deep burgundy carpet and that is illuminated by ornate gas lamps and by sconces lit with dainty globes, there

Josef Hoffmann, *Das Rheingold*, Scene 2: Valhalla Landscape, 1876.

are sofas, settees and armchairs, and those "curule" chairs used by ancient Roman dignitaries – all in great number and choice, in red velvet, blue satin, oriental embroideries, gold covers and so forth. Bookshelves run around all the walls, lined with thousands of volumes bound in that rich old French way, bright and gold'. Nina remembered 'a small portable table for tea standing in front of the red velvet sofa, leaning against the soft cushions', while 'Madame Cosima did the honours, pouring the tea into cups in turn', while never taking her eyes off her husband. And at the same time, she chatted with the men in the room about the consequences of the interbreeding of human races and of racial selection, all with astonishing ease and in an affected manner that

Josef Hoffmann, *Das Rheingold*, Scene 3: Nibelheim's Underground Chasms, 1876.

quite frankly took some getting used to. 'The immediate impression she made upon me was decidedly unfavourable'. Meanwhile, Wagner himself was 'wearing purple stockings and black buckled shoes with large rosettes, black knee-length pantaloons, a black velvet doublet with satin lapels and fitted sleeves, out of which white cuffs obtruded and covered his wrists. And he wore a black velvet beret that cast a shadow over his broad, bony forehead, his deep-set burning eyes, and slightly askew nose, and his strong chin that maintains control over his mouth, which trembles between anger and pleasure. This was the impression I had of the gentleman from Bayreuth.'[56]

During the course of the evening, it was agreed that 'the maquettes would be ordered over from Coburg again',[57] and Hoffmann begrudgingly agreed to 'negotiate any alterations that may – perhaps – be necessary'.[58] But the Brückner brothers were starting to lose patience: 'Conflict between the painters Brückner and Hoffmann – God knows how it should be resolved', wrote Cosima in her diary. And further, 'it appears that the Brückners in fact no longer want to work with Hoffmann at all anymore. For his part, Hoffmann is asking for money from our board of directors, which doesn't have any to give.'[59]

The point of no return had been attained; on 12 October, Hoffmann relinquished his role as the lead scenographer and was paid 600 Thalers in compensation despite 'his inactivity over the past few months', according to Cosima.[60] Wagner wrote Hoffmann a conciliatory letter that, according to his wife Nina, was a 'balm' to her husband. 'Honourable sir and friend!' wrote Wagner. 'It had not been my wish for you to resign; I proved to you that it was personally important to me to have you and the other two gentlemen to whom the execution of your designs were entrusted work together amicably. It is not the time now to go into the reasons why this turned out to be an impossibility. Suffice to say that the unworkable situation has become apparent to you as well. My only real wish is that you and I – two honourable men – say goodbye in peace ... With the request to commend me to your esteemed wife, I shake your hand in farewell, and remain yours sincerely, Richard Wagner.'[61]

A couple of days later the Brückners arrived in Bayreuth, 'and were visibly relieved to be freed from Hoffmann. They made no extra requests and are now happily going about their work back in Coburg.'[62] On 1 December, Wagner and Cosima travelled to Coburg to view the background scenes for themselves: 'Enormous dimensions', wrote Cosima in her diary.[63] Wagner had finally completed his score for *Götterdämmerung* shortly before that, on 21 November, some twenty-six years and three months after he had begun to work on the *Ring* back in Dresden.

So now, with the painting of the background scenes well underway, and the musical score for the *Ring* complete, Wagner turned his mind in earnest to the staging of his *Meisterwerk*. By the following summer, he was ready to begin with the preliminary rehearsals. On 24 June 1875, the huge assembly of singers, musicians and stagehands all gathered to review the Festspielhaus, and the general impression was very positive. Then the rehearsals began, and the acoustic resonance was found to match the visual one; but Wagner wanted to be sure that this would also be the case during actual performances, so he arranged for a group of soldiers stationed at Bayreuth to serve as a test audience. Since the seating was still on its way, they sat themselves down on the raked floor of the auditorium, and Wagner was overall very satisfied with the way the rehearsal went. He in fact considered the army reservists to be the ideal audience; they were seated before the music began, were quiet for the duration of the performance, and made no claim afterwards to have understood anything.[64] In all, that summer of 1875 was a kind of gentle warm-up for the one that would follow; the cast and orchestra dispersed for their winter seasons elsewhere, but the camaraderie that had developed in Bayreuth returned when the performers did too, in the final days of May 1876.

And Wagner began at the beginning, with the *Rheingrund* (In the Depths of the Rhein) which is the prelude to *Das Rheingold*, itself the *Vorabend* (preliminary evening) to the *Ring*. These are Wagner's staging instructions: 'Greenish twilight, lighter towards the top, darker towards the bottom. Surging waters fill the upper space, flowing restlessly from right to left ... Everywhere steep rocky reefs rear up out of the depths, bordering the stage and defining its space; the entire bottom of the river is fractured by a maze of jagged edges, making it nowhere completely flat and suggesting deeper ravines on all sides stretching out into a chain of darkness. – The curtain remains closed when the orchestra starts playing.'[65]

Swimming apparatus for the Rhinemaidens in *Das Rheingold*, Bayreuth Festspielhaus, *c* 1876.

The music is at first an almost inaudible rumble – a sustained deep E-flat in the double basses. And then five bars in, bassoons add a pair of B-flats. Together, these notes form the interval of the perfect fifth, 'an emanation of primordial nature, the hum of the cosmos at rest',[66] in the words of the music critic for *The New Yorker*, Alex Ross, who provides a vivid description of the remainder of this opening sequence: 'Then eight horns enter one after another, in upward-wheeling patterns, which resemble the natural harmonic series generated by a vibrating string. Other instruments add their voices, in gradually quickening pulses. As the mass of sound gathers and swirls and billows in the air, the underlying tonality of E-flat does not budge.' 'The prolonged stasis engenders a new sense of time', writes Ross, although just what kind of time is difficult to say; perhaps it is 'an instant passing in slow motion, perhaps eons passing in a blur.'[67]

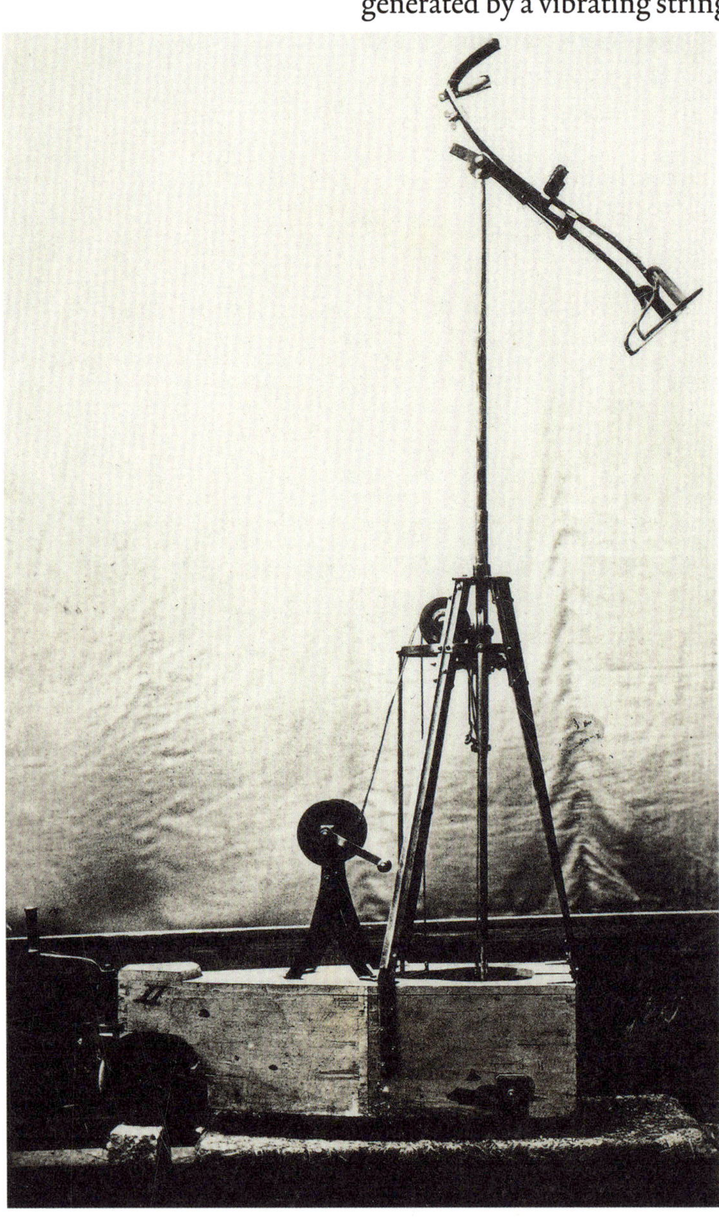

Remarkable in performance, this beginning is just as arresting in the musical score, though in the realm of the visual. Back in 1854, twenty-one years before rehearsals began, Wagner prepared his first draft of the partiture for *Das Rheingold, Vorspiel und erste Scene (auf dem Grunde des Rheins)* and the deep constant E-flat harmony of the eight *Contrabäße* (double basses) is plain to see, as is the moment when the *Fagotte* (bassoons) come in at B-flat, before the horns arrive and take off 'in upward wheeling patterns' – they accumulate and rise – toward the right-hand side of the page, and then beyond.[68] The swell of sound that the partiture brings to the level of visual representation is that of the mighty Rhine.

In his staging instructions, Wagner indicated precisely the moment that the curtain was to be raised, which was after 126 bars had been played by the orchestra: 'With graceful swimming movements at the centre of the stage, one of the *Rheintöchter* (Rhinemaidens) circles a reef, its slender pinnacle towering upwards into a denser flood of water and brighter dawning light.' The Rhinemaiden, Woglinde, swims up from the depths, singing a mixture of nonsensical syllables and German words: '*Weia! Waga! Woge, du Welle, walle zur Wiege! Wagaweia! Wallala weiala weia!*'[69]

facing
Richard Wagner's first draft of the musical score for the prelude to *Das Rheingold*, 1854.

The preparation of this opening scene had been a trial, certainly for the three Rhinemaidens who were required to sing and swim, but also for the stage technician Brandt, whom Wagner had charged with the design of the swimming apparatus into which the Rhinemaidens would be strapped. The machine he devised was composed of a kind of corset attached atop a tall

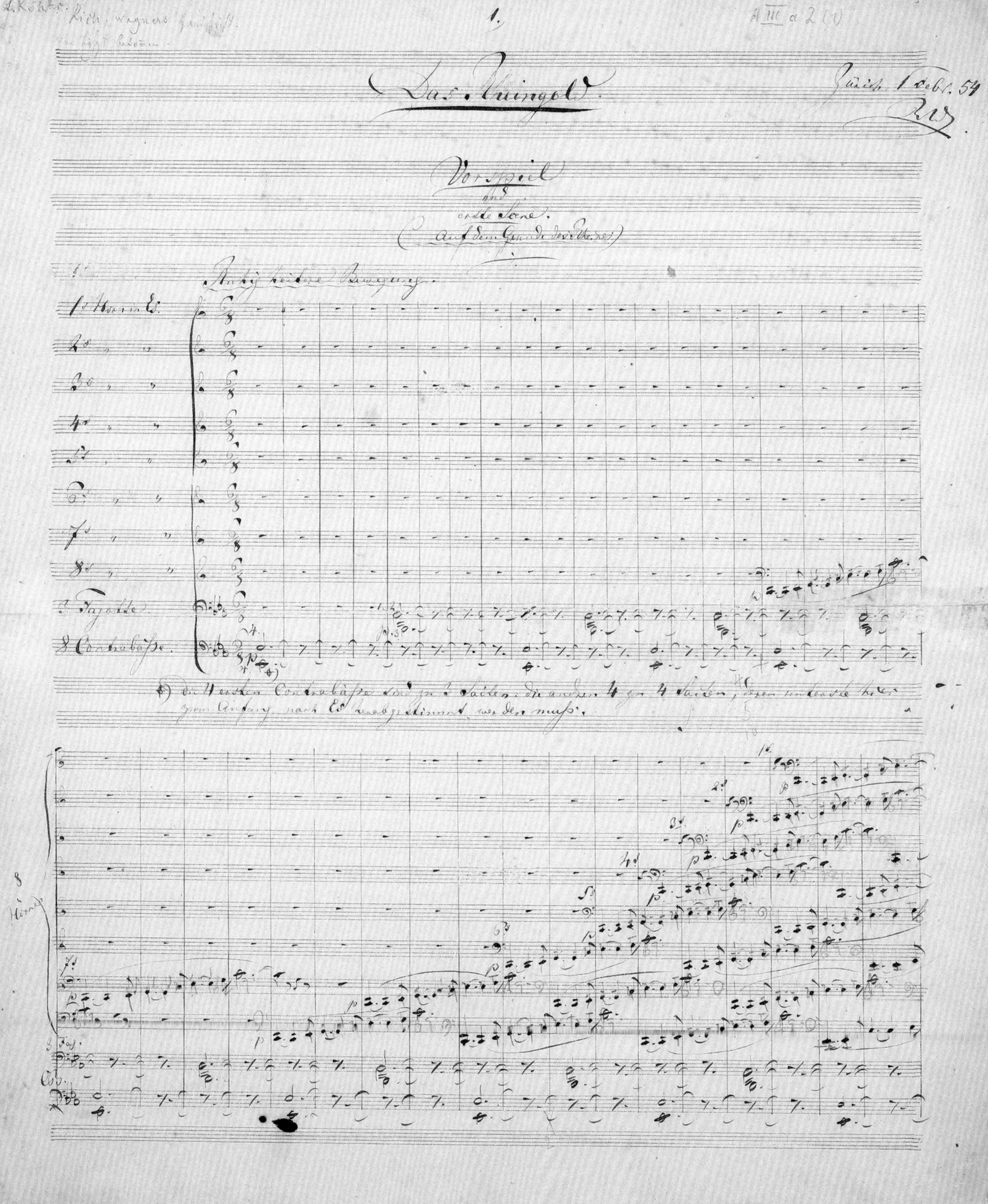
1.
Das Rheingold.
Zürich 1 Febr. 54
RW
Vorspiel
und
erste Scene.
(Auf dem Grunde des Rheins)
Ruhig heitere Bewegung.
1r Horn in Es
3 Fagotte
8 Contrabässe
*) Die 4 ersten Contrabässe sind zu 5 Saiten, die andern 4 zu 4 Saiten, deren unterste Saite
zum Anfang nach Es herabgestimmt werden muss.
8 Hörner

iron pole that was stabilised at its base by a square pyramidal frame attached in turn to a timber coffin-shaped box on wheels, all linked together and mobilised by a complex mechanism of cogs, chains and gears. While the cart was driven around the stage, the pole could be raised, lowered and tilted, all provided that each of the Rhinemaidens was willing to endure the resultant movements. Wagner developed a choreography for the Rhinemaidens, making coloured marks in a copy of the vocal score – indicating left, right, forward, backward, up and down movements – to be interpreted by three different musical directors following the score, each of whom was then required to instruct two stagehands seated on each of the three said machines, one steering and the other controlling the vertical movement of the Rhinemaidens strapped in way above the fretful activity down below.

Franz Betz as Wotan in the premiere season of *Der Ring des Nibelungen*, 1876.

But ultimately Wagner gave up on the idea of trying to choreograph the movements of the Rhinemaidens in advance, which, given their movements were through three-dimensional space and were controlled by others, would have amounted to the denotation of three complex sequences of Cartesian coordinates. Wagner decided to rely upon his *Balletmeister* Richard Fricke, whom he had employed as a kind of stage director for the *Ring* (the profession of stage director did not yet exist: the *mise-en-scène* was usually negotiated by a combination of composer, ballet-master, stage manager and librettist). Rather than spending too much time thinking about it in advance, Fricke strapped occupants into the swimming machines, though they were not yet the actual Rhinemaidens, but rather local Bayreuth gymnasts whom Wagner had summoned to try out the unproven contraptions on their behalf. After four days of rehearsals, the *Balletmeister* was satisfied that the swimming movements of his willing athletes were indeed graceful and that it was time for the Rhinemaidens to try out the machines for themselves.

The Rhinemaidens were less willing swimmers than the gymnasts had been, as Fricke recorded in his diary entry for that day, 3 June 1876: '"No", said Lilli. "Nobody can expect me to do that. I will not do that under any circumstances. I have just arisen from my sick-bed, and I am also continuously dizzy." The other two were quiet. I said, "Fräulein Marie, have courage. Try it just once, and I'll wager the fear will disappear, and a feeling of pleasure in swimming will prevail." They brought the ladder; Brandt and I helped her get in. Amid her *ooooh* and *eeeee* screechings and squeaks we strapped her in firmly, and the voyage began, very slowly. She started to lose her terrified expression, began to laugh, and said it was going very nicely. Now Lilli has agreed, and *voilà*! in a few minutes she has become the bravest one. Fräulein Lammert now follows, and all three are swimming, amid happy laughter.'[70]

When daily rehearsals began in earnest, it became apparent there were creases to be ironed out. For example, at a rehearsal for the third scene of *Das Rheingold*, the steam serving as the sulphurous vapours of the underground chasms of Nibelheim seeped through the wall of the orchestra pit and the harps went out of tune. And on another occasion, a member of the orchestra complained of an 'unbearable draft', to which Wagner replied: 'I composed the opera, now you want me even to close the windows!'[71]

But overall, Wagner was pleased with the way that it was all coming together, particularly when the enormous stage sets that the Brückner brothers had painted based on the sketches made by Hoffmann finally arrived in Bayreuth – two weeks after the rehearsals had begun.[72]

Amalie Materna as Brünnhilde, 1876.

The final full ensemble rehearsal of *Das Rheingold* was held on 15 July, and by that time everything was humming along nicely; the orchestra was finely tuned in its mystical abyss, and the singers on the stage up above them all knew their parts by heart. And they also now looked the part, since the costumes that Carl Emil Doepler had designed for them had arrived. Doepler proudly stated that his costumes were based on 'the latest discoveries of pre-historic times',[73] though this was disputed by some actual historians who told him that the colour blue was not used in prehistoric Nordic times. Cosima got involved – blue was retained. And she also had an opinion on other aspects of the costumes and accessories, including the sword Nothung, which she thought was too short, though Doepler had reproduced it from the longest Germanic sword in existence.

There was a great deal of weaponry involved – swords, shields and helmets, but also spears, staffs and of course Donner's mighty hammer, which the Bohemian baritone singer Eugen Gura wields with purpose in the *Costümporträt* (studio portrait) of him in character.

Franz Betz sang the bass-baritone role of Wotan, first among the gods. In his studio portrait, Betz is seen holding the spear Gungir, carved from the wood of the world ash tree Yggdrasil and engraved with the contracts from which Wotan derives his power. The mightily-bearded Betz is wearing a great winged helmet but is otherwise dressed much like Gura; they both wear a heavy woven tunic and cloak, leggings wound with leather straps, wrist- and armbands, and above all an aspect of godly intent.

The Austrian soprano Amalie Materna played Wotan's favourite Valkyrie daughter, Brünnhilde, and she too wears a winged helmet and is armed with a sword, shield and impressive chainmail vest. More impressive still is the well-rounded cuirass that one of her Valkyrie sisters is wearing to go along with the round shield resting at her feet, on which her own spear leans.

Otto Brückwald, Bayreuth Festspielhaus, 1876.

All that was needed now was an audience to perform before, and it began to build one member at a time. The single attendee at the dress rehearsal on 9 August was the *Märchenkönig* (Fairy-tale King) Ludwig II, who arrived by train at night and was met at the station by Wagner. But the rehearsal was all the fairy-tale king saw, since he left before the performances of the *Ring* began, and before the Kaiser arrived.

Kaiser Wilhelm of Prussia, who had not responded to Wagner's appeals for financial assistance, arrived on Saturday – the day before the premiere of *Das Rheingold* – and the composer was at the station to greet him too, more so out of obligation than anything else. Many other Germanic nobles – *Könige, Prinzen, Großherzöge* and *Herzöge* – also travelled to Bayreuth, and some came from even further afield, including Grand Duke Vladimir Alexandrovich

from Russia and Dom Pedro II of Brazil, who at the hotel gave his name as 'Pedro' and his occupation as 'Emperor'.

And of course, since the premiere of *Das Rheingold* was a major musical event, many composers also made their way to Bayreuth, among them Edvard Grieg, Anton Bruckner and Wagner's father-in-law, Franz Liszt. Pyotr Ilyich Tchaikovsky came as both a composer and a journalist, and he filed an account of the main problem facing visitors to Bayreuth – food. 'The little town offers, it is true, sufficient shelter to the strangers, but it cannot feed all its guests. So it happened, on the very day of my arrival, I learnt the meaning of the words "struggle for existence". ... One can only obtain a piece of bread or a glass of beer with immense difficulty, by dire struggle, or cunning stratagem or iron endurance ... Throughout the whole duration of the *Festspiele*, food forms the chief interest of the public; the artistic representations take a secondary place.

Cutlets, baked potatoes, omelettes – all are discussed much more eagerly than Wagner's music.'[74] Regarding the range of backgrounds of the hungry patrons, Grieg wrote that 'there are people here from all social classes, the gentry in their grand attire and jewels, young fanatical intellectuals and hundreds of artists and musicians of all kinds, all united by the excitement of the unique occasion.'[75]

Appia's leaving certificate from the Collège de la ville de Vevey.

Je certifie que Adolphe Appia, fils de Louis Paul Amédée, de Genève, né le 1er septembre 1862, a été admis, en novembre 1873, comme élève régulier au Collège de la ville de Vevey et a dès lors, jusqu'en avril 1879, suivi en cette qualité les classes VI, V et IV de la Section classique, puis les classes III et II de la Section industrielle de cet établissement.

Je puis ajouter que pendant ces cinq ans le travail et la conduite de cet élève ont toujours été très satisfaisants.

Le directeur du Collège:

Dr Dumur

DIRECTION DES ECOLES OFFICIEL DE VEVEY

Vevey, 12 septembre 1881.

Virginia Woolf was not in Bayreuth in that first year of 1876, but she travelled over to the festival years later, and exercised her powers of observation and expression in her 1909 essay, 'Impressions at Bayreuth', which she published in *The Times*. Woolf wrote of the landscape around Bayreuth, the direct setting of the Festspielhaus, and also the temporal arc of an evening spent watching one of Wagner's three-act *Wort-Tondramen*: 'From the hill above the theatre you look over a wide land, smooth and without hedges; it is not beautiful, but it is very large and tranquil. One may sit among rows of turnips and watch a gigantic old woman, with a blue cotton bonnet on her head and a figure like one of Dürer's, swinging her hoe. The sun draws out strong scents from the hay and the pine trees, and if one thinks at all, it is to combine the simple landscape with the landscape of the stage.'[76] In a letter to King Ludwig II, Wagner had stipulated precisely the time at which the first act of each evening of the four-part performance of the *Ring* was to commence, and except for *Das Rheingold* (which is the *Vorabend* and started later), that starting time was 4pm. The audience were mustered indoors by a brass ensemble playing the motif with which Donner summons the mist. At the conclusion of the first act, the audience are freed once again to take in their surroundings, as Woolf recalled: 'When the music is silent the mind insensibly slackens and expands, among happy surroundings: heat and the yellow light, and the intermittent but not unmusical noises of insects and leaves smooth out the folds.'[77] The appreciable interval seemed to have the effect that Wagner intended; he wanted the audience to 'stroll in the parks around the theatre and to take refreshments outdoors in the charming neighbourhood', so that 'thoroughly refreshed, they gather again – following the sound of the brass from the heights of the theatre – with the same receptivity they had for the first act'. This second act began at around 6pm, followed by another interval that the patrons spent out of doors before they were

Jean-Baptiste Lesueur, Le Conservatoire de Musique de Genève, 1858.

summoned in again, this time for the third and final act, after which the indoor performance was complete – though in Woolf's account, the audience arrived outside to find 'another act out here also: it is now dusky and perceptibly fresher; the light is thinner, and the roads are no longer crossed by regular bars of shade. The figures in light dresses moving between the trees of the avenue, with depths of blue air behind them, have a curiously decorative effect. Finally, when the opera is over, it is quite late; and halfway down the hill one looks back upon a dark torrent of carriages descending, their lamps wavering one above another, like irregular torches.'[78]

There were another three evenings like that one in August 1876; *Das Rheingold* was followed by *Die Walküre* on Monday 14; *Siegfried* on Wednesday 16 (postponed by one day because Wotan – Franz Betz – was unwell); and finally, *Götterdämmerung* on Thursday 17. Nietzsche summed up the significance of the occasion, realising that what Wagner had created was not just of special interest and relevance to lovers of music and performance; rather, the 'new language, new body, new sound, new interior world' that the *Meister* had ushered into being was a cultural phenomenon: 'Wagner sums up modernity; it can't be helped, one must first become a Wagnerian.'[79]

And in time, a Wagnerian is precisely what Appia became. As one of his relatives recalled, 'Wagner had even taken the place for him of religion, of love, of everything.'[80] However, he first had to complete his secondary education, which he did in the spring of 1879: 'Over the course of these past five years, the work and conduct of your son have always been most satisfactory', was the underwhelming verdict on the leaving certificate addressed to Appia's father.[81] By now, Appia was eighteen years old, and his overbearing parents begrudgingly assented to his desire to study music at the Conservatoire de musique de Genève, which in turn meant that he was able to learn about opera *in situ* at the Grand Théâtre de Genève, completed only the year before. Before that, Appia had only heard opera spoken about on a handful of occasions, and then only in very conventional terms that entirely failed to satisfy his curiosity. Now a whole new world opened up for him.

The first performance Appia ever saw was Charles Gounod's five-act opera *Faust*, which was loosely based on Johann Wolfgang von Goethe's *Faust – Eine Tragödie*. 'As soon as the curtain rose', the future scenographer later wrote, 'I was amazed to see, or rather to feel, that the scenery was made only of fabric, with no material presence, and I thought to myself: What, are they just screens?' Appia was similarly disbelieving about the fact that the stage was just one continuous horizontal surface: 'I had assumed that the stance of the actors – and in fact all of their postures – would be determined and highlighted by diverse arrangements.' As the opera wore on, Appia found that his 'gaze became ever more – finally, almost exclusively – trained on the performers, finding it odd that each of the acts was not better *situated*'.[82] For Appia, it was as though the actors were wandering around aimlessly in an urban plaza. When the performance finally drew to a close and the lights came up, he walked all about the theatre by himself, muttering: 'What good are all these heavy walls, this solid building?'

Emile Reverdin and Gaspard André, Grand Théâtre de Genève, 1879.

Reflecting on these formative years in his life, Appia noted: 'Only once did I pose a question that now in hindsight testified to my as-yet unconscious dispositions, and that I would say was the beginning of my career.' The question that he posed was to a fellow student who had been to see a staging of one of Wagner's works in Germany but had only provided Appia with vague recollections of it upon his return. 'I wanted him to be more precise, and asked of him whether it had really been the case that the performers were situated in one location, and what did this location look like?' But his friend failed to understand Appia's question: 'I remember pressing him with mounting concern – Where were their feet?' So, wrote Appia, 'in my general ignorance of the theatre, to my mind it was the location occupied by the actor that took precedence over everything else'.[83]

In his own words, the theatre by now had a 'delicious hold' on Appia, but the embrace was an uneasy one: 'I had a kind of intimate ill-defined feeling of moral and aesthetic decline that was all-pervasive. The moral aspect was natural; my education had prepared me for it; but the aesthetic, that was more symptomatic of what was to come.'[84]

Appia at age eighteen in 1880, the year he enrolled in the Conservatoire de Musique de Genève.

After attending the conservatory a mere 500 metres down the road from his family home for two years, Appia decided to transport himself to a new country to study at the famed Hochschule für Musik und Theater in Leipzig, the city in which Wagner had been born. The Canton of Geneva issued his passport on 14 July 1882, valid for one year and for the express purpose of travelling to Germany. Since passport photographs had yet to be introduced, the method that the canton used to identify its citizens in the late nineteenth century was a twelve-line matter-of-fact list of physical characteristics, which in the case of Adolphe François Appia read as follows: Age: 20, Height: 1.7 metres, Hair: Brown, Forehead: Medium, Eyebrows: Brown, Eyes: Brown, Nose: Medium, Mouth: Medium, Beard: Brown, Chin: Round, Face: Oval, Complexion: Pale. With the official document now in his pocket, Appia was free to travel northward, crossing that border which divided the *Conféderation Suisse* from *Deutschland*, the land of Richard Wagner.

But Appia never really committed himself to his musical studies in Leipzig. Not long after he arrived in the city, he recognised that the increase in latitude was social and sexual as much as it was geographical. Far from the doctrine of Calvin that dominated the city in which he was born (and even more so the household he grew up in), Appia 'set out to discover where reality resides'. 'Naturally', he wrote, 'I took the wrong path. Within a few months, everything that gives passionate pleasure was revealed to me, and I gave myself over without defence or question ... The joys were those of art – such as I was able to taste them – mingled with a brand-new kind of happiness born of camaraderie and friendship, of things savoured in common, of freedom. The exuberant intoxication was too sudden and violent, and there was nothing to temper it.' One relationship came to stand above all others: 'Among my friends, there was one who soon came to dominate all the rest ... This relationship replaced *Life* for me ... I recovered from the debacle, but the damage had been done.'[85]

The name of the man with whom Appia had his first meaningful homosexual relationship is unknown; a fact that is unfortunate regarding our understanding of Appia and his companion as two individuals, but even more so regarding the times they lived through. In the latter half of the nineteenth century, a gay man, 'who had a sexual nature opposed to common custom', was generally considered dissolute and decadent – a sinner. That Appia himself never spoke very directly of his sexual orientation is unsurprising, not only for the stigma attached to it, but for the fact that the word 'homosexuality' had only recently been invented, meaning that all was allusion.[86]

facing
Appia's passport, issued on 14 July 1882; Appia's letter of acceptance into the Hochschule für Musik in Dresden, 1 September 1886.

Appia only stayed in Leipzig for two years – as he later related to his doctors, his homosexuality drove him out of town. This time the young musician moved westward to Paris, that great theatrical city of intoxication, enrolling in the conservatory and immersing himself in the rich informal theatrical milieu that orbited around it, and meeting frequently with members of *La Revue Wagnérienne*, including the Symbolist poets Stéphane Mallarmé and Paul Verlaine.[87] At the time, Verlaine was constantly battling drug addiction and alcoholism, as Appia would later do too.[88]

Apparently the one meaningful relationship Appia had during his stay in Paris was with a 'man of letters', who as it turns out was married and had a young family back home in Switzerland. Other than that, he only had brief liaisons, mostly with working-class men including vintners and fishermen, plus the occasional chance encounter, on a train journey for example. Each time, Appia would disappear for a couple of days before reappearing without warning. It seems that his moments of exultation were usually followed by a period of profound despondency, even depression, during which time Appia said he was 'sick' and needed to take to his bed, unable to read or write.[89] One of his friends later wrote of these forlorn episodes: 'Alas, it is always the same with him. Things get better for a while, and then there is a fall – alcohol and idleness, not to mention the terrible vice that assails him and that being congenital, is incurable.'[90]

After a couple of years in Paris, during which he was officially registered at the conservatory but rarely attended any classes, Appia returned to Germany in an attempt to finish off his studies, enrolling at the Hochschule für Musik in Dresden on 1 September 1886. Although he was ostensibly becoming a musician, even taking first prize for a fugue he composed,[91] Appia was not so much devoted to his formal musical training as he was captivated by the world it opened up to him. For instance, his unique roaming education had included an informal apprenticeship with the innovative lighting technician Hugo Bähr at Dresden's Royal Court Theatre,[92] which in turn allowed him to take drawing lessons with Benedikt Kietz, an acquaintance of Wagner's who had also drawn his portrait.[93]

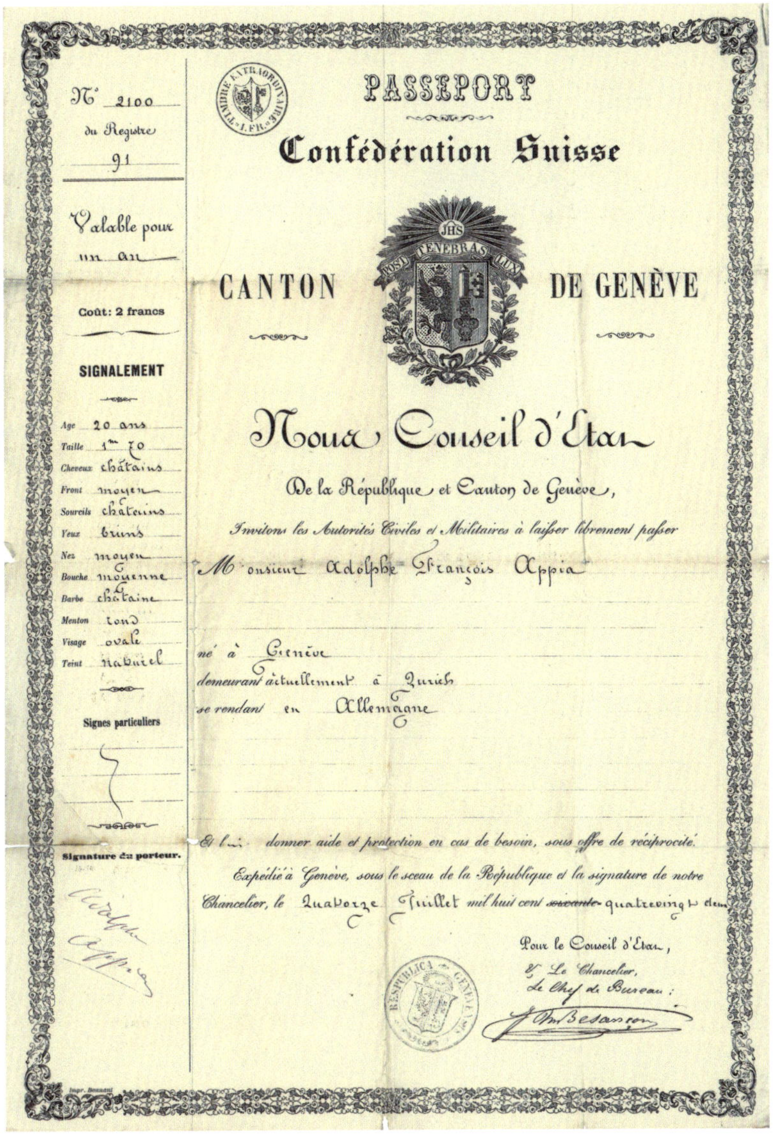

N° 2100 du Registre 91

Valable pour un an

Coût: 2 francs

SIGNALEMENT

Age 20 ans
Taille 1m 70
Cheveux châtains
Front moyen
Sourcils châtains
Yeux bruns
Nez moyen
Bouche moyenne
Barbe châtaine
Menton rond
Visage ovale
Teint naturel

Signes particuliers

Signature du porteur. Adolphe Appia

PASSEPORT

Confédération Suisse

CANTON DE GENÈVE

Nous Conseil d'Etat

De la République et Canton de Genève,

Invitons les Autorités Civiles et Militaires à laisser librement passer Monsieur Adolphe François Appia

né à Genève

demeurant actuellement à Zurich

se rendant en Allemagne

et lui donner aide et protection en cas de besoin, sous offre de réciprocité.

Expédié à Genève, sous le sceau de la République et la signature de notre Chancelier, le Quatorze Juillet mil huit cent ~~soixante~~ quatrevingt deux

Pour le Conseil d'Etat,
Le Chancelier,
Le Chef de Bureau:
J. M. Besançon

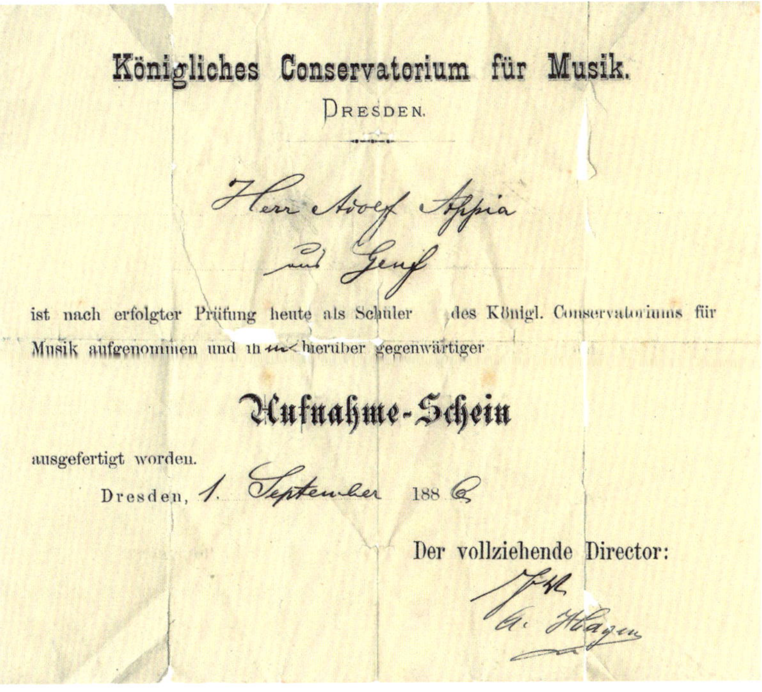

Königliches Conservatorium für Musik.
Dresden.

Herr Adolf Appia
aus Genf

ist nach erfolgter Prüfung heute als Schüler des Königl. Conservatoriums für Musik aufgenommen und ihm hierüber gegenwärtiger

Aufnahme-Schein

ausgefertigt worden.

Dresden, 1. September 1886

Der vollziehende Director:
G. Hagen

It seems likely that his tutor's personal connection to Wagner was the aspect that most appealed to Appia, rather than any of his artistic insights. 'Kietz seems to have been one of those men whose whole life is a preparation for something that never happens', was the brutal assessment of Ernest Newman, author of the four-volume *Life of Richard Wagner*.[94] And Cosima herself had written the following to a friend: 'This brings me to good old Kietz, who – yes, you are right – is a kind-hearted soul, his look always reminds me of – you won't misunderstand me – that of a faithful lapdog, and even if in the beginning I didn't exactly think of him as gifted, now I think that, yes, actually he does have some talent.'[95] Though his talent was modest, and he only ever achieved moderate renown, the artist's characteristic method – of drawing with pastels on tinted paper to deliver high and low lights – did appear to make a decisive impression on his student.

Portrait of Richard Wagner by Benedikt Kietz, with a fragment from the musical score and libretto for Wagner's opera *Rienzi*.

Shortly before finishing his studies in Dresden, Appia suffered the first of what would come to be a series of debilitating, almost fatal depressive episodes. He attempted suicide in 1888 at the age of twenty-six, and again in November 1890, recuperating at the Burghölzli psychiatric clinic in Zurich. Though the affliction that sent Appia to recuperate was psychological, at the *fin de siècle* there was a vogue for treating all manner of health conditions in spas and sanatoria that were small worlds unto themselves. Thomas Mann's *Der Zauberberg* (The Magic Mountain, 1924) is set in one of these sanatoria, high in the rarefied mountain air of the Swiss Alps, to the east of the clinic in which Appia was recovering. For Mann, the sanatorium was a place to examine the social manners and neuroses of a series of characters who made up a kind of microcosm of pre-war Europe, first among them the young German merchant Hans Castorp, whose *Bildungsroman* it is – what he comes to realise, Mann later wrote in a discussion of the novel, is that 'one must go through the deep experience of sickness and death to arrive at a higher sanity and health; in just the same way that one must have a knowledge of sin in order to find redemption'.[96] It is a notion that one might imagine Appia agreeing with, or at least recognising in himself.

In the writing of his book, Mann used a technique that Appia was most certainly familiar with – that of the Wagnerian leitmotif, which the novelist defined as a 'magic formula which works both ways, and links the past with the future, the future with the past. The leitmotif is the technique employed to preserve the inward unity and abiding presentness of the whole at each moment.'[97] In Wagner's late *Wort-Tondramen*, the leitmotif is a distinctive musical phrase that announces an individual character, the locale in which they find themselves, or a plot that is momentarily developing. Though he never used the word himself, Wagner was the inventor of the leitmotif, a 'sonic tag'[98] which impresses itself in the way that satellites do – here now, then gone again but ever to return. Leitmotifs are not only demonstrative of the action but indicate what it is that the characters are seeing and thinking, even if that perception is occluded to the characters themselves. Mann brought the leitmotif into the world of words. 'To me', wrote Mann, 'the novel was always like a symphony, a work in counterpoint, a thematic fabric; the idea of the musical motif plays a great role in it. People have pointed out the influence of Wagner's music on my work. Certainly I do not disclaim this influence. In particular, I followed Wagner in the use of the leitmotif, which I carried over into the work of language.'[99]

Appia at age twenty-eight in 1890.

Appia was well enough to leave Burghölzli by the end of February 1891, and on the advice of his doctors he continued his recuperation away from the city with all its temptations. But rather than ascending to the Alps, he moved out to the small village of Gennersbrunn, renting a room in a farmhouse where he could write and draw in solitude: 'I began to sense my own inner resources and the responsibilities impressed upon me. I retired to the countryside and set to work on what I regarded as my imperative task.'[100]

The mission to which Appia committed himself was no minor undertaking – a fundamental reform of the staging of Wagnerian drama. He immediately set about writing down his ideas in a manuscript, later entitled 'Notes de mise-en-scène für den Ring des Nibelungen', and he also made his first drawings.[101] Appia's pivotal conviction was that the *mise-en-scène* was immanent in the musical score itself, and that additional scenic instructions were unwarranted, even discarding Wagner's own written directions to develop a type of staging based on the libretto and score alone: 'The musical score is the sole interpreter for the director; whatever Wagner has added to it is irrelevant ... his manuscript contains by definition the theatrical form, its projection in space; therefore any additional remarks on his part are superfluous, even contradictory to the aesthetic truth of an artistic work. Wagner's scenic descriptions have no organic relationship with his poetic–musical text.'[102]

As Appia later recalled in his 'Expériences de théâtre et recherches personnelles': 'I set to work on the first scene of *Das Rheingold*, without having the slightest idea whether I was equipped to prepare all four scenes in such a way that they would be differentiated one from the other in such a way that would have pleased Wagner – had he found within himself the gift of synthesis that I inherently possess.'[103]

The libretto for *Das Rheingold* that Appia possessed was the original small leather-bound edition with gold trim published by Schott's Söhne in Mainz in 1876, the year of the premiere performance in Bayreuth.[104] He bought it during his second year of study at the Hochschule für Musik in

Dresden – on the inside cover he wrote in pencil 'Adolphe Appia / Dresden Mai 87'. And under that he wrote – as though signalling a new beginning – 'Gennersbrunn 91–92'.[105]

Appia at first worked intuitively and compulsively, impelled by a force that he felt to be outside of himself: 'I had nothing to do with it – I just obeyed.'[106] It was only later that he realised that his *vision scénique* could be theorised, thus forming the basis for a fundamental reform of the staging of Wagnerian *Wort-Tondramen*.

Das Rheingold is elemental, encompassing water (Prelude and Scene 1: In the Depths of the Rhine), air (Scenes 2 and 4: Valhalla Landscape) and fire (Scene 3: Nibelheim's Underground Chasms). The three elements, wrote Appia, 'must be represented with the clearest distinction possible', requiring one to 'adhere to a high degree of simplicity'. To achieve this profound simplicity – and this was Appia's key insight – it was important to listen to what the music itself had to say, regardless of what Wagner had to say. 'No hesitation possible – I took out a sheet of drawing paper, and also my copy of the musical score for *L'Or du Rhin* (piano and vocals, in quarto, Klindworth) and began to study the first scene.'[107]

This first scene is that of the *Rheingrund* (Depths of the Rhine) and its corresponding element is that of water, surging and flowing restlessly while the three Rhinemaidens – Woglinde, Wellgunde and Floßhilde – gambol around the steep rocky reefs that rear up out of the depths, soon to be interrupted by the lustful Nibelung dwarf Alberich, who will steal the *Rheingold*, thus setting in motion the vast four-part drama of the *Ring*.[108] The graphite drawing on beige paper that Appia made for this scene in 1892 does indeed attain the high degree of simplicity that he had set for himself. Formally, it is composed of three rocky reefs – corresponding to the three Rhinemaidens – which are drawn in outline only and appear to be pierced by four straight lines, all approximately the same length, that each intimate motion since they are skewed off the horizontal. What one comes to realise is that these lines are 'notations'; they are a representation of the four performers in the underwater scene, but there is no attempt whatsoever at naturalism. What the lines do is locate the performers in space – both in respect to their surroundings, and more fundamentally, in respect to each other – in a manner that is analogous to musical notation, which also is a graphic representation of a phenomenon that in reality has duration but that through abstraction can be frozen in time on the page.

Appia made a similarly pared-back drawing for the second scene, which is the open mountaintop area near the Rhine over which Valhalla ranges majestically, as described by Wagner in his staging instructions: 'The light of breaking day falls with growing splendour on a fortress with gleaming battlements visible on a rocky pinnacle in the background; between it and the foreground, a deep valley with the Rhine flowing through it is to be imagined.'[109] Again, the topographical features are few in number and Appia drew them in outline only, starting with Valhalla, the mighty fortress of the gods that dominates the scene, though it stands in the background.[110] The foreground is where all of the action takes place, and again Appia has precisely indicated the location of the characters using his newly invented technique of notation – straight lines that provide no sense of figuration, but which situate human bodies in both plan and elevation; that is, in space. And these lines, all vertical in this drawing since the characters are standing, diminish in height the further back they are in the scene, which Appia wrote 'must be entirely practicable, without any detail that is not three-dimensional'.[111] So these drawings are in fact perspectival, although that is not how they at first appear, since there are no forms with lines perpendicular to the picture frame that might guide our eyes towards the vanishing point on the horizon. This realisation is worth a pause, since it is for the perspective drawings that Appia made in his middle years – his *Espaces rythmiques* – that the scenographer is best known, since they make explicit his intent for the stage to become a genuinely three-dimensional proposition. And yet, the idea is here already, *in nuce*.

Appia, 'Notes de mise-en-scène für den Ring des Nibelungen', 1891–92.

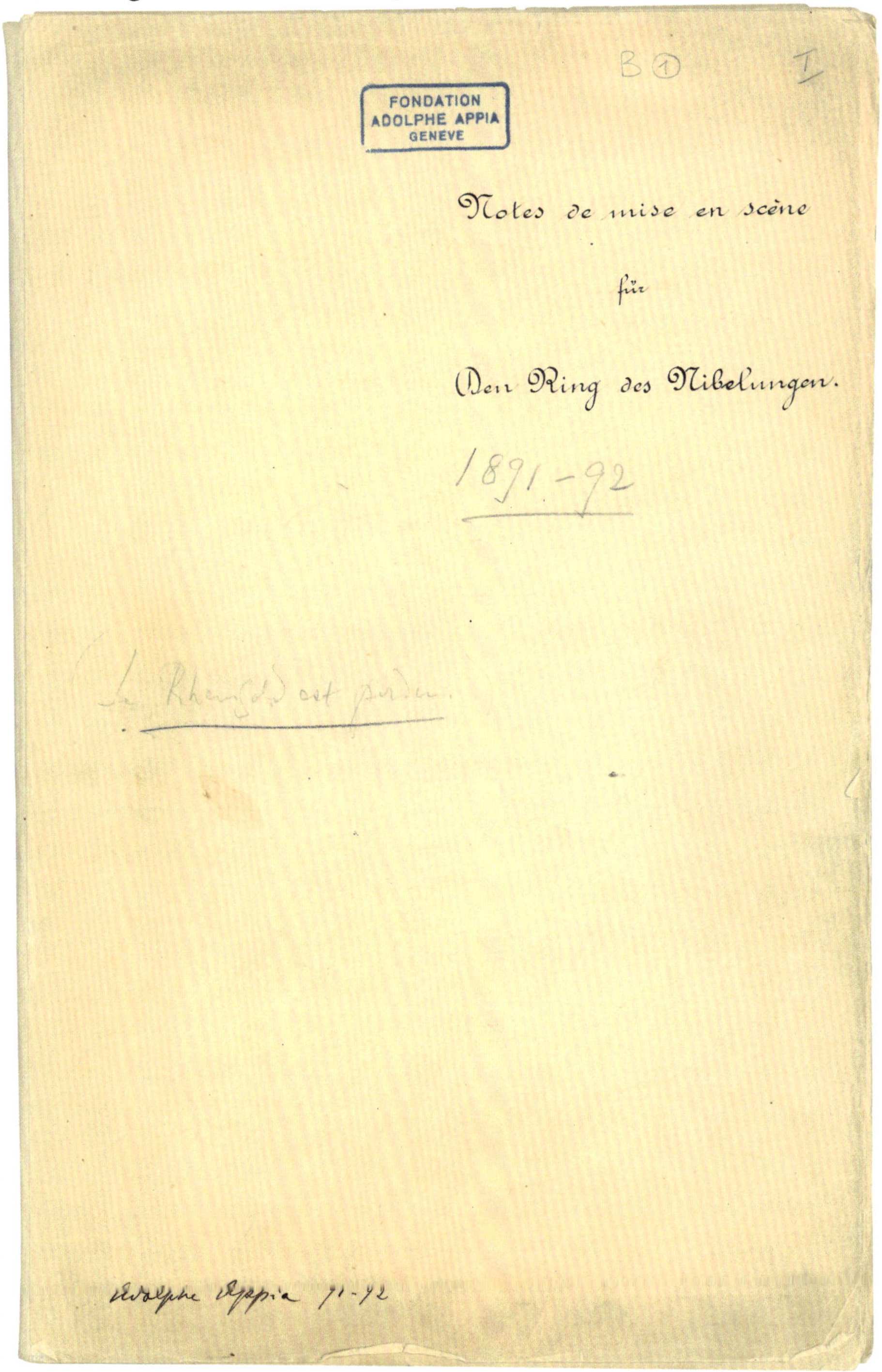

In addition to the outline drawing that Appia made in 1892 for this second scene in *Das Rheingold*, he made a handful of others, of which three still exist. And these three drawings are very different in character to the first insofar as they are full renderings of distinct moments in the scene and demonstrate the importance to Appia of not only form, but also colour and illumination. What these drawings convey, above all, is atmosphere. The first of them, so far as the action goes, is for the very opening of the scene, as 'the light of breaking day falls with growing splendour' on Valhalla, which in Appia's words stands 'precisely in the centre ... rising majestically, its summit invisible to the audience'.[112] The dawning sun that is rising above the horizon directly behind us has cast its full light only on Valhalla, and it is here that we can see what Appia yielded from his drawing teacher Benedikt Kietz in regard to working with tinted papers and pastel – though the two ultimately used the technique for contrary purposes. For Kietz, and the more talented artists who came before him, all the way back to Leonardo da Vinci, it was a way of generating a translucent vivacity seen as highlights in the faces of his portraits. For Appia, in contrast, it was a means to create a faint luminosity – white pastel can be added to shift parts of the drawing to the lighter end of the visual register, which is what he has done here in the upper reaches of the monumental, illuminated peak of Valhalla.

Appia later emphasised the importance of the colouring of this scene, writing that he would 'like to remind the reader that, particularly regarding the Valhalla landscape, colour plays a major role'. The entire traversable foreground terrain on which the performance takes place 'glows in that fresh, uninterrupted, lush green of Alpine meadows. Only in the two raw clefts (for Nibelheim and for Erda) are bare soil and rock to be seen.' 'Over and above all of these greens Valhalla rises, mighty, rocky – artificial.'[113] Appia only ever drew with charcoal, graphite and white pastel, meaning that what he added to the page was entirely monochrome. However, he carefully selected the colours of his drawing papers – mostly in hues of beige and pale blues and greens in these early drawings – to give each drawing a distinctive ambient undertone.

In the second of his three atmospheric drawings for this second scene in *Das Rheingold*, the sun has risen and the contours of the rocky landscape at the foot of Valhalla are more distinct, as too are the banks of the mighty river that flows horizontally through the scene, dividing the three-dimensional foreground from the two-dimensional background that is now palely illuminated. In his third drawing, Valhalla has disappeared from sight, in accordance with Wagner's staging instructions: 'A hazy fog fills the stage with increasing density; within it the gods turn pale, taking on the appearance of old age more and more; all stand with a worried and expectant gaze on Wotan, who, his mind elsewhere, fixes his eyes on the floor.'[114] He has only now come to proper realisation of the price of Valhalla, which is Freia – goddess of youth, love and beauty – whom he promised to the two giants Fasolt and Fafner in return for the fortress they built for him. The brothers agree to renounce their claim on Freia in return for the ring, but that is a treasure that Wotan does not possess, and which is not his to trade, at least not yet: 'Get up! Descend with me! Let's get down to Nibelheim: I need to win the gold', is his impassioned entreaty to Loge, who agrees to lead the way. The two gods descend into the cavern that Appia decided to place on the right-hand side of his drawing, and out of which sulphurous vapour now pours, spreading over the entire stage and quickly enveloping it with a dense cloud.[115]

The subterranean world of the Nibelung dwarfs, skilled metalsmiths who mine the spoils of the earth and forge them into new forms, is the setting for the third scene.[116] According to Appia, the 'element' for this scene is fire, and since 'fire only illuminates the area from which it derives, in a forge it cannot come from above'. He notes that the lighting should be obviously artificial, contrasting with the previous open-air scene. And furthermore, this light should come in irregular flashes, deriving as it does from the fires excited by the bellows. 'Showers of glimmering sparks will suddenly uncover this or that detail of the set, and the spatial arrangement, by being an obstacle to the light, will create with its heavy shadows a sense of chaos.'[117] 'Here is being forged that which will ruin the world', wrote Appia dramatically, before reiterating his conviction that it is to the music that the scenographer must turn for guidance regarding the character of this setting, leading away from naturalism towards a 'high degree of simplicity'. 'A reading of the libretto alone cannot possibly make us expect the tragic grandeur with which the music invests this space', he wrote. 'The general impression will be one of subjugation and a lack of light. The mere proportions of the set will have to be somehow crushing.'[118]

Appia once again made an outline drawing for this scene, and the overall sense that it conveys is indeed a crushing one; the weight of the earth above the cavern is palpable. In the language of architecture, the part of the setting above the oblique line that sinks from the right-hand side of the page to the left – and that vertically divides the drawing approximately in two – is seen in section, but Appia himself referred to it as a 'geological slice'. That is, all the action takes place in the cramped area below that slice, which is supported by a powerful central column of stone that occludes the forges of the Nibelungen yet allows their 'showers of glimmering sparks' to indirectly illuminate the scene.

Alberich, who was taunted and tormented by the Rhinemaidens in the first scene, has now turned tormenter, and it is his brother Mime who bears the brunt. 'Over here, cunning dwarf!' hollers Alberich at his brother, who has diligently forged for him a magical helmet, the Tarnhelm. Alberich places it on his head and vanishes, just as Wotan and Loge lower themselves down out of a shaft above. The dwarf takes a long and mistrustful look at the two gods, takes off the helmet, then starts to brag to them about his newly won powers of invisibility and shapeshifting. Wily Loge tricks Alberich into transforming himself into a toad, and Wotan traps him underfoot before tying him up and dragging him up through the chasm through which they first entered the scene. That same sulphur that enveloped the stage at the end of the second scene reappears and the transformation takes place again, though in reverse order; the setting is once more 'an open mountaintop area near the Rhine'.

Fettered and humiliated, Alberich is forced by Wotan to give up his ill-obtained hoard of treasure, which his tyrannised Nibelung brethren haul through the chasm and pile up in the foreground of the stage. As a final insult, Wotan takes the ring from the dwarf, who quickly vanishes into the chasm as the scene begins to grow lighter. And now it is Wotan's turn to be humiliated: In order to fill the final crack in the pile of treasure, the giants Fasolt and Fafner demand the ring. Wotan refuses, that is, until the prophetic earth goddess Erda emerges and delivers him a warning: 'All that is, – will end! A dark day is dawning for the gods: – I advise you, avoid the ring!' With sudden resolve, Wotan throws the ring onto the pile and the giants bicker over it. Fafner kills Fasolt with a single stroke then tucks the ring into his sack, leisurely gathering what remains of the hoard along with it. 'All the gods are rooted to the spot in horror', wrote Wagner. 'Portentous silence.'

Donner determines to clear the air, and summons the weather to order, disappearing at first inside an 'increasingly dark accumulation of thundercloud' that he then disperses with a blow of his hammer and a flash of lightning. A dazzling rainbow bridge becomes visible, stretching across from the valley to Valhalla. 'Wotan and the other gods are lost in speechless amazement at the glorious sight.' But then Wotan gathers his senses, takes his wife Fricka by the hand and walks slowly toward the bridge, followed by Froh, Freia and Donner. Loge lingers in the foreground and warns that the gods are 'speeding on to their destruction', before eventually falling into line behind them. The curtain falls.

following spread
Das Rheingold, Scene 2: Valhalla Landscape, 48.1×62.8 cm, 1892.

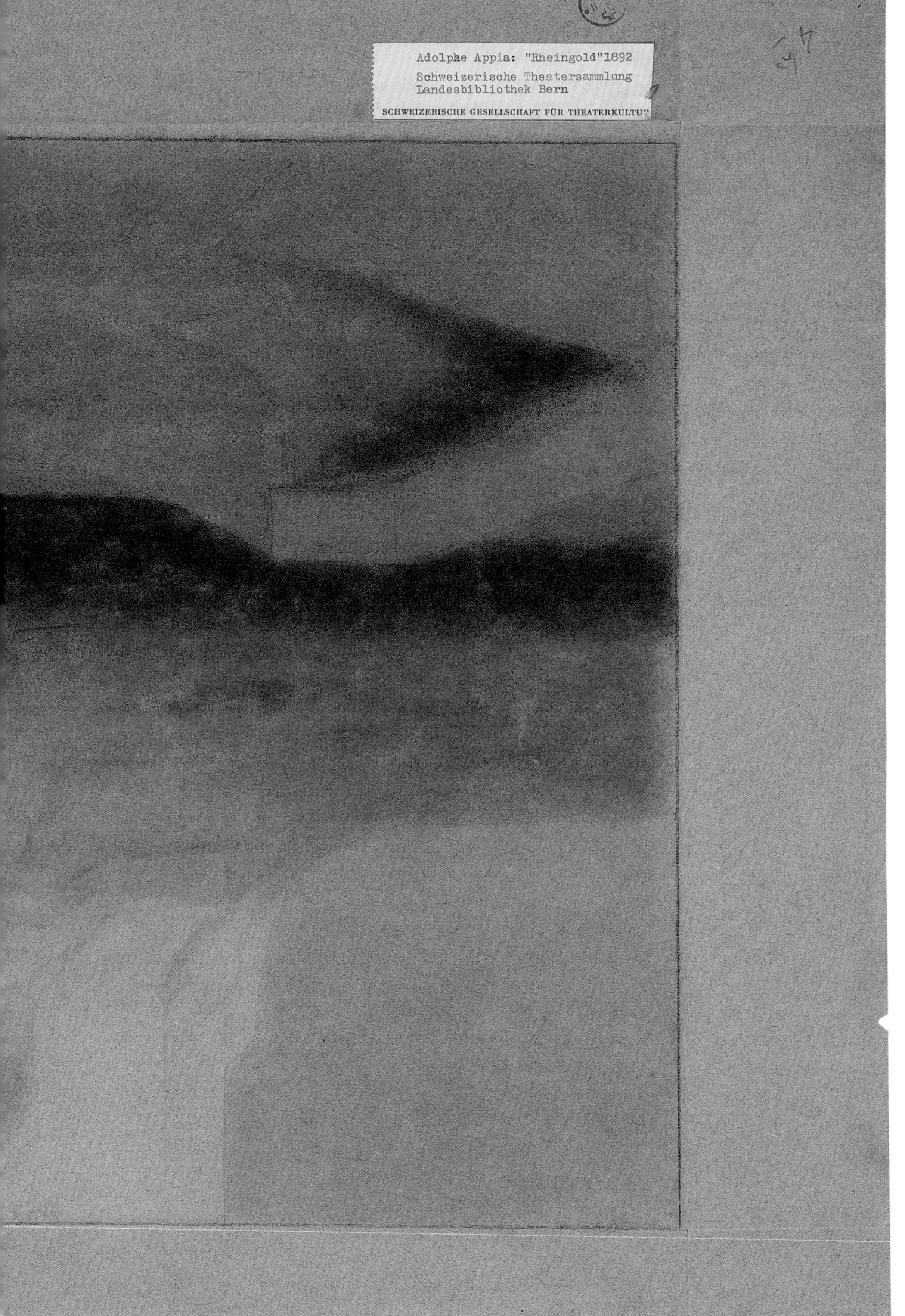
Adolphe Appia: "Rheingold"1892
Schweizerische Theatersammlung
Landesbibliothek Bern
SCHWEIZERISCHE GESELLSCHAFT FÜR THEATERKULTUR

Das Rheingold, Prelude and Scene 1: In the Depths of the Rhine, 18.1×22.5 cm, 1892

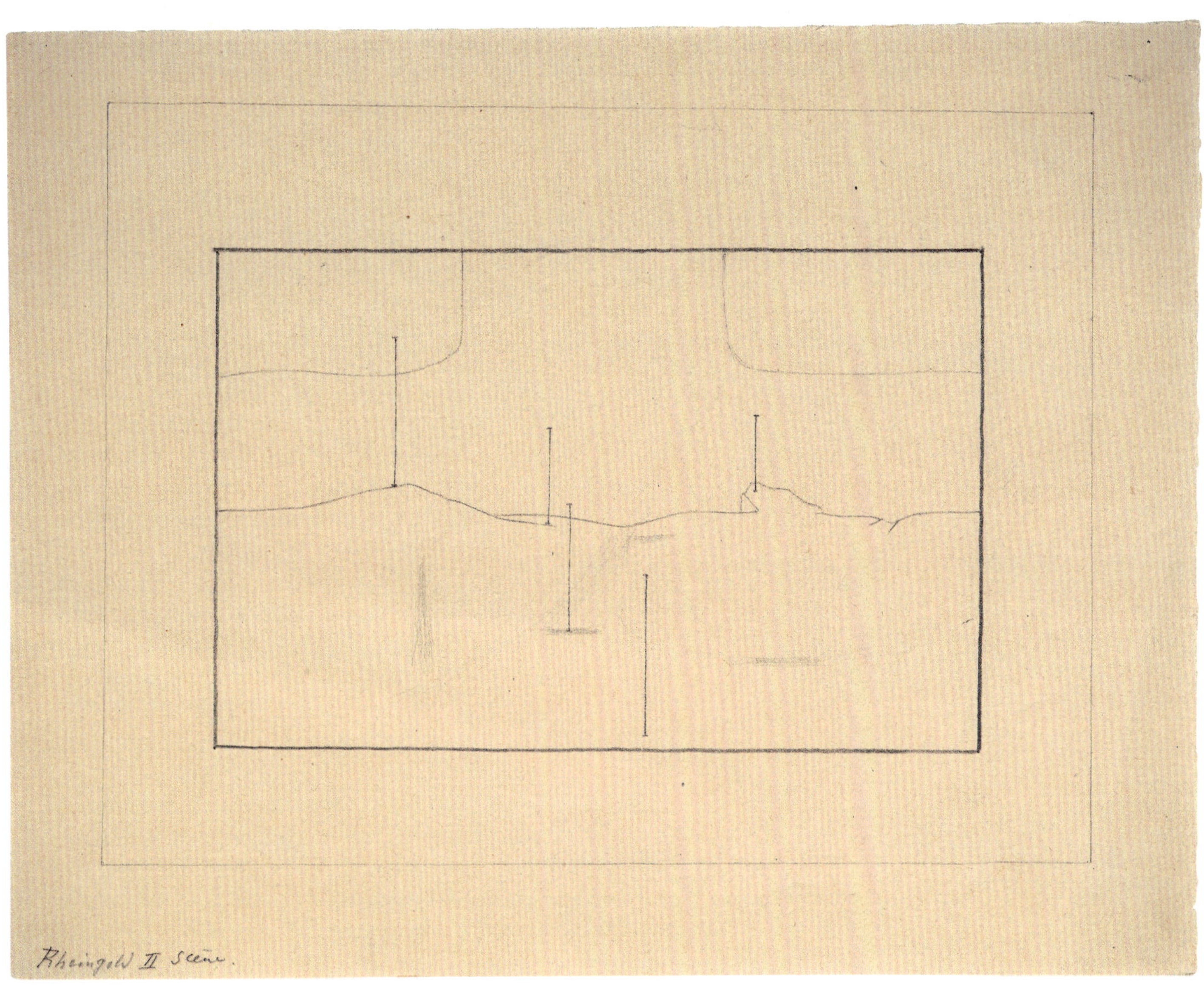

Das Rheingold, Scene 2: Valhalla Landscape, 18.1×22.5 cm, 1892

Das Rheingold, Scene 2: Valhalla Landscape, 47.0×61.5 cm, 1896

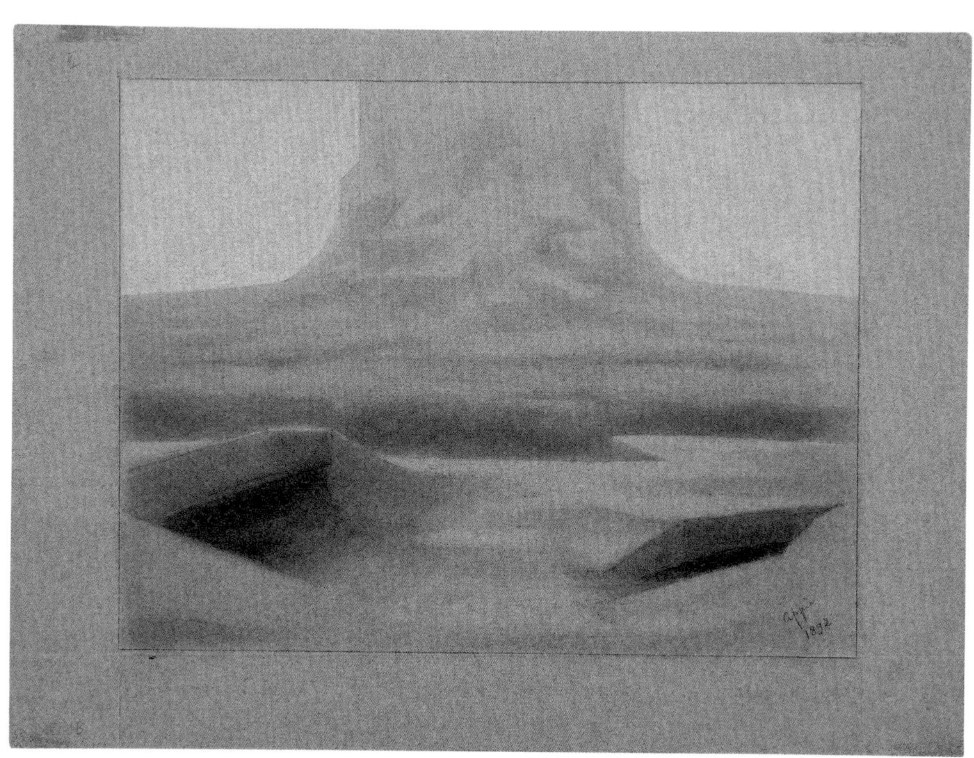

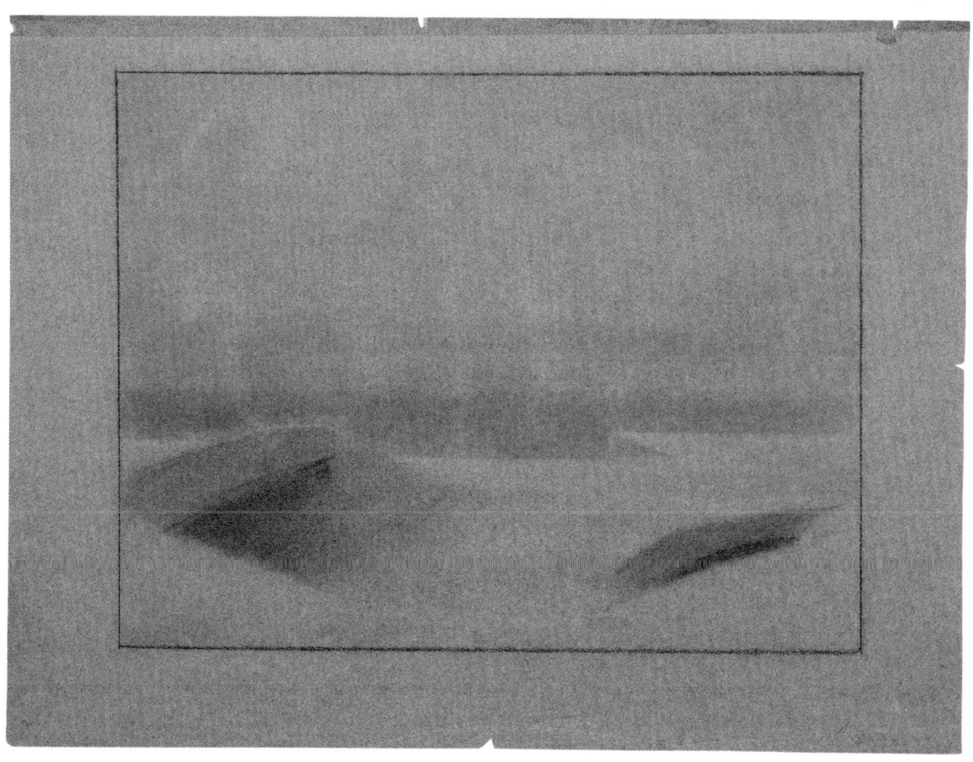

Das Rheingold, Scene 2: Valhalla Landscape, 48.0×62.9 cm; Close of Scene 2
Opening of Scene 4: Valhalla Landscape, 47.0×61.5 cm, 1892

following spread *Das Rheingold*, Scene 3: Nibelheim's Underground Chasms, 18.1×22.5 cm, 1892

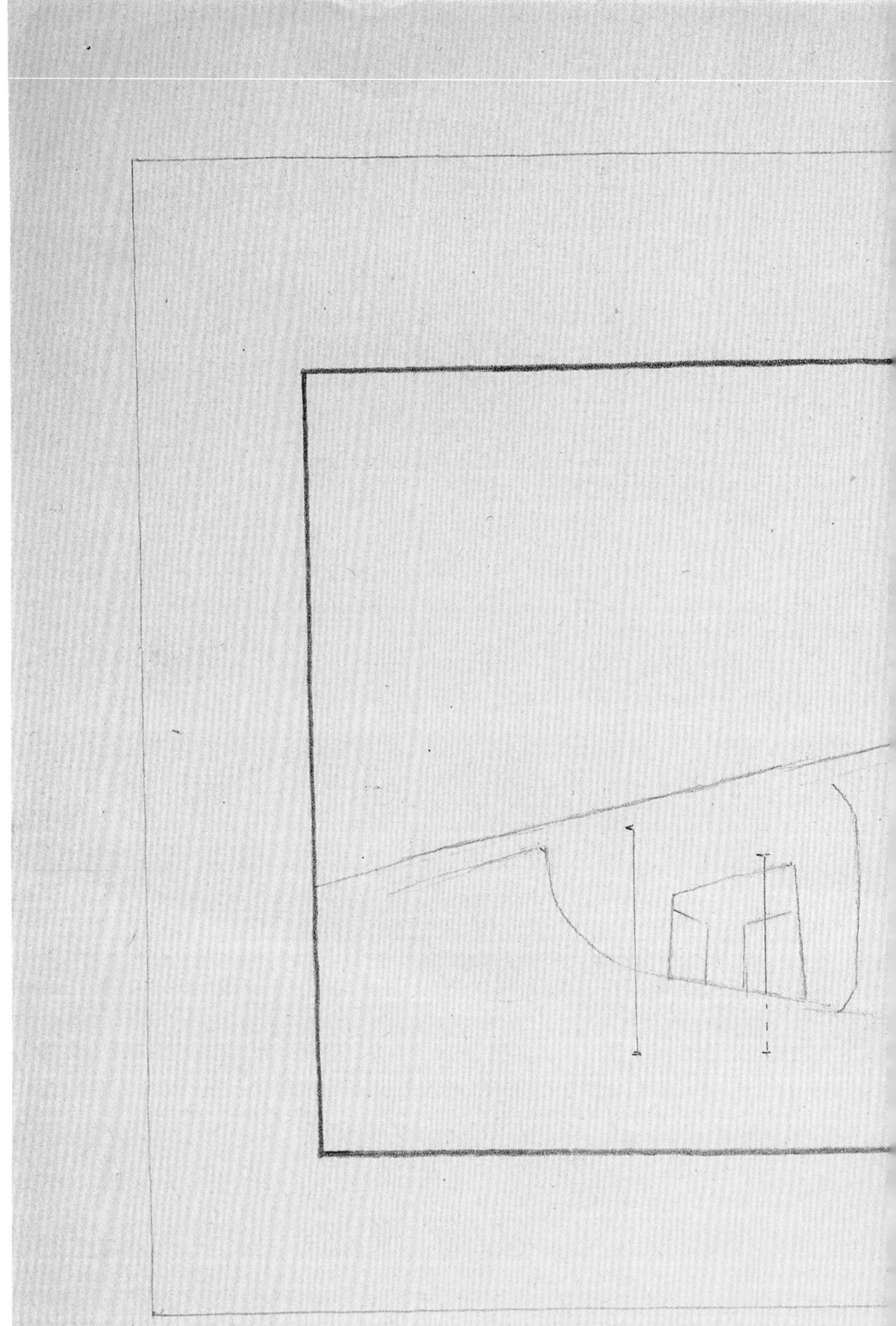

Rheingold III Scene.

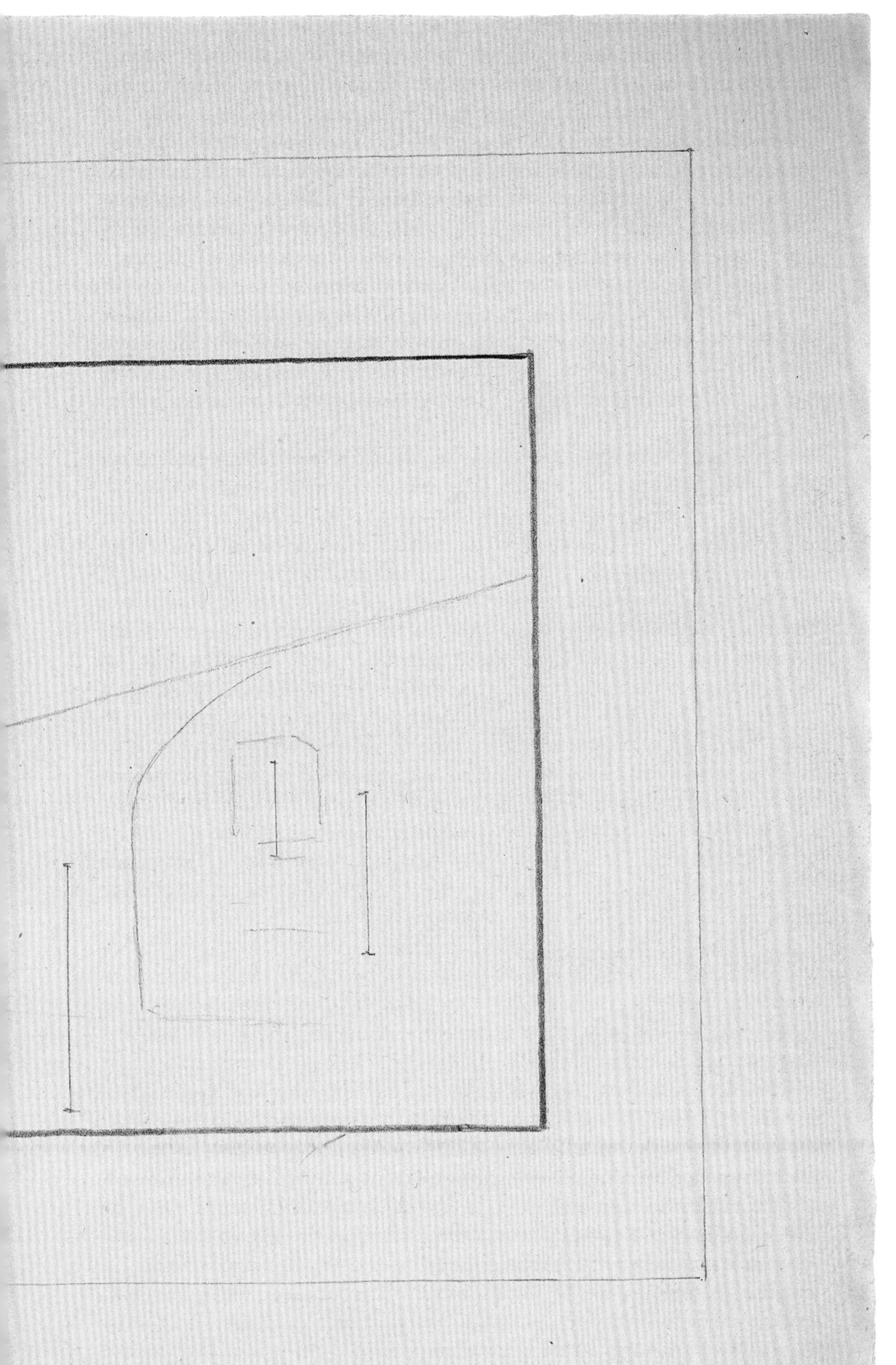

When the curtain rises for the opening scene of act one of *Die Walküre* the setting that stands before the audience is of a different order to those of *Das Rheingold* in that it is architectural rather than elemental; the heftily crafted timber interior of a hunting lodge that has been built around a mighty ash tree occupies the centre of the stage.[119] In Wagner's staging instructions, the branches of the tree pass through the roof here and there, which is exactly what they do in the set that the Brückner brothers painted for Wagner based on Hoffmann's sketches. A hearth with a chimney stands on the right-hand side of the stage, and on the other side there is a rustic dining table and chairs like those found in taverns. Bearskin rugs lie on the floor in the foreground.

Appia wrote that at the beginning of this first scene, the sole source of illumination is the flickering fire in the hearth, which 'burns brightly enough to light up the surroundings, casting fantastic shadows'. The trunk of the tree occludes the light from the hearth, sinking the left-hand side of the stage into darkness, while its branches 'cast shadows that dance on the roof beams above'.[120]

The aspect of the physical setting that Appia pays most attention to in his staging instructions is in fact the floor, which is earthen and uneven, displaced by the sturdy roots of the ash tree that have grown up through it, but that have been worn down again on one side by the traffic of feet between the table and the hearth.[121] And it is the hearth that first attracts the attention of the weary stranger who enters the lodge owned by Hunding, who is still out hunting. 'Whoever's hearth this is, I must rest here', he announces, before throwing himself down dead tired on one of the bearskins. Taken aback by his presence, Hunding's wife wakes him: 'Water Water!' the parched stranger implores her, and she brings him a drinking-horn filled to the brim with cool water. Now slaked and grateful, he begins to tell his story: for days now, he has been harried by a vengeful pack of hunters, and then, to make matters worse, a raging storm descended, driving him to the lodge in search of refuge. His tale apparently fully told; the stranger gets up to leave. But the woman beseeches him to stay, and it is apparent that a secret bond is growing between them: 'She raises her eyes slowly to look at him; with an expression of great emotion, they gaze in long silence into each other's eyes.'

Hunding arrives home at the beginning of the scene that follows, and he is immediately irritated by the presence of the foreigner. Though instinctively distrustful, he grants the stranger hospitality – just for the night – on the condition that he reveals his name. The stranger says that he calls himself Wehwalt, which means 'ruled by sorrow', and by way of explanation, he recounts the woebegone story of his childhood. Hunding gradually realises that the stranger is in fact the very man that he himself had been looking for, and challenges him to combat the next day, the laws of hospitality protecting the stranger for the moment. Hunding retires to bed and on his way orders his wife to prepare his nightly drink. 'She leaves carrying the torch that has been illuminating the scene', wrote Appia, 'leaving the stage very dark'. The stranger is now all alone, and his thoughts turn to the duel that he will have with Hunding the following day. He recalls his father's promise to avail him with a sword should he find himself in just such a situation, and as a hint to what will come, Appia wrote that during this scene 'a gentle light should fall on the hilt of the sword'.[122] Hunding's wife returns, having sent her husband to sleep by lacing his drink, and she draws the stranger's attention to a sword driven into the ash tree, all the way up to its palely illuminated hilt. It was thrust there during her wedding by a stranger, and nobody at that time or since has had the strength to draw it from the tree – she is waiting for her saviour to do so.

Max Brückner, *Die Walküre*, Act 1: Inside Hunding's House, 1896.

The woman and the stranger passionately embrace as the great door behind them springs open to let in the light of the moon on a beautiful spring night. This moonlight, according to Appia, 'should fall obliquely on the floor, from as high up as possible. It must fall on the couch that stands at the foot of the hearth, plus the area of the floor that leads up to it from the door. And it

should just graze the trunk of the ash tree. Everything that the light hits directly must be three-dimensional. The colour of this light should be rather golden than too blue, and it must be constant. It does not need to be very bright since that would be disadvantageous for the faces of the actors. The door height is regulated by the requirements of this illumination, but it will be preferable to keep it within the bounds of typical dimensions.'[123] The relations between the man and the woman are soon revealed to be beyond the bounds of the typical – they are siblings. 'Let me call you as I love you – Siegmund – that is your name!' announces the woman – Sieglinde – to her twin brother sitting close beside her on the couch. Emboldened, he springs to his feet and grips the hilt of the sword that he then names: 'Nothung!

Max Brückner, *Die Walküre*, Act 2: Wild Rocky Mountains, 1896.

Nothung! Pitiless steel! Show your sharp edge!' Siegmund pulls his sister close to him 'with unruly passion', instructs Wagner. The curtain falls quickly. The setting for the opening scene of the second act of *Die Walküre* is once again an outdoor one, this time in the craggy mountains, where a ravine stretches upwards, leading into a high pass in the rocks, from where the ground again dips down towards the front of the stage, into a 'dark void', in Appia's words. 'The setting is delimited', he wrote, 'by a slice of darkness that resembles a geological slice, following the contours of the terrain'.[124] Wotan is armed for war and so too is one of his Valkyrie daughters, Brünnhilde, who leaps to the task of ensuring victory for Siegmund in his duel with Hunding: '*Hojotoho!*

Hojotoho! Heiaha! Heiaha! Hojotoho! Hojotoho! Heiaha! Heiaha! Hojotoho! Hojotoho! Hojotoho! Hojotoho! Heiahaja! Hojoho!'[125]

Sounds of Hunding's approach are heard, summoning Siegmund to battle. According to Wagner's instructions, 'the stage becomes gradually darker; heavy storm clouds gather in the background and one by one settle down until they envelop, little by little, the mountain walls, the ravine, and the heightened mountain ridge'. As the foes hurl insults at each other, a lightning flash reveals them engaged in ruthless battle. In regard to the staging of this pivotal scene, Appia wrote that although the audience must be able to recognise the characters and grasp the purpose of their movements, 'it is not necessary for them to be perfectly distinct all the time; in addition to the projections that must envelop the scene and create a vital atmosphere, gauzes can be combined in such a way as to pass in front of the characters, without harshness, appearing as a trail of mist'. Brünnhilde arrives on the scene determined to protect Siegmund with her shield, and according to Appia she is accompanied by a 'light furnished by an apparatus placed behind some rock that has been specially placed for this purpose, as near to her as possible. It is not a white, pale light, but rather *golden*. The two combatants are *in silhouette*; Brünnhilde alone stands in the light.'[126]

Max Brückner, *Die Walküre*, Act 3: On the Summit of a Rocky Mountain (Brünnhilde's Rock), 1896.

Having now attained the upper hand in his duel with Hunding, Siegmund steadies himself to deliver his foe a final deadly blow with Nothung, but then

– exactly on the fourth beat of the bar 165/5, according to Appia – a 'blood-red light begins to glow on the left-hand side of the stage, then it breaks through the clouds'. Wotan appears from behind one of the rocks, and though Brünnhilde's light fails to illuminate him, his light 'suddenly tinges her with a bloody gleam', according to Appia.[127] Brünnhilde takes a step back in horrified despair – Wotan intends to intervene in the battle. As Siegmund flashes Nothung towards Hunding, the sword shatters on the god's spear. And then, on the second beat of the bar 166/1, Hunding drives his own spear into the defenceless Siegmund, who falls lifeless to the ground.

The two kinds of light – golden for Brünnhilde and blood-red for Wotan – vanish, replaced by dense, gloomy clouds. Out of this darkness, Brünnhilde emerges with her horse Grane from a gorge on the right-hand side of the stage. 'If I am to save you, get on the horse!' she implores Sieglinde, before taking matters into her own hands, hoisting her up. As the two of them ride off in haste, the clouds part so that Hunding, who has just pulled his spear out of Siegmund's chest, can clearly be seen. Wotan stands behind him on a rock, leaning on his spear and gazing in distress at Siegmund's corpse, according to Wagner's staging instructions. Appia focused on the music, writing that it is on the penultimate beat of 167/1 that Hunding tears his sword from Siegmund's body, and re-sheathes it with force in his scabbard. With a wave of his hand over the corpse, he indicates that his revenge has been satisfied. It is important, wrote Appia, that his gestures have that character of a pantomime, serving as a foil for Wotan whose actions now are 'brutal, violent, but not rushed. Wotan, body motionless, turns only his eyes to Hunding'. On the third beat of bar 167/3, wrote Appia, 'Wotan makes a very sober gesture with his spear, and he says '*geh!*' (go!) almost without emotion. Wotan repeats the word, still not shouting, but scornfully and with greater emphasis, and with a contemptuous wave of his left hand.[128] Hunding sinks to the ground, dead.

'Now for Brünnhilde! That delinquent will be sorry!' announces her father in a sudden rage. 'Special projections surround him with clouds, while the lightning starts again, at first very moderate, and there is also a dull roll of thunder', wrote Appia.[129] And then there is a terrible peal as Wotan climbs up to the high pass in the rocks, 'accompanied by a whirlwind of projections'. Finally, according to Wagner's staging instructions, 'Wotan vanishes in thunder and lightning. – The curtain quickly falls.'

According to Appia, the third and final act of *Die Walküre* – 'On the Summit of a Rocky Mountain' – is a particularly difficult one to stage. The dramatic events that unfold require topographical features that are not usually found together in nature: 'Wagner demands the impossible', wrote Appia, referring to the fact that there is to be a rocky summit above which a second peak rises, a cave and also a fir tree.[130] 'A cave at the top of a mountain is very rare, and the mass of a tree would annihilate the effect of a summit', he observed. 'The author has sought, however, to reconcile the irreconcilable,' wrote Appia in the third person, 'and it was the score itself that guided his pencil'.[131]

The score for the opening scene of this third act of *Die Walküre* is, in Alex Ross's words, 'Wagner's finest action sequence – a virtuoso exercise in the massing of forces and the accumulation of energy'.[132] It is the mustering of the Valkyries – Gerhilde, Ortlinde, Waltraute, Schwertleite, Helmwige, Siegrune, Grimgerde and Rossweisse – in full battle armour, each carrying on their horse a slain hero destined for the hall of Valhalla. Ross describes the galloping music: 'At the beginning, winds trill against quick upward swoops in the strings; horns, bassoons, and cellos establish a galloping rhythm, at medium volume; then comes a trickier wind-and-string texture, with staggered entries and downward swooping patterns added; and, finally, horns and bass trumpet lay out the main theme. Successive iterations of the material are bolstered with trumpets, more horns, and four stentorian trombones.' The last two Valkyries to arrive at the assembly are Rossweisse and Grimgerde, and when they do, 'the contrabass tuba enters fortissimo beneath the trombones, giving the sense of maximum reinforcements arriving'.[133]

Appia's fully rendered drawing of this moment in Wagner's action sequence is the most vital among his 1891–92 settings for the *Ring*. The eight battle-ready Valkyries are gathered on the rocky summit that stands on the left of the scene, silhouetted against the sky as portentous storm clouds roll in from the right. Siegrune is stationed as a lookout atop the final peak with her spear held high, and in the action that immediately follows she calls out to her Valkyrie sisters down below: 'Brünnhilde riding this way at break-neck speed!' She arrives, bearing Sieglinde on the saddle of her horse, which is floundering from the wild ride. Brünnhilde is fleeing, furiously pursued by Wotan for whisking away and protecting the woman. In Appia's next drawing, Wotan's imminent arrival is announced by the dark storm cloud that gathers in the north and now arrives on stage with full force. 'Rescue me, brave one!' implores Sieglinde. Brünnhilde offers herself up to her father Wotan's revenge, delaying the angry god while the woman escapes. 'Just know one thing, and never forget it', she calls out after Sieglinde. 'It is the world's noblest hero that you are bearing in your womb.' She takes the pieces of Siegmund's shattered sword out from under her armour and hands them to Sieglinde: 'Keep these sturdy pieces of the sword safe ... let him, who will one day forge and flourish the sword anew, take the name I give to him now: "Siegfried" – joyous in victory!' Wotan arrives: 'Stop! Brünnhilde!' The Valkyries surround their imperilled sister as Wotan gets down from his horse in a rage, 'with unforgiving strides'. Appia captured him mid-stride and centre-stage, girded by the storm clouds that are dissipating as he pronounces his stony-hearted sentence: 'I divorce you from the company of the gods, disowned by the immortal lineage; our bond is rent asunder; from my presence you are banished.' To the horror of the Valkyries, Wotan condemns Brünnhilde to lie defenceless in unguarded sleep, vulnerable to the first man who finds her. They protest, but Wotan is resolute: 'Your treacherous sister is banished from your company; no longer shall she ride the skies with you on horseback.' The Valkyries disperse with wild screams of woe as black clouds gather, then break apart with the discharge of a garish flash of lightning which reveals an image of the battle maidens in tight formation, riding off wildly at full speed. The storm soon settles down and the clouds disperse. Twilight descends, followed by night.

It is all music scored for cinema, though that medium was yet to be invented in Wagner's time and was still some way off even when Appia was writing his notes and making his drawings. He recognised the filmic potential though, and while the cinematic lexicon was yet to be formulated, there is no doubt that the silver screen is what he had in mind: 'Until the means of *photographie électrique* – which involves the quasi-simultaneous projection of a series of images to give the illusion of one continuous moving image – is introduced into theatre practice, *Die Walküre* will never be staged satisfactorily.'[134]

But back to the becalmed drama of the stage on which Wotan and Brünnhilde stand alone. She is wondering whether her actions really were so wrong, to which he responds: 'Yes'. And yet Wotan promises to protect his Valkyrie daughter – to an extent. 'Let the rock that is aglow with flaming heat scatter the fainthearted ... Only one is destined to wed the bride, one freer than I, the god!' he announces, placing long kisses on both of her eyes, lulling

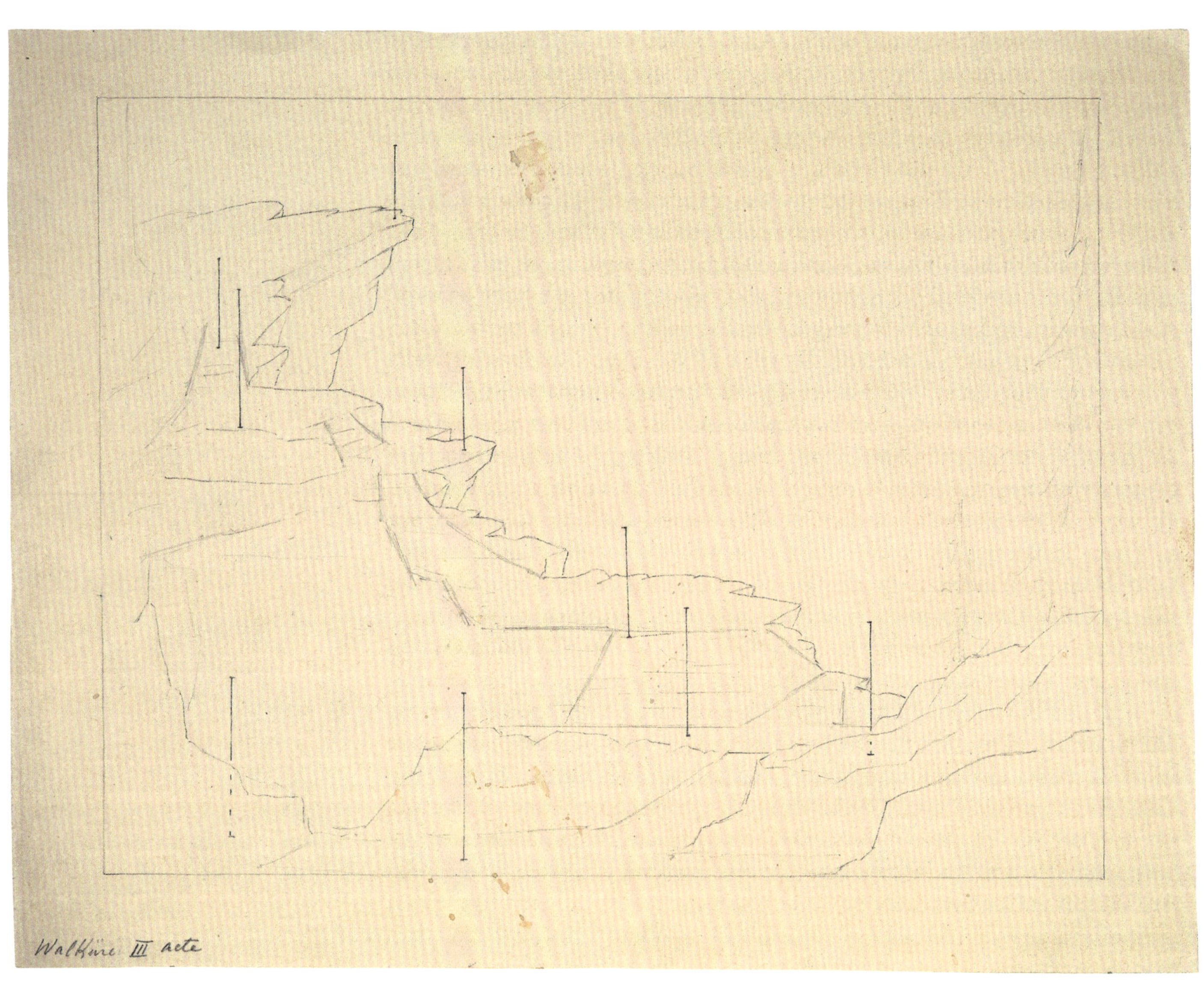

Die Walküre, Act 3: On the Summit of a Rocky Mountain (Brünnhilde's Rock), 17.4 × 22.0 cm, 1892

Die Walküre, Act 3: On the Summit of a Rocky Mountain (Brünnhilde's Rock), 18.8×23.9 cm, 1892

Die Walküre, Act 3: On the Summit of a Rocky Mountain (Brünnhilde's Rock), 48.3×62.7 cm, 1892

Die Walküre, Act 3: On the Summit of a Rocky Mountain (Brünnhilde's Rock), 32.0 × 49.0 cm, 1892

following spread *Die Walküre*, Act 3: On the Summit of a Rocky Mountain (Brünnhilde's Rock), Before the Arrival of Wotan, 31.5 × 48.5 cm, 1892

1892

Die Walküre, Act 3: On the Summit of a Rocky Mountain (Brünnhilde's Rock), 48.5×62.9 cm and 48.0×63.0 cm, 1896

Die Walküre, Act 3: On the Summit of a Rocky Mountain (Brünnhilde's Rock), 31.5 × 48.2 cm and 48.0 × 62.7 cm, 1892

following spread *Die Walküre*, Act 3: On the Summit of a Rocky Mountain (Brünnhilde's Rock), Brünnhilde's Sleep, 48.0 × 63.0 cm, 1892

1892

her to sleep, before leading her tenderly to a low mossy bank beneath the fir tree that Appia alluded to rather than described on the right-hand side of his drawing, revealing only an outstretched low-hanging branch in silhouette. Wotan lays Brünnhilde down then summons Loge: 'Arise, swirling inferno. Girdle the rock with flame!' And that is what Loge does, encircling the Valkyrie in a wild flickering blaze. In Appia's drawing, Brünnhilde has become almost at one with the ground – the contour of her torso and head in profile is all that distinguishes her from it. 'Whoever fears the tip of my spear, never through this fire shall they walk', announces Wotan before he vanishes through the protective ring of flames as the curtain falls on *Die Walküre*.

When the curtain rises on the third evening at Bayreuth – for the prelude of Siegfried – the audience sees a cave in the foreground, with a large rock-formed forge set against the back wall to the left of the scene.[135] Its chimney is fed by large bellows that are likewise naturally formed, issuing upwards through the roof of the cave. Blacksmiths' tools are scattered around, and an oversized anvil stands in the foreground. Mime stands bent over the anvil in frustration – though he slaves and slogs, the swords he forges fail in the hands of Siegfried, who presently blusters in from the forest leading a bear on a leash, no less. Disdain is what he has for Mime, the dwarf feigning to be his father. Pressed on this point, the Nibelung unravels: 'Father this! Mother that! Pointless question!' Grabbing Mime by the throat, Siegfried demands to know: 'Out with it, you scabby rascal! Who are my father and mother?' The Nibelung capitulates under duress and tells the intriguing story that began a long time ago with a woman lying prone in the forest, moaning. Though Mime helped her to his cave and nursed her by the warmth of the hearth, the woman died in childbirth. But the boy survived and, standing now before the dwarf, he demands to know his mother's name, which Mime strains to recall: 'Did I really forget it? Just a second! Maybe it was Sieglinde, the one who anxiously gave you into my care.' But as for his father, Mime has no recollection at all, knowing only that he was slain in battle, his mighty sword was broken into pieces, and – fetching the fragments – in shards it remains. Now full of enthusiasm, Siegfried demands of the dwarf that he re-forge the sword by the end of the day. He bounds out of the cave as Mime trudges back to his anvil, stooping to his task, wondering how he will 'ever be able to match the pieces of the elusive steel'.

The scene that follows is dominated by Wotan, though in his Wanderer guise. Swathed in a long dark-blue coat and wearing a broad round-brimmed hat that hangs low to veil his missing eye, the enigmatic visitor arrives at the threshold of the cave and, leaning on the rune-bedecked spear that is also his walking staff, addresses Mime: 'I salute you, wise smith! Be so kind as to grant a travel-worn visitor the favour of your house and hearth.' The pensive dwarf rises to his feet and attempts to send the Wanderer away, but his visitor is undeterred, walking slowly over to the hearth and taking a seat down beside it. According to Appia, when the Wanderer sits down his form is to be lost in shadow, 'save for the dancing light cast by the occasional flickering ember'.[136] 'Now, dwarf, tell me this', asks the Wanderer of Mime, 'Which sword fit for Fafner's death must Siegfried now wield?' 'Nothung is the name of the pitiless sword', answers Mime, worried since he knows he is not capable of re-forging the broken pieces of the sword himself, of making the damned steel yield. 'Only he who has never felt fear shall forge Nothung anew', offers the Wanderer with a smile, before turning his back and vanishing into the forest.

Max Brückner, *Siegfried*, Act 1: A Rock Cave in the Forest, 1896.

Mime slumps down on the stool behind his anvil as Siegfried arrives at the cave, stomping out of the undergrowth. 'How is the forging of the sword going?' he enquires of the cowering dwarf. Poorly, is the answer: 'Only he who has never felt fear shall forge Nothung anew – I am too wise for such work.' They both turn towards the forge and then Siegfried strides over to it: 'My father's steel will submit to me: I will forge the sword myself!' He pitches in a load of coal and stokes the flames up to maximum heat, before tossing the

rent pieces of Nothung into a melting-pot that he places in the radiant forge. 'Nothung! Nothung! Pitiless sword!' intones Siegfried as he works the bellows. '*Hoho! Hoho! Hahei! Hahei! Hoho!* Bellows blow! Stoke up the flames!' Now that it is molten, Siegfried pours the steel that was once his father's sword into a mould, then plunges it into a bucket of water that hisses and spits. He sets about hammering, sharpening and polishing the blade at the anvil before fastening the mighty sword to its hilt. 'Nothung! Now you are home in your hilt again.' Aglow with pride and self-assurance, he turns to Mime: 'Look, smith that you are – Siegfried's sword cuts like this!' He strikes down on the anvil, cleaving it in two, before holding the sword jubilantly aloft. The curtain falls, quickly.

Max Brückner, *Siegfried*, Act 2: Deep in the Forest, 1896.

According to Appia, the setting the audience is to see before them when the curtain rises for the second act – *Tiefer Wald* (Deep Forest)[137] – must be profoundly verdant. 'Everything is to be *green*, either naturally or through the transparency of the foliage and its reflections; when the light increases at the beginning of the act, the impression of green must captivate the spectator; it must remain with them until the curtain falls', he wrote. The yawning mouth of a cave stands at the back of the stage, while the forest floor in front of it rises to form a small plateau centre-stage. A fissured rockface stands to the left, and that is where Alberich stands darkly brooding, hoping still to recover the treasure for himself: 'I keep watch before Neidhöhle: my ears alert, my eyes strain-

ing to see.' A storm wind is gathering in the forest to the right, accompanied by a bluish light that is 'dancing closer ... hurtling this way'. The wind dies down, and the light fades away, as the Wanderer steps out of the forest into the clearing. According to Wagner's staging instructions, 'as if from the sudden parting of a cloud, moonlight streams in and illuminates the Wanderer's form'. 'Fafner! Fafner! Dragon, wake up!' the Wanderer shouts down into the cave, seeking to alert him to Siegfried's imminent arrival. The dragon stirs but is dismissive of the threat. Fafner yawns: 'Here is my place and here I prevail – let me sleep!' So, the Wanderer takes his leave, escorted by a storm wind and a shaft of light, both of which quickly die away. Alberich slips to one side into a chasm. 'The stage remains empty – *Morgendämmerung* (daybreak).'

As Siegfried and Mime arrive on the scene in the promising light of the dawning day, Fafner rouses himself from his lair and trundles through the undergrowth. Appia was concerned that the dragon would appear ridiculous if his form was fully revealed to the audience, so for him 'a method must be found to present to the audience a vague, ungraspable form ... a menacing, moving mass, nothing more'. At bar 162/1 in the musical score, the dragon's head is to become visible as he makes his way towards the central plateau, which is where he pauses for a yawn (which must be very violent according to Appia, otherwise it would be farcical). He and Siegfried trade barbs, then begin their battle. Appia made a diagrammatic sketch for this action sequence

Max Brückner, *Siegfried*, Act 3: A Wild Region at the Foot of a Rocky Mountain, 1896.

that is remarkable for the fact that it is a plan view, seemingly the only one he ever drew. 'The plan specifies the movements of Fafner (- - - + - - - + - - -) and Siegfried (|||||||||)', he explained. The path marked out for Fafner is in fact a trench deep enough for the actor operating the mechanism that animates the head and body of the dragon to stand in, out of sight of the audience. According to Appia, the tail of the dragon is operated independently of the body and is to be 'set in motion by the advanced techniques used for snakes in fairgrounds'. Fafner coils back his tail on the first measure of bar 165/1, then takes an almighty sweep with it at Siegfried. But the 'dauntless boy' leaps over it and plunges his sword into the dragon's heart, right up to the hilt. Siegfried reveals his name to his dying foe 'in a conversational tone', according to Appia 'while the orchestra provides its own commentary'. Fafner cries out 'Siegfried!' as he raises himself up one last time then dies. Siegfried plucks the Tarnhelm from the cave that Appia has indicated is on the left side of his plan drawing and shoves it into his belt, then slips the ring onto his finger before heaving the corpse of the dragon to the entrance of the cave, blocking it off entirely.

The rugged setting for the opening of the final act of Siegfried is at the foot of Brünnhilde's rock, which rises steeply up to the left, its summit out of view.[138] A thunderstorm is raging: 'Projections of clouds, as dark as possible, moving across the entire stage ... the lightning does not illuminate the stage but appears, varying, amidst the projections of clouds, indifferently on the sky or on the mountain. The wind and thunder are very violent at the rise of the curtain', wrote Appia. These darkly projected clouds abate as the Wanderer strides on stage, marching with determination towards the cave in the foreground. Leaning on his spear, he shouts down into the subterrane: 'Waken, Seeress! Seeress! Awaken! ... I am summoning you: Get up! Get up! Out of your foggy vault, out of those murky depths, get up! Erda! Erda! Woman eternal!' A bluish ray of light gradually begins to dawn in the vault of the cave, emanating from the left wall according to Appia, 'spreading softly veiled, throughout the interior of the cave'.

The Wanderer is seeking the advice of Erda, but the earth goddess, the one who knows what the deep hides, says she has none to offer to him. 'Let me return to the deep! Let me lock my wisdom away', she implores. But before he lets her go, the Wanderer lets Erda know that a hero – one without fear – will awaken their daughter Brünnhilde, and then she will 'carry out the deed that redeems the world'. Erda closes her eyes and sinks down, disappearing into the cave as the blue light fades. At bar 227, according to Appia, 'the sky and landscape are entirely clear, calm and *colourless*'.

As the rising moon begins to cast its light over the stage, the Wanderer greets Siegfried, who has arrived on the scene and is enquiring about a rock encircled by fire where a 'woman is asleep ... I want to wake her'. The Wanderer points with his spear to the top of the rock, where a swirling glow of fire appears. According to Appia, the appearance of the fire is 'not one of *colour*, but rather a *movement* – a moving fire; a small amount of steam can be used, *but without noise*, and projected from *top to bottom*'. The Wanderer entreats Siegfried to abandon his quest, but the boy who knows no fear is resolute. 'Presenting the same magnificent silhouette as in the third act of *Die Walküre*', according to Appia, the Wanderer brandishes his spear on the third beat of bar 244 and then announces: 'I hold in my hand the symbol of sovereignty: this shaft did once shatter the sword you now flourish: so, yet again my eternal spear will rend it asunder!' 'Wield your spear: my sword will cut it apart', retorts Siegfried, who, true to his word, rends the Wanderer's spear in two with a single stroke of Nothung. 'Move on! I can't stop you!' says the Wanderer as he vanishes instantly in total gloom. The fire flares up with ever brighter tongues of flame, and Siegfried dives into the inferno as it surges downwards from the heights, spreading into the foreground. The flames burn at their brightest at bar 250, and from then on begin to gradually dissolve into a gentle cloud that looks to be illuminated by a sunrise.

The cloud disperses into a fine veil of rose-coloured mist that, according to Appia, vanishes entirely by the first beat of bar 253, revealing a 'sky entirely blue except for a faint pinkish tinge in the vapours behind the ridge' of the mountaintop setting that had already appeared in the final scene of *Die Walküre*. Brünnhilde lies deep in sleep under the outstretched branches of the fir tree, wearing her helmet and full battle armour, and with her long shield covering her body. Contrary to the Bayreuth tradition, Appia lies Brünnhilde down so that the audience see her silhouetted in profile, which for him was 'the only way to blend her into the landscape ... directing the audience towards the horizon, which is thereby expanded'. Siegfried lifts off her brilliantly shining shield, loosens her helmet, then cuts away her chain-mail armour. Eyes closed, he presses his lips to Brünnhilde's, and she draws herself up to a sitting position, awakening to the world: 'I greet you sun! I greet you light! I greet you, glorious day!' Appia made a fully rendered drawing of this moment of jubilation, capturing Brünnhilde as she separates herself from the landscape that she was 'blended together with' and gazes upward to Siegfried standing before her with his arms expectantly outstretched. 'Be mine! Be mine! Be mine!' he implores. 'Yours I have been forever!' responds Brünnhilde. Impassioned, they summon the end – the *Götterdämmerung* (Twilight of the Gods).

When the curtain rises slowly for the prologue to *Götterdämmerung*, the three Norns – daughters of Erda – are revealed, weaving their rope of destiny.[139] It is night, and glowing fires shine out of the deep, palely illuminating the statuesque women in dark, richly pleated robes as they stand together atop the rock of the Valkyries as Siegfried and Brünnhilde had done at the end of the previous act. In the past, the Norns had tethered their rope of destiny to the world ash tree, whose 'verdant limbs, blessed, big and strong, blossomed forth from its trunk'. But that was now impossible, since Wotan had cut the shaft of his spear from the mighty tree, draining it of its strength. So, the fir on the mountaintop is serving as its surrogate. According to Appia, the rope is to be golden so that it will stand out against the dark background of the scenery and costumes, and it is to be weighted at one end so that it is convenient for throwing. He wrote that the Norns are to 'perform their work with precision, and grand dignified gestures should characterise each of their movements so that *nothing is confusing* for the audience'. The first Norn unwraps the golden rope from her body and fastens one of its weighted ends to a branch of the tree, then passes it to the second Norn, who continues the story of Wotan, the world ash tree he disfigured, and the calamity that will follow. As the sky reddens with the dawn, the Norns lose their thread as the rope of destiny becomes entangled. 'Eternal knowing at an end! Nothing more have the wise to say to the world ... Down! ... To mother! ... Down', wrote Wagner in his libretto. Siegfried and Brünnhilde emerge from the cave and he gives her the ring as a solemn pledge of his faith, while she in turn gifts him her horse Grane. 'Hail! Hail! Hail! Hail!' they exclaim together, before Siegfried leads Grane to the rocky slope and descends, leaving Brünnhilde on the stage alone as the curtain closes.

As far as Appia was concerned, the atmosphere of the prologue to *Götterdämmerung* was the 'final echo of all that came before in the *Ring*; the remaining scenes are to be treated quite differently. Set designers and costume designers can be given free rein to indulge their imagination and erudition; the general impression is to be a tumultuous overflowing of colour and

Siegfried, Act 1: A Rock Cave in the Forest, 14.5×18.6 cm, 1892

Siegfried, Act 1: A Rock Cave in the Forest, 48.0×62.5 cm, 1892

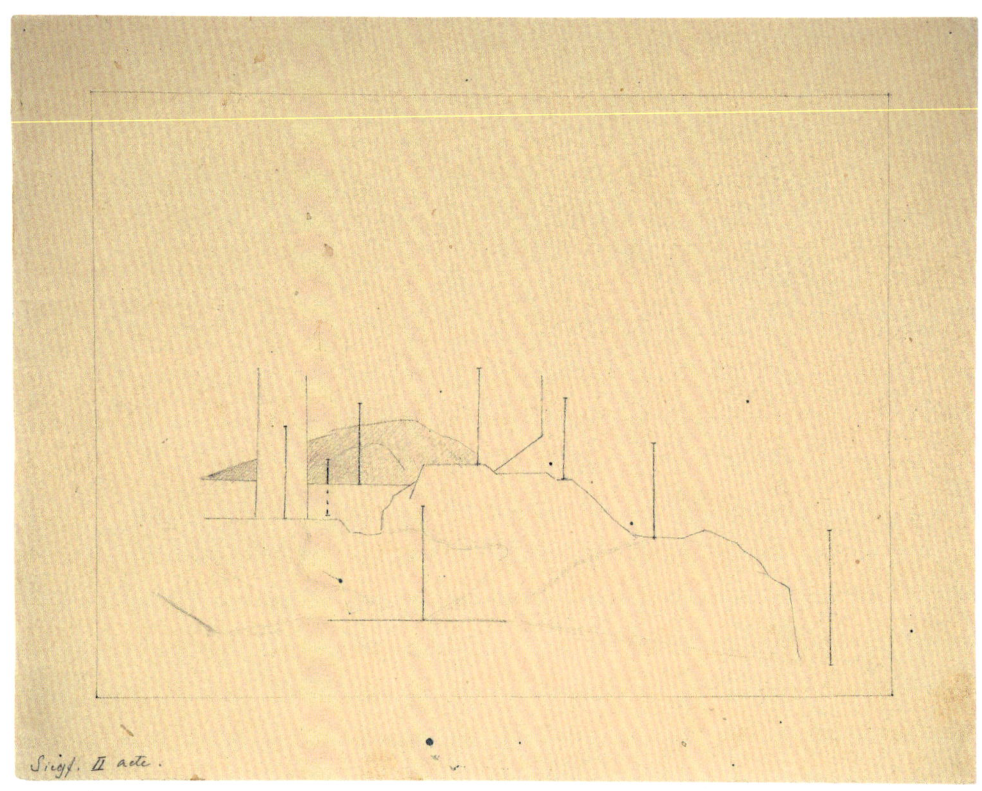

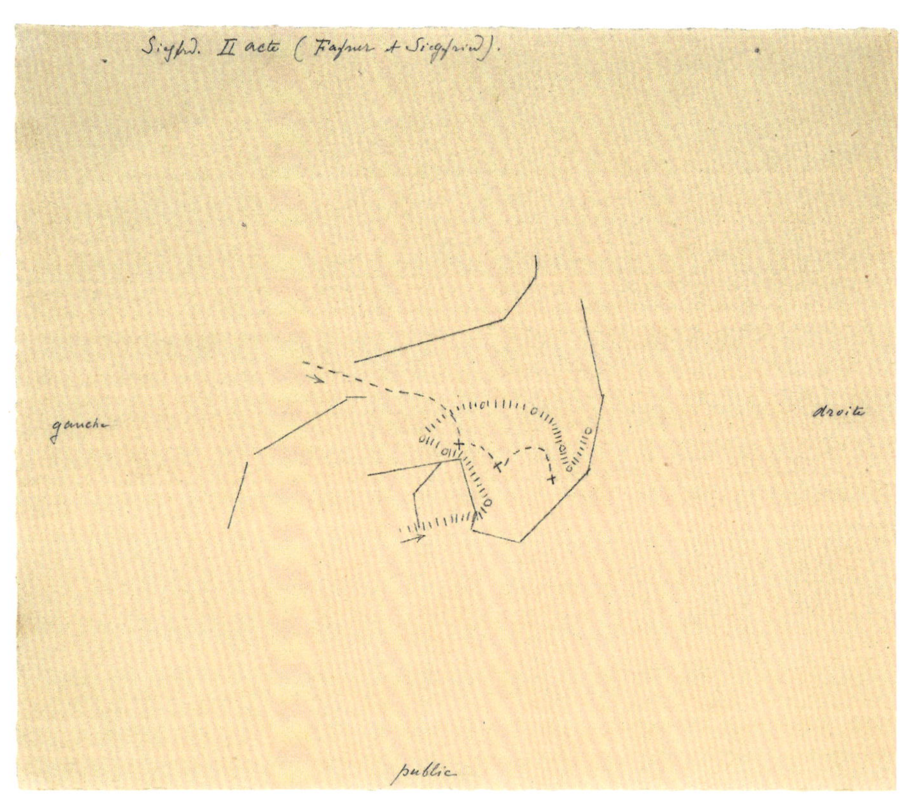

Siegfried, Act 2: Deep in the Forest, 14.2×18.7 cm and 15.6×18.1 cm, 1892

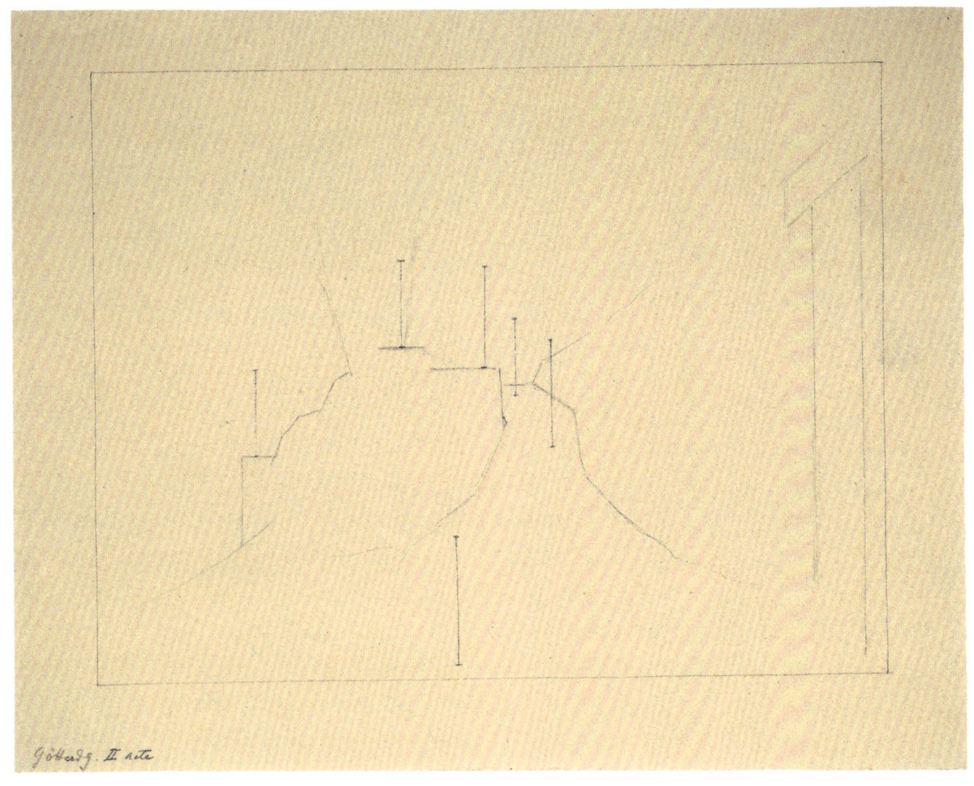

Götterdämmerung, Act 2: in Front of Gunther's Hall, 18.0×22.4 cm; Act 3, Scene 2, 18.0×22.5 cm, 1892

Siegfried, Prelude and Act 1: A Rock Cave in the Forest, 31.3×24.3 cm, 1892

Siegfried, Act 3, Scene 3: On the Summit of a Rocky Mountain (Brünnhilde's Rock), 31.4×24.5 cm, 1892

form. The costumes are to be varied, richly adorned, and *arbitrary* in comparison to the previous scenes; the overwhelming sense one of restlessness.' The first agitated scene takes place in the mighty timbered hall named after the former king Gibich. His son and heir Gunther sits on a throne centre-stage, as does his sister Gutrune. Hagen – their half-brother and adviser, and the dwarf Alberich's son – counsels them each to marry for the good of their dynasty, proposing Brünnhilde, 'the world's most glorious woman', as a bride for Gunther, and Siegfried, 'the strongest hero', as a husband for Gutrune. The prospect is as appealing to the siblings as it is unlikely – how should Brünnhilde and Siegfried be wooed? Conspiratorially, Hagen leans toward Gutrune and reminds her of a potion that sits in the cupboard next to her, one that makes whoever drinks it 'forget any woman he has seen before'. Just then, a horn sounds, strong but distant. Hagen peers down the river and shouts back: 'He rows the boat hard against the stream ... It is Siegfried, no one else!' For Appia, the boat with furled sails should be primitive in appearance, at odds with the decorative interior of the Gibichungs' hall. 'Siegfried arrives *in motion*, occupied with his weapons, his horse, directing the boarding with his spear, etc.', wrote Appia. Hagen cups his hands and shouts towards the river, 'Where are you bound for, blithe hero?', to which Siegfried responds: 'For Gibich's sturdy son.' He guides his boat to the shore and moors. 'Hail! Siegfried, cherished hero!' exclaims Hagen, joined on the riverbank by 'Gibich's sturdy son', Gunther. 'Do battle with me, or be my friend!' declares Siegfried, to which Gunther, inclined towards the latter, replies, 'Forget the fighting! Feel welcome!' He invites Siegfried to accompany him to the hall, where Gutrune greets him with a laced wine drinking horn that he empties in one draught before fastening his eyes on her, his passion aflame: 'Would you think me too bold if I offered myself to you in marriage.' She humbly bows her head and exits the hall with faltering steps as Siegfried turns to Gunther and enquires whether he himself has a wife. 'I am yet unmarried, and the prospect of a wife is unlikely ... though my heart is set on one, there is no way she will ever be mine', is his despondent response. 'She lives high on a rock encircled by a fire that protects her from all but the bravest suitor.' 'I fear no fire', declares Siegfried. 'I will woo the woman for you ... I will fetch you Brünnhilde', which he intends to do by using the Tarnhelm's devious power to assume Gunther's form. The two conspirators board the boat that Appia tells us Siegfried should 'push away with his spear thrust against the shore'. Turning technical, Appia notes that at measure 90/2 the boat should be shunted onto a second set of below-stage tracks that are further back than the first, and that will send the boat downriver. Siegfried, facing the landscape rather than the audience, 'grabs the oar and begins to row in time with the music, while Gunther attends to the sail, etc. Departure in full motion to accentuate the subsequent stillness', are Appia's final staging instructions as the curtain, once girding the hall's forefront, descends.

In the concluding scene of the first act of *Götterdämmerung* the action returns to the rock of the Valkyries. It is evening, and Brünnhilde is brooding at the entrance to the cave, wondering when Siegfried will come back to her. The radiance of the flames encircling her intensify, 'extending along the ridge and all around the summit. Showers of sparks and flames break out here and there – the atmosphere must be menacing', wrote Appia. Siegfried's horn sounds out as he leaps through the licking tongues of fire. However, to Brünnhilde's dismay, the man wearing the Tarnhelm is not Siegfried. 'Who has invaded my world?' she wonders. In the guise of Gunther, Siegfried claims Brünnhilde for his wife. 'Show willingness and follow me', he demands, before demanding ominously: 'Night is closing in: you must marry me in your cave!' 'Don't even dare to get near me!' she retorts. Siegfried persists, removing the ring from her finger, eliciting a violent scream. 'Now you are mine, Brünnhilde, Gunther's bride.' She relents, crushed, and with shaking, faltering steps, walks into the cave followed by Gunther. The curtain falls.

For the second act of *Götterdämmerung*, the action moves from the interior to the exterior of the hall of the Gibichungs, opening up to the landscape beyond.[140] Appia wrote that the general effect should be 'dense, abundant and oppressive'. For him, the drama and its evocation in the music of this second act 'demands a richly coloured rugged setting, so the hues will be vivid and saturated'. An altar devoted to Fricka is visible part way up a narrow rocky pass that rises to the right from the shore, flanked by two others: one to Donner and the other to his brother-in-law Wotan. Hagen's warning horn summons vassals down mountain paths, gathering on the shore before the hall. Hagen intends to honour Gunther's marriage to Brünnhilde with a slaughter of great beasts: 'Strong bulls; let their blood gush on that altar for Wotan!' Then a boat arrives, and some of the vassals leap into the water and haul it ashore, shouting: 'Hail to you, Gunther! Hail to you, and our bride!' The crowded tumult of vassals on shore falls into line once Gunther makes a move to disembark. Appia wrote that there should be enough of them to be 'arranged in two or three rows, somewhat like irregular steps', but they should not obstruct the main characters of Siegfried and Brünnhilde as they make their way towards the hall and meet the bridal procession that is emerging from it. Siegfried is being borne aloft on his shield, and Gutrune on a throne. Shocked and astonished, Brünnhilde stammers, 'Siegfried ... he doesn't know me!' Catching sight of the ring on his finger, she screams in anguish: 'Trickery! Trickery! ... Treason! Treason! Siegfried forced pleasure and love from me.'

The forest region near the Rhine that is the setting for the prelude and first scene of the third and final act of *Götterdämmerung*[141] is to be 'shady and *damp*', according to Appia. A plenitude of overgrown, slender-trunked trees dominates the right-hand side of the scene, 'growing even in the water among heavily moss-covered, dark rocks'. Ascending to the left and towards the back of the stage, the terrain dries out and becomes lighter. Distant horns are heard as the curtain rises to reveal the three Rhinemaidens – Woglinde, Wellgunde and Floßhilde – swimming to and fro, singing '*Weialal, weialala leia leia wallalalaleialala leilalala la lei la la*'. Their to and fro swimming is no easier to stage than it was in *Das Rheingold*, and Appia battled to come up with a viable solution just as Wagner had done before him. 'It will only be possible to stage this scene satisfactorily', wrote Apapia, 'if the three Rhinemaidens are able to move *independently*. Therefore, the stage technician will have to fabricate a rolling device for each of them. It will be powered by pedals in the manner of old velocipedes, which will significantly reduce the weight of the device and will deliver movements on the ground akin to those of swimming. The Rhinemaidens will be able to embark and disembark at will. They should be provided with soft-soled slippers that have a kind of moulded support mounted on springs, so that they can bounce into position. A lighter horizontal support, likely made from metal rods, will support the upper body in a prone position; the wheels, rubber coated, should achieve maximum velocity. Brakes that are easy to operate will be indispensable.'

Siegfried appears atop a cliff and the Rhinemaidens who have braked to a standstill jest with him as he makes his way down to the river's edge. But they soon turn serious, warning Siegfried that the ring on his finger will do him harm: 'The trickster who forged it and lost it ingloriously put a curse on it, damning to death any person who wears it.'

In the distance, Hagen's voice calls out '*Hoi-ho!*' and Siegfried answers with his hunting horn. 'Come down! Here it is fresh and cool!' he shouts out

Setting for *Götterdämmerung*, Act 1: The Hall of Gunther's Court Near the Rhine, Bayreuth Festspielhaus, 1896.

to Hagen and Gunther as they arrive at the cliff edge. The brothers climb down to meet Siegfried, who sits himself down between them as they unpack a wineskin and drinking horn to celebrate their successful hunt. Hagen fills the horn and passes it to Siegfried, who takes a draught before passing it on to Gunther in turn. Two ravens fly up out of the bush, circling above Siegfried. 'Can you unlock these ravens' whispers', asks Hagen, as Siegfried follows the flight of the birds with his eyes. 'Their advice to me is vengeance!' he shouts, plunging his spear into Siegfried's back. With his last words, Siegfried recalls Brünnhilde – 'sacred bride'. In Appia's words, he dies 'without a shiver, very calmly, in the arms of the men'. There is to be complete stillness from everyone as the darkness enfolds them all. The four strongest vassals take charge of Siegfried's body, lifting it onto a shield. 'The men carrying him must be strong enough to do so with dignity, those at the back with their arms held high', wrote Appia. They walk in slow procession over the high rocks. The moon breaks through the clouds, casting an increasingly bright light on the funeral procession as mists emanate from the Rhine, gradually enveloping the entire stage. During the interlude, the stage becomes entirely shrouded.

Setting for *Götterdämmerung*, Act 2: In Front of Gunther's Hall, Bayreuth Festspielhaus, 1896.

These mists dissipate in the final scene, revealing the Gibichungs' hall, behind which the moon's radiance reflects in the Rhine. 'Get up Gutrune! Greet your Siegfried!' shouts Hagen as the procession moves towards the centre of the hall, and the vassals carefully place the body on an improvised resting place. 'A wild boar's prey: Siegfried, your deceased husband', announces Hagen. Gutrune prostrates herself over the lifeless body and accuses Gunther of Siegfried's murder, exclaiming, 'Get away, treacherous brother, you, the

killer of my husband!' Gunther discloses that Hagen is the true culprit, stating, 'He is the wild boar that fatally wounded this noble man.' Hagen admits his guilt, declaring, 'So be it! I killed him.'

Gunther and Hagen clash swords, despite attempts by vassals to intervene. A single stroke from Hagen's sword claims Gunther's life. 'The ring is mine!' he declares in triumph. Brünnhilde strides purposefully from the rear of the stage to the front of it and instructs the vassals to heap up a huge funeral pyre. While they are doing that, Brünnhilde undergoes a tender transformation, losing herself in rapt contemplation of Siegfried's lifeless face. 'Oaths were never taken by a man more honest; contracts never honoured by a man more loyal; no man ever loved more innocently than he!' She signals the vassals to place Siegfried's body on the pyre, and at the same time removes

following spread
Setting for *Götterdämmerung*, Act 3: Closing Scene, Bayreuth Festspielhaus, 1896.

Paul von Joukowsky, setting for *Parsifal*, Act 1, Scene 2, 1882.

the ring from his finger: 'I take possession of my heritage now. The accursed ring!' She vows to return it to the Rhinemaidens, those 'knowing sisters of the water's depths'. They are to take it from her ashes: 'The fire that burns me to death shall purge the ring of its curse!' Slipping the ring onto her finger, Brünnhilde turns to the pyre and wrests a massive firebrand from one of the vassals. 'Now the destruction of the gods is truly dawning. Like this – I throw the firebrand into Valhalla's brilliant fortress'. Spying her horse led by two young men, she exclaims, 'Grane, my horse!' rushes to unbridles it and then asks aloud: 'Do you also know, my friend, to where I shall lead you? … *Heiajoho*! Grane!' Brünnhilde vaults onto Grane and steadies him to jump. At full speed, she rides into the burning pyre. The crackling fire swiftly ascends, filling the entire space in front of the hall.

At the same time, the Rhine forcefully bursts its banks, flooding the scene. The three Rhinemaidens swim along the waves, emerging at the site of the funeral pyre. Hagen hastily discards his spear, shield and helmet, plunging into the water. Woglinde and Wellgunde entwine his neck, dragging him into the deep: 'Hands off the ring!' Floßhilde, swimming ahead, jubilantly celebrates the recovery of the ring, holding it aloft. A reddish blaze grows brighter through the spreading layer of cloud on the horizon, illuminating the Rhinemaidens, who are swimming in circles and playing with the ring in the becalmed waters of the Rhine that has receded back into its bed. According to Appia, the water will be simulated through a combination of projections and a heavy cloth waved by stagehands in such a way as to depict a tranquil current flowing from right to left. The lighting is to be 'calm, lunar, very moderate', and 'nothing is to impede the gaze, which loses itself, totally immersed in the atmosphere'. The assembled gods and heroes appear as the inferno of Valhalla attains its crescendo in the rear of the scene, while the hall of the Gibichungs slowly collapses, 'without noise or dust, or in fact anything that would disturb the sky', wrote Appia. The crowd of men and women in the foreground buckle in terror, kneeling as a unified dark mass. 'When the gods are completely engulfed in flame, the curtain falls.'

Settings for *Parsifal*, Act 1, Scene 2, Bayreuth; Act 2, Scene 2: Klingsor's Enchanted Garden, Bayreuth.

While it was the powerful mythical world of the *Ring* that inspired Appia's first drawings and theoretical musings in 1891 and 1892, the landscape all around him chimed with Wagner's music and libretti for *Das Rheingold, Die Walküre, Siegfried* and *Götterdämmerung*, and he missed it sorely when he returned to the city: 'I have had veritable *Heimweh* (homesickness) for Gennersbrunn since the very day I left, and I am beginning to get seriously worried. It really is a marvellous landscape, and I met the rare conditions for happiness there by chance. Just yesterday I realised something that would have caught somebody else's eye sooner: the landscape is that of the *Ring* – every corner of the forest and the clearings, every furrow, meadow and orchard – everything is quickened, down to the gardening tools – rakes, spades and pitchforks, even the saddle room. I am in the midst of sorrow for that time; nothing in the world will give it back to me – and I cry for it. I am almost indifferent about the four elegantly bound musical scores for the *Ring* that sit here before me on my piano.'[142]

But his apathy passed, and Appia set about condensing his ample staging notes for *Der Ring* in order to have them published with the funds that he had available to him. He pared his manuscript back to a mere fifty pages that amounted to more of a prolegomenon than a treatise – the central chapter was entitled 'Some Preliminary Thoughts' – and with the help of friends, including the French writer Édouard Schuré,[143] Appia secured a contract with the publisher Léon Chailley in Paris. And so, in 1895, at the age of thirty-three, he became a published author. A neat 500 copies of *La mise en scène du drame Wagnérien* (Staging Wagnerian Drama)[144] were printed, and the slim unillustrated paperback was sent out for review in the French-language musical press of France, Belgium and Switzerland. The responses were encouraging, if not glowing – most reviewers found it 'concise and interesting', and one thought it would

following spread
Carl Emil Doepler, setting for *Parsifal*, Act 2, Scene 2: Klingsor's Enchanted Garden, 1882.

make good summertime reading: 'Mr Adolphe Appia's booklet, which is very concise and is clearly written, deserves to be studied by all *régisseurs* and *directeurs* who believe in the artistic worth of their vocation. May they all use their summer holidays to read these few pages. They will thereby mix the useful with the pleasant – *utile dulci* – and it will not be long before we are reaping the rewards.'[145]

The only one of Wagner's *Wort-Tondramen* that Appia made explicit staging notes for in *La mise en scène du drame Wagnérien* was the *Ring*, partly since he had a limited number of pages at his disposal, and partly since 'of all the dramas of Wagner, *Der Ring des Nibelungen* offers the greatest variety and the widest range of potential development'.[146] But Appia increasingly concerned himself with Wagner's other *Wort-Tondramen*, including the composer's final work, for which he had even coined a neologism: *Parsifal*, a reformulation of the chivalrous coming-of-age quest for the holy grail, became a *Bühnenweihfestspiel*, or ritualistic festival transposed onto the stage.[147]

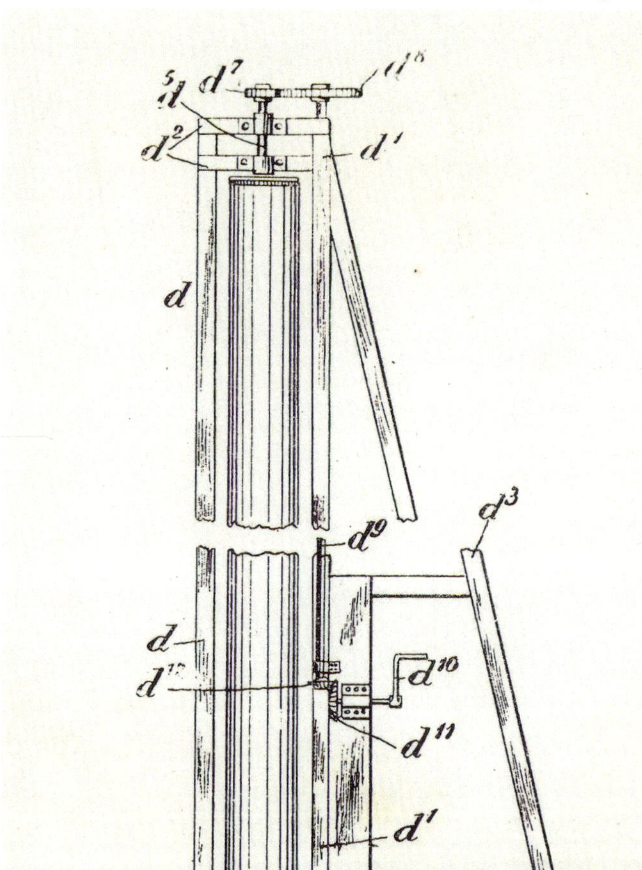

Technical drawing for the rotating scenery mechanism at the Bayreuth Festspielhaus, *c* 1882.

And it had been on the stage of the Festspielhaus that Appia had seen *Parsifal* under Wagner's own direction, while on a similarly Parsifalian quest of his own – his first annual pilgrimage to Bayreuth for the premiere performance, in the summer of 1882.[148] Although profoundly moved by what he heard, Appia was terribly disappointed by the conservatism of the opera's romantic imagery and also by the ungainly techniques of stagecraft that were used to transition between scenes. Ironically, these were also a cause of vexation for Wagner, who was adamant that the audience should experience Parsifal's physical quest as also an inner spiritual awakening that should be both gradual and dreamlike, demanding that changeovers between scenes be seamless. The solution that his stage technician Carl Brandt came up with involved Parsifal pretending to walk along while the landscape – painted on three huge canvas scrolls running between vertical rollers on either side of the stage – moved behind him. But unfortunately, the scenery took longer to pass between the rollers than the music took to play, so Wagner composed a few extra bars, and when it turned out during rehearsals that even that was not enough, he allowed some of the music to be repeated. And yet this failed to synchronise music and backdrop, since the rollers were turned by hand and the timing was difficult to coordinate – in the early performances, including the one that Appia witnessed, the music tended to arrive in the *Gralstempel* (Temple of the Holy Grail) before the scenery. 'If everything in the auditorium at Bayreuth expressed Wagner's genius', recalled Appia many years later, 'then on the other side of the footlights everything contradicted it'.[149]

Appia set about remedying the situation, so far as Parsifal was concerned, and in 1896 – the year after the publication of *La mise en scène du drame Wagnérien* – he prepared staging instructions and three drawings, one for each act of the *Bühnenweihfestspiel*, and described how transitions between the scenes in each act would be accomplished, which was gradually, and within full view of the audience.[150] Wagner himself describes the setting for act one – *Waldlichtung und Gralsburg* (Clearing in the Forest and Castle of the Grail) – as a 'forest, shady and solemn but not gloomy, with a clearing in the centre. On the left, a path rises to the castle. The background slopes down in the centre to a deep-set forest lake. Daybreak.'[151] In his drawing for this opening scene made on beige Canson & Montgolfier paper, Appia guides our eyes from a location within a dark cave-like forest, which he worked up in charcoal and graphite pencil, through to a central luminous landscape of gently contoured hills, which he sculpted back from an evenly shaded field of grey towards the ambient colour of the paper using his characteristic method of erasing, rubbing and smudging.[152] Contrary to custom, rather than opening with this forest setting and then switching part way through to the interior of the temple, Appia proposes a gradual metamorphosis of one into the other. 'The setting must already possess a temple-like character, in order to convey a transfiguration of nature into architecture', he wrote.[153] 'In the fantastic and tragic splendour of the orchestra, the trunks will, little by little, come to bear down on flat masonry foundations – the vegetation will disappear.'[154] At the same time, the natural light of day will give way to the 'supernatural light shining out from within the Temple of the Holy Grail', and as the columns 'gently replace the great boughs of the forest', we are transported from 'one temple into another'.[155]

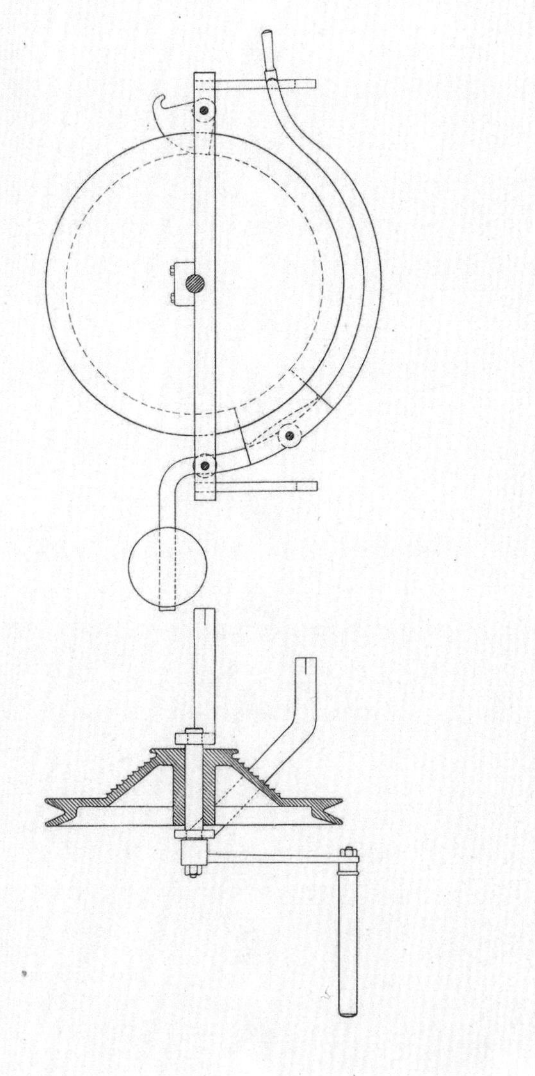

Stage machinery at the Bayreuth Festspielhaus, *c* 1882.

Wagner describes the setting for act two – *Klingsors Zauberschloß* (Klingsor's Enchanted Castle) – as 'the inner keep of a tower open to the sky'.[156] For Appia, it is the 'dwelling place in abysmal darkness' of the sorcerer, Klingsor, who 'strives to drag humanity down to the irresolvable despair in which he himself is entangled. His castle is therefore a place of nameless dread ... it is not a torture chamber, rather an abyss of moral despair.'[157] For the drawing that he made to accompany his notes on this 'place of nameless dread', Appia chose pale blue Canson & Montgolfier paper, on top of which he patiently built up the fathomless depths of the cyclopean masonry in soft charcoal, then articulated the details with a sharp graphite pencil. The mood is portentous and menacing: 'My *Zauberschloß* lures the fool, whom I see approaching from afar', announces Klingsor in the opening

Parsifal, Act 1: Clearing in the Forest and Temple of the Holy Grail, 47.7×62.3 cm, 1896

Parsifal, Act 2: Klingsor's Dungeon, 47.8×53.0 cm, 1896

following spread *Parsifal*, Act 3: The Meadow in Bloom, 47.2×62.3 cm, 1896

scene, before setting alight incense that 'instantly fills the background with blue smoke'.[158] Parsifal 'appears in the luminous plain',[159] according to Appia, who directs our eyes towards it with an illuminated patch of sky. The journeying youth is out of sight for us, down in the depths as we are, but Klingsor, 'standing on the lower terrace overlooking the abyss – has seen him in his necromancer's mirror'.[160] Unaware of the danger, Parsifal approaches the castle and – in Appia's interpretation – 'in order to gain a better vantage point from which to contemplate the scene', he 'climbs rapidly up towards the luminous sky and leans against the tower that dominates the horizon. To mark the contrast, the entire sky will be the most intense blue, while in the depths the livid horror of suffering and death will reign.'[161] Klingsor summons forth his enchanted knights to battle with Parsifal, who overcomes them one by one, much to the disbelieving sorcerer's dismay. Klingsor steps in himself and hurls a spear at Parsifal, but miraculously it comes to a standstill above the head of the young hero, who seizes the weapon and makes with it the sign of the cross, thereby banishing the sorcerer's powers. The castle – a dwelling place of abysmal darkness – collapses and disappears, along with Klingsor. According to Wagner's own staging notes, 'the bluish light is extinguished, leaving total darkness down below, in contrast to the bright blue sky above the walls'.[162]

The setting for act three – The *Blumenaue* (Meadow in Bloom) – is described by Wagner as a 'pleasant spring landscape with a background of gently rising flowery meadows'.[163] Appia tells us that 'we are now back in the hallowed land of the Grail, as indicated by the tree trunks and the general aspect of the landscape',[164] and to reinforce this awareness, the drawing that he made for this opening scene of act three is a visual echo of the one that he made for the opening of act one; the trunk-columns on the right-hand side of the foreground page possess the same 'temple-like character'. In accordance with Wagner's instructions, a 'hermit's hut stands against a mass of rock' in the middle ground,[165] and the same landscape of gently contoured slopes that extended into the background of the opening scene of act one reappears in this one, though this time it rises up from left to right, and eventually – later in this final act – it dawns on us that what Appia has disclosed, though not entirely, is the Castle of the Grail. Parsifal is revealed as the Redeemer, and along with Kundry and Gurnemanz he sets off for the castle, where distant bells have announced the funeral of Titurel. This is Appia's description of the scene: 'The three figures ascend to the right among the trunks. The forest soon envelops them, slipping imperceptibly from right to left, and we once again enter the Temple of the Holy Grail.'[166]

Appia published his three Parsifal drawings together with a brief explanatory essay in which he wrote that 'the drawings should – as far as this is achievable outside of the context of the performance and the accompaniment of music – demonstrate how by carefully following the information that is in fact hidden within the score itself (the libretto and music) the stage director is provided with the opportunity to arrive at a style that is full of expression'.[167] For Appia, this style, which is 'no longer rooted in the personal imagination that the director happens to possess, forces a change in the way the setting is conceived and then technically executed: the entire *mise-en-scène* must arise from the very plot of the drama itself'.[168]

La musique et la mise en scène was the title Appia gave to the manuscript that would be the closest he would ever come to a full explication of his scenographic theories. In 1895 he relocated from the village of Gennersbrunn to the town of Bière, lodging once again on the outskirts with a farming family in order to live a quiet life in the countryside, with plenty of time to focus on the writing of his book, a task that absorbed him completely: 'You cannot imagine the passion that I pour into the writing of my book! It is an artistic work – and my soul is in it', Appia wrote to his Germanophile friend Houston Stewart Chamberlain in January 1896.[169] The close friendship between the two had developed on the basis of their shared devotion to Wagner: Chamberlain had contributed numerous articles to the *Revue Wagnérienne* in Paris, and his book, simply titled *Richard Wagner*, would be published by the right-leaning Munich publisher Hugo Bruckmann that same year.[170] At the time, Chamberlain considered himself to be a writer – more than an ethno-nationalist political philosopher, as he would later become – whereas Appia, by his own admission, struggled to capture his ideas in words: 'Above all, my hand is unaccustomed to the pen, and besides that, the topic that I have addressed concerns an element – music – which, more than every other, evades analysis.'[171]

Appia sent what he thought was the final draft of *La musique et la mise en scène* to Chamberlain in the summer of 1896, together with an explanatory note regarding his writerly ambitions for the book: 'I would like my book to be a kind of poem ... a technical and tangible dream proposition.'[172] Chamberlain's response was full and frank. Appia must have realised what he was in for after reading the first couple of lines: 'With all the best intentions of a friend, I will here provide an honest critique of your writing style, rather than entering into a discussion of your ideas ... In my opinion, your writing style has major flaws, and these flaws are serious enough to damage your work.' The chief problem, according to Chamberlain, was that Appia had failed to properly attune himself to the demands of the actual task at hand, namely the writing of a book: 'There is no doubt that your way of speaking and your way of being are very closely related, but one should not write as one speaks.'[173] Chamberlain told Appia that his 'uniquely enigmatic literary style' made him difficult to comprehend, and that even he needed to re-read some passages two or even three times before he was sure that he had understood the meaning – a serious flaw, in his opinion.

That is when Chamberlain began to offer his friend writing advice: 'When you sit down to write, it is absolutely necessary to tell yourself that *writing is an art*. You – an artist – seem not to suspect this at all. Your writing lacks relief, colour, contrast and nuance; it is as though you write in much the same way as you would plant potatoes ... How the devil can it be that when you – the artist – write, there is no discernible trace of organisation, of "composition"; the topic stretches out endlessly in a straight line, without relief for the eye, without forms on the horizon?'[174]

The quality of his writing aside, Appia's devotion to Wagner was beyond dispute; in *La musique et la mise en scène* he referred to him variously as *Meister*, *Genie*, *Schöpfer* (creator) or *Wort-Tondichter* (word-tone poet). Appia praised Wagner's compositions as the culmination of the centuries-long development of *Deutsche-Drama*, accurately predicting that *Wagner-Drama* would soon become epoch-defining. At the same time, Appia remained convinced that the unimaginative sets at Bayreuth and elsewhere were woefully ill-matched to the greatness of Wagner's epic works. He was equally convinced that a new staging of those works had to be attuned to its time, even titling the third section of his book 'The word-tone drama *without* Richard Wagner'.

Appia's key insight, which became the source of such vitality later, was that light itself could create a physical space that would be profoundly attuned to the music in a way that traditional two-dimensional painted scenes never could be. 'The word-tone poet paints his picture with light', he wrote, insisting on the fundamental importance of illumination.[175] Having stated his premise, Appia went on to distinguish two different types of lighting: *gestaltendes Licht* (forming, sculpting or shaping light) and *verteiltes Licht* (distributed light) or, more generally, *Helligkeit* (brightness).[176] The first was generated by directed lighting that cast precise shadows to evoke 'the moon in the night, a fiery torch or a supernatural apparition'.[177] The second, on the other hand, was a kind of all-pervasive, directionless illumination that could be 'tuned'. Appia also refers to this second kind of lighting as *Transparentenbeleuchtung*, or transparent illumination, which would be achieved via 'certain transparent panels in the décor that would bring parts of the stage to appearance, insofar as the light would fall on the rear side of the canvas'.[178]

Appia had initially hoped to complete *Musique et la mise-en-scène* in the spring of 1897, but soon found that: 'The subject grows, the material multiplies and my seriousness increases as I feel the universal scope of my work.'[179] By the time he had finished writing, more than 500 pages of text in a series of notebooks numbered 1–22 sat stacked on his desk in front of him, and Appia was ready to set out to look for a publisher. But none of the French-language publishing houses showed an interest, so Chamberlain put in a good word for him with Bruckmann, and Appia committed to translating his book into German. *La musique et la mise en scène* became *Die Musik und die Inscenierung*. Appia was assisted in the task of translation by Princess Elsa Cantacuzène (the daughter of a penniless aristocrat), who within the year married into the publishing house and its social circles – and became Elsa Bruckmann.[180]

La mise en scène du drame Wagnérien had gone unillustrated for want of funds, but Appia negotiated better terms for *Die Musik und die Inscenierung*, including the provision for a number of drawings to be reproduced as collotypes.[181] So he turned his attention to these, first of all revaluating the atmospheric charcoal and pastel drawings that he had made for *Das Rheingold* back in 1892, deciding that they should be 'simpler, more sculpturally schematic'.[182] 'I need to go to Geneva to buy some drawing supplies essential for the transcription of my shaded sketches', Appia wrote to Chamberlain, adding that 'within a couple of days I will be able to present Bruckmann with a sample drawing – the *Walhall-Landschaft* for the second scene of *Das Rheingold*, a setting that 'should be hieratic'.[183] In all, Appia included eighteen drawings in *Die Musik und die Inscenierung*, most of them settings for the *Ring* – two for *Das Rheingold*, six for *Die Walküre*, three for *Siegfried* and one for *Götterdämmerung*. But he also included six drawings that he had recently made for *Tristan und Isolde*, and that a quarter of a century later would serve as the basis for the staging of *Tristan* at La Scala in Milan which Appia prepared with the Italian maestro Arturo Toscanini.[184]

Appia introduced his drawings to the readers of *Die Musik und die Inscenierung* in almost apologetic terms: 'The drawings that follow make no artistic claims. The setting for a word-tone drama only exists while it is being performed; outside of the performance it can merely be technically apprehended, much in the same way that music is denoted in the score, or in the material conditions of the instruments of the orchestra or the bodily organism of the actor. In order to make the drawings somewhat palatable, and to make a positive impression on the reader, the author has attempted to give them more relief through certain "painterly" features, thereby halfway compensating for their lack of "life".'[185]

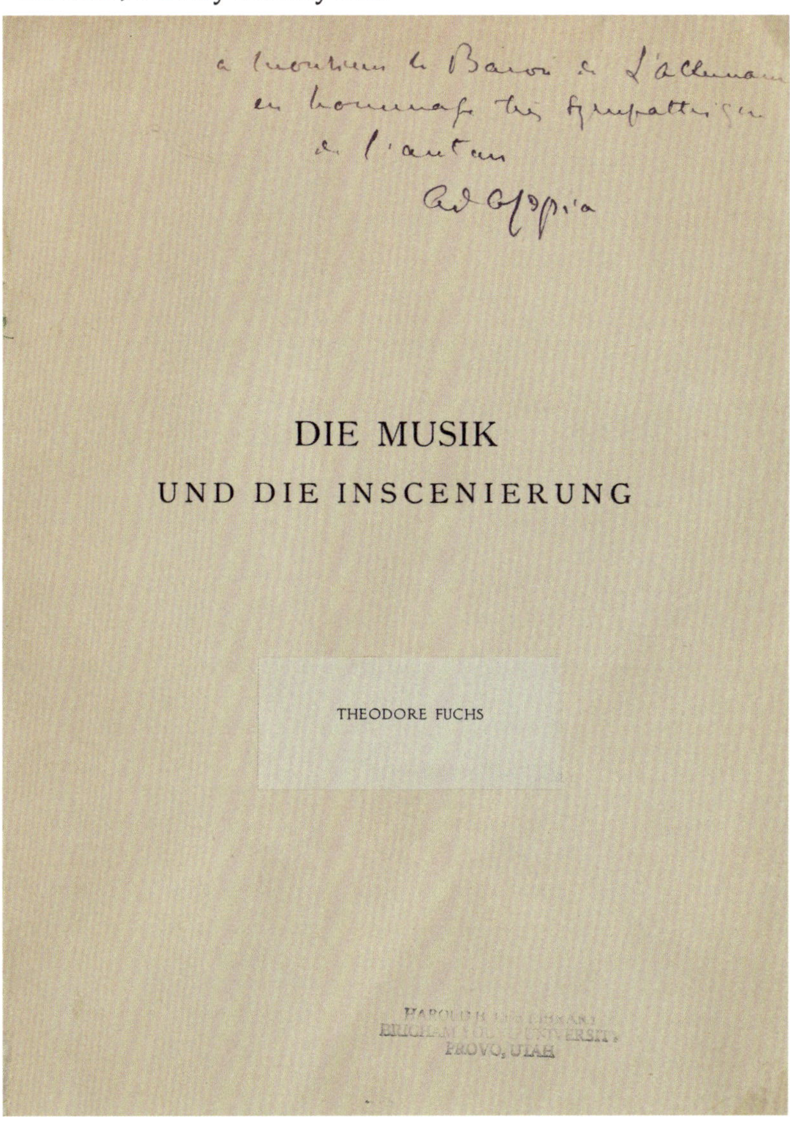
DIE MUSIK
UND DIE INSCENIERUNG

THEODORE FUCHS

Title page of Appia's book *Die Musik und die Inscenierung*, 1899.

By early 1898, Cantacuzène had just about finished translating Appia's manuscript, and with his drawings now also ready, Appia travelled to Munich to discuss the finer details of the publication of *Die Musik und die Inscenierung* with Hugo Bruckmann. This accounts for the fact that Appia was in the Bavarian capital when news of the death of his domineering father Louis reached him, prompting the scenographer's immediate though not swift return to Geneva; Appia cycled all the way home, some 571 kilometres. 'I pedalled myself almost to death, so as not to do it some other way', he wrote.[186]

Die Musik und die Inscenierung was published in March 1899, by which time Appia was thirty-seven years old. Though his second book was more widely reviewed than his first, Appia was again disappointed by the critical response: 'So far, I have received very little encouragement for my book – it feels a bit as though I have tossed my book out into the streets to feed fish that don't eat paper ... On the one side there is the overblown exultation of Schuré, and on the other there is the complete indifference of Bayreuth.'[187] (Cosima, the composer's widow and guardian of his cult, sent Appia a personal letter, but this is all she wrote: 'Dear Sir, My son and I appreciate the kind attention that prompted you to send us two copies of your book *Die Musik und die Inscenierung*. I am not able to say exactly when we will be able to attend to it, but when we have the leisure to do so, we will read with interest, since of course the theme interests us greatly. Receive, Sir, with the expression of our thanks and assurance of our most distinguished consideration. C Wagner.')[188] Even those among his supporters saw little prospect for the immediate uptake of Appia's ideas: 'Though it will slumber for a time on the shelves of specialist libraries, there is no doubt that its time will come', wrote Alfred Dufour in his review of *Die Musik und die Inscenierung* for *Journal de Genève*.[189]

Tristan und Isolde, Act 2, Scene 2: The Garden in Front of Isolde's Chambers, 47.8×62.0 cm, 1896

Tristan und Isolde, Act 2, Scene 1, 48.3×63.0 cm, 1896

Tristan und Isolde, Act 2, Scene 2: The Garden in Front of Isolde's Chambers, 48.3×62.9 cm, 1896

Tristan und Isolde, Act 3, Opening Scene: The Courtyard of Kurwenal's Castle, 47.4×62.3 cm, 1896

Having poured himself into the writing and publication of his far-reaching proposals for a reform of the staging of Wagnerian *Wort-Tondramen*, which at times almost overwhelmed him completely – on one occasion he wrote to Chamberlain: 'I have just endured twenty-four hours of insomnia, anguish, incapacity',[190] Appia was spent. He packed his bags, and in the first year of the new century, set off on what he would later refer to as his 'yearlong exile' to Italy. His first stop was Florence, then Rome in the spring. In the middle of the year – summer by now – Appia made his way to Naples and reflected there upon the drives behind his journey: 'What determined me to exile myself, glowing and sad, nobody knows; how I got to be the way I am today, nobody knows. The greatest experts on homosexuality (my sister Hélène for example – my confidante) know no more than the most ignorant. What I have suffered this year, no one in the world can know … (yet) what pleasure to discover oneself where there are no boundaries. Perhaps, but I have within myself a certain proud resistance which taints this incomparable pleasure. … Up until the end (when, how can I say?), I shall have resonating in my soul "wild desire", a kind of "burning longing". Alas, I am incorrigible in this regard, and all the Sorrentine intoxication with its beautiful people will not change anything.'[191] Appia made his way through the beautifully intoxicating streets of Sorrento to its wharves, and from there sailed to the island of Capri, before finally coasting home to Switzerland when the weather turned cold at the close of the year.

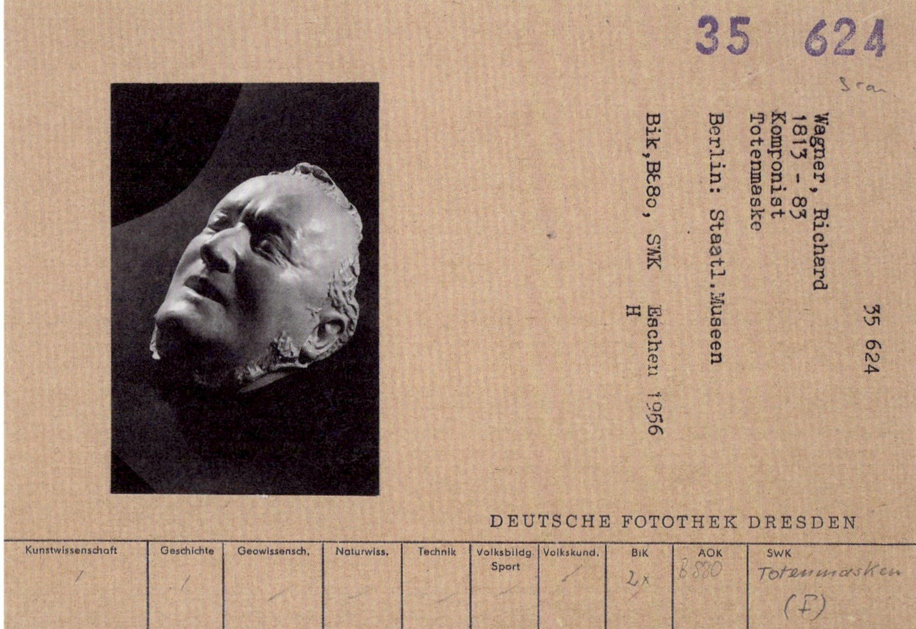

Carl Wölfel, Villa Wahnfried, Bayreuth, 1874; Richard Wagner's death mask, 1883.

Reinvigorated, Appia's first move was to seek an audience with Cosima, a formidable individual about whom a philosopher no less formidable than Nietzsche once wrote: 'There is one single case where I acknowledge my equal – I recognise it with profound gratitude. Frau Cosima has by far the noblest nature.'[192] As noble as her nature might well have been, it was one that had no time for Appia: she ignored every one of his entreaties for a meeting.

And yet Appia was undeterred, deciding to send his friend Chamberlain as an envoy. Back in the summer of 1888, Chamberlain had visited Wahnfried for the first time and met with Cosima, and later recalled that she had 'electrified' him. He felt the 'deepest love' for her, while Cosima herself wrote to a friend that she felt a 'great friendship' with Chamberlain 'because of his outstanding learning and dignified character'.

That Chamberlain's character was dignified has been generally disproved by history – Alex Ross has described him as a 'remarkable and repellent man',[193] one who came to embrace the *völkisch* belief of the unity of race, art, nation and politics. It was for these beliefs that Bruckmann commissioned Chamberlain's follow-up book for his publishing house, one that was intended to summarise all of the achievements of the nineteenth century and which later appealed particularly to *völkisch* movements[194] – Chamberlain has been referred to as Hitler's John the Baptist.[195] The principal thesis of Chamberlain's frankly racist book, *Die Grundlagen des neunzehnten Jahrhunderts* (Foundations of the Nineteenth Century), is that modern Western civilisation,

Richard Wagner's grave in the grounds of Villa Wahnfried, 1883.

manifest most splendidly in the German Empire, is rooted in the 'awakening of the Teutonic peoples – *Germanen* – to their world-historical destiny'.[196]

Wagner was Chamberlain's own John the Baptist, and it had been the music of Wagner that brought Appia and Chamberlain together, certainly more so than any political inclinations. In fact, it seems to have been Chamberlain's strident support for Germany in the First World War that caused the rift in their friendship that never healed. In 1914 Appia wrote to Chamberlain that he had seen peaceful doves flying by his window in Switzerland and that in contrast to the German ones, these doves spoke the truth. (The first German military planes, light biplane bombers, were colloquially known as *Rumpler-Tauben*, Rumpler-doves.)[197]

But that was much later. At the beginning of the century, Chamberlain was willing to side with his Swiss friend when it came to the question of the

following page
Bust of Cosima Wagner, *c* 1876; Carl Wölfel, Cosima Wagner's study in Villa Wahnfried, Bayreuth, 1874.

renewal of the staging of Wagner's *Wort-Tondramen* in Bayreuth. He was, however, careful to temper Appia's expectations, warning his friend to expect little from Cosima: 'I basically have no hope on that side, none. The Great Wall of China is a trifle compared to that which stands before you.'[198] And that is indeed the way that things turned out to be. After his first visit to Wahnfried, Chamberlin reported to Appia on his progress: 'Madame Wagner tells me that she will read your brochure "in due course" although she doesn't expect to find anything of interest to her.'[199]

One of the reasons Cosima was not expecting to find anything of interest was her conviction that, in fact, there was nothing at all left to discover. Appia never stood a chance, and she wrote as much in a letter to one of his friends, Hermann Graf (Count) Keyserling: 'And now I come to the main question – the application of Herr Appia's ideas to our art. You seem to have forgotten one thing – dear Count – the *Schöpfer* of our works of art (Wagner), the *Schöpfer* of the drama from out of the spirit of the music, has provided us with every one of the instructions necessary for the staging of his works, right down to the very finest detail. All one needs to do is read the staging directions that he wrote down in his scores.' According to Cosima, there was 'nothing yet to be invented – only the details can be perfected – and the *Schöpfer* of the drama would certainly not have demanded or established anything that would be disadvantageous to his works. In short, everything must remain exactly as stipulated by the *Meister*.'[200]

Cosima found Appia's drawings as unimpressive as his theoretical formulations. Chamberlain recalled that after showing her some of them, he 'could hardly see her face because she had turned the same colour as the tablecloth, into which she seemed to be vanishing'. The pale tablecloth had presumably been spread out in Cosima's salon which was otherwise gaily furnished. An earlier visitor – Nina Hoffmann – described the décor as follows: 'The furnishings are all of lilac velvet and satin, complementing the patterned yellow wallpaper. But despite the harmony of the colours, the overall impression is one of exquisite tastelessness.'[201]

Exactly which drawings Cosima reviewed in her tasteless salon is unknown, but Appia learned that on another occasion she compared what were likely to have been his 1892 designs for *Das Rheingold* – cool blue evocations of the monumental setting for the Valhalla landscape – with the desolate ice fields of the North Pole.[202] Appia in fact recounted the episode himself: 'Bayreuth refused to even take my book

Die Musik und die Inscenierung into consideration, and furthermore accused my drawings of recalling the Nansen expedition.' He added, despondently: 'I was simply not able to articulate myself any more clearly than I had done in my book', and that 'Bayreuth had flat out refused to even read my screenplay for the *Ring*, which in fact should have arrived at just the right time, since a performance was being prepared for the 1896 festival'.[203]

Appia at age thirty-seven in 1899, the year in which he published *Die Musik und die Inscenierung*.

The settings for that 1896 festival were designed by Max Brückner, who had, of course, prepared some of the stage sets for the original 1876 production that the *Schöpfer* himself had prepared, and which for that fact served as the template from which the new settings were to deviate very little – 'nothing new was to be invented, only the details could be perfected'. This is how Brückner himself understood the artistic duty with which Cosima had entrusted him, as stated in his introduction to a folio of lithographs of his paintings published on the occasion of the 1896 Bayreuth Festival, at which these very same paintings were reproduced at the 'colossal dimensions' of the Bayreuth stage: 'Mighty, marvellous scenes of nature in affecting moods. That is what this poetry demands and prescribes, and I have endeavoured – as faithfully and intimately as possible – to represent the scenic locations as intended by the *Meister*, thereby making but a small contribution to the memory of the performances of the *Ring* – that sublime work of our immortal *Meister* Richard Wagner.'[204] Brückner's settings had, of course, been vetted and commented upon by Cosima, who was overwhelmingly positive in her appraisal of the preparatory drawings that he sent to her for approval in 1894: 'Your sketches arrived today, and I think they are wonderful! Thank you, from the bottom of my heart, for the great joy that they have delivered to me!' It was their realism that she admired most: 'Your sketches are of the most beautiful and true naturalism – everything in them is organic and therefore belongs to the great works that will follow!' She was grateful to Brückner for the wonderful hour that she 'spent withdrawn from the everyday, immersed in that poetry which, perhaps like no other, allows us to feel the divinity of nature. Greetings, my dear Herr Professor', she wrote, 'in friendship and with gratitude!'[205] The tone that Cosima reserved for Appia could not have been more different to the exultant one she used in her correspondence with Brückner, rejecting and belittling him behind his back as she did – on one occasion she asked Chamberlain whether it was too late for Appia to become something 'useful', say a *costumier* or a lighting technician.[206] Realising that the door

Fridtjof Nansen, *Midnight Sun on the Polar Ice Cap*, 1894.

following page
The front door of Appia's family home at 5 rue Calvin, Geneva.

of Wahnfried had been firmly – and permanently – shut on him, Appia suffered a crisis of faith that threatened his very existence. At one point he even wrote a will, which he ominously posted to his sister Hélène in case he should 'die suddenly'.[207] He roamed around Switzerland for the next few years working odd jobs in the countryside, where (writing from the farmhouse at Bière in 1904), by his own account, he felt better than in the city with its temptations: 'I must live absolutely reclusively, without the least thing to disturb the monastic regularity of my days.'[208] Appia also picked grapes on those steep terraced hillsides that rise from Lake Geneva all around its pebbly shores, before finally making his way back to the city where he was born.

That is where Appia found himself at his drawing table in a melancholy mood in 1905, lonesome and writing down his *notes personelles*: 'At my age, that of forty-three, I ought to be presiding over a large workshop in which stage scenery is fabricated and painted; I ought to possess a private studio in which to compose and execute drawings and models; I ought to be constantly active on the stage – directing rehearsals and supervising performances. But above all, for the sake of my spiritual and mental wellbeing, I ought to regularly experience that singular happiness that comes with witnessing one's work attain its highest realisation – the performance. Instead, I am increasingly isolated, ever-more estranged from the theatre, and from other artists.'[209]

MIDDLE

Appia's prospects, thankfully, soon brightened. In the spring of 1906, he went along to a lecture that Émile Jaques-Dalcroze was giving at the Conservatoire de Musique on the topic of eurhythmics – the technique of musical instruction that the Swiss music teacher had himself invented and was now vigorously promoting.[1] Eurhythmics was described at the time as 'a scientific method of utilising our natural instincts for rhythm in the acquisition of an intimate knowledge of musical construction, in the development of a more perfect co-ordination between mind and body, and in the creation of a new outlet for artistic expression'.[2]

Jaques-Dalcroze had been appointed 'Professor of Harmony' at the conservatory back in 1892 at the age of just twenty-seven,[3] and over the next decade honed his musical pedagogy, which – as he later articulated in his essay, 'Rhythm as a Factor in Education' – was founded on his conviction that fundamentally there are 'two physical agents by means of which we appreciate music'.[4] The first of these is the ear, to receive sound, and the second is the 'whole nervous system as regards rhythm'. Based on his experiences with his guinea-pig music students, Jaques-Dalcroze came to the conclusion that it is wisest to undertake the study of these two fundamental elements independently, at least at first. He further reasoned that 'tone is evidently secondary, since it has not its origin and model in ourselves, whereas movement is instinctive in man and is therefore primary. That is why I begin the study of music by careful and experimental teaching of movement.'[5] He devised a whole system of bodily movement to teach time measures and note duration, based on precise and incremental positioning of the arms and hands as one register, and the legs and feet the other. Exercises included: 'Beating the same time with both arms but in canon, beating two different tempi with the arms while the feet march to one or other or perhaps march to yet a third time, e.g., the arms 3/4 and 4/4, the feet 5/4. There are also exercises in the analysis of a given time unit into various fractions simultaneously, e.g., 'in a 6/8 bar one arm may beat three to the bar, the other arm two, while the feet march six'.[6]

Émile Jaques-Dalcroze at age thirty in 1895.

Musical education and expression thus became spatial, which was one decisive step towards making it architectural. Consider the correspondence between the diagrammatic illustrations that Jaques-Dalcroze used to illustrate his method in *La Rythmique* and conventional architectural drawings. Both of them abstract aspects of reality for the purpose of representation, such as by using arrows to indicate movement through space – say over a stage in an exceptional performance, or up a flight of stairs in an everyday building. They furthermore both privilege the orthographic viewpoints of plan and elevation. While such drawings come across as narrow or focused

Émile Jaques-Dalcroze, 'Eurhythmics: The Five Species of Vertical Movement'.

scientific descriptions of reality, eurhythmic ambitions were holistic, as Jaques-Dalcroze exclaimed: 'The body can become a marvellous instrument of beauty and harmony when it vibrates in tune with artistic imagination and collaborates with creative thought.' He announced that music resides inside us all, and 'should obtain free and complete development, and that the rhythms which inspire their personality should enter into intimate communion with those which animate the works to be interpreted'.[7]

The conservative authorities at the conservatory kept Jaques-Dalcroze at arm's-length, unsympathetic to his ideas. In order to pursue them, he started offering his own experimental classes outside the traditional curriculum and out of hours. But in the spring of 1902, he was offered the ideal opportunity to give a very public demonstration of eurhythmics when the Canton of Vaud commissioned him to prepare a large-scale event, the Festival Vaudois, in celebration of the canton's century of independence. After spending many months working away on the score of the festival and determining its eurhythmic choreography, Jaques-Dalcroze was ready to supervise rehearsals, and much like a pastoral circuit rider, he travelled to towns and cities all over the canton for the next six months to prepare the vast cast of 2,500 actors, singers and musicians – both professional and amateur – for the performance and to 'preach' to them on eurhythmics. The Festival Vaudois was presented in Lausanne in the summer of 1903 and was a great popular success. Fortified by this enthusiastic response, and now convinced of the merits of eurhythmics both within and beyond the academy, Jaques-Dalcroze began fleshing out a full syllabus, developing lectures and delivering them to increasingly large audiences at the conservatory.

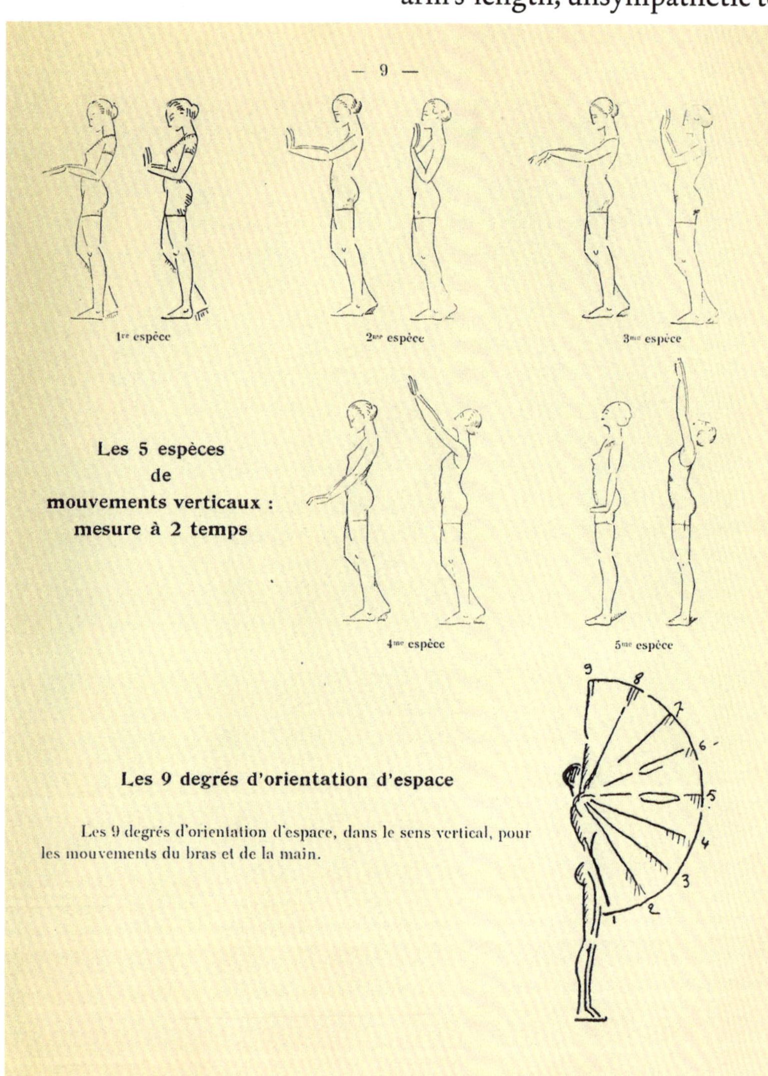

Although formulated and promoted as a new method of musical instruction, the origin of eurhythmics – both the word itself and its foundational ethos – were ancient, deriving from the Greek word εὐρυθμία (eurhythmia), which in turn is made up of εὖ (well) and ῥυθμός (flow or symmetry), so 'harmoniously proportioned'. Jaques-Dalcroze himself wrote in his essay, 'The Inner Technique of Rhythm', that every person should have music within themselves: 'I mean what the Greeks called music – the totality of our sensorial and psychic faculties, the ever-changing symphony of spontaneous feelings created, modified, then refined by the imagination and ordered by rhythm.'[8]

So, it was to ancient Greece as a cultural–spiritual ideal that Jaques-Dalcroze made his appeal, which could be done at a safe remove from the actual country that is to be found on maps of the Mediterranean. But there were other, more adventurous characters for whom such nautical maps were an invaluable practical necessity, among them the photographer Frédéric (Fred) Boissonnas, who like Jaques-Dalcroze was based in Geneva, but whose spirit of discovery led him much further afield.

Frédéric Boissonnas at the Acropolis in Athens, 1903.

Boissonnas was born into the trade; his father Henri-Antoine had set up his photographic studio in Geneva and built up a reputation for family portraits.[9] Fred also took portraits, but as often as not they were of himself. He took some time to properly commit to photography – flirting with architecture, music and even mountaineering – before undertaking apprenticeships at studios in Stuttgart and Budapest, then returning to his home city of Geneva. Fred threw in his lot with his younger brother and brilliant chemist, Edmond-Victor, to purchase their father's photographic studio. And while their bread-and-butter business of Geneva society portraits kept the account ledgers in the black, behind the velvety backdrops the two brothers toiled to perfect their new invention. After three years of experimentation, they patented their orthochromatic plate and its yellow-sensitive emulsion, which accurately rendered in greyscale the tonal values of natural colours and so dispensed with the tiresome process of printing from two separate plates in order to reconcile, say, the bright clouds in an azure sky with a dark landscape below. The brothers' invention was a great success, but Edmund-Victor was lured away from Geneva by the cashed-up manager of Kramer's Dry Plate Works of St Louis, Missouri, who was keen to keep pace with the Europeans. It was a fatal move: he died of typhus less than six months after setting foot in the New World.

But Boissonnas continued to innovate. He teamed up, for example, with Auguste Vautier-Dufour – an amateur photographer, industrialist and inventor whose passion was astrophotography and faraway landscapes – to develop and then take to market a brand-new camera, the Téléphot. Frustrated with the bulky camera equipment required for the kind of distant landscape photography he was most interested in, Vautier-Dufour consulted with friends and colleagues – including the deputy astronomer at the Observatoire de Gèneve – and carried out a series of experiments that eventually led to his invention of a wholly original compact camera that delivered the long focal length he desired, via two internally mounted mirrors which extended the distance the light entering the lens had to travel, running back and forwards the length of the camera

Frédéric Boissonnas, view of the west pediment of the Parthenon in Athens, 1903.

thrice.[10] But without sufficient personal capital to market his invention, Vautier-Dufour went on the lookout for a business partner, and found one in Boissonnas. They founded Véga – with the tagline 'Anonymous Photography and Optics Company' – to manufacture and sell various models of the Téléphot.

In the spring of 1903, Boissonnas loaded up a charter boat with trunks brimming over with photographic equipment – including the latest Téléphot – and embarked with sails trimmed for Greece. But it took some weeks to get there, and Boissonnas whiled away his days on board exposing plate after photographic plate to the vast watery horizon in all its moods – sometimes

still and benign, sometimes choppy under a dark, stormy sky. Disembarking in Piraeus, the forty-seven-year-old photographer made his way into Athens, unpacking his cameras periodically to capture the majesty of the Acropolis on approach, before finally arriving at the Parthenon, which was his final destination – a building that one of his fellow countrymen would describe as a 'cry hurled into a landscape made of grace and terror', a 'monument to strength and purity', after his own first revelatory journey to the East.[11]

Boissonnas took photograph after close-up photograph of the Parthenon, before turning his back on it and sailing home, with the architectural grandeur of classical Athens now exposed on his glass photographic plates. It was perhaps while he was out on the open sea with time on his hands that Boissonnas devised the idea for an exhibition of his 1903 photographs – especially those atop the Acropolis – but not only those; he came up with the idea of pairing his photographs of the actual remains of classical Athens with a suite that was rather infused with what he imagined to be its spirit.

Poster for Frédéric Boissonnas's exhibition *Greece: Celebrated Sites, Forgotten Corners,* 15 April–15 May 1904.

Before leaving for Greece, Boissonnas had befriended Émile Magnin, a Swiss hypnotist and professor at the École de magnétisme in Paris. Magnin had a muse, Magdeleine G, who would come to be known as *Die Schlaftänzerin* (sleep dancer) or *Traumtänzerin* (dream dancer), for dancing always and only when hypnotised. For philosopher and theoretician of the theatre Georg Fuchs, her performances were nothing less than an 'artistic miracle', evoking a *menad, bacchante* or *dionysiaque* – strongly instinctive figures from antiquity.[12] Magnin asked Boissonnas to take the photographs with which he would illustrate *L'Art et l'hypnose* (Art and Hypnosis), the book on his 'findings'. The images show Magdeleine G dancing, entranced, in flowing diaphanous robes, arrested in dramatic, expressive poses. There is no hint of an actual geographical context to give away site or history, though the world that is invoked is undoubtedly that of ancient Greece – albeit ancient Greece through the lens of Northern Europe: the music that Magdeleine G was dancing to was Wagner's *Die Walküre*.[13] And while the motivation behind Boissonnas's photographs of Magdeleine G might have been communion with mythology, his motor was modern Swiss technology: he shot the *Traumtänzerin* with a Téléphot fitted out with a lens which, in addition to reducing exposure time to 1/300 of a second, allowed Boissonnas to blur the background while sharpening the subject in silhouette. The result was akin to a bas-relief.

A prominent gallery in Geneva hosted Boissonnas's unique photographic exhibition, *La Grèce. Sites célèbres et coins perdus* (Greece: Famous Sites and Forgotten Corners), which paired 100 photographs that Boissonnas had taken in Greece with 500 of the *Traumtänzerin*. The show ran from mid-April to mid-May 1904 and was a resounding success.[14]

The landscape and architecture that he had seen first-hand in Greece – and the reception that his photographs received back home – evidently whetted Boissonnas's appetite, and in 1907 he set sail once again, this time with a travelling companion, his art historian friend Daniel Baud-Bovy, who by that time had become curator of the Musée Rath, the original home of Geneva's

Musée d'art et d'histoire.[15] The project the two had in mind was an ambitious one: a survey of classical Greek architecture, written by Baud-Bovy and photographed by Boissonnas. Once again, the Parthenon was the high point, and this time Boissonnas wanted to get up closer to it. He commissioned a local carpenter to nail together for him a climbable apparatus best described as a cross between a tripod and a ladder, but three storeys high. When he arrived at the Acropolis, having ascended the grand stairway from the Agora and paced through the ceremonial gateway of the Propylaea, Boissonnas set up his timber tripod-ladder on the ruin-strewn ground and stabilised it with spiderweb-like guy ropes. We know this since Boissonnas seemed to spend almost as much time in front of the lens as he did behind the viewfinder. There are, for example, a whole suite of photographs of him perched atop his tripod-ladder like a sailor in his crow's nest. There are others of Boissonnas shifting around ladders and planks and cameras high up inside the roof of the Parthenon, and even one of him posing on the south porch of the Erechtheion, casting a friendly arm around a caryatid.

Magdeleine G being hypnotised by Emile Magnin in 1903.

The fruit of this survey was a sumptuous large-format book, *En Grèce par monts et par vaux* (Greece by Mountain and by Valley), which, despite its eye-watering price tag of 1,000 francs, soon sold out.[16] Critically acclaimed as well as commercially successful, the book raised Boissonnas's stock as a photographer to such an extent that he could charge handsomely for adventurous excursions that one suspects he would have taken on without charge.

The Swiss Hellenist Victor Bérard came to Boissonnas in 1912 with a proposition that was as alluring as it was dubious. Bérard was convinced that Homer's topographical descriptions in the *Odyssey* corresponded to actual locations in and around Greece, and was determined to find and document them. The two travellers set sail for the Greek islands – one with a pen in hand, the other clutching a camera. Cruising comfortably aboard their cutter *Olive*, the two men examined maps and read stories below deck over pinot noir and gruyère, eager to reconcile mythology with concrete reality. Whether they managed that or not, the speculative-hopeful titles of Boissonnas's photographs radiate promise: one of them, 'The Sirens and the Boat of Ulysses', was taken at a safe distance from 'the island of the Sirens, those creatures who spellbound any man alive'. The enchanting goddess Circe tells homesick Odysseus that 'whoever draws too close, off guard, and catches the Sirens' voices in the air – no sailing home for him'.[17] Boissonnas and Bérard avoided such calamity, and after they had safely steered *Olive* back home over the Ionian Sea, past the island of Ithaca – home of the great exile

Odysseus – the two seafaring comrades compiled all of their notes and photographs for publication as *Dans le sillage d'Ulysse* (In the Wake of Ulysses).[18]

The eurhythmics of Jaques-Dalcroze might also be said to have come about in the wake of Ulysses, or at least of the classical world which Homer's wily man of twists and turns famously roamed around – a sublime mythical world which humans shared with giants, goddesses, gods and fantastical creatures of all kinds. This description also holds true for the Nordic myths that were the font at which Wagner sipped, and which the *Meister* retold in his *Word-Tondramen* that had so enthralled Appia until the time that he discovered eurhythmics. Profoundly moved by Jaques-Dalcroze's lecture at the Conservatoire, he described how, 'Without changing my orientation, eurhythmics freed me from too inflexible a tradition, and, in particular, from the decorative Romanticism of Wagner ... From that day on, I saw clearly the route my development would take. The discovery of the basic principles for the *mise-en-scène* could only be the point of departure; eurhythmics determined my future development.'[19]

Magdeleine G dancing under hypnosis to Richard Wagner's *Die Walküre* in 1903.

Invigorated, Appia enrolled in a 1908 short course on eurhythmics at the Conservatoire that would be taught by the Swiss dancer and teacher Suzanne Perrottet, one of Jaques-Dalcroze's first students and, over time, his *Lieblingsschülerin* (favourite student).[20] A photograph taken between classes shows Appia in his *Lieblingspullover* – a striped nautical *pull marin* – and with his face framed by a heavy black beard and crop of greying hair. His right arm is cast around one of his six companions, all of whom share an evident camaraderie. One of them stands proud in his fashionable short-sleeved slim-fit button-down shirt and suspenders, and two others are wearing white skivvies. All are well-groomed and are playing for the camera; although studying rhythm, they are an offbeat crew.[21]

The following year, Appia attended the Casino de Saint-Pierre in Geneva to watch a performance staged by the creator of eurythmics himself. Immediately after the performance he wrote a letter to Jaques-Dalcroze, who later recalled: 'Fortunately, on the day following the demonstration ... I received a letter from Adolphe Appia, whom I did not yet know, and in which he expressed his confidence in me and saw in the clearest way the future of my research. This was a great consolation for me, and a powerful encouragement.'[22] Appia had in fact been encouraged and discouraged in equal measure by what he had experienced. As had been the case at Bayreuth twenty-seven years before, Appia was dismayed by what he identified as a profound disconnect between the wonder of what he heard and saw of the performers

Frédéric Boissonnas and Victor Bérard aboard their boat *Olive* in 1912.

themselves, and the abjectness of their scenography. He later wrote: 'I took up paper and pencil and designed two or three *Espaces rythmiques* every day with feverish determination.'[23]

The setting in which Appia designed his *Espaces rythmiques* was a sparsely furnished room in the truncated tower of Château de Glérolles, a medieval château perched alone on the pebbled lakeshore of Lake Geneva, close to the small town of Rivaz.[24] Appia rented two small rooms in the tower from 1909 to 1919, and it was the closest he ever came to settling down.[25] The French theatre critic and scenographer Jacques Copeau, who has been referred to as 'Appia's finest disciple',[26] recalled his first meeting with the man he would later refer to as the 'Hermit of Glérolles'. And it was Jaques-Dalcroze who made the personal introduction in the summer of 1913: 'When I first met Appia – almost fifteen years ago now – at Château de Glérolles on Lake Geneva where Jaques-Dalcroze had brought me to meet him, Appia was already this magnificent and smiling solitary man with whom I would eventually spend many unforgettable hours. He had sparkling wide eyes that were always a little moist, and a sensual mouth from which his words came out hesitantly – sometimes cooing and sometimes explosively.' Copeau wrote that Appia 'stuttered slightly, and this defect doubtless added apprehension to his native timidity. Although he actually loved to be in society and was convivial in company, he said that in friendship as in art he needed authentic presence, and he often dreaded contact with the world.'[27]

So Appia mostly kept to himself, though he took part in the quiet life around him. Every autumn, he helped the owner and his family of vintners, the Ruchonnets, harvest their grapes, all of which were varieties of red – pinot noir, merlot, cabernet franc, syrah and humagne rouge – that had ripened on their ancient vines spreading out in rows over five hectares of steeply terraced south-facing hillside behind the château. Appia took his meals with the family all year round, but otherwise led a largely solitary life, leaving plenty of time for him to think, write, and most importantly, to draw.[28]

Appia's long-time friend, Jean Mercier, wrote that Appia used a collapsible drawing board which could 'easily be carried along whenever he changed residence'.[29] In the château, which takes its name from the Gallo-Roman village that originally stood on the site, itself derived from the Latin glarea (gravel) – Appia kept his table close to the window. 'Lifting his eyes', wrote Mercier, 'he could see the mountains and the sky; lowering them he could watch the waves rolling against the walls of the tower'.[30]

It was Mercier who took the only existing photograph of Appia at his collapsible drawing board, gazing past lightly patterned curtains towards the distant horizon in the summer of 1909. He was working on his *Espaces rythmiques* at the time, all of which are spartan configurations of steps, platforms and terraces, staged before a watery horizon under a lustrous sky. It was probably one of these mass and light drawings that lay on the drawing board before Appia, tilted gently away from Mercier's camera.

These drawings, numbering about thirty-five, which Appia made 'with feverish determination', retain a vigour equal to those made in the thrall of Wagner, but this time dispense with the libretto, infusing the performances with movement. They marry an atavistic appeal to primordial experiences with sober perspectival precision, framing a series of monumental yet minimal scenes that might be the fragmentary remains of a past culture or the

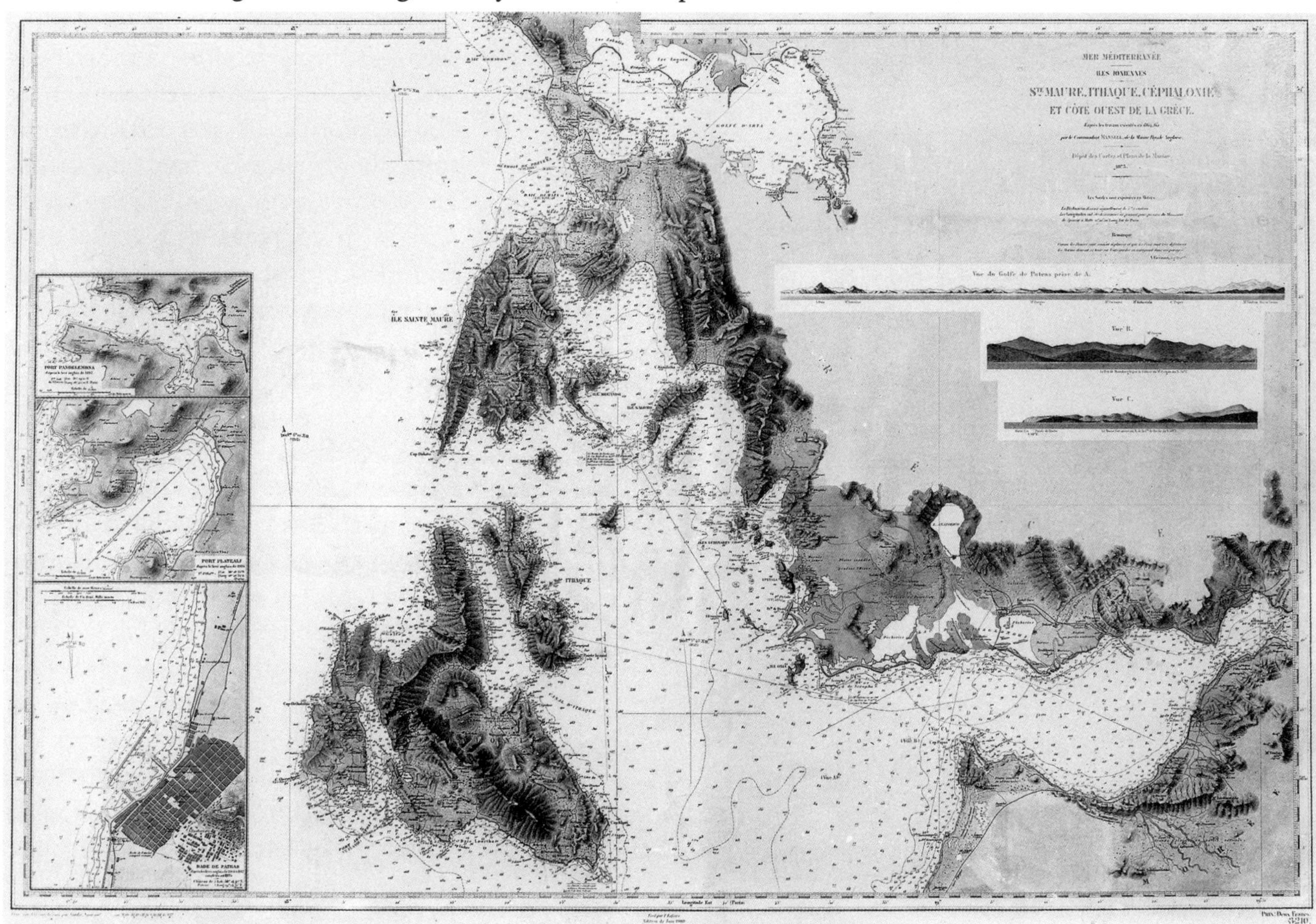

Nautical chart used by Frédéric Boissonnas and Victor Bérard aboard their boat *Olive* in 1912.

inauguration of one to come. The Romantic *Landschaftsseele* (expression of a landscape's soul) – a surrogate for the absconded God – is a constant, spectral presence in Appia's drawings, and they expose a certain tension in the German Romantic view of art as the synthesis of the secular and sacred.

Friedrich Schiller's brisk statement – 'the temples remained sacred to the eye, when the gods had long become ridiculous'[31] – identified a nascent modernist tendency of Romantic artists to retain the characteristics of traditional religions, including their architectural settings, without observing their spiritual obligations. Appia is similarly evasive, with his semi-sacred chthonic settings for gods just departed or soon to arrive offering a reading of modernity's simultaneous desire for radical newness and nostalgia for an ancient past.

Frédéric Boissonnas, 'Scylla: Reefs and Waves', 1912.

Though no two of Appia's *Espaces rythmiques* are quite the same, some of them are similar in composition and are best thought of as a pair, including *Steps in the Foreground* and *Addiction*. In both of these drawings there is a slim ledge of rough-hewn masonry that spans right across the drawing in the immediate foreground, and an expanse of still water which begins in the middle ground and extends to the horizon – though some of it is occluded by two sheer cliffs which plunge down into the water on both sides of the drawing in the case of *Steps in the Foreground*, and only on the left-hand side in the case of *Addiction*. If they are overlaid, one can see that Appia traced out basic forms from one drawing to the other.[32]

And then there are others that the scenographer evidently composed as a set, for example the three drawings *The Game of the Hills*, *Jest* and *Ditto*. They are formally very similar, made up as they are of three narrow ranks of masonry walls with assortments of steps, ramps and platforms in the immediate foreground, standing before a large luminous patch of sky which extends to the top edge of each of the drawings, all on the same beige-coloured paper.

The *Espace rythmique* that Appia named *The Quay* resembles the trio, except that its three ranks of low masonry walls are all neatly orthogonal and a small amount of the terrace that they stand on the edge of is visible in the foreground. There are also three tall tree trunks which appear almost as columns on the right-hand side of the drawing, and their shadows fall on the terrace, since the sun must be off to the right-hand side of the page, coloured a warm burnt sienna. *The Clearing* also has three tall tree trunks as part of its composition, although they stand in the foreground – two on the left and one on the right – and we peer between them to a forest clearing lit by bright pools of dappled sunlight in abstract shapes. About this drawing, Appia wrote: 'This is an example of a forest that is simply evoked by curtains with cut-outs, and with appropriate lighting. This can be done in any room – even a bedroom. The light is filtered as desired by the use of the cut-outs and by cardboard boxes out of the line of sight, and the shadows that fall on the performers can thus become animated. The fusion is complete.'[33] He concluded with a final, self-admonishing sentence: 'The three trunks in the foreground are likely extraneous.'[34] He made such critiques on a number of occasions, sometimes jotting down his remarks on the very drawings themselves. For example, on the bottom edge of the reverse side of the *Espace rythmique* that he gave the simple title *Opening*, Appia wrote in pencil: '*L'escalier est tout à fait superflu!* (The staircase is completely superfluous!)'

Photograph taken by Frédéric Boissonnas of the island of Ithaca, viewed from Arkoudi in 1912.

The Ring Dance of the Evening Sun distinguishes itself from Appia's other *Espaces rythmiques* by virtue of its formal repertoire – curves and symmetry. Two shallow steps in the foreground rise to a platform which fronts onto an expanse of water that reaches into the far distance. The brightest point on the horizon is at its centre; the sun must be presently about to rise or has just moments ago dipped down out of sight. There is an unusual formation in the sky; two concentric rings of clouds encircle the sun. *On the Edge* also sets itself

apart from Appia's other *Espaces rythmiques*, this time because the setting is almost a building, though the temple-like architecture is of an indeterminate ancient style, and we only see part of the building, standing on a ledge – either of a quay or a cliff. There are two ramps, the first of which ascends from the bottom right-hand side of the drawing to an intermediate platform in the centre of the composition, and the second, which rises from that platform to arrive at what reads as the stylobate to the mysterious temple.

One of the few drawings amongst Appia's *Espace rythmiques* that follows a narrative is the one that was inspired by the philosophical poem, *The Legend of the Isle of Sounds*, which his cousin Henri Odier had written under the pseudonym Roger d'Auryanne,[35] but which had not yet been published. Appia's drawing was in fact intended to serve as the basis for a theatrical

following spreads
Photograph taken by Frédéric Boissonnas aboard *Olive* in 1912; and *Espace rythmique: Cataracts of the Dawn*, 50.2×64.6 cm, 1909.

Les cataractes de l'Aube

Espace rythmique: The Ring Dance of the Evening Sun, 49.9×71.7 cm, 1909

Espace rythmique: Nine Columns, 50.2×72.4 cm, 1909

Espace rythmique: On the Edge, 52.5×72.4 cm, 1909

Espace rythmique: The Great Curtains of the Sky, 49.0×72.0 cm; *Opening*, 49.9×72.0 cm, 1909

interpretation which never materialised. The isle of the title was named Alabaster, for the chalky whiteness of its shores and the translucent white marble of its seaside palace in which a chimerical princess had taken shelter. Seduced by the harmonies of the Elements, she boarded a boat with sails which would be swollen by the wind, which would be an enchanting haven of eternal peace upon the rolling seas. In Appia's interpretation, the boat is a *barque lémanique* – a workmanlike oak-hulled boat native to Lake Geneva – with its distinctive twin sails set in a butterfly arrangement to catch a strong tailwind, its jib gathered in. Here the boat is still docked, and the hull is obscured by the terrace and the steps that lead down to it, but the sails are unmistakable. Another, more subtle element in the drawing which accords with the narrative is the cladding of the steps and terrace. Nowhere else does Appia tile his momentous stone ashlar blocks. He does so here because the island, Alabaster, is sheathed in silky white marble.[36]

Appia at age forty-six (third from left) attending classes on eurhythmics given by Suzanne Perrottet in 1908.

The symmetrical setting of the *Espace rythmique* that Appia matter-of-factly named *Nine Pillars* is much more contained than *On the Edge*. The nine square-section columns which give the drawing its name stand close together on top of a long, low, continuous masonry base that in turn rests upon a sturdy terrace paved with massive rectangular stones. We can see a horizon of water through the screen of columns which stand parallel to the picture plane, but not the sun, which must be lying just on it, occluded by the central column; the column's shadow is cast directly towards the viewer.

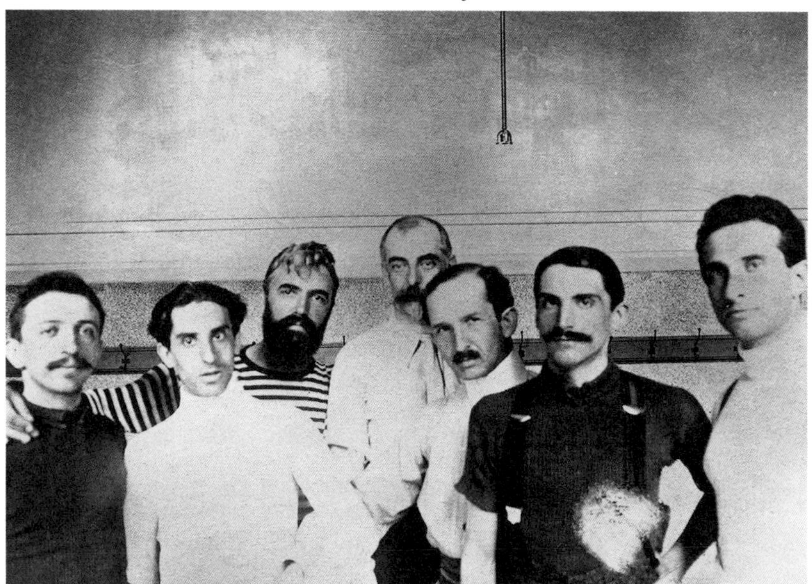

That watery horizon appears again in *Three Steps*, though it is tightly framed by the two tall masonry walls which the three steps in the image rise between. The composition of *Closed Sky* is almost identical, but as the name suggests, the horizon which meets the sky is not to be seen – a wall in the background blocks the view – but an oblique shaft of light coming from the left shows that passage in that direction is possible. It is the role of light that Appia always emphasised, for the way that it masters form and colour: 'When shapes and colours seek to express something, Light says: "I am; shapes and colours will only derive from me." ... Light will lead us, even precede us; rather than throwing before us the ever-deepening shadow of our egoism and our passivity.'[37] In *Before an Invisible Hand Opens the Door*, it is darkness rather than light which dominates, but in a drawing titled *The Opened Door* which depicts the same scene at a different time, light streams in from the right-hand side where a now-opened door is situated.

In the section of *L'Œuvre d'art vivant* that Appia devoted to his *Espaces rythmiques*, he wrote: 'Let us take, as an example, a square vertical column, with sharply defined right-angled edges. This column rests, without a base, on a horizontal slab. It conveys an impression of stability and resistance. A body approaches. Due to the contrast between the motility of the body and the quiet stillness of the column, there is an immanent feeling of expressive life, which the body alone without a column, or a column alone without a moving body, would not have achieved ... But the body now comes closer, to touch the pillar, the opposition is growing stronger. And then, finally, the body leans against the column, the immobility of which offers it a solid point of support: the column resists; he acts! The opposition has created life in the inanimate Form: space has become alive!'[38] His meaning is most evident in three drawings which again might be thought of as a set: *The Two Columns*, *Terrace with Three Columns* and *The Three Columns*, all of which seem to be different views of the same abstract temple, made up as they are of a broad terrace in the foreground, then three shallow steps which rise to a second terrace on which equally spaced sturdy orthogonal columns stand, casting raking shadows from a sun just rising or just setting over the distant waterline that is the ultimate horizontal line, on Earth as it is on the drawing board.

In fact, when one takes a step back and views Appia's *Espaces rythmiques* as a set, it is the ultimate line of the horizon that makes the greatest impression. One of the earliest admirers of the drawings, Prince Serge Wolkonsky, wrote that 'when we gaze upon Appia's drawings, it is always the horizon that impresses itself first upon us, and indeed the horizon is the most profound phenomenon that they render visible. Of all that there is here on earth, the "most distant" is the horizon line of the sea; that place where sky and water encounter one another, where there are no bounds to space nor to the imagination. Within the realm of the possible, the horizon is the most material manifestation of infinity, and therefore it is also the visual expression of eternity.'[39]

Château de Glérolles, *c* 1909.

The watery horizon of the three *Espaces rythmiques* that Appia most certainly created as a set and that he gave the names *The Waterfall*, *The Waterfall 2* and *The Final Columns of the Forest* is that of a lake or a broad river; the drawings are dominated by the same slim, centrally located waterfall plunging down into a broad expanse of still water from a very tall sheer cliff in the background. *The Waterfall* has the most minimal foreground, made up of two slim masonry walls with sloping upper surfaces: the wall on the left slopes downwards to the right, and the one on the right slopes down to the left and slides in front of the other wall, arriving at the bottom left-hand side of the drawing. The line of the water at the base of the cliff in the far distance is marked almost imperceptibly. Appia must have very gently drawn an eraser across a straight edge to remove a thin horizon line from the cliff face that he had shaded in an even field of grey. Appia worked up *The Waterfall 2* in more detail, adding white pastel to the sky to make it more luminous, and this time the full expanse of water, not just its horizon, has been rubbed back almost to the naked colour of the beige paper. The rocky composition in the foreground is also more highly wrought, made up of a rough collection of walls and rocks that might either be ruinous or recently hewn and yet to be dressed. The background of *The Final Columns of the Forest* is identical to that of *The Waterfall 2*, and the foreground is also similar, except that it is a more natural setting; the rocks seem to have been dragged into place, fringing what looks to be an informal gathering place in the very near foreground. And again, there are three tall, column-like tree trunks – two to the left of the central waterfall, and one to the right – framing the scene.

Amongst Appia's *Espace rythmiques*, which are otherwise mostly made up of the elements of earth, water and air, there are three drawings depicting identifiable vegetation, and in all three it is in the distinctive evergreen form of a cypress tree – an ancient symbol of the afterlife, embodied for example in *Die Toten Insel* (The Isle of the Dead), by Appia's countryman, Arnold Böcklin, a remarkable painting which found admirers amongst both the general public and those in public office.[40] Two of Appia's cypress drawings are named simply *The Cypress*. In one of these, a grove of fully mature trees stands tall just beyond the walls that bound a neatly trimmed lawn; a straight, narrow, paved path runs through the centre of it and through a gap in the boundary wall. In the other drawing, it is the tops of the trees which are visible, meaning that the tight composition of steps and terraces flanked by massive walls must overlook the stand of cypresses. In the third drawing, entitled *The Shadow of the Cypress*, the cypress tree itself does not appear. Alongside a reproduction of this drawing in *L'Œuvre d'art vivant*, Appia wrote, in the third person: 'For this *Espace rythmique*, the author at first proposed an avenue of cypresses. But little by little he removed the trees, retaining only their shadows. And then finally, at the end, only this solitary shadow remained – because it is sufficient to evoke an entire landscape.'[41]

There is one other *Espace rythmique* in which cypresses were originally an integral part of the composition but came to haunt the drawing in the same way a phantom limb reminds a body of that which is lost. *The Diver* was published only once in its original state, to accompany the article on Adolphe Appia that Wolkonsky wrote for an obscure Russian-language literary journal.[42] It reveals that Appia initially drew three tall, distinctively silhouetted cypresses on the left-hand side of the drawing, attesting to the abstractly classical landscape that he had in mind as the setting for Schiller's eponymous 1798 poem. In the poem, a humble squire accepts a king's challenge to dive from a tall rugged cliff to retrieve a golden goblet from the violent sea below, which 'boils and roars, hisses and seethes, as when water and fire first blend'.[43] The squire emerges with the goblet after a turbulent undersea trial: 'in a darkness of purple-tinged dye', he saw 'crowded in a union fearful and black, and in a horrible mass entwined, all manner of sea creatures'.[44] Taken by his bravery, the king awards the goblet to the squire but demands that he once again visit the depths. The king's daughter, now enamoured with the squire, pleads with her father not to tempt fate, but her lover plunges in. The yearning gathering gapes over the gulf. They listen to the thundering breakers roll in, and back out, but 'the youth is brought back by no kindly wave'.[45]

At some point, Appia decided to lop off the cypresses, resulting in the square final composition of the drawing that exists today, which is by far the largest and most spatially rich of Appia's *Espaces rythmiques* and warrants particular attention for its complexity. In the end, Appia's monumental setting for Schiller's tragic poem is an asymmetric orthogonal configuration of stairs, landings, platforms and terraces which intimate an ancient city wall on the edge of a cliff. Massive flanking walls recede far into the distance, and a sliver of sea horizon is visible to the left of the composition. The quasi-ceremonial character of the foreground attests to a civilised world, with a neatly tended lawn and path facing the viewer, while sublime nature endures beyond. The temporal setting of the drawing is likely the day after the heroic squire's second dive and his forever mute, Romantic death. However, it could also be the moment before his first leap, making the drawing a fusion of hopeful anticipation and commemoration. While Appia carefully delineated those parts of the narrative setting that are in view, he was just as judicious in

Frédéric Boissonnas, *Landscapes of Greece*, 1912.

his occlusion or omission of others – not least the violent ocean, which inhabits the scene as an absent presence.

Appia's drawing *The Diver* is a one-point perspective, as are all of the scenographer's other *Espaces rythmiques*, placing him in a long line of artists who used the drawing technique of perspective – from Latin *perspicere*, 'to see through' – as a method for representing three-dimensional reality on a two-dimensional page in a manner both reliable and convincing.[46] It is a history which begins with the Renaissance, particularly with Leon Battista Alberti, who formulated the insights and observations of those who came before him into a simple, universal and readily demonstrable method which even in his own time came to be recognised as indispensable for making drawings and paintings. Alberti accompanied his axiomatic written assertions with elemental diagrams of extraordinary clarity, the most famous

Appia, *Espace rythmique: The Diver*, 1909.

– justifiably so – of which appears at the end of the first book of his three-part treatise, *Della pittura* (On Painting, 1435).[47]

Alberti began by drawing a horizontal line in the bottom right-hand quadrant of the page. This baseline is the 'sill' of the 'window' through which the creator, and eventually the observer, of the drawing will view the scene in front of them. 'I inscribe a quadrangle ... which is considered to be an open window through which I see what I want to paint', wrote Alberti.[48] He then divided his 'sill' into six measures, and directly above its centre placed a point representing the target of sight, 'a point that occupies that position where a centric ray would strike'.[49] He then drafted lines from each of the divisions of the baseline up to this point. These 'visual rays' represent lines that are

parallel to each other in plan but that converge on a position in the infinite distance of perspectival space – the vanishing point.

That which has been marked out thus far is the bilaterally symmetrical frontal view, and now the same equal divisions of the baseline and the vanishing point are used to regulate the vertical measures. A horizontal line is drawn across the page at the height of the vanishing point – the horizon line of the drawing. A point is then placed on this horizon at a distance along the plane of representation which must be slightly greater than the distance between the 'eye' of the spectator and the picture plane, meaning that the point necessarily stands outside the frame of the 'window'. Lines are then drafted between the original baseline divisions and this point, intersecting with the frame of the window. These points of intersection establish the diminishing intervals of the baseline divisions and are transferred across to the frontal view as horizontal lines that cross the foreshortened 'visual rays', meaning that now a 'chequerboard' has been marked out in perspective, which will guide the construction of figures and buildings in correct proportion. Since in Alberti's method the eye of the creator-observer and the vanishing point are necessarily located directly opposite each other – a conjunction of the viewing and the viewed – the vanishing point is a 'counter-eye, so to speak, to the true eye that views it and is inseparably and reciprocally connected to it'.[50]

A vast literature on the construction of perspectival drawings accumulated in the wake of Alberti's concise theoretical formulation, his *costruzione legittima*, including critical commentaries and texts proposing alternative systems which were nevertheless tied to the original through concepts such as that of the relation between the eye and the vanishing point. Thus there were many tomes to be considered by the time the precocious Prussian architect Friedrich David Gilly was assembling his library in Berlin as a teaching resource for his proposed Bauakademie lecture course on 'Optics and Perspective as the Foundation of Theoretical-Artistic Instruction in the Art of Draughtsmanship, Especially for Architects' in the final decade of the eighteenth century.[51] It is impossible to review his extensive and discerning collection of books here, but on the basis that they accord in many ways and generally share a common lexicon for the parts of a perspective drawing and the procedures followed to arrive at them, a look at one of them – Jean Dubreuil's *The Practice of Perspective: Or, An Easy Method of Representing Natural Objects According to the Rules of Art* – can serve as the basis for discussion of some of the important themes that come to the fore in one of Gilly's own one-point perspective drawings, and are equally important for an understanding of Appia's *Espaces rythmiques*.[52] Appia's *The Diver* seems at least partially indebted to the theme, tenor and technique of Gilly's pen-and-wash *Perspective Study in a Landscape Setting*, made in 1798, the same year Schiller wrote his poem. The configuration of forms in both drawings is remarkably similar; in both, a central ramp-stair rises via intermediate landings to arrive at a platform flanked by walls which frame a view towards the distant water horizon.

But the set-out of Gilly's drawing is as interesting and informative as its composition. By his time, the 'sill' of Alberti's 'window' was referred to as the 'terrestrial line', but just as the Renaissance architect had done before him, Gilly divided it into equal lengths that can be thought of as one unit of measure within the particular world of his perspective drawing. He then drew a perpendicular line through one of the points that he had marked out along the 'terrestrial line', near the centre of the page. This vertical line would become the hinge for the bilaterally symmetrical perspectival setup, and in recognition of its special importance within the hierarchy of lines in the drawing, it was called the 'principal ray'.[53] At a distance of four units of measure along the horizontal line from this principal ray – right and left – he drew lines that met up at the same four-unit distance below the terrestrial line, which they therefore met at a forty-five-degree angle – making a right angle turned through forty-five degrees, as it were. He extended each of these lines – which were called 'extreme rays' – above the terrestrial line for the same distance as they projected below it. The endpoints of the two extreme

following spreads
Espace rythmiques:
The Diver, 71.5×74.3 cm;
Steps in the Foreground, 46.2×61.2 cm; *Untitled*, 69.2×102.3 cm, 1909.

appia
1909-10

Espace rythmique: Addiction, 51.2×71.7 cm, 1909

Espace rythmique: The Game of the Hills, 47.4×56.3 cm; *Jest*, 48.1×54.6 cm; *Ditto*, 48.1×54.6 cm, 1909

Espace rythmique: The Quay, 47.2×56.4 cm, 1909

Espace rythmique: The Alleyway, 47.0×56.3 cm, 1909

Espace rythmique: Door at the Base, 47.8 × 61.5 cm, 1909

Espace rythmique: Before an Invisible Hand Opens the Door, 47.7×63.5 cm; *The Open Door*, 47.7×63.5 cm, 1909

rays are termed 'points of distance', and they lie on the horizon, as of course does the vanishing point – Alberti's *punctus centricus*, or Dubreuil's 'point of sight'. The distance along the horizon line between the point of sight and each of the points of distance is crucial to the success of a perspective drawing: 'For as the beauty of a perspective depends on the point of distance, so the eye ought never to be placed too near the object, nor too far from it, but at a convenient distance, for in this situation the visual angle will be at a right angle or ninety degrees, and this is the largest angle that the eye can well discover at one cast.'[54]

Gilly joined up all the units of measure along the terrestrial line to two points of distance to create a pair of radial sets of lines, resulting in a dense web of 'visual rays' that tile the ground plane on which the stereometric prisms sit. These tiles would be squares if seen in plan, or in 'ichnographic projection', to use Dubreuil's terminology. The term he used for a 'projection made on a plane perpendicular to the horizon'[55] – what we would now refer to as an elevation drawing – was 'orthographic projection'. On the principal ray that in the picture plane stands perpendicular to the horizon, Gilly marked out the same regular measure – four units in total – spanning the distance between the terrestrial line and the point of sight. By drawing a line parallel to the horizon through one of these measures until it intersects with a given vertical line drafted up from one of the intervals on the terrestrial line, and then joining this point of intersection back to the points of distance, the corner of a volume that is one unit high is delineated. By way of demonstration, Gilly drew a dashed line across to the left from the point that is one unit up until it met with a dashed vertical line which he extended from the point where the terrestrial line meets the 'extreme ray' – that is, four units across. Finally, he joined this point of intersection back to the left-hand point of distance.

These kinds of dashed lines were called *linee occulte* (concealed lines), as they brought to vision the three-dimensional, cubic grid that despite its omniscience was invisible. Sebastiano Serlio had used the same term for the regulating lines which served as a practical guide when setting out the armature of a perspective drawing on the drafting table. For the Renaissance architect, these *linee occulte* also brought to the level of visual appearance the underlying order of natural – and potentially also constructed – forms: they occupied the province between the vanishing point on the horizon, at which all lines converge, and the terrestrial line in the foreground that is the very first line drawn upon the page – the one from which 'all things have their beginning', according to Serlio.[56]

That the intrinsic revealing–concealing character of *linee occulte* is naturally part of the appeal of perspective drawing is shown in Gilly's *Perspective Study* by the way the prisms stand in the liminal context of a shoreline – between water and land that is in constant flux, as the tide ebbs and flows. It is unclear whether the prisms have just been revealed by the ebbing of the tide, or whether they will soon vanish out of sight under the incoming waters, washed over by sand, never to be seen again. It is possible that when making this instructional drawing, Gilly had in mind the notion that those same processes of decay and renewal that animate the natural world were also at play in architecture, and that it would be on the basis of the geometric-optic discipline of perspective that a new architecture for his time would be created.

Karl Friedrich Schinkel was among the very first cohort of students in Gilly's lecture course at the Bauakademie and was awarded his teacher's highest grade, *ausgezeichnet und viel Fähigkeit* (excellent, and much ability).[57] After graduating, Schinkel applied himself to designing a multitude of important public buildings that included the Königliches Schauspielhaus (Royal Theatre), Altes Museum (Museum of Antiquity) and the Neue Wache (New Guardhouse), all within a stone's throw of each other on one side or the other of Unter den Linden in Berlin – as was his new Bauakademie, which replaced the one in which Gilly had given his lessons. Though Schinkel was ultimately an architect, he was much else besides, including a scenographer, artist and draughtsman.[58] His various guises came together to great effect in his speculative drawings, including the one that he made in 1815 for a 'Classical Palace, Staircases and Triumphal Arch'. The repertoire is one that Appia also played: stairs are what the drawing is really about. A broad sweep of them rise from the base of the drawing to an expansive platform on which the architecture that is nominally the content of the drawing resides. It is certainly classical, though non-specific – drawn, it seems, at speed. A run of stairs in the foreground rises to the right, and another to the left which kinks through ninety degrees to a view of the horizon that dominates the whole image. And there are more stairs, a run of which rises to the right in the background and then once again kinks around to gaze towards the horizon. The rises and runs

Friedrich Gilly, *Perspective Study in a Landscape Setting*, 1798.

(height between treads and depth of the treads) of the stairs in their multiple ranks are all different; the drawing is an experiment. As a theatrical setting, it resembles the one that terminates the Via Appia in Brindisi, where the twin columns that mark the final milestone measure from the Forum in Rome stand proud above a broad sweep of stairs leading down to the harbour, the gateway to the east.

Stairs, too, are what the perspective drawing that Alberto Sartoris made a century after Schinkel, as an eighteen-year-old final-year architecture student at the École Supérieure des Beaux-Arts in Geneva, is all about. Locatable within the same disciplinary tradition as Gilly and Schinkel, it is testament to

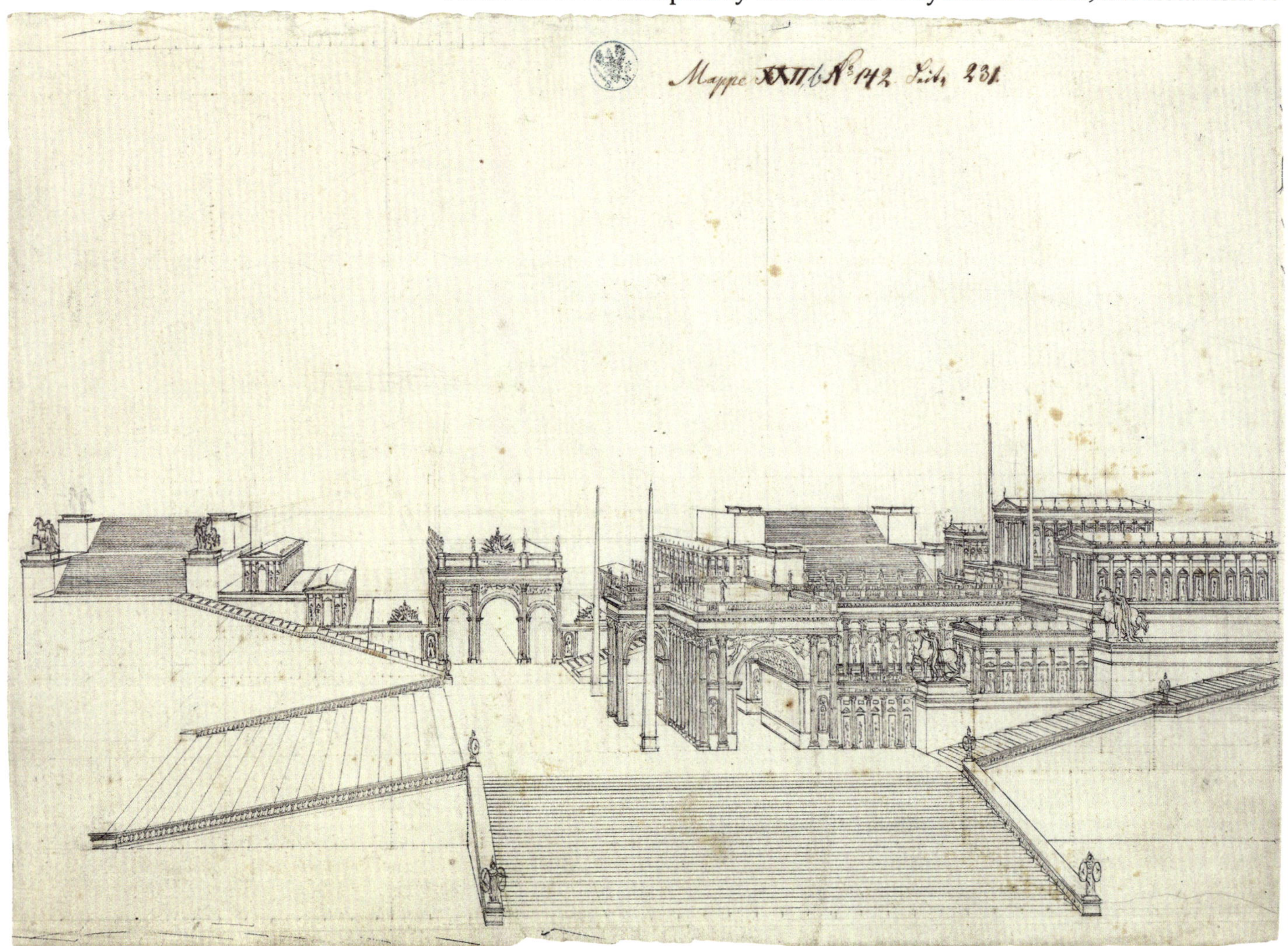

Karl Friedrich Schinkel, *Classical Palace, Staircases and Triumphal Arch*, 1815.

the fact that the ability to execute a perspective drawing accurately was regarded as essential to becoming an architect. At the same time, it equally serves to foreground the creative opportunities afforded by the increasing malleability of perspectival representation that emerged between the time of the Bauakademie and Sartoris as the 'rules' of perspective drawing, codified by Alberti and Serlio, became more malleable. They were tried and tested procedures that had been found to work well on the drawing board, and that could now be treated more freely, adjusted, combined and occasionally discarded in the service of the expression of modern architectural ideas and forms.[59]

Sartoris's minimal orthogonal composition – everything is either parallel to the picture plane or perpendicular to it – involves a long wall of continuous height which starts out parallel to the picture plane and proceeds from the left-hand side of the drawing towards the right, halting approximately two thirds of the way across and pivoting through ninety degrees to return towards us – the viewers – before turning again and covering the short distance that remains to the right-hand edge of the picture frame. One set of stairs runs most of the length of the first section of wall, ascending to the right and meeting in the corner with a second set of identically composed stairs – six treads, an intermediate landing, and then another six treads – that is turned through ninety degrees, running almost the entire length of the second section of wall that stands perpendicular to the first. They arrive at a common top landing that is short of the upper horizon of the walls by the height of a balustrade. So, a notch that accords with the width of the landing is cut out of the first section of wall to permit passage through it. Whether the walls are freestanding or retaining, and what lies beyond them, is a mystery, since they are taller than we are: the horizon beyond is at the height of the tenth step. The architectonic expression is an abstract stereometric one; the opaque walls and stairs cast shadows but offer no clues as to their materiality. It is as though the whole monochromatic composition has either been cast in plaster or carved from alabaster.

Since Sartoris's drawing is at least as much an educational demonstration as it is an architectural proposition, it is unsurprising that the elements making up the composition – the stairs foremost amongst them – are to a certain extent paradigmatic for perspective drawings, recalling Serlio's assertion that 'of all the elements which have a great power of demonstration in perspective, I find that staircases come out best'.[60] And again, bearing in mind that the drawing is an illustration of technique, it is no surprise that the perspectival setup and the steps that the young student of architecture correctly followed to arrive at his composition of walls and steps, as well as the shadows that they cast on each other, can be clearly read; he drafted everything in coloured pencil first – magenta for forms, pale blue for shadows – and left these lines on the drawing as evidence for his teacher after carefully outlining with sharp black lines the final composition that they delivered to him.

The composition of one of Appia's own 'stair' drawings, his *Espace rythmique Moonlight*, which takes in a scene that might be a fragment of an ancient citadel or the forecourt of a temple, is very similar to Sartoris's perspective drawing. A run of stone steps ascending parallel to the picture plane up and to the left – one shallow step, then a platform, then six more steps rising to another platform which extends beyond the bounds of the drawing. The run of steps and platforms abuts a wall of carefully laid ashlar masonry, above which there is an evenly illuminated slot of sky. What might lie beyond the wall is a mystery and, unlike in Sartoris's drawing, there is no gap in it through which one might pass. The lower part of the drawing is cast in the shadow of a bright but low-lying moon off to the right, beyond the frame of the drawing. The angle and height of the shadow it casts intimate that there is a right-angle return to the ashlar wall, back towards us, the viewers.

There is both less and more in Appia's perspective drawing than in the one made by Sartoris, which is concerned to maximise the legibility of the perspectival armature – to push the hidden lines to the surface, both figuratively and literally – in order to demonstrate what can be achieved by mastery of technique. Appia's presses in the opposite direction, since he erased all traces of its setting-out, preferencing a diffusion of form and contour within an overarching mood or atmosphere, that of a calm moonlit night. In Appia's drawing there is much more in the way of material expression: the unyielding ashlar masonry has clearly been hewn, probably a long time ago and by masons both capable and strong. It reads as a semi-sacred nocturnal setting for gods just departed or soon to arrive, and the German Romantic *Landschaftsseele* is a spectral presence in this drawing as it is in Appia's other *Espaces rythmiques*. This invites comparison with paintings that were made at about the time Gilly was drawing his *Perspective Study*, but which seem to be unconditioned by perspectival geometry, made by artists who were part of the project of German Romanticism, and who in Joseph Leo Koerner's words navigated the purgatory 'where the artist fashions his works again as altars but must leave out the gods'.[61]

The best-known German Romantic painter of all is Caspar David Friedrich, whose enigmatic paintings mediate a religious experience. In Koerner's words, what his canvases are finally about 'remains always only almost visible'. While Koerner was referring to content, the 'almost visible' also generally holds for what one literally sees in Friedrich's paintings, master as he was of 'all transitions between the visible and the invisible'.[62] That is certainly so under normal lighting conditions, but when his paintings are seen under other conditions, a great deal more is revealed. Infrared radiation has a greater wavelength than visible light, and penetrates deeper into the structure of a painting, making any otherwise hidden underdrawing visible. As part of its recent restoration, an infrared reflectogram was made of Friedrich's *Abtei im Eichwald* (Abbey in the Oakwood), which shows a sombre wintry scene centred on the ruined remains of an abbey dimly lit by a sliver of crescent moon.[63] The reflectogram discloses that the building was in fact diligently set up in one-point perspective; the columns of the fragmentary remains of the nave of the abbey recede behind the west façade towards the point of sight that with symbolic significance is located on the altar. In Koerner's words, Friedrich allows 'loss, absence, the departure of things close to us, all to occur within our immediate experience of the image: as the fog that renders nature fugitive'.[64]

One of the things that has been 'rendered fugitive' in *Abtei im Eichwald* is its perspectival setup, which is also the case in Appia's likewise palely illuminated *Moonlight*. In this respect, they extend our understanding of *linee occulte* by introducing the theme of occultation and shadowy concealment alongside the summoning of form seen in the sunlit drawings by Gilly, Schinkel and Sartoris which make the geometric-optic construction explicit.

As fragmentary 'set pieces', all these perspective drawings can be thought of as a conjunction of architecture and scenography. They exist not in the two-part world of 'ichnographic projection' (plan) and 'orthographic projection' (elevation), but rather in the third projection in a triumvirate, which is defined in one of those books on perspective that Gilly based his lecture course on: 'When the projection of any object is made by rays flowing from the several parts of the object, uniting in one point where the eye is supposed to be placed', the representation is called the 'scenography' of that object, so that to 'draw the scenographic projection of any object is to draw the several parts of it as they will appear to the eye situated at a convenient distance from the object upon a plane placed perpendicular to the horizon, and in a proper situation to receive the object; and how this is to be done, is the proper business of perspective'.[65]

At first, it is the variety – of theme, composition and atmosphere – in Appia's scenographic drawings that is arresting, but when his *Espaces rythmiques* are considered as a suite, it is in fact the constancies that impress themselves. The carefully considered details and faint evidence of the techniques used to achieve them are only evident at close range; for example, the sequence of light construction lines that Appia used to set up his one-point perspectives, or the tiny pinholes he used to trace an early iteration of a drawing. One

Alberto Sartoris, perspective drawing exercise made in 1919 while a student at the École Supérieure des Beaux-Arts in Geneva.

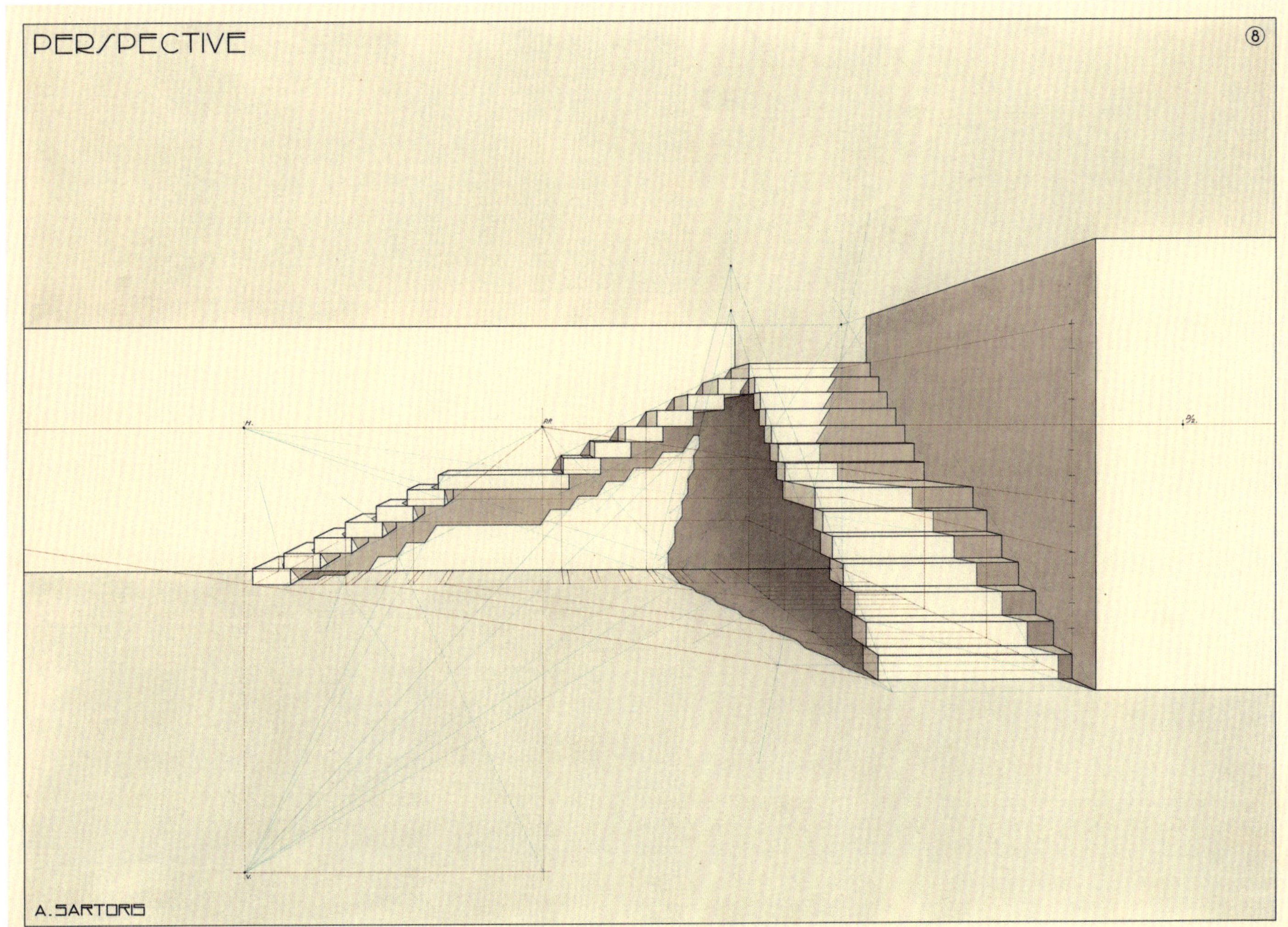

also comes to realise the extent to which he limited his palette, only ever drawing with charcoal, graphite and white pastel. The drawings are monochrome – though not completely, since the colour of the paper, mostly in hues of pale blue, green, beige or amber, provides each drawing with a distinctive ambient undertone and an upper limit of brightness. Appia very occasionally added white pastel to shift parts of the drawing even higher toward the lighter end of the visual register. For him this was a means to create a faint luminosity, mostly in the rectangular slot of sky in the upper reaches of his drawings, framed by the edges of the page and by the horizon below. But for the most part, he articulated highlights by working back towards the ambient colour of the paper from an evenly shaded field of grey.

following spread
Espace rythmique: Moonlight, 49.2×66.5 cm, 1909.

F 7f

L'escalier pourrait commencer plus à droite et monter plus haut

Aerial photograph of the terraced hillsides around the Rivaz area, including Château de Glérolles.

following spread *Espace rythmique: The Waterfall,* 50.7×72.2 cm, 1909.

This method of erasing, rubbing and smudging was used to sculpt the light of early dawn gently radiating from behind the imposing central mountain in *Cataracts of the Dawn* and the cataracts themselves, which cascade down towards the three heavy stone steps in the foreground of the stage facing the viewer. Appia was also diligent at the other end of the gradient, patiently building up the ashlar masonry in soft charcoal, then articulating the details with a sharp graphite pencil.

What also becomes apparent is that Appia only ever drew on the Ingres papers made by Canson & Montgolfier, famed for their constancy of texture and colour. The cotton-rag paper mills at Vidalon-lès-Annonay in southern France date back to the sixteenth century, and the papers are still made there today in three factories sited on adjoining lots strung out over a distance of a mile along the banks of the fast-flowing River Dêume. By Appia's time, the company had set up two international branches: one of them in the United States, on 8th Avenue in New York, but the other much closer to home. The Dêume is a tributary of the Rhône, which on its way from the Swiss Alps to the Mediterranean flows through Geneva, where the second branch was just twenty minutes' walk from the Conservatoire, at 46 route de Frontenex. Appia restocked his paper supply there, every sheet of which bore the distinctive embossment CANSON MONTGOLFIER <> VIDALON-LES-ANNONAY <> ANCNE MANUFRE.

All of the *Espaces rythmiques* that Appia drew into existence on the collapsible drawing board set up in his modestly furnished lodgings in the Château de Glérolles, which mostly had only its view across the lake towards the majestic Alps to recommend it, are devoid of people. And yet, the human form is always present, since the steps, platforms and landings all anticipate the presence of the performers whose role it is to navigate them. It might be that the performers are just about to step onto the stage, or they may well have just exited and are now milling out of breath in the wings.

Appia parcelled up his drawings and posted them to Jaques-Dalcroze, together with an accompanying note in which he griped that eurhythmics students, who always moved about on a flat surface, give the impression of 'mountain climbers who are climbing the Matterhorn in bas-relief'.[66] Unoffended, Jaques-Dalcroze wrote straight back, and in fact, as Appia later recalled, 'was greatly enthused when he saw my drawings, and I was convinced that – both for his sake and for mine – I had brought to realisation something convincing. The *Raumstil* (spatial style) for eurhythmics had been found.'[67]

appia
1909

Espace rythmique: The Final Columns of the Forest, 50.7×71.5 cm, 1909

Espace rythmique: The Waterfall Two, 47.5 × 63.5 cm, 1909

Espace rythmique: Cypresses, 48.3 × 57.8 cm, 1909

Espace rythmique: Cypresses, 46.5×53.0 cm, 1909

following spread *The Legend of the Isle of the Sounds*, 62.7×80.7 cm, 1909

'We gather here in Hellerau this afternoon to celebrate the laying of the foundation stone for our Bildungsanstalt. The youngest pupil – a local eight-year-old Hellerau lad – will strike the first three hammer blows for this building that is one of the few to be consecrated to the future.'[68] Brimming with optimism, Wolf Dohrn delivered his speech to the smiling cosmopolitan audience that had gathered around on the beautiful spring afternoon in 1911. The Bildungsanstalt was to be a place of education and performance – a Festspielhaus. And though for Wagner that would have been a national cause, for Dohrn the clods of earth being turned over were *europäisch* before they were *deutsch*: 'We are like one large family numbering in the hundreds ... no fewer than fourteen countries are represented here today, all united under the sign of *Rhythmus!*'[69]

Jaques-Dalcroze had taken up a position in the front row and stood there full of satisfaction – the Jaques-Dalcroze Bildungsanstalt für rhythmischen Erziehung (Institute for Rhythmic Education) had been named after him – whereas his reclusive chief collaborator, Appia, was characteristically absent.[70]

The Bildungsanstalt was to be the centrepiece of Hellerau, the newly founded garden city located on the edge of the gently undulating landscape of Dresden Heath, a 'wide and sandy plain where daisies and the occasional pine tree grew', as recorded by the composer Darius Milhaud in his memoir *Notes Without Music*.[71] And the writer and journalist Alfred Günther wrote that 'you could breathe freely on the hills, where grain was ripening, heather and lupines were blooming, and dirt roads led far out into the countryside. It was a simple barren moorland – but you had to love it.'[72]

The affectionately recalled city of Hellerau could be reached in about half an hour by tram from Dresden, the city which it stood a hundred metres above, and whose sea of lights down below were visible on clear evenings such as the one on which the Bildungsanstalt was consecrated.[73] Hellerau had been modelled along the lines proposed by Ebenezer Howard in *Garden Cities of To-morrow*, which had been translated into German in 1907.[74] Howard himself in fact visited the garden city and recorded his impressions in a letter to the editor of a local newspaper, the *Dresdner Anzeiger*: 'The first impression that Hellerau made on me was a positive one, and no less positive was the final overall feeling that I took away with me. Hellerau is not merely an imitation of the English garden cities, but rather it is testimony to that characteristic quality that Germans possess, namely, to learn from others but not to slavishly copy them, going their own way instead.'[75]

The particular direction that Hellerau went was governed by the guiding leitmotif that permeated all of life there, both cultural and economic – that of rhythm. The garden city was intended to be an antidote to the arrhythmia that the German economist Karl Bücher had identified in his 1896 book *Arbeit und Rhythmus* (Work and Rhythm) as the primary affliction of urbanised modern industrial society.[76] Having studied the rhymes, chants and songs of traditional craftspeople, as well as the physical movement each craft demanded, Bücher had determined that in ancient times work and art existed in harmony. This harmony, he argued, had been disrupted by the artificial, mechanised tempo of industrial machinery, and so advocated a rediscovery of traditional rhythm, ushering individuals back into healthy accord both with their original selves and with their community.

'In the beginning there was a man by the name of Karl Schmidt', wrote Peter de Mendelssohn of the founding of Hellerau in the section of his memoir dedicated to his childhood years, a time that he remembered with great fondness: 'Never again have I basked in such radiant sunshine and breathed in such fragrant air as I did during my childhood in Hellerau.'[77] It was the sights and smells, but also the cosmopolitan sounds that so captivated him: 'I marvelled as the voices of all of Europe – French and Russian, English and Italian, Swedish, Danish and every kind of German – resounded in my ears.'[78]

Schmidt, the man who was there in the beginning, was a carpenter, furniture maker and businessman who, according to Mendelssohn, began

Laying of the foundation stone for the Bildungsanstalt Jaques-Dalcroze in Hellerau, 1911.

a 'revolution in furniture design' that was intended to replace the mass-produced jumble of styles that prevailed at the end of the nineteenth century with a new contemporary aesthetic based on the qualities of materials themselves, and on handicraft. Schmidt founded the Dresdner Werkstätten für Handwerkskunst in 1898, and by 1909 his business was doing so well that he required a larger factory to manufacture his modern furniture.[79] He bought a large plot of land in Dresden Heath and commissioned the Munich-based Jugendstil architect Richard Riemerschmid, a fellow co-founder of the Werkbund, to build the factory and to devise a master plan for a residential settlement of single-family houses for the workers. Schmidt, who came to be known to his friends as 'Holz-Goethe' (Timber-Goethe),[80] wrote about these

Photographs from 1910 of Appia's *Espaces rythmiques: Left Portal; The Shadow of the Cypresses*, 1909.

early years in his memoirs, excerpts of which have been published as *Die Gründung von Hellerau* (The Founding of Hellerau). In one brief passage, Schmidt wrote of his invention of the name for the garden city: 'It was during a performance of an opera at the Semperoper in Dresden that I came up with the idea (which I had heard from some farmers who spoke of the *Au am Heller*), to give it the name "Hellerau".'[81] In his own memoirs, Mendelssohn wrote that he was not sure how the settlement gained its name: 'Sometimes you read that it derives from a guesthouse named *Zum letzten Heller* that is said to have existed on the heathland. But as a child, I knew every last corner of the area, and I have never seen or heard of such a guesthouse. However, it is true that the large, sandy heathland surrounded by pine forests that lay between us and the city of Dresden – in the summer we children literally trudged up to our calves in the hot sand – was simply called Der Heller.'[82]

The other individual who became a driving force behind Hellerau – as an idea as much as a place to actually live and work – was Wolf Dohrn, a philanthropist, curator and journalist. He was also the first General Secretary of the Werkbund, which he helped to found in the summer of 1908. According to Wolkonsky, Dohrn was 'a tireless supporter of the Werkbund and its projects, lecturing widely, serving on planning committees and acting generally as its spokesman and publicist. He was a man of very substantial gifts: he had an enormous capacity for enthusiasm and hard work, a talent for communicating his ideas and inspiring others with them and, most significantly, a deeply felt idealism.'[83]

Dohrn channelled his idealism into the enterprise of eurhythmics and, according to Wolkonsky, the full realisation of Jaques-Dalcroze's ideas in Hellerau became his primary goal: 'Dohrn devoted to this idea all his strength, extraordinary personality, confident will and great perseverance.'[84] Having been immensely impressed by a performance of eurhythmics in Dresden that Jaques-Dalcroze himself directed in November 1909, Dohrn drafted a proposal to the Swiss musical pedagogue on behalf of the Werkbund, offering him a ten-year contract and promising to build a *Festspielhaus* that would be the architectural, educational and cultural beating heart of the garden city.[85]

Having secured the signature of Jaques-Dalcroze, Dohrn set about identifying an architect up to the task of designing the festival theatre. He settled on Heinrich Tessenow, a then thirty-three-year-old architect and professor at the Technische Hochschule in Dresden who according to Mendelssohn 'worked unconditionally with clean straight lines and smooth surfaces'.[86] The German art historian Karl Scheffler, who would in time become one of Tessenow's greatest advocates, wrote that the architect's particular talent was to 'think in terms of masses, to live in the cubic'.[87] His further general characterisation of Tessenow's architecture is apposite: 'If other architects of our time seek ambitiously to be classicists, then Tessenow with his buildings is, silently, a classicist full of discretion.'[88] And finally, if one were to attempt to sum up Tessenow's architecture, 'one might speak of a rural classicism, of a Hellenic austerity born of North German peasantry'.[89]

Photographs from 1910 of Appia's *Espaces rythmiques*: *The Three Columns*; *Terrace with Three Columns*, 1909.

The task with which Dohrn charged young Tessenow was no minor one; in addition to a focal Festsaal, the Bildungsanstalt was to contain rehearsal spaces, changing and shower rooms, and areas for rhythmic exercises, comprising what one critic characterised as an amalgamation of an ancient Greek temple and *palaestra*, or wrestling school. It was also proposed that the Bildungsanstalt would 'replace the missing church', in accordance with the ambition voiced in 1906 by Theodor Fischer, an architect and yet another co-founder of the Deutscher Werkbund. In his essay 'Was ich bauen möchte' (What I Would Like to Build), Fischer imagined 'not a school, nor a museum, nor a church, nor a concert hall, nor an auditorium! ... something of these and also something more!'[90]

In the summer of 1910 – a year after Appia had drawn his *Espaces rythmiques* – Tessenow travelled down to Switzerland to discuss his preliminary plans for the Bildungsanstalt with Jaques-Dalcroze. The key reason the meeting was set up in Switzerland – at the Hotel Terminus in Lausanne – was because Jaques-Dalcroze had come to rely heavily on Appia for aesthetic guidance, having been beguiled by his drawings, and was adamant that the self-effacing, travel-shy scenographer should be personally present at discussions regarding the design of his Bildungsanstalt.[91] Jaques-Dalcroze wrote the following to Appia in advance of the four-way meeting: 'You will meet Salzmann, a Russian painter, who admires you enormously and who will be the ideal collaborator for you', and 'Tessenow will show you his plans, which I like very much.'[92]

following spread
Espace rythmique: The Three Columns, 46.2×61.2 cm, 1909.

Espace rythmique: Terrace With Three Columns, 43.7×49.4 cm, 1909

Espace rythmique: The Two Columns, 47.9×55.8 cm, 1909

Espace rythmique: Three Steps, 47.4×53.5 cm; *Closed Sky*, 48.0×63.0 cm, 1909

Espace rythmique: Oblique Shadow, 47.0×53.4 cm; *Left Portal*, 47.2×53.6 cm, 1909

Heinrich Tessenow, Bildungsanstalt Jaques-Dalcroze, Hellerau, 1912.

Appia's *Espaces rythmiques* are cumbersome to transport; they are sizeable and subject to smudging. But Jaques-Dalcroze had a clever idea; he arranged for his friend Boissonnas to photograph all of Appia's drawings in his studio in Geneva. Jaques-Dalcroze then had copies printed off, which he could carry along to meetings – such as the one in Lausanne with Tessenow. These photographs by Boissonnas are excellent – the next best thing to being in the presence of the drawings themselves. However, they are of course monochrome, and this stripping of the ambient colour, coupled with the enhanced contrast, makes them more sharply profiled and, for want of a better term, more architectural.

The extent to which Appia's *Espaces rythmiques* impressed themselves on the young architect Tessenow is unknown, but it is certainly worth drawing

attention to the uncanny resemblance between them and the configuration and proportions of the long shallow steps and heavy stone pilasters that greet visitors to the temple-like Bildungsanstalt.[93]

Appia himself was not at all concerned by the similarity and was, in fact, effusive in his praise for the design of the building, writing in a letter to Jaques-Dalcroze: 'The more I think over Tessenow's plans, the more it seems to me that no other design could possibly accommodate and unify in itself so many of those conditions that are fundamental and indispensable for your work. Tessenow has understood in an absolutely ingenious way that the architecture of the Bildungsanstalt must come second to the life that you will arouse inside of it. He has fully grasped that the style of the Bildungsanstalt is to derive from the absolute and refined restrained silence of every line and surface because these lines and surfaces must meet the needs of life and, above all, the movements that they must limit and embrace. Indeed, from this point of view we could not have done better, and Tessenow's intuition, it seems to me, is nothing short of astonishing.'[94]

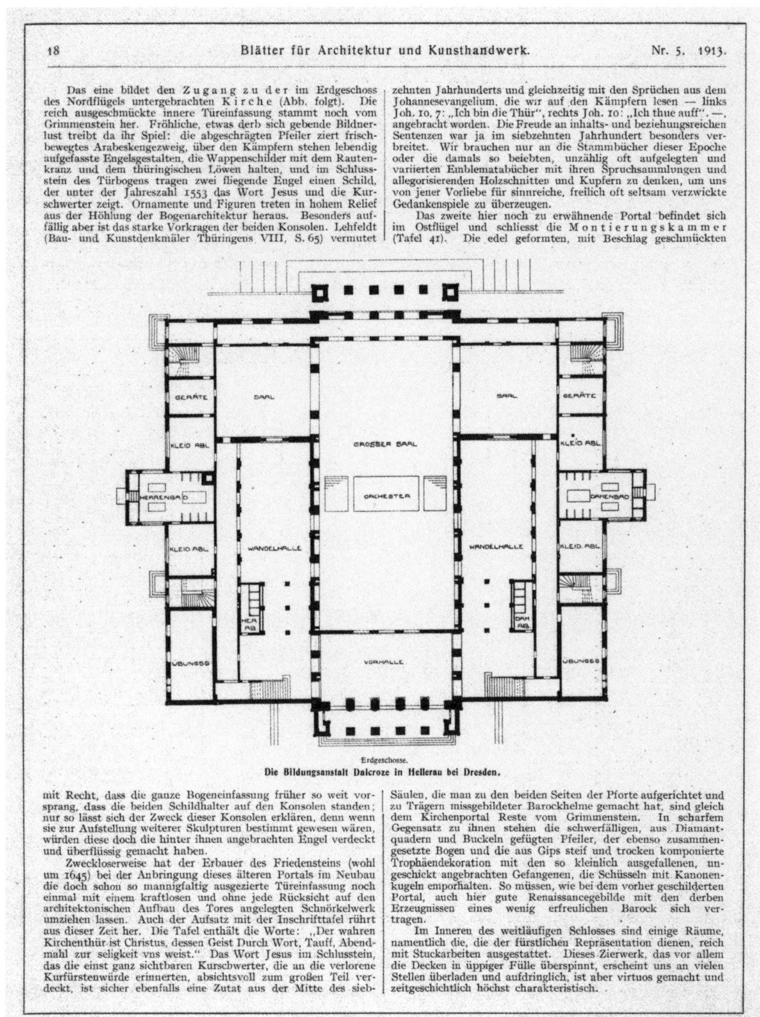
18 Blätter für Architektur und Kunsthandwerk. Nr. 5. 1913.

Das eine bildet den Zugang zu der im Erdgeschoss des Nordflügels untergebrachten Kirche (Abb. folgt). Die reich ausgeschmückte innere Türeinfassung stammt noch vom Grimmenstein her. Fröhliche, etwas derb sich gebende Bildnerlust treibt da ihr Spiel: die abgeschrägten Pfeiler ziert frischbewegtes Arabeskengezweig, über den Kämpfern stehen lebendig aufgefasste Engelsgestalten, die Wappenschilder mit dem Rautenkranz und dem thüringischen Löwen halten, und im Schlussstein des Türbogens tragen zwei fliegende Engel einen Schild, der unter der Jahreszahl 1553 das Wort Jesus und die Kurschwerter zeigt. Ornamente und Figuren treten in hohem Relief aus der Höhlung der Bogenarchitektur heraus. Besonders auffällig aber ist das starke Vorkragen der beiden Konsolen. Lehfeldt (Bau- und Kunstdenkmäler Thüringens VIII, S. 65) vermutet zehnten Jahrhunderts und gleichzeitig mit den Sprüchen aus dem Johannesevangelium, die wir auf den Kämpfern lesen — links Joh. 10, 7: „Ich bin die Thür", rechts Joh. 10: „Ich thue auff". —, angebracht worden. Die Freude an inhalts- und beziehungsreichen Sentenzen war ja im siebzehnten Jahrhundert besonders verbreitet. Wir brauchen nur an die Stammbücher dieser Epoche oder die damals so beiebten, unzählig oft aufgelegten und variierten Emblematabücher mit ihren Spruchsammlungen und allegorisierenden Holzschnitten und Kupfern zu denken, um uns von jener Vorliebe für sinnreiche, freilich oft seltsam verzwickte Gedankenspiele zu überzeugen.

Das zweite hier noch zu erwähnende Portal befindet sich im Ostflügel und schliesst die Montierungskammer (Tafel 41). Die edel geformten, mit Beschlag geschmückten

Erdgeschosse.

Die Bildungsanstalt Dalcroze in Hellerau bei Dresden.

mit Recht, dass die ganze Bogeneinfassung früher so weit vorsprang, dass die beiden Schildhalter auf den Konsolen standen; nur so lässt sich der Zweck dieser Konsolen erklären, denn wenn sie zur Aufstellung weiterer Skulpturen bestimmt gewesen wären, würden diese doch die hinter ihnen angebrachten Engel verdeckt und überflüssig gemacht haben.

Zweckloserweise hat der Erbauer des Friedensteins (wohl um 1645) bei der Anbringung dieses älteren Portals im Neubau die doch schon so mannigfaltig ausgezierte Türeinfassung noch einmal mit einem kraftlosen und ohne jede Rücksicht auf den architektonischen Aufbau des Tores angelegten Schnörkelwerk umziehen lassen. Auch der Aufsatz mit der Inschrifttafel rührt aus dieser Zeit her. Die Tafel enthält die Worte: „Der wahren Kirchenthür ist Christus, dessen Geist Durch Wort, Tauff, Abendmahl zur seligkeit vns weist." Das Wort Jesus im Schlusstein, das die einst ganz sichtbaren Kurschwerter, die an die verlorene Kurfürstenwürde erinnerten, absichtsvoll zum großen Teil verdeckt, ist sicher ebenfalls eine Zutat aus der Mitte des sieb- Säulen, die man zu den beiden Seiten der Pforte aufgerichtet und zu Trägern missgebildeter Barockhelme gemacht hat, sind gleich dem Kirchenportal Reste vom Grimmenstein. In scharfem Gegensatz zu ihnen stehen die schwerfälligen, aus Diamantquadern und Buckeln gefügten Pfeiler, der ebenso zusammengesetzte Bogen und die aus Gips steif und trocken komponierte Trophäendekoration mit den so kleinlich ausgefallenen, ungeschickt angebrachten Gefangenen, die Schüsseln mit Kanonenkugeln emporhalten. So müssen, wie bei dem vorher geschilderten Portal, auch hier gute Renaissancegebilde mit den derben Erzeugnissen eines wenig erfreulichen Barock sich vertragen.

Im Inneren des weitläufigen Schlosses sind einige Räume, namentlich die, die der fürstlichen Repräsentation dienen, reich mit Stuckarbeiten ausgestattet. Dieses Zierwerk, das vor allem die Decken in üppiger Fülle überspinnt, erscheint uns an vielen Stellen überladen und aufdringlich, ist aber virtuos gemacht und zeitgeschichtlich höchst charakteristisch.

Heinrich Tessenow, floor plan of the Bildungsanstalt Jaques-Dalcroze, Hellerau, 1912.

As built, Tessenow's Bildungsanstalt presented the pronounced nave, side aisle and transept arrangement of a church, but on closer examination the governing dimensions of the floor plan are not so much ecclesiastical as geometrical, based around the 'dance' or 'play' of a single governing square module along a north–south axis. For example, the twin stair halls that flank the entry foyer are one quarter of this module, as are the rehearsal rooms either side of the theatre, while a 'slipped' repetition of the same square defines the elongated service zones along the eastern and western extremities of the plan. This modular play is entirely in accord with Jaques-Dalcroze's own regulations for eurhythmic movement, as explained in 1914: 'Note duration is expressed by the forward movement of the feet and the body. A quarter note, the length of an average step forward, forms the unit. Eighth notes are stepped rapidly; half the length of the quarter note, and sixteenth notes are so short that they become light running steps.'[95]

At the centre of the composition is the Festsaal (auditorium), conceived as a kind of alchemical vessel invoking a special temporality – the time-out-of-time of ritual and ceremony – and the fundamental or original conditions for the re-enactment of dramatic performances, which at Hellerau were seen to be embodied in the play between the metaphorical play between dark earth and bright ethereal light. And it is here that Appia, at Jaques-Dalcroze's invitation, collaborated with the Russian artist Alexander von Salzmann in fabricating an electric lighting apparatus that could regulate and temper the ethereal light. The pair had initially undertaken a series of highly imaginative, albeit hazardous, experiments in the school's provisional lodgings in Dresden's baroque Landhaus, using carbide lamps, car headlights, mirrors and phosphorescent paint. They eventually hit on a proposal whereby both the walls and ceiling would be made of taut canvas screens impregnated with cedar oil and illuminated from behind by thousands of electric globes – a 'luminous organ' that would envelop the audience in the same mysteriously diffuse glow as the performers.[96] Salzmann later recounted the transformation of the entire theatre – all four walls and the ceiling – into a single great lighting apparatus: 'We stretched pre-prepared lengths of fabric over the light bulbs, and in the end we had created a space that was itself luminous, rather than a space that was illuminated. Light emits into the space itself

– the distraction of visible light sources has been eliminated. And the traditional brutal contrast between the dark auditorium and the brightly illuminated stage has likewise been eliminated – the two can now be attuned.'[97] Salzmann went on to describe the purpose of this attunement, which was 'not to tell anecdotes about the sun, the moon and the stars. No, we don't call upon it for effects, but rather for atmosphere.'[98]

This luminous, atmospheric theatre was a unique proposition, and visitors to Hellerau were eager to inspect it at close quarters. One of the sightseers was the Irish playwright and critic George Bernard Shaw, who recalled 'the great expanses of white fabric that cover the walls and ceiling, and the multitude of lights behind and above them. All that would additionally be needed in order to stage every conceivable performance under heaven would be a transparent floor, illuminated from below.'[99] And in a similar vein, the Austrian novelist Franz Werfel wrote: 'We now possess in Hellerau a Festsaal that envelops the entire tremendous life of the theatre, stage and auditorium alike, in that same great element – light. Everything nestles inside the Festsaal with its ever-present, transforming, invisible light, in the same way that all the events of the earth take place under the arch of the sky.'[100]

The vast ranks of globes that fashioned what Appia himself described as the 'omnipotent light'[101] of the theatre were cabled back to a master control console with forty-six circuits, where their intensity and distribution could be played by a single operator at the 'luminous organ'. At the same time, more powerful directional lights used to underscore movement were similarly housed in the cavity behind the silky white canvas screens lining the entire theatre, while internal baffles shielded spectators from glare. This concerted play between two classes of illumination – one luminous and ambient, the other sharp and focused – perfectly aligned with Appia's *verteiltes Licht* and *gestaltendes Licht*, finally giving life to the theory he had articulated a decade earlier. Devoid of illusionistic affectation and stripped of proscenium, curtain, footlights, raised stage, flies, traps or wings, the Festsaal was therefore the first embodiment of Appia's ideal theatre – 'only an empty room waiting'.[102]

And it was in this apparently empty space that everything suddenly seemed possible. 'I never enter it without the frisson of happiness ... and apprehension', wrote Jaques-Dalcroze in a letter to Appia. 'I ask myself whether we will know how to profit, if you like, from this suggestive space. Will we be able to breathe life into the virgin space, animate its lines and awaken its echoes?'[103]

What was at stake here was more than an educational enterprise; it was a matter for the spirit. As Dohrn wrote: 'Rhythm alone gives form to life. So, for us, rhythm has become an almost metaphysical concept – it spiritualises the bodily and embodies the spiritual.'[104] And Jaques-Dalcroze himself wrote that 'the artist must spiritualise himself before desiring or being able to spiritualise matter'.[105] In time, the Bildungsanstalt did in fact become a beacon for a brand new bodily-spiritual culture, imbuing the garden city with a semi-sacred atmosphere; as Scheffler wrote, visiting Hellerau was 'like stumbling upon a secular monastic order of the youth'.[106] And the visual cues were both myriad and ill-quoted. According to Peter de Mendelssohn, for example, 'The painter Alexander von Salzmann designed the Hellerau emblem emblazoned on Tessenow's pediment, viewable from afar: a circular disc in which two flowing, tapering black and white semicircles were composed. Salzmann declared that it was an ancient Indian symbol. My father, who knew more about symbolic ornamentation than anybody else, assured me that it was a sun-wheel and that Salzmann had drawn it the wrong way round; the wheel was spinning backwards. And it was. Nevertheless, it was not changed.'[107] Those 'flowing, tapering black and white semicircles' were not in fact a sun-wheel, or from ancient India, but a yin-yang symbol.

The collaborators' first attempt to awaken the echoes of the virgin space of the semi-sacred theatre was the staging of the second act of Christoph Gluck's *Orfeo ed Euridice* at the first Hellerau *Schulfest* (school festival), planned for the following summer. Two of the bright-eyed eurhythmics students who would perform in the Schulfest were the Norwegian sisters Inga and Ragna Jacobi, who sent their parents a large number of letters and postcards between May 1911 and July 1912. Their cache of correspondence provides illuminating insights into the daily routine at Hellerau,[108] which centred on the lessons that Jaques-Dalcroze and his assistants delivered daily in the remarkable glowing Festsaal that, according to Ragna, was illuminated by a 'mystical lighting apparatus'.[109]

Cher ami, pardonnez-moi mon silence. Cette année je réorganise tout, et je pense que vous serez content de cela. Je vous écrirai prochainement. Bonne santé.
Votre fidèle
Jaques-Dalcroze

Postcard from Émile Jaques-Dalcroze to Appia, 1 November 1912.

Musical Ear Training, Improvisation, Breathing, Anatomy, Gymnastics and Dance were the main subjects taught in the Bildungsanstalt – four to six hours per day, Monday to Saturday.[110] Each lesson was 'varied to a remarkable degree. Every day he [Jaques-Dalcroze] has new ideas, consisting of new movements, or of new uses for old ones, so that there is never a dull moment. It must be understood, however, that the alphabet and grammar of the movements remain the same, it is the combinations of them that are limitless. The music is, of course, always improvised.'[111] At times, the way that the students communicated with each other was also a matter of improvisation, as Inga Jacobi wrote in one of her letters: 'On any given day I speak English, French, Norwegian and German, and every now and then all of them at once – a most curious blend, I can tell you ...'[112]

The classes that Jaques-Dalcroze delivered in French, and that the students followed as best they could, were evidently very well received. Ragna told her parents: 'The lessons with Jaques are held in an atmosphere of joy

Émile Jaques-Dalcroze Eurhythmics, 1913.

and humour, and that gives everything great impetus.'[113] In addition to his teaching at the Bildungsanstalt, Jaques-Dalcroze delivered public lectures in Hellerau and throughout Saxony, often holding forth on what he believed to be the far-reaching educational benefits of eurhythmics, which went well beyond musical training. During one of these, given in Leipzig, he said: 'The effect of rhythmic training on the timetable and life of a school is like that of a hot water heating system which spreads an equal warmth through all parts of a building. Teachers of other subjects will find that such training provides them with pupils more responsive, more elastic and of more character than they would be otherwise.'[114] And in another lecture, this time in Dresden, he said matter-of-factly: 'I expect much from education in rhythm in elementary schools, provided it be given regularly, completely and sufficiently. The exercises should be begun at the age of six, with half an hour's lesson three times a week, but these lessons can quite well be taken from playtime.'[115]

Jaques-Dalcroze further sought to promote eurhythmics by illustrating its purpose and verve with photographs commissioned from Boissonnas, who by this time had firmly established himself as Jaques-Dalcroze's photographer of choice. The Swiss photographer's assignment was to come up with an image that would serve as an emblem for the whole Hellerau-eurhythmic endeavour – and it required a source of light strong and direct; one that would burn bright and fast on his photographic plates, capturing in freeze-frame agile youths in dynamic motion, their bodies emanating an entrancing mix of gaiety and tightly framed common purpose. In the frontispiece image to the inaugural volume of the institute's yearbook, *Der Rhythmus* – printed in summer 1911, and as much a manifesto as a chronicle – four lithe young women (including Suzanne Perrottet, Appia's eurhythmics teacher), spring aloft in unison over a brightly lit summer meadow.[116] They are wearing flowing tunics, and with their hands all clasped together and faces thrust skyward, they embody Jaques-Dalcroze's split dream of ecstatic abandonment and collective order.

The inaugural yearbook is rounded out with mostly dry facts and tallies, including the 'Annual Report of the Bildungsanstalt Jaques-Dalcroze for the Teaching Year 1910/11', after which comes a numbered inventory of all the eager eurhythmics students who were enrolled in that first teaching year, and where they had come from, which was far and wide.[117] Some arrived from the neighbouring countries of Switzerland and Austria to the south, Poland and Bohemia to the east, the Netherlands to the west. Some came from the north, from Finland, Sweden and Norway. And then others travelled to Hellerau from countries further afield, including Russia, Spain and England, and even the United States. But of course, many students came to Hellerau from other parts of Germany, some from as far away as Munich, but others from locations much closer to the garden city, including the young daughter of the architect of the Bildungsanstalt: '488. Lotte Tessenow, Hellerau'. Another notable entry is '9. Ada Bruhn, Berlin', a dancer who had just recently begun courting the Aachen-raised, Berlin-based son of a stonemason, Maria Ludwig Michael Mies. Bruhn was sharing a small townhouse with another young dancer – Mary Wigman – who later in life, and by then a celebrated cultural figure in her own right, recalled that Mies 'regularly came to Hellerau to visit Bruhn'.[118]

below and following spread
Émile Jaques-Dalcroze Eurhythmics, 1913.

Appia's former eurhythmics teacher Perrottet described Bruhn as a 'tall, powerful, quiet, lovely woman', a description that accords with the one offered by Mies's biographer Franz Schulze: 'Bruhn cut a stately figure and was, from all accounts, very good-looking, tall with long, straight brown hair, solemn eyes, and a junoesque carriage.'[119] The dancer and the architect continued their liaison, despite the initial disapproval of Bruhn's authoritarian tax inspector father; Friedrich Wilhelm Gustav was cool on Mies,[120] unimpressed by his name that in German means wretched, miserable, out of sorts. He accepted the relationship, however, acknowledging that Mies 'looked like a man with a future'.[121]

That is certainly the way Mies looks in a photograph taken of him the year before the wedding. Dressed in a finely fitted dark suit and tie, the architect stands with his arms firmly folded, holding a cigar in his right hand. His bearing is both brooding and confident. The half-open doorway in which he is standing belongs to his first independent architectural commission, a house built on a steeply sloping site just outside Potsdam – 'Schinkel-Behrens country'[122] – for the philosopher Alois Riehl, in 1907.[123]

What motivated the philosopher of 'critical realism' to call on the untried twenty-year-old 'architect' to design his house is not clear, since at that time

Émile Jaques-Dalcroze Eurhythmics, 1913.

Mies had little to offer beside his personality; architecturally speaking, he was a *tabula rasa*.[124] In any case, the decision turned out to be an inspired one, since the building Mies delivered is remarkably accomplished. 'The architecture is so utterly impeccable that it would never, ever occur to one that it might be the very first independent building by a young architect', announced the admiring author of the first assessment of the house to appear in print, in an article concerned with the 'new artistic generation'.[125]

Its transformation from a bourgeois villa on the entrance façade into a temple atop a monumental podium on the adjacent one is the building's most exceptional feature. Mies achieved the feat by employing a great retaining wall that severs the house and its tended garden, which takes up the upper third of the site, from the remaining two thirds down below. It was the first of many times in his career that Mies used a podium to elevate a building above its ground (this rather than, say, arranging a series of terraces to connect the house to nature). The definitive line of the high wall serves to compose a panorama juxtaposing the foreground setting with the distant view out towards the horizon; a view of the landscape and sky carefully framed by the four pared-back 'temple' columns that rise flush with the outer edge of the retaining wall, and also by the parapet created by the wall on the *Wohngarten* (living garden) side, which steps up ever so slightly as it reaches the veranda, 'maintaining the erasure of the middle distance that transforms the landscape into a pictorial experience'.[126]

The Riehls baptised their home *Klösterli*, or 'little cloister' – both, perhaps, for its walled garden and for its conduciveness to intellectual retreat – and it became the centre of a vibrant intellectual and artistic life that Mies was welcomed into, as attested by the frequent appearance of his name in the guest book. It was, in fact, on one of these visits that Mies had first met Ada, and the young architect seemed to acknowledge the professional and personal importance of the house to him when he signed the guest book on 15 October 1911, not as 'Ludwig Mies' but rather as 'Ludwig Klösterli'.[127]

It was in that same month of October 1911 that the Bildungsanstalt in Hellerau was completed, and now it was indoors – in the glowing space of the Festsaal – that the students would show what they had learned. Ragna wrote to her father: 'Imagine it – the *grosser Saal* (large hall)! We were inside it!! Daddy, you know the small halls, they were already big, weren't they. But they almost vanish alongside the large one; we only needed one third of it, and almost all the students could be accommodated in a square formation. There were some seventy of us (some others were unwell and did not come along). And now Jaques has tried out all sorts of things with us – yes – you will see at the festival.'[128] And in another letter she wrote: 'Oh, now we are already working towards the festival. It is the second act of Orpheus that we are going to sing and perform. Oh, it is going to be marvellous.'[129]

At the same time as Ragna and her classmates were readying themselves for the festival, they were also working towards their diploma examinations, overseen by Jaques-Dalcroze and a watchful committee that included Herr Appia. Shaw attended the evaluations of a couple of students, as he later recalled in a letter to a friend: 'The two examinees, wearing a bathing suit that had not an inch of sleeves or leggings, stood before their examiners – a line of elderly gentlemen. Each of them in turn took a class of similarly robed victims and played rhythms on the piano that the students then marched along to.'[130]

These examinations and the rehearsals that led up to them evidently demanded a great deal of energy from the students: 'At the end of a day such as this one you are dead tired', wrote Ragna. 'Eurhythmics for 1 hour, or rather 3/4 of an hour, but in the 1/4 hour break I keep going since it is so much fun; then *Soflège*, then another break in which I practise piano. After that, I had a nap at the table at lunchtime, then read a few pages of Heinrich Heine (since you are not supposed to play during this time), but from 3–4 you are, during which time we have tea, and I also practiced the violin. Then we had dance from 4–6 o'clock.'[131]

Afterwards, Ragna and her bone-tired classmates retired to their lodgings in the two-storey Großes Pensionshaus (large dormitory) that stands to the South of the Festspielhaus.[132] The Pensionshaus was a place of accommodation, but also one of socialisation. There are large gathering areas, especially on the first floor, which is where the students' dormitory rooms were located, surrounding the central dining room, which also had access to the garden and terrace. According to the 1911 annual report, the food that was served up in the dining room was, 'good and wholesome (many vegetables)'.[133] What the young women thought of their wholesome diet is unrecorded, but one visitor to Hellerau who (briefly) lodged in the Pensionshaus later recalled his experience there: 'I was first of all put up in the Pensionshaus for girls that Paul Claudel called the "*Gazellengehege*" (gazelle enclosure). But my youthful appetite was too powerful to be satisfied with a diet consisting of nuts, raw tomatoes, and tea. So, I took a room with a baker, where the fare was heartier.'[134]

Maria Ludwig Michael Mies, Haus Riehl, Potsdam, 1907.

It was most likely one of Ragna's fellow students who snapped a photograph of Jaques-Dalcroze and Appia in the spring of 1912, since it was taken from the terrace of the Großes Pensionshaus, which the dining room serving wholesome fare opens onto. Jaques-Dalcroze, more central to the composition, wears a well-fitted dark suit and tie, a smart fedora that partially shades his face and a flamboyant handlebar moustache. The more enigmatic Appia is

Prometheus Bound, Act 1, 70.2×100.1 cm, 1910

Prometheus Bound, Act 2, 66.8×100.4 cm, 1910

following spread *Prometheus Bound*, Act 3, 72.9×102.8 cm, 1910

1910

Der Rhythmus: Yearbook of the Bildungsanstalt Jaques-Dalcroze, vol 1, 1911.

dressed in black, with a dark limp-brimmed hat obscuring his full beard and he is clutching a swollen folio of drawings. The countenances of the two comrades accord with the description of them provided by Appia's biographer Walter Volbach, for whom a pair less similar than Appia and Jaques-Dalcroze could hardly be imagined: 'Appia, fairly tall, had bright shining eyes, a sharp Roman profile, and a beard that made him look like a prophet ... Gentle and reticent, he was particularly shy in the presence of strangers. Dalcroze, by contrast, was below average height. His friendly round face had a goatee; his small near-sighted eyes twinkled behind glasses. He was jovial, outgoing.'[135]

On this occasion, the pair both look well-content, having perhaps just concluded rehearsals for their staging of Gluck's opera *Orfeo ed Euridice* that they had been working on with their students since the start of the year, and that would be the focal performance of the first Hellerau *Schulfest* held that summer.

The setting that Appia – the prophet – developed for Orpheus' famous descent into the underworld was described by the Swiss conductor Ernest Ansermet as being 'stripped of anecdote'.[136] It comprised a flight of stairs spanning from upstage right across the full width of the theatre to upstage left, a narrow centre-stage landing and a final dramatic run of full-width stairs down to the polished black floor. It also offered an uncanny reflection of the theatre's tiered seating, implicating the audience in the performance. Appia had repeatedly outlined his ambition to diminish what he saw as the abyss between stage and seating, arguing that traditional theatres dulled their audiences, who only ever sat in semi-darkness in a state of total passivity. In 'Über Ursprung und Anfang der Rhythmischen Gymnastik', written at the Château de Glérolles in 1911, Appia boldly announced that 'Eurhythmics will overthrow this passivity. Musical rhythm will enter all of us, to say "you yourself are the work of art"!'[137] At the Festsaal, both the audience and performers entered the hall through twinned tripartite doors located in the middle of the long edges of the theatre, having mingled in the adjacent common areas.

Stepping out onto the polished black floor, the audience then took their places in the 600 dark chairs banked in rows at the rear of the space, while the performers assumed their positions opposite. The few existing photographs of the Festsaal in use show choreographed figures in motion against the brilliant, silky whiteness of the walls and ceiling. As one witness, Wolkonsky, attested, 'when the light goes on, one seems to drown in a bath of light'.[138] Appia, who placed exceptional importance on light as the carrier of moods and atmosphere, particularly when carefully calibrated with music, declared: 'The human bodies, bathed in this vital atmosphere will recognise it and salute *Music in Space*. For Apollo was not only the god of music; he was also the god of light!'[139]

Eurhythmics students gathered outside the Pensionshaus Hellerau in 1911; Appia and Émile Jaques-Dalcroze photographed in front of the Bildungsanstalt Jaques-Dalcroze from the terrace of the Pensionshaus in 1912.

Characteristically, Appia contrived to absent himself from the throng of bodies at the opening night of the 1912 festival. During the final dress rehearsal, he and Jaques-Dalcroze had disagreed on the costumes that would be worn during Orpheus' descent into the underworld. Appia favoured a light-coloured toga for Orpheus and white tunics for the chorus of Furies, since regular black tights would absorb light and would fail to reveal bodily contours. But Jaques-Dalcroze was adamant that Orpheus' toga should be dark grey, and that the chorus should wear black tights, as was the custom. Appia refused to acquiesce and retreated to his lodgings in the Château de Glérolles.[140] As a result, the accolades the production received were instead passed onto his collaborators – chiefly Jaques-Dalcroze – and this despite Jaques-Dalcroze having written to Appia in June 1911 that he looked forward to working with him through the winter to 'make the buds of our joint venture blossom in the sun. Be assured, my friend, that you are intimately associated with this work ... and that the festival in Hellerau shall be signed with your name beside that of your faithful and affectionate E J Dalcroze'[141]

The second annual festival was a decidedly more ambitious undertaking than the first, as noted by Appia's former teacher, Perrottet: 'The *Schulfest* ran for three days. Every evening, the performance began with rhythmic gymnastics demonstrations, ranging from very simple movements to the most complex of forms, carried out to the improvised notes and rhythms that Jaques-Dalcroze played on the piano. And then came the programme proper, performed on the stage-setting that Appia had designed, and for which Salzmann had prepared the lighting. Now that was a tremendous thing – the atmosphere – all these big names who came to Hellerau. And all the students and the teaching assistants felt as though they were actors in the service of a singular great idea – yes, I felt that they were rather more like priests than artists.'[142]

Orfeo ed Euridice, Act 1, Funeral Scene, 48.1×63.1 cm, 1926

Orfeo ed Euridice, Act 2, Scene 2: The Elysian Fields, 71.3×101.0 cm, 1910

following spread *Orfeo ed Euridice*, Act 2: Descent into the Underworld, 48.2×63.0 cm, 1926

Orfeo ed Euridice was again the pivotal performance, but this time all three acts were staged. There are no photographs of the first act – 'Orpheus Before the Tomb of Eurydice' – nor of the scene that closes the second act – 'The Elysian Fields' – but there are some images of the broad cascading steps that in the opening scene manifest 'The Descent into Hades'. Many years later, Appia made a drawing for this first act, presumably reprising the one he would have made in preparation for the Hellerau performance. He also made a new drawing for Orpheus' descent into Hades, the event on which the second act turns, and described his proposition for the setting of that scene: 'Orpheus crosses over into the Underworld to retrieve Eurydice. The scene of the Underworld is composed of ranks of stairs interrupted by terraces, all supported by columns embedded in the supporting walls. It is therefore the *escaliers* that characterise the Underworld.'[143]

There is one drawing still in existence that Appia made in preparation for the *Orfeo ed Euridice* performance at Hellerau, rather than in memory of it. This drawing is for the scene that closes the second act – 'The Elysian Fields' – an otherworldly place in which, as Homer tells us, 'Life glides in immortal ease for mortal man; no snow, no winter onslaught, never a downpour there. Night and day, the Ocean River sends up a breeze, singing winds of the West, refreshing all mankind.'[144] For Appia, this setting must only be made up of inclined planes, 'without the slightest vertical line interrupting them', since that is the only way to express the 'perfect serenity of the place'.[145] The arrangement of these inclined planes is particularly difficult, writes Appia, but then asserts, 'fortunately, the score gives valuable clues – in such a place, the gait is naturally calm and quiet and the soft light – with its uniformity and its gentle mobility – transforms the material reality of the actual construction into a kind of rocking

preceding spread
Eurhythmics performance in the Festsaal; children performing eurhythmics exercises in the Festsaal; audience seating in the Festsaal; eurhythmics performance in the Festsaal of the Bildungsanstalt Jaques-Dalcroze in 1912.

movement that is wavelike in its effect. Thanks to the lighting, the performers partake in this irreal atmosphere.'[146]

This is how Wolkonsky remembered that irreal atmosphere, as he experienced it in 1913: 'As Orpheus's song gradually transforms the angry roar of all Hell into benevolent compassion, one perceives perfectly that he sings not for us, the audience, but for those on stage – they hear him and react instead of, and differently from us: we hear only the music – whilst they, however, live in it.'[147] At that moment, wrote Wolkonsky, 'I can assure you that you forget you are listening to music, and have been watching a performance. You have observed a portion of life which has become a holy act; the mystery of life and death, of hate and love, of asking and forgiveness.'[148] Wolkonsky attributed the profound effect that the performance had upon him to the 'harmony between movement and music – the seen and the heard became an aural and visual unity which involved one's entire perception'.[149]

Emmi Leisner was Orpheus' Eurydice, and her performance at Hellerau is generally considered to mark the beginning of the German opera singer's career (she went on to perform at Bayreuth, most notably in the role of Erda [the earth goddess] in *Der Ring des Nibelungen*). In his glowing appraisal of what to his mind was one of the best ever productions of *Orfeo ed Euridice*, Shaw wrote that Leisner 'sang very well (although she was too slow in some parts of "*che faro*")'. And that the staging was most remarkable: 'Just a few more rehearsals under my direction and it would have been perfect.'[150] Jaques-Dalcroze and Appia had decided to change the traditional happy ending of the opera: in the final scene, when Orpheus and Eurydice appeared upstage, ascending a few steps to face and approach the audience, a curtain closed behind them. Orpheus continued downstage a few steps further, and at the moment at which – unable to resist her pleas further – Orpheus turned at last to look upon Eurydice, the scene darkened, and she vanished into the folds of the curtain. The light returned to reveal Orpheus standing alone on the empty stage.

A total of 5,000 other visitors also watched the performances over two weeks, many of them famed European inspired types: choreographers and dancers, composers and musicians, dramatists and actors, painters, poets and architects. They included the Austro-Hungarian dance theorist Rudolf von Laban, the Russian prima ballerina Anna Pavlova, the Bohemian-Austrian poet Rainer Maria Rilke, the Austrian scenographer Alfred Roller and two of his countrymen, the librettist Hugo von Hofmannsthal and the writer Stefan Zweig, plus the architect Hans Poelzig and the architecture critic Karl Scheffler, both from Germany.

One enthusiastic visitor on his way to Tessenow's Bildungsanstalt, with its 'incomparably clean lines', wrote that the flags of every land under the sun 'fluttered up high on tall masts'.[151] And another recalled that 'festivals were held every summer in the great *Lichtsaal* (light hall) inside the Festspielhaus that resembles a theatre-temple from antiquity. The settings were composed of a diffused light – rather than scenery – and the audience that attended them was a cosmopolitan one. Kilometre after kilometre, the streets were adorned with countless flags of all nationalities, waving high up on their masts – people from all over the world came to see the Hellerau "Olympiad of the Arts".'[152]

The visiting Olympian multitude required lodgings, which the sole guesthouse in Hellerau provided. The Waldschänke might be thought of as the carnal, earthly counterpart to the otherworldly theatre, and it attracted guests like moths to the flame, in part because it was the very first building that the visitors came across: 'On approach, Hellerau is dominated by the Waldschänke with its Dutch gabled-roofed form, multiple hips and bold chimneys, rising above the low service wings and the open colonnade that make up the building ensemble.'[153]

Rehearsal of *Orfeo ed Euridice* in the Festsaal of the Bildungsanstalt Jaques-Dalcroze, 1912.

Franz Kafka was one of these guests at the Waldschänke, and he recorded his Kafkaesque stay there in his diary: 'Hellerau. ... Waldschänke, a reading of "Narcissus" in the garden of Paul Adler, visit to the Dalcroze House, evening in the Waldschänke ... Failed ... wrong tram to Hellerau, no room in the Waldschänke; forgot that I wanted E to phone me there, so, back again; ... Dalcroze in Geneva; arrived too late at the Waldschänke the next morning.'[154]

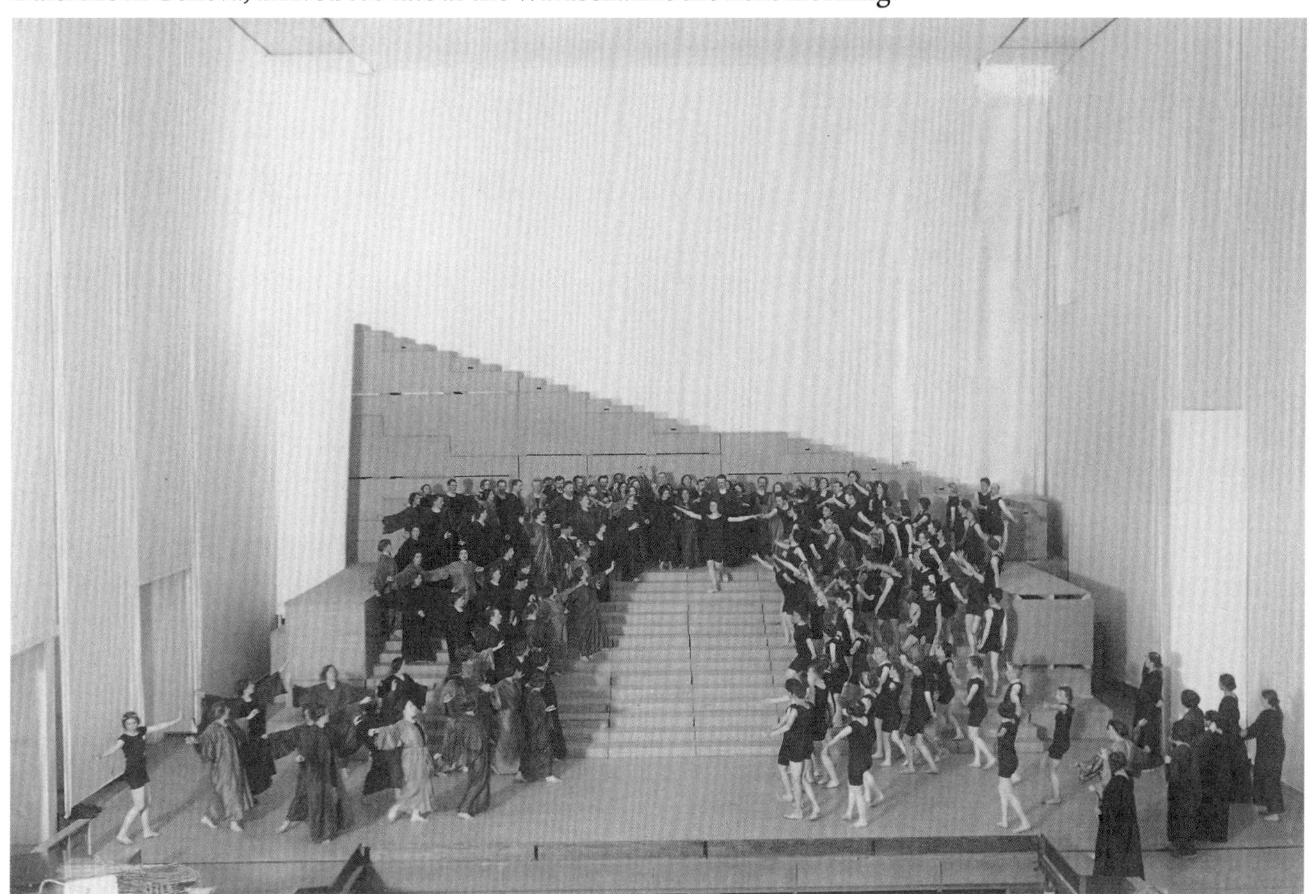

The journeyman Swiss architect Charles-Édouard Jeanneret – the future Le Corbusier – also made a record of the evening meal that he took with his brother Albert Jeanneret at the Waldschänke in the lead-up to Christmas in 1910, which he published as the dedication to his *Journey to the East*: 'To My Brother, the Musician Albert Jeanneret', he wrote, 'Your face made the journey from the beginning to the end – through the Danube, Stamboul, Athens, but was mislaid, unknown to me, amongst old papers. It had your features, but not exactly. I sketched it, unbeknown to you, at the Waldschänke in Hellerau during the Christmas of 1910: you were devouring slices of blood sausage on buttered bread (one of those menus forced on us by our pocketbooks in that country!). The voracious way you were eating that sausage and butter disgusted me. At certain times – and precisely at that moment – you struck me as incredibly gluttonous.'[155] In a letter that he mailed to his

following spread
Appia's setting for *Orfeo ed Euridice* in the Festsaal of the Bildungsanstalt Jaques-Dalcroze, 1912.

Richard Riemerschmid, Waldschänke, Hellerau, 1911.

parents at the end of that same visit to Hellerau – sent on New Year's Day 1911 – Le Corbusier wrote 'Prosit Neujahr Amen!' (Cheers, Happy New Year, Amen!), and retold the events of the long night before, which he spent drinking with his older brother Albert and with Appia. He mocks his brother for 'pulling in his paws before midnight' only to be found at four in the morning reading Goethe in German. But never mind, *camarade Appia* was up to the challenge, and 'like pure Parisians, the two of us waited until the first trams passed before finally heading off to bed'.[156]

Le Corbusier was in Hellerau to visit his brother, 'the Musician Albert Jeanneret', who like Appia had studied at the Conservatoire in Geneva but had performed better than the scenographer, graduating as a violinist with the Premier Prix de Virtuosité in 1909. Albert then followed Jaques-Dalcroze

to Hellerau and completed a course of studies in eurhythmics that culminated in a final examination (Appia was on the jury) qualifying him to become a 'Teacher of Eurhythmics Following the Method of Jaques-Dalcroze'.

As brothers do, they kidded around, as captured for example in a sequence of photographs that the two of them took of the other in turn. Their three companions (two women and one man) stay put, seated in a springtime meadow, plucking and then smelling the flowers now in bloom, while the two brothers are each time standing, having just released the camera's shutter before returning to its frame.[157]

But Le Corbusier too had educational reasons for travelling to Hellerau. On his initial visit to the garden city, two months before his end-of-year escapades, the architect met with Dohrn, Schmidt and Jaques-Dalcroze, and was greatly enthused by what he encountered. In Hellerau, he wrote, 'the greatest artists of Germany' were enjoying 'the most favourable circumstances so that genius might be manifest, so that artists can produce almost total works of art'.[158] In another brief, unpublished text, 'La sale, cathédrale de l'avenir?', Le Corbusier wrote: 'Hellerau opened a reign of kindness with Jaques-Dalcroze, and an era of utility with Tessenow. A million people have gathered for these two men of rhythmic music ... in this great and irreproachable room (the Festsaal) ... in which city? Hellerau.'[159]

Now that he was a member of staff of the Bildungsanstalt, Albert became friendly with his former examiners, including Appia, with whom he exchanged letters and postcards. On one of them he wrote: 'Dear Mr Appia, we always think of you with affection. Yours, Albert Jeanneret.'[160] His younger brother was less of a friend, writing to his parents that he came across Appia once again, this time in Hellerau, and describing the scenographer as 'an energetic *garçon* whom I had known as a dreamer and poet in Paris'.[161] Le Corbusier doesn't add anything further. And the letter that he wrote to them after his second meeting with Appia was even more cursory and cutting than the first: 'Appia, the founder of grand unpatented systems and inventions, barbed all those who would grant him ten minutes of their time with Parisian jargon'[162] – a verdict that could easily have been applied to Le Corbusier himself. The grounds for this slight are uncertain; it might have been a matter of personal disinclination, or simply a lack of awareness of the extent of Appia's decisive contribution. But tellingly, it did mark a moment when the same themes Appia had been exploring in his *Espaces rythmiques* started to occupy Le Corbusier.

Albert Jeanneret and friends at Hellerau in 1911; Charles-Édouard Jeanneret (Le Corbusier) and friends at Hellerau in 1911.

Rather like his 'gluttonous' brother, Le Corbusier was hungry, though for knowledge and inspiration. It was directly after his fourth and final visit to Albert in Hellerau at the end of May 1911 that he departed for his famed voyage to the Orient, where he incessantly sketched, wrote and mulled over the remains of classical antiquity. The fledgling architect eagerly absorbed it all, just as Boissonnas had done before him. And, as with the photographer, when it really came down to it, the journey was all about arriving at the Parthenon. Later in life, Le Corbusier recalled: 'To see the Acropolis is a dream one treasures without even dreaming to realise it ... A long time ago I accepted the fact that this place was like a repository of a sacred standard, the basis of all measurement in art.'[163] Though he took pride in making his own judgements about what he discovered *in situ*, Le Corbusier was also more or less influenced by what he had read beforehand, which probably included *Prière sur l'Acropole* (Prayer on the Acropolis) by Ernest Renan.[164] He had asked William Ritter where he could find a copy of the French philosopher's text: 'I will travel through historic lands, but because I am ignorant of everything, their stones will not reveal their secrets, their stories, their evocations! Couldn't I begin my initiation with some useful readings? ... Books! Books! Where can I find Prayer on the Acropolis, in which volume of Ernest Renan?'[165]

One sketch that Le Corbusier made, amid the vast strewn piles of stones at Delphi rather than on the Acropolis in Athens, reveals a premonition of an architecture both archaic and modern, exposing an allegiance not just to Appia, but also to Sigfried Giedeon who in *The Eternal Present* avowed the abstract nature of all art, which proceeds via 'simplification and concentration of natural form'.[166] The drawing itself takes in three blocks of stone, possibly building foundations, that face across the valley towards the mountains. Significantly, this view looks away from the more emblematic ruins of Delphi – the temple, altar and theatre – offering instead a kind of original architecture made up of just a couple of square-hewn stones responding to the phenomenon of 'place' in a savage landscape. Years later, Le Corbusier recalled the scene: 'Dominating the gulfs and the valleys of Delphi, these three dice of stone bear violent and pure testimony. They speak of the sublime.'[167]

Jaques-Dalcroze and Appia too travelled away from Hellerau, though it was later and was only supposed to be temporarily, in order to prepare the Fête de Juin in their home city of Geneva. Jaques-Dalcroze's fame was soaring on the back of his achievements at Hellerau – circulated via the photographs of Boissonnas and the writings of others – and in 1914, the powers-that-be in Geneva approached him with an irresistible offer to choreograph an extravagant public spectacle. The Fête de Juin, which was ten years in the planning, and was actually scheduled for July because the weather was supposed to be more predictably kind, was to be a grand week-long celebration of the canton of Geneva's century-long membership of the Swiss Confederation.

The event was embraced with patriotic fervour and the organising committee decided to devote most of their 200,000-franc budget to the staging of a glorious festival celebrating the previous century of Geneva's history. Boissonnas's one-time travelling companion, and now director of the École Supérieure des Beaux-Arts de Genève, Daniel Baud-Bovy, was entrusted with the weighty responsibility of composing a century's worth of historical episodes into a four-act, three-hour performance, interspersed with eurhythmic *intermezzi* arranged and choreographed by Jaques-Dalcroze. The setting was to be prepared by Appia, who had some radical ideas that he expressed in jovial terms to his old friend Houston Stuart Chamberlain: 'It will be Hellerau-Appia mixed with the necessary *Genevoisisme*! No painted decorations! No curtain! The audience will look towards the huge stage, with its 50-metre opening. At the end of the performance, the back will open up onto the lake and the *barques des confédérés* will sail up right into the scene; the stage is entirely on pilotis!'[168]

There was no theatre in Geneva that was appropriately situated, nor capacious enough, to accommodate the vast numbers of spectators expected to attend the festival, so one was custom-built. Framed up with enormous broad-spanning timber trusses and carried on pilotis that took it half out over the edge of the lake, the 1,200-square-metre theatre resembled nothing so much as a gigantic aircraft hangar. Rows and rows of raked seating were installed – facing lake-ward down towards the broad stage fronted by a deep orchestra pit. Everything – even the enormous 'classical' columns that framed the stage – was crafted from timber, more than warranting the posting of *défense absolue de fumer* (smoking strictly prohibited) signs throughout the theatre, which after hosting 1,200 performers for months of rehearsals was finally opened up to a 6,000-strong premiere audience on Saturday, 4 July.

Charles-Édouard Jeanneret (Le Corbusier), sketch at Delphi, 1911.

Ironically, they came in rain-soaked, but when the festival got underway at 9am, the mood of the audience soon brightened. The spectacle certainly was just that; troupe after troupe of performers in extravagant period costume strode on and off the giant stage in front of a backdrop on which the

view of the very lake behind had been painted in painstaking detail. At the conclusion of the performance, around lunchtime, all the performers thronged in from the wings and back onto the stage for the final *coup de grâce*. As choreographed by Appia, the backdrop was slowly furled up to reveal the expansive watery horizon of the real lake itself, and a large boat with Latin sails – a *barque lémanique* – gradually drifted into view. With its Swiss flag fluttering proudly in the breeze, the *Confédérés* sidled up to the theatre and docked ceremoniously at the rear of the timber stage. A hefty number of the performers piled onto the boat, and it sailed off and away into the watery distance.

Boissonnas captured all the performances at the Fête de Juin on 6 July 1914.[169] He also stayed on in the afternoon to take photographs of the crowd who lingered afterwards, and who were mostly as elaborately outfitted as the performers they had just seen on the stage. In one of these photographs, a group of six people – two men, three women and a young girl – stand on the lakeshore promenade with their hands clasped together. The girl wears a simple cotton blouse and is shoeless, and the women are wearing modest full-length dresses and dark shawls. But the two men are extravagantly dressed. One of them in particular demands attention, resplendent in pantaloons, grey stockings, knickerbockers, a crisp white shirt with pleated neckcloth, and an ornate tailcoat buttoned up over a smart vest. His gaze is averted from the camera, and his full-bearded face is further obscured by his dark broad-brimmed felt hat. It is Appia.

After a rehearsal for one of the Hellerau performances, Appia had been photographed together with Jaques-Dalcroze, wearing the very same felt hat that he has on in Boissonnas's photograph. And his dark monochrome clothing accords with the description of his general manner of attire, which was described by one of his friends as 'always black or light grey, not at all conventional. However he dressed, he had "style" – one unique to him.'[170]

Henry Maillard, sectional perspective drawing for the Fête de Juin Théâtre in Geneva, 1914.

The day's festivities were yet far from over – the hangar-like theatre where Boissonnas photographed Appia was only one station on the celebratory voyage of the *Confédérés*, which had, in fact, begun in the morning in Nyon, some twenty-five kilometres away. Accompanied by a flotilla of smaller craft, it had set sail with actors playing their parts in the political events that had led to Geneva joining the Swiss Confederation. A century before, representatives of the cantons of Solothurn and Fribourg had sailed south and across the lake and were eventually welcomed with great fanfare at the Port Noir at Cologny, a small municipality just to the north of Geneva. This time, they docked at 5pm to salvoes of artillery and the sounds of ringing bells. 8,000 enthusiastic Genevans dressed up in period costume were there to greet them, ready to set off in a convoy headed for the city centre, along four kilometres of promenades and streets lined by 100,000 cheering spectators. Some of the marchers came in fancy dress as Switzerland's original tribal Helvetti, swathed in bear skins and wearing horned helmets over long braided hair, while others came as their tormentors – the Romans – kitted out in shiny armour and shields, presided over by a gold-wreathed Caesar.

They all arrived at Geneva's famous Treille promenade at around 7:15pm, in time for the official ceremony, which included speeches by Henri Fazy, president of Switzerland's Conseil National, and by foreign dignitaries including the Greek statesman Ioannis Kapodistrias, who pronounced Geneva 'the musk that perfumes Europe'. Afterwards, some of the crowd decamped to the Salle Communale de Plainpalais for a 500-seat banquet in the appropriately named Salle de Spectacles, and ate, drank and danced the night away.

While Genevans were making merry at the Fête de Juin, political events were cascading elsewhere in Europe, centring upon Germany, which is where Jaques-Dalcroze returned to after the festival – though only briefly, to collect his belongings and his family. Mendelssohn recalled that the events that preceded the First World War scattered the entire enthusiastic community of Hellerau to the four winds. 'Jaques-Dalcroze himself departed at dawn, leaving a ruined work in his wake; crying, Gaby said goodbye to me. "We must go", he says. "Why then?" I asked. "*Sais pas, isch wieß nisch* (I don't know), *la guerre* (the war) – we must".'[171]

And so, in 1914 the great experiment that was Hellerau unravelled, precipitated in part by continental events that destroyed much else besides, but also by one event of direct consequence for the garden city – the tragic death of its co-founder, Dohrn, in a skiing accident in Switzerland. His memorial service was held in the Festsaal of the Bildungsanstalt that he himself had spoken about in such lofty, optimistic terms when the foundation stone was laid three years before. 'In an hour the service for Wolf Dohrn will take place in the Bildungsanstalt. Hopefully it will be suitably simple and dignified. This afternoon, all the shops in Hellerau are completely closed for a couple of hours ...'[172] wrote one eurhythmics teacher in a letter to a friend in advance of the ceremony. And afterwards she wrote: 'The introduction to the service was Beethoven's funeral march and then came a string quartet, followed by a male choir. Then Karl Schmidt, the *Werkmeister*, gave a speech so fine, so warm, so clear, so straight from the heart – now, that was fabulous.'[173]

The politician Friedrich Naumann gave the eulogy and recounted Dohrn's full life that had been cut short: 'How many ideals, interests, desires, whims and calculations passed through his mind, right up until – at the age of thirty-six – he lay with a broken skull at the foot of Mont Blanc! There are people who grow to be twice his age and yet live half the life he did.'[174] And then he spoke of Dohrn's unwavering passion for the project that was Hellerau: 'At this serious hour, I would like to reiterate what Herr Jacques-Dalcroze said earlier today: Ultimately it was this school, and its *musikalisch-rhythmische Kultur*, that the soul of our dear departed friend was focused upon.'[175] Naumann concluded his fulsome eulogy with the following words: 'The flames now possess his body. Earth to earth, ashes to ashes, fire to fire, and soul to soul!'[176]

Later in that fateful year of 1914 Geneva's newspaper, *Journal de Genève*, printed 'A Swiss Protest against the Bombardment of Reims', signed by ninety-three Swiss artists and intellectuals: 'The undersigned, Swiss citizens, intensely moved by the unjustified assault against the Cathedral of Reims,

following spreads
Spectators at the Fête de Juin performance on 6 July 1914; the Fête de Juin performance from the point of view of the audience.

Eurhythmic performance at the Fête de Juin on 6 July 1914.

following page
Appia at age fifty-one at the Fête de Juin with friends.

occurring after the arson of the historic and scientific wealth of Louvain, denounce with all their might an act of barbarism which wounds all humanity in one of its most noble testimonies of moral and artistic grandeur.'[177] One of the signatories was Jaques-Dalcroze, who was subsequently banned from returning to Germany, while Appia simply decided not to go – both spent the war years in Switzerland and never returned to Hellerau.

That theatre and war are both dramatic, and can be thought of in some of the same terms, has often been remarked upon, most explicitly in the formulation *Kriegstheater* (theatre of war), coined and defined by Carl von Clausewitz: 'A *Kriegstheater* is not merely a microcosm of the whole war, rather it is its own entirety, and one in which those events that are at any one time occurring elsewhere in the war have no direct influence, rather only indirect.'[178]

To a certain extent, Hellerau might be thought of in such terms regarding its relationship with modernism: 'Hellerau should not be pictured as a quaint, peaceful village that existed in an atmosphere of tranquil contentment. Rather, it was a battleground for spirited opinions – a kind of testing ground – where the many ideas for reform that were in the air at the time all came together and were tried out. Hellerau was always intended to be an experiment',[179] wrote a former eurhythmics teacher reflecting upon her time living and teaching in the garden city. Significantly, the Bildungsanstalt designed by Tessenow, which can be seen to preview strains of modernism – and which attracted the likes of Le Corbusier, who described the focal Festsaal as a 'great and irreproachable room' – is both figuratively and literally on the outskirts. It is neither a work of *Großstadt Architektur*, as is, say, the Semperoper, where Wagner once conducted with a baton that Semper himself had designed for him, nor is it the kind of modest building out in the countryside that one might find in a Caspar David Friedrich painting nestling in the Albertinum in that same city of Dresden.

It is in part for its peripheral location that the architectural legacy of the Bildungsanstalt für rhythmische Erziehung is yet to be uncoiled, and in part because the years of its vital existence were so few. The Bildungsanstalt was a building consecrated to the future, and indeed it seemed to hold such great promise inside itself – in the remarkable Festsaal: 'Gradually glowing red like the dawn in coming, the walls cloaked in white fabric – and the ceiling too – shone as one: a room composed only of light', recalled one eyewitness. 'At that time, I imagined how everything material could become spiritualised under the sway of the mystery and "sound" of light. The play of colours seemed to be the final flare-up of a great artistic legacy. And then, the lamps were extinguished forever.'[180]

LATE

The wartime years and those that immediately followed were a fallow time for Appia so far as his own creative output was concerned. However, the works he had already made up to that time – particularly his *Espaces rythmiques* – were beginning to gather quiet renown. They were spoken about, but more importantly, they were shown, for example at the *Theaterkunst* (Theatre Art) exhibition held in 1914 at the Museum of Applied Arts in Zurich.[1]

And that was the occasion on which Appia first met the individual with whom he is to this day customarily compared – the Englishman Edward Gordon Craig – who was in fact on the platform to meet Appia when he stepped off the train in Zurich. Though Appia knew no English and Craig could not hold a conversation in French, they apparently got by mostly in German, and when that failed, they sketched their ideas.[2] In the third volume of his *Daybook*, Craig recalled the first time they met: 'Yesterday Appia and I had our first talk. It was very good, very enjoyable. Today our second talk, and it was exciting. He spoke much of Wagner and of Hellerau and Jaques-Dalcroze ... I had to say that Wagner hated the Theatre and used it as a Prostitute is used. This made him divinely angry.' For Craig, Appia's devotion to Wagner and then to Émile Jaques-Dalcroze was his weakness. Nevertheless, Craig recalled how much he enjoyed Appia's 'laughing and strong disagreement on several points, how bracing it is – I have not been so braced for years. And what a fine fellow he is; the only *Man* I have yet met in the world around the theatre – for he is not quite in it, he flutters round it – rightly he fears the unrest which entering the theatre would bring him – but he fears and

The 'Adolphe Appia' room at the 1914 *Theatre Art* exhibition held at the Museum of Applied Arts in Zurich.

therein is he weaker if wiser than our old stage carpenter who descends into Hell and is unharmed.'[3]

It must have seemed miraculous to Craig that he was able to meet the fine fellow Appia at all, as he had thought the reclusive scenographer had passed away years before; in the very first footnote to the preface of the second edition of his most important book, *On the Art of the Theatre*, Craig corrected himself: 'Appia, the foremost stage-decorator of Europe, is not dead. I was told that he was no more with us, so, in the first edition of this book, I included him among the shades. I first saw three examples of his work in 1908, and I wrote to a friend asking, "Where is Appia, and how can we meet?" My friend replied, "Poor Appia died some years ago," This winter (1912) I saw some of Appia's designs in a portfolio belonging to Prince Wolkonsky. They were divine, and I was told that the designer was still living.'[4]

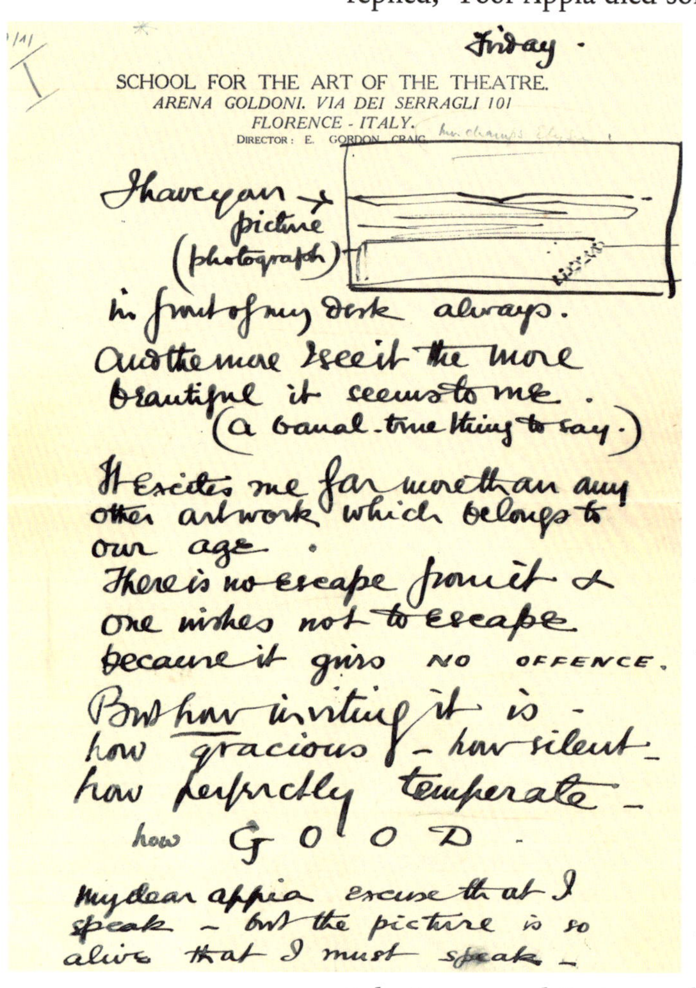
Friday ·
SCHOOL FOR THE ART OF THE THEATRE.
ARENA GOLDONI. VIA DEI SERRAGLI 101
FLORENCE - ITALY.
DIRECTOR: E. GORDON CRAIG
I have your picture (photograph)
in front of my desk always.
And the more I see it the more
beautiful it seems to me.
(a banal-true thing to say.)
It excites me far more than any
other artwork which belongs to
our age.
There is no escape from it &
one wishes not to escape
because it gives NO OFFENCE.
But how inviting it is -
how gracious - how silent -
how perfectly temperate -
how G O O D -
My dear appia excuse that I
speak - but the picture is so
alive that I must speak -

Letter from Edward Gordon Craig to Appia, 4 May 1914.

The two living scenographers exchanged signed copies of their books at the *Theaterkunst* exhibition – Craig was gifted *Die Musik und die Inscenierung* and Appia *On the Art of the Theatre* – and they also saw each other's drawings in the flesh rather than in portfolios. Two photographs of the room in the exhibition devoted to Appia's drawings still exist, both mounted on pastel-coloured card, one olive-green and the other cream. The way that the exhibition is presented is revealing of its time, which was one before art galleries had become the white boxes that they are now. The setting is more domestic than artworld; the ceilings are low, lighting is natural, there are heavy patterned rugs on the floor and comfortable rattan armchairs for visitors to rest their limbs. The drawings are heavily framed and these frames dangle on wires from picture rails that circumscribe the room.

After the opening of the homely exhibition, Appia and Craig went their own ways; Appia retreated to his lonesome medieval château on Lake Geneva and Craig travelled back over the Alps to Italy, where he had set up his own 'School for the Art of the Theatre' in Florence.[5] It was from his school that Craig wrote one of the first of the many letters he sent to Appia, penning the following exulted lines, accompanied by his own thumbnail sketch of Appia's serene drawing of the Elysian Fields in Act 2, Scene 2 of Gluck's *Orfeo ed Euridice*: 'I have your picture (photograph) in front of my desk always. And the more I see it the more beautiful it seems to me (a banal but true thing to say). It excites me far more than any other artwork which belongs to our age. There is no escape from it + one wishes not to escape because it gives NO OFFENCE. But *how* inviting it is – how gracious – how silent – how perfectly temperate – how G.O.O.D. My dear Appia, excuse that I speak – but the picture is so alive that I must.'[6]

No doubt it was due to the self-evident aesthetic rapport between Appia and Craig – plus their strident public declarations regarding the need for a fundamental reform of the outmoded staging techniques that their time had inherited from the nineteenth century – that their friendship blossomed into kinship, which is the word Appia himself used to describe their relationship: 'Our kinship is too obvious to separate us, and our differences are all the more curious and instructive for the public. We could not have done our work in any other way than we did; in this we are indeed brothers in suffering as in joy!'[7]

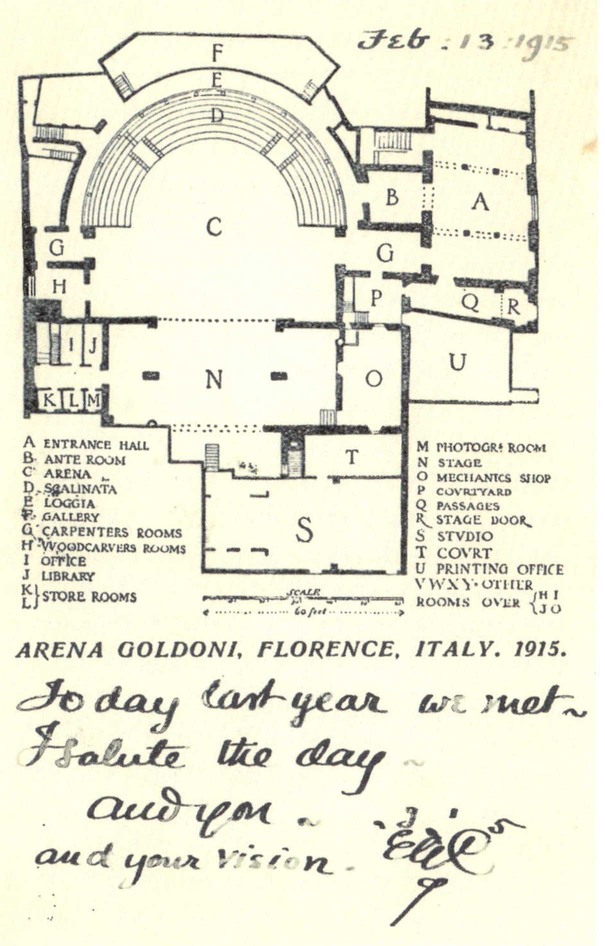

Postcard from Edward Gordon Craig to Appia, 13 February 1915.

Though they shared convictions and sensibilities, the two scenographers adopted differing subject matters and artistic techniques to embody them; while the drawing by Appia that Craig so admired was for the staging of an opera, he himself was most interested in the theatre, particularly the famous tragic plays by his countryman William Shakespeare, chief among them *Hamlet*. And he also used representational techniques foreign to Appia – watercolour sketches, and scale models cast in plaster – to convey his pared-back settings and to invest them with atmosphere.

Jaques-Dalcroze saw Craig's settings for the 1912 production of *Hamlet* at the Moscow Art Theatre and was adamant that their aesthetic debt to Appia in fact amounted to plagiarism. He wrote a letter to his friend the very day after he had seen the performance: 'I have just seen Hamlet at Konstantin Stanislavski's with sets by Craig, the Englishman who claims to be revolutionising scenography; there are some very beautiful things – all copied from you – and to such an extent that I am still foaming with rage after nine hours of restless sleep, or rather insomnia.' And further: 'I have the impression that this man must have seen your drawings but does not know how to make use of them. That you are copied by others is quite natural; every man of genius is.'[8]

Critics also started to think about Appia and Craig in the same terms and at the same time, both in Europe and abroad; one perceptive exhibition reviewer wrote: 'Once we have made our way through all the rooms, it becomes abundantly clear that a new tendency is all-pervasive: painted canvases, with their false spaces and false volumes, are being replaced by architecture and light. So now the actor no longer moves about *in front* of a scene, *in front* of an atmosphere, but rather *among* the elements of the scene. This is the principle that the great Bernes director Mr Alfred (sic) Appia follows.'[9] He wrote that a 'certain gravitas' emanated from the room devoted to Appia and Craig, the two 'stars of modern scenography', and that though they belong together, 'a discerning eye readily perceives the differences that exist between these two "bosses". Craig – don't forget he is English – is more of a painter than an architect, whereas Appia is, above all, an architect. Craig particularly employs draperies and vertical

following spread
The Adolphe Appia and Edward Gordon Craig rooms at the 1922 *International Theatre* exhibition in Amsterdam.

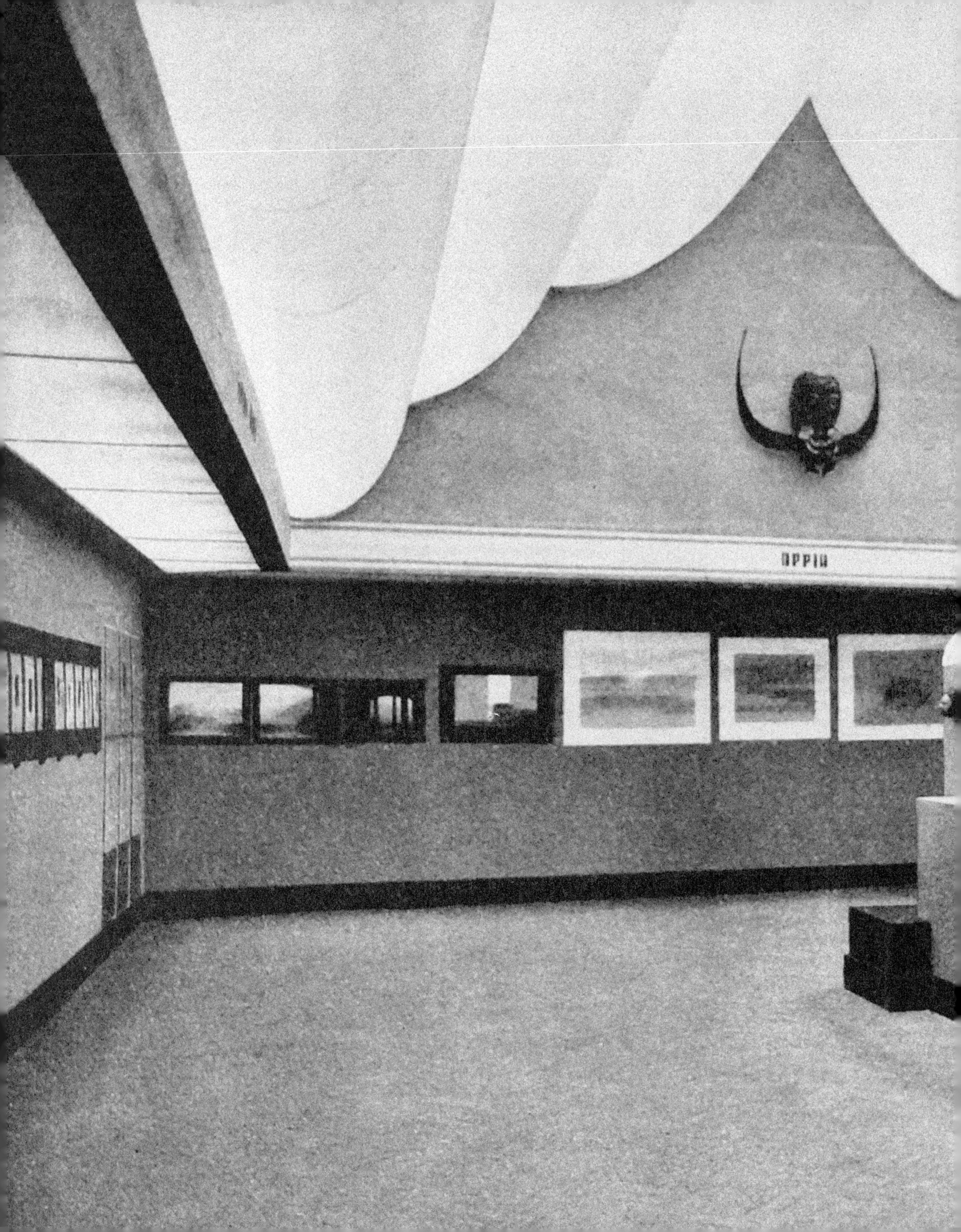
APPIA

GORDON CRAIG

planes; Appia has a predilection for horizontal planes. In short, Craig works with curtains and columns, Appia works with stairs, masses and light.'[10]

The American critic Carl Van Vechten was less amenable to the idea that the two scenographers were equals, asserting that it was Appia who was responsible for the fundamentally modern *mise-en-scène*, and that Craig followed after him. Van Vechten published a lengthy article simply entitled 'Adolphe Appia and Gordon Craig', which mounted that very argument.[11]

Lyonel Feininger, cover of the Weimar Bauhaus Manifesto and Programme, 1919.

Craig was incensed and fired off a letter to his friend: 'Dear Appia, a surly American critic has just published an insolent article to say (well, not to say, but rather to insinuate) that I could not have written my book (the poor thing that it is!) without having read both of your books, and that I have STOLEN all your ideas! ... POOR YOU, POOR ME, because you cannot read my book and have not, I am sure, and alas, I have not read yours. I often take it out and stroke it, but I cannot read German any more than I can read French or even Italian. Tell me, what should be done about this American who is trying to pit one friend against the other. He deserves a good reward, but which one?'[12] To which Appia responded: 'How often I think of you! And how I would like for us to be together; you who represent so well that which I am not, alas; and me, who seeks with all my soul to be and develop that which I do not know how to be ... So, we would not only be together, but we would also be one. Do not stop writing to me – your little words of presence, I need them ... I think of you and love you with all the ties that bind us indissolubly and that are so soft, so strong, and so light all the same.'[13]

Then, though it was not his wont to communicate with theatre critics, Appia wrote directly to Van Vechten: 'I don't understand what it is that you wish to say by placing on my shoulders the *sole* responsibility for the actual reform of the *mise-en-scène*. Without a doubt, I have contributed to it, but so too have others. And if my particular aesthetic pleases you, that is no reason to bestow on me *all* of the honour, which I refuse.'[14] Appia forwarded a copy of this letter on to Craig, accompanied by a brief note: 'You write of things that take me by the heart ... and I don't know what to say to you, other than that I know that you could not have my desires! Our two natures are different – you have infinite charm; me, I have (and only have), this: [Here Appia includes a small sketch of his Elysian Fields]. You have a thousand ways of expressing yourself to others. Me, I am a wolf in his lair who gazes upon the light that crosses his hole ... luminous – very luminous!'[15]

Later in that same year of 1914 in which Appia and Craig had adjoining rooms at the *Theaterkunst* exhibition in Switzerland, they were invited to participate in the now-famous Deutscher Werkbund exhibition in Cologne.[16] This time 'pride of place had been given to Appia', the English-born theatre producer Maurice Browne attested in his chatty autobiography, *Too Late to Lament*, and his 'work filled one large room; the designs of his third period left us breathless with their beauty'.[17] Appia himself later recalled that 'in the order of thirty of my original drawings were shown',[18] these being for the most part his recent *Espaces rythmiques*, but he exhibited some of his earlier Wagnerian settings too. Appia needed encouragement to take part in the 1914 Werkbund exhibition at all, and voiced his frustration with the organising committee to Craig, who responded: 'I very much want to meet with you, and speak about Cologne. If you will exhibit there – so will I. If you will not – I will not. I have no care any longer to exhibit anywhere if your works are not there too.'[19] Appia wrote back four days later, on 8 May (the exhibition was scheduled to open on 16 May): 'Still nothing from Cologne; it would be impossible to be ruder. If it were solely up to me, I would withdraw from the exhibition. But since you wrote to me in such solidarity, I will wait to hear what you decide to do. It seems impossible to me to acquiesce, but please do let me know of your decision right away. No doubt it is our duty to exhibit, but surely, we should not be obliged to do so under such conditions; they are not gatekeepers, but rather vulgar doormen who fail to see us properly for who we are.'[20]

Just how many of the exhibition architects sighted the works of the two aggrieved modern scenographers is unknown, though one assumes it was no small number of them given the age-long relations between drawing and building – whether for the purpose of describing a project that is already fully formed in the mind of the architect or for presenting radical visions for an architecture yet to come. It was this deep-seated importance of drawing to architecture that caused the young Walter Gropius to despair of ever being able to follow in the footsteps of his architect father, as recorded in an anguished letter he sent to his mother Manon in 1907: 'My absolute inability to jot down even the simplest thing on paper tarnishes some beautiful ideas, and often leaves me worried about my future profession. I am unable to even draft a straight line; as a 12-year-old boy, I was able to draw much better. It seems to be almost a physical disability that I have: I immediately get a cramp in my hand; the tips of my pencils are constantly breaking off; and after five minutes I need to stop for a rest. My handwriting is the same – it gets worse every day. Even in my darkest hours, I never feared that it would be so bleak. How on earth should things ever work out for me?'[21]

By 1914 Gropius's spirits had risen, along with his standing in the profession, which was now such that he was able to successfully convince the organisers that he was just the architect to design the model factory that along with Bruno Taut's Glass Pavilion would become one of the exhibition's most memorable buildings[22] – one that, so far as the disposition of the plan goes, is in fact

Walter Gropius and Lászlo Moholy-Nagy, eds, *Bauhausbücher 4: Die Bühne im Bauhaus*, 1924.

as ancient as it is modern, since it is that of a church, complete with a nave, side aisle, atrium, narthex and even a 'baptistry'. The symmetrical cross-section, with its tall, pitched roof, is also very much that of a religious building, even as the materials from which it is made, and the construction techniques used to piece it all together, point towards the future. This future would have to wait, however, since the First World War placed all thoughts of it in abeyance – as one critic reported, the Werkbund exhibition was 'forced to close its gates, and now all the buildings are filled with wounded soldiers and those who are convalescing. Never has the contrast between peaceful labour and malicious destruction been more glaringly obvious than here – the industrious striving of an entire *Volk* that was here united has been scattered to the four winds in the blink of an eye.'[23]

In the same month that the gates of the Werkbund exhibition were forced to close, Gropius was drafted into the German Imperial Army. And the direction the wind cast him was west – Gropius served first as a sergeant major on the Western Front, during which time he was wounded – almost fatally – and then after that as a lieutenant in the signal corps. Gropius was awarded the Iron Cross twice, 'when it still meant something', as he confided to a friend some years later.[24] Maria Ludwig Michael Mies – that other modern architect who cut his teeth as a 'lieutenant' in Peter Behrens's architectural office in Neu Babelsberg – went in the other direction. His wartime feats were much less heroic, though this probably had more to do with opportunity than daring, since as the son of a modest stonemason, and without a university education or some other signifier of social rank, he was relegated to the ranks of the non-commissioned and never raised a rifle in anger – though he did once lock horns with a sergeant and was despatched to Romania, where he ended up 'in an outlying region guarding railway sidings'.[25]

Gropius was released from military duty on 18 November 1918, by which time he was thirty-five years old. Formerly politically conservative, the architect later recalled that, 'as in a flash of light', he became progressive: 'it dawned on me ... the old stuff was out'.[26] Chastened by his experiences of machine-led killing, Gropius experienced, as he put it, 'a mixture of deep despondency – following Germany's defeat in the war and the disintegration of intellectual and economic life – and fervent hope and desire to build something new on these ruins'. He founded the Weimar Bauhaus. And since 'a sober call for sober work would have spoiled the concept, which was to offer young people who are full of new ideas a broad basis to purify and test them',[27] he wrote a catalysing manifesto and programme that was published in April 1919, fronted by Lyonel Feininger's prismatic expressionist woodcut *Cathedral of the Future*. He redirected his earlier enthusiasm for industrial production to the pre-industrial motif of the Gothic cathedral, the new (and old) exulted locus for creative endeavour, pronouncing that 'the ultimate, if distant, aim of the Bauhaus is the *Einheitswerk* (unified work of art) – the great building'.[28] Although clearly operating in separate social and artistic circles, Appia shared Gropius's ambition. For him, too, it was the cathedral of the future – more as a glorious motif rather than anything actually buildable – that ignited the imagination. In a short text published in the same year as Gropius's manifesto, Appia wrote with great enthusiasm that 'Sooner or later we will arrive at what we shall call the *Saal* (hall) – the cathedral of the future – which will accommodate, in a free, large, transformable space, the most varied manifestations of our social and artistic life.'[29] And in the same year he finished the final draft for his book *L'Œuvre d'art vivant* (The Work of Living Art), which was finally published in 1921. In it, he exclaims: 'We are, moreover, beginning to sense an ever more compelling need to unite with others, whether outdoors, or in a hall not restricted in advance to one or the other of our public activities to the exclusion of others.' On the contrary, this hall 'exists solely and simply to enable us to come together with one another, as once we did in our cathedrals ... The term escapes me! I cannot recall it. Ah, yes: it is in a cathedral of the future that we must take our vows!'[30]

Treppenwitz being performed by Oskar Schlemmer and others in the Bauhaus building, Dessau, 1927.

When the Bauhaus moved to Dessau in 1925, its guiding principle shifted from the cathedral of the future to the *Wohnmaschine* (machine for living), a change also advertised by the stark, factory-like school designed by Gropius himself. The Bauhaus building's pin-wheeling composition comprised three interlocking volumes. Two of these – the workshop block and the apartment block – were linked on the ground floor by a single-storey bridging structure accommodating an auditorium, a cafeteria and a stage that could be opened up to face an audience on either side.[31]

With its stripped-back disposition and flexibility, the Bauhaus stage presented itself (knowingly or otherwise) as the high modern equivalent of the Festsaal at Hellerau. Spatially and conceptually central to the new school, it hosted performances that were more radically modern in expression than those staged at the Bildungsanstalt, though Appia figured in the conception of some of them through some written advice that he gave to the dancer Albert Burger, who, together with his wife Else Hötzel, had undertaken a five-month study trip to Hellerau in 1912 to learn more about eurhythmics, and according to some reports even played parts in *Orfeo ed Euridice*. When the two professional dancers returned home to Stuttgart they got together with the painter – and recently trained dancer – Oskar Schlemmer, and together the three of them invented the *Triadisches Ballet* (Triadic Ballet).[32]

POSTKA[RTE]
IM AUFTRAG DER VERWALTUNG ...
DEUTSCHES REICH
HELLERAU (AMTSH. DRESDEN)

Cher Monsieur
Appia,
Nous pensons toujours à vous avec affection
votre Albert Jeanneret

Monsieur
Adolphe Appia.
Sanatorium du
Dr. Reymond,
Rivaz-St Saphorin
Canton de Vaud
"Schweiz"

Postcard from Albert Jeanneret to Appia, 14 April 1913.

Burger wrote to Appia asking for advice, and the scenographer responded, though not immediately. 'If I was not so unwell you would have heard word from me a long while ago, since I often think of you with the deepest empathy and fondness', wrote Appia, who then apologised in advance for 'sending but a few lines'. After this first brief, unpromising opening, he gets straight to the heart of the matter: 'Your project interests me very much: Every one of Jaques-Dalcroze's students should become a *Mitarbeiter* (collaborator) in order to propel the great ideas for reform forwards. But it is difficult for one such as I, who was never actually a student of Jaques-Dalcroze, at least not for a long period of time, to give really good advice. Even more so since for many a year now I live in solitude ...' Appia signs off at the top of page two, but then has second thoughts, jotting down ideas and declarations at pace: 'Rather sleek and simple than sumptuous and Russian etc. It is the aesthetic purity of the intentions alone that makes for beauty.' And then, 'You will probably also have terraces, steps, columns etc.? Do not forget that the vertical lines are necessary for the body to make an impression and express itself creatively. This was lacking somewhat in *Orfeo ed Euridice* at Hellerau.' And then, at the top of page three, Appia suggests that once Burger's plans become more concrete, he should be so kind to share them, so that Appia can see in what way he might be able to help. Finally, he signs off – once again – this time circling back to the location where he is pencilling the letter: 'In regard to this old château on the lake where I have rented a little *Einsiedelei* (hermitage), would you like to visit? Appia!'[33]

In 1924 Gropius published *Die Bühne im Bauhaus*, the fourth in the Bauhausbücher series. It was, apparently unknowingly, infused with notions and propositions articulated by Appia many years before in *Die Musik und die Inscenierung*, but this time couched in more ecstatic terms – for example, Oskar Schlemmer's stated conviction that 'the laws of cubical space are the invisible linear network of planimetric and stereometric relationships. This mathematic corresponds with the interiorised mathematic of the human body … It is the geometry of calisthenics, eurhythmics and gymnastics.'[34] László Moholy-Nagy wrote that the Bauhaus stage was 'envisaged as a great, dynamic-rhythmic design enterprise', which 'out of the greatest possible clashing and piling up of sources that engender qualitative and quantitative tensions, fuses into a primal form'.[35] And of his proposition for a 'mechanised eccentric' as though it were a new idea, he wrote: 'individual flats on the stage will have a double-skin made of stretched linen, which transmits and diffuses light from both spotlights and low lamps'. In an even more direct gloss of Appia, he proclaimed, 'a further improvement would be to abolish the isolation of the stage. In the theatre of today, the stage and audience are far too separated from one another, too much divided into active and passive for creative relationships and tensions to be generated.'[36]

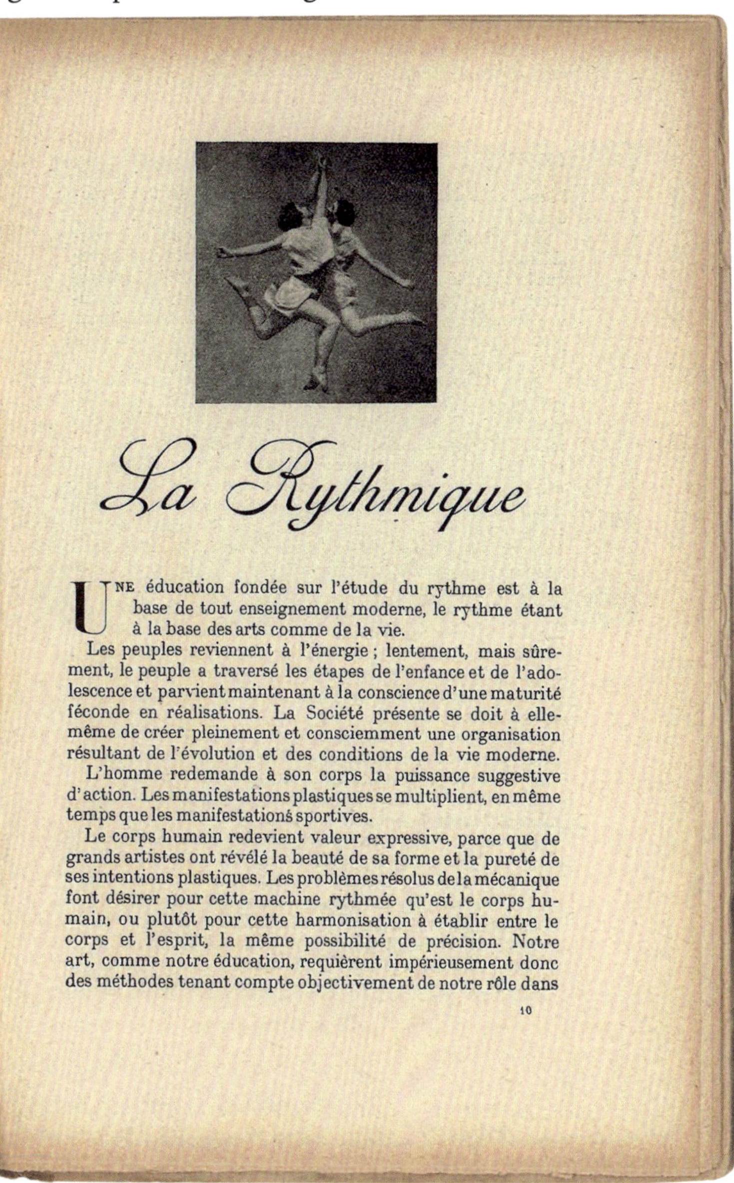

La Rythmique

Une éducation fondée sur l'étude du rythme est à la base de tout enseignement moderne, le rythme étant à la base des arts comme de la vie.

Les peuples reviennent à l'énergie ; lentement, mais sûrement, le peuple a traversé les étapes de l'enfance et de l'adolescence et parvient maintenant à la conscience d'une maturité féconde en réalisations. La Société présente se doit à elle-même de créer pleinement et consciemment une organisation résultant de l'évolution et des conditions de la vie moderne.

L'homme redemande à son corps la puissance suggestive d'action. Les manifestations plastiques se multiplient, en même temps que les manifestations sportives.

Le corps humain redevient valeur expressive, parce que de grands artistes ont révélé la beauté de sa forme et la pureté de ses intentions plastiques. Les problèmes résolus de la mécanique font désirer pour cette machine rythmée qu'est le corps humain, ou plutôt pour cette harmonisation à établir entre le corps et l'esprit, la même possibilité de précision. Notre art, comme notre éducation, requièrent impérieusement donc des méthodes tenant compte objectivement de notre rôle dans

10

Albert Jeanneret, 'La Rythmique', *L'Esprit nouveau*, no 2, 1920.

A photograph taken by T Lux Feininger down low at the foot of the Bauhaus stage during a 1927 production of Schlemmer's humorous pantomime *Treppenwitz* (esprit de l'escalier) captures the three performers up above in dramatic action – one of them is literally hanging from the rafters. Modern harlequins they are, all wearing burnished metal masks and one-piece costumes, two of them dressed in monochrome while the third – Schlemmer himself – is in a two-tone outfit as he descends a set of demountable timber stairs that stand before a plain white flat hanging from one of the four tracks that have been mounted in the shallow fly-tower that scarcely warrants its name. The whole *mise-en-scène* has a provisional look about it, which is not surprising since three-dimensionality and flexibility were top of the agenda – 'the ceiling of the *Bühnenraum* (stage area) is equipped with a set of four tracks on which walls, props and so forth can be attached and moved around. And then there are 72 square metres of practicables that on the one hand enable the entire floor of the stage to be raised by 50 cm and, on the other hand, can serve as scenic building material', ran the caption to a photograph of the Dessau stage on the cover of an issue of its own periodical, *Bauhaus: Zeitschrift für Bau und Gestaltung*, dedicated entirely to the theatre.[37] Schlemmer guest-edited the

Le Corbusier-Saugnier, 'Architecture III: Pure Creation of the Mind', *L'Esprit nouveau*, no 16, 1922.

issue, which was published to coincide with the major exhibition of German theatre held in Magdeburg in 1927.

Schlemmer does not mention it, but it was Appia who came up with the idea for *Praktikabeln* ('practicables')[38] – building blocks of uniform size and shape that could be assembled to create a three-dimensional setting on the stage and then afterwards readily unpacked and reconfigured for a new performance. And it was in the mighty composition of cascading stairs in the Festsaal at Hellerau that Appia employed these to most dramatic effect, consummating the vision of a new architecture for the stage he had first expressed in the *Espaces rythmiques*. Appia also invented the name *Praktikabeln*, though this fact apparently was not well known, and if it was, it went unacknowledged. The drift of the time was toward self-promotion, largely via publications that served that very purpose; the Bauhaus had its own periodical and series of publications, and Ludwig Mies van der Rohe (formerly Maria Ludwig Michael Mies) had *G: Journal zur elementare Gestaltung* (G: Journal for Elemental Form-Creation). But before each of these came *L'Esprit nouveau*, founded in 1920 by Amédée Ozenfant, Paul Dermée and Charles-Édouard Jeanneret, who would soon become Le Corbusier.

The first line in the first issue of *L'Esprit nouveau* proclaimed it the 'first journal in the world devoted to the aesthetics of our time, in all of its manifestations'.[39] It was mostly devoted to the arts, but there was much else besides – issue 2 alone contained: an essay on the composer and pianist Erik Satie; excerpts from letters written by the post-Impressionist Paul Cézanne along with full-page reproductions of some of his paintings; Knut Hamsun's short story 'The Queen of Sheba'; along with full-page advertisements for hot water systems, Suchard Cocoa, Omega watches and Ford, makers of the 'Universal Car', plus the latest results in local cycling, rugby and boxing competitions. And then there were also two articles on architecture, the first of them being Adolf Loos's now famous essay 'Ornament and Crime',[40] and the second was the now equally famous essay that Le Corbusier wrote together with Amédée Ozenfant but that he ultimately claimed for himself: 'Three Reminders to Architects. II: Surface'. The architect's musician brother Albert Jeanneret also contributed a two-part essay – 'La Rythmique' – which was illustrated throughout with those photographs of lithe spirited eurhythmics students that Boissonnas shot outside in the bright spring light of Hellerau in 1913.

It was back to his time at the Bildungsanstalt in Hellerau that Jeanneret turned his mind when he sat down to write 'La Rythmique', in part because his apprenticeship there with Jaques-Dalcroze determined his future development as a musician and teacher. Jeanneret had set up his own École de Rythmique in Paris, had designed himself a logo based upon one of Boissonnas's photographs,[41] and was now promoting his lessons in full-page advertisements in the back pages of *L'Esprit nouveau*. But he also genuinely believed that the study of rhythm should in fact be the very foundation of modern education, since it is 'the basis not only of the arts, but of life'.[42] Jeanneret recounted some of the basic exercises of eurhythmics, such as 'walking in a regulated, even tempo; *accellerandos* and *rallentendos*; substitution of one movement for another, a step replaced by a clap of the hands, for example; execution, while walking, of a jump, a pirouette or a change of direction on a given command'.[43] But then he quickly moved on to the activities that took place inside the 'sober and firm' architecture of the Bildungsanstalt, 'a work by Tessenow that incorporates a large auditorium hung with smooth white fabric', which can be 'readily transformed' from a setting for lessons 'into a configuration of level and inclined planes – architectural forms – such as the setting for *Orfeo ed Euridice*, performed in August 1913'.[44] Le Corbusier's brother then described how the three-dimensional setting in which Orpheus 'slowly descended from the top of a 10-metre-high wall, repelling the menacing mass of Furies', consisted of a 'system of *Praktikabeln* designed by Adolphe Appia' that made it possible to construct a 'potent and important architectural setting in a quarter of an hour'. The pupils soon learned to easily move about on these steps and inclined planes, wrote Jeanneret, and 'performing together as one rhythmic, stylised form, they transformed into the Furies barring Eurydice's lover from the gates of Hell, and then into the mystical figures that inhabit the Champs-Elysées'. Jeanneret remembered how the auditorium had been illuminated by '60,000 electric globes concealed behind the translucent fabric that covered the entire surface of all of the walls', and how this 'luminous organ was able to be played easily, offering a range of luminosity that went from full shadow to sharp illumination, bathing both the performers and spectators in the same atmosphere'.[45] Jeanneret concluded his essay with the kind of spirited statement that was typical of *L'Esprit nouveau*, announcing that 'we are living at an important time in the modern period, one of common action that is the result of both intuition and deliberate effort – constructive, conscious of the moment in which we live'.[46]

That same spirit was alive in the essays which Le Corbusier himself published in *L'Esprit nouveau*, beginning with 'Three Reminders to Architects. I. Volume' in the premier issue of the journal, an essay that contained the architect's memorable definition of architecture as 'the masterful, correct and magnificent play of volumes brought together in light',[47] a definition that he would repeat again and again as a kind of refrain, including in 'Architecture III: Pure Creation of the Mind', an essay devoted to the Parthenon – for Le Corbusier the climax of the Doric,[48] a building that he later said 'made me

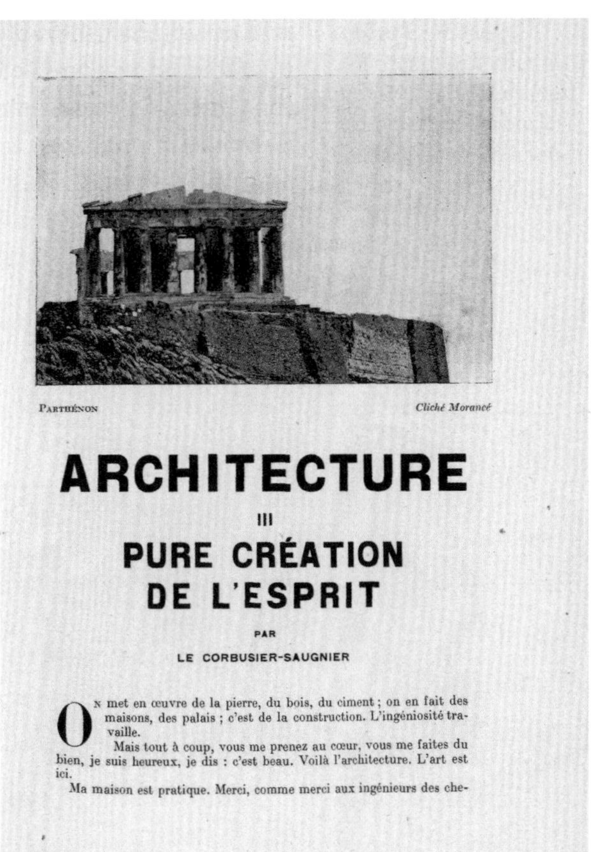

PARTHÉNON *Cliché Morancé*

ARCHITECTURE

III

PURE CRÉATION DE L'ESPRIT

PAR

LE CORBUSIER-SAUGNIER

On met en œuvre de la pierre, du bois, du ciment ; on en fait des maisons, des palais ; c'est de la construction. L'ingéniosité travaille.

Mais tout à coup, vous me prenez au cœur, vous me faites du bien, je suis heureux, je dis : c'est beau. Voilà l'architecture. L'art est ici.

Ma maison est pratique. Merci, comme merci aux ingénieurs des che-

PARTHÉNON. — *Voici la machine à émouvoir. Nous entrons dans l'implacable de la mécanique. Il n'est pas de symboles attachés à ces formes ; ces formes provoquent des sensations catégoriques ; plus besoin d'une clé pour comprendre. Du brutal, de l'intense, du plus doux, du très fin, du très fort. Et qui a trouvé la composition de ces éléments ? Un inventeur génial. Ces cailloux étaient inertes dans les carrières du Pentélique, informes. Pour les grouper ainsi, il ne fallait pas être ingénieur ; il fallait être un grand sculpteur.*

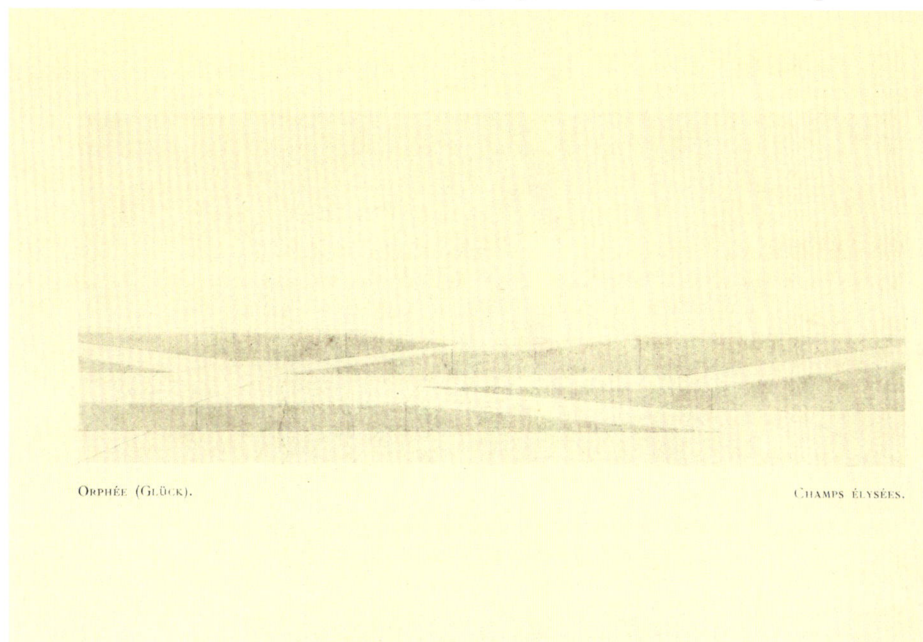

Appia, drawing for Christoph Willibald Gluck's *Orfeo ed Euridice*, Act 2 (The Elysian Fields), as published in *L'Œuvre d'art vivant*, 1921.

a rebel ... I have kept this certitude: Remember the clear, clean, intense, economical, violent Parthenon.'[49] Le Corbusier prefaced his essay with a photograph of the Parthenon taken front on from some distance, which turns out to be a heavily cropped reproduction of one of the suite of photographs that Frédéric Boissonnas shot back in 1903 with his recently invented Téléphot camera.[50] All of the other photographs that illustrate the essay were also taken by Boissonnas. Le Corbusier found them in two books – *Le Parthénon* and *L'Acropole* – which he described as 'genuinely accurate documents' that were made possible 'thanks to the skill of the photographer Frédéric Boissonnas, whose perseverance, enterprise and qualities as a plastic artist have revealed to us the most important Greek works of the great period'.[51] Le Corbusier was, of course, agitating in favour of mechanical precision in architecture, and he co-opted the Parthenon and Boissonnas's photographs of it – particularly those taken atop his tripod-ladder – to serve his polemical purpose. Under one close-up of a masonry detail, he boldly asserted: 'The impression is of naked polished steel'; and further that: 'For two thousand years, those who have seen the Parthenon have felt: this was a decisive moment for architecture', before finally asserting that we too 'stand before a decisive moment'.[52]

Le Corbusier would redeploy his definition of architecture as 'the masterful, correct and magnificent play of volumes brought together in light' to great effect in his book, *Vers une architecture*, which he had given the working title 'Architecture or Revolution'. It came out in 1923 and was promoted in *L'Esprit nouveau* with vigour: 'Just published. This book is implacable. It is unlike any other.' And Le Corbusier even wrote a kind of review of his own book, describing himself in the third person as 'the most vibrant, the most lively of the theoreticians who has taken an interest in the problem of a new spirit in architecture'.[53] Le Corbusier sold many copies of *Vers une architecture*, but he also gave plenty away to friends and colleagues, including Jaques-Dalcroze. 'You are one of the personalities who have contributed most to the development of a true *esprit nouveau*' is what Le Corbusier wrote in the copy that he posted to the inventor of eurhythmics.[54] He also mailed a copy to Boissonnas, who was somewhat confused as to the identity of the sender, since he knew Le Corbusier by his birth name Charles-Édouard Jeanneret. 'Dear Mr, it is no doubt to your kindness that I owe receipt of Le Corbusier-Saugnier's book *Vers une architecture*. I am still to decipher the signature that accompanies the kind dedication, but I am sure that it can only be you – and I wonder whether perhaps you are in fact tied to the author of the book by way of a pseudonym,' wrote Boissonnas. 'In any case, I made it my bedside reading and read it dry. I was enthralled and see eye to eye with you regarding your comparisons.

In short, you fiendishly knocked me backwards, but I accept it as an educational experience. So, this is to offer you my sincere gratitude, but with the smallest of niggles – to do with the authorship of the photographs, which were attributed to the publisher. It was not (Albert) Morancé who risked his bones one hundred times atop my ladder!!'[55]

The question of attribution is one that has been raised not only regarding the images that Le Corbusier published in *L'Esprit nouveau*, but also regarding some of his words. In the chapter of his book *L'Œuvre d'art vivant* entitled 'Les éléments', Appia wrote 'l'architecture est l'art de grouper les masses dans le sense de leur pesanteur; la pesanteur est son principe esthétique', which translates cumbrously as 'Architecture is the art of grouping masses in the direction of their weight; gravity is its aesthetic principle'.[56] Pierre Saddy, for one, concluded the short text that he wrote on Appia for the catalogue accompanying the major 1988 retrospective exhibition, *Le Corbusier: Le passé à réaction poétique*, with the assertion that Le Corbusier in fact adopted Appia's conception, which he 'summed up in the famous formula "Architecture is the masterful, correct and magnificent play of volumes brought together in light".'[57]

Appia, drawing for Christoph Willibald Gluck's *Écho et Narcisse*, as published in *L'Œuvre d'art vivant*, 1921

Saddy's claim is very difficult to either confirm or refute given that the dates of publication of Appia's book and Le Corbusier's essay almost coincide,[58] and also because there is no evidence that the architect ever read *L'Œuvre d'art vivant* (nor any of Appia's other writings).[59] But the aesthetic affinity is evident. 'Architecture is the art of creating determined and circumscribed space ... It expresses this fact in both height and depth, and by a superposition of solid elements whose weight ensures solidity. It is the art of the real,'[60] wrote Appia. And by way of a real example, he turned to the Parthenon, as Le Corbusier so often did too. Appia had long been inspired by Friedrich Schiller's pithy assertion that 'when music reaches its noblest power, it becomes form',[61] and he wondered whether it was the Parthenon that the German writer had in mind: 'Perhaps contemplation of the Parthenon inspired him; his gaze went from column to column, as in a succession of silent chords; the frieze, the pediment testified to his eyes of a definitive order, of a harmony henceforth fixed. While resting on the ground, he will have felt the weight of the construction resting directly, without intermediate foundations, on the slabs of the temple, by the rough bases and the sincerity of the columns.'[62] For Appia, it was the architectural self-restraint of the Parthenon that served to magnify the mighty Doric temple's power, which is what Le Corbusier also thought: 'We can speak of "Doric" when man, having raised his sights and completely sacrificed the accidental, has attained the uppermost region of the mind: austerity.'[63]

Le Corbusier, Villa Le Lac, 1923.

Although it was the quality of austerity that they professed to admire in architecture, both Appia and Le Corbusier often couched their theoretical musings in terms that were exultant and beckoning. The concluding chapter of *L'Œuvre d'art vivant* is entitled 'Les porteurs de flamme' (The Keepers of the Flame), and in the final passage of it, Appia wrote that 'in order to harness and nourish this flame of aesthetic truth, it has been necessary to trample over those torches that belong to the old false aesthetic culture', words that one could easily imagine Le Corbusier writing at the time.[64]

While Le Corbusier committed his thoughts to paper and considered himself to be 'the most vibrant, the most lively of the theoreticians', he also considered himself 'the most original of architects'.[65] In that same year of 1923 in which he published *Vers une architecture*, he built an original *petite maison* with 'a precise, functional floor plan' that corresponded exactly to its programme – 'an authentic little machine for living in', as he later wrote.[66] It was his elderly parents who would be moving into the *petite maison*, which Le Corbusier had in fact already designed for them before he knew where it was going to be built.[67] In his own words, the architect had been strolling around with the plans for this house in his pocket 'for a long time, looking for a site',[68] one that would have to be greater in length than breadth, since the precise, functional floor plan was a slim rectangular form with a length to width ratio of four to one. One of the two long façades would be closed, save for the main entry door that opened into the flowing interior, which would have as its principal feature a *fenêtre en longueur* – a long ribbon window – that would be the 'central player in the house', and that would occupy almost the full length of the other long façade.[69]

This is Le Corbusier's pithy recollection of the providential moment the site that he later described as a *salle de spectacle* (theatre)[70] revealed itself: 'We discovered the correct site (for the house) from the top of a hill. It was on the lakeside and might be said to have been waiting especially for this little house. The vintner and his family who sold it were very obliging and agreeable – we toasted the sale.'[71]

According to Le Corbusier, the view over Lake Geneva, south towards the Alps that reign above it, is 'one of the most beautiful horizons in the world',[72] and this was his opportunity to commune with it, principally via the 11-metre strip window that he later said 'unites and illuminates all of the elements, making the majesty of the magnificent site enter into the house: the lake with its movement, the Alps with their miraculous light'.[73] This long window 'introduces the immensity of the outdoors, the unfalsifiable unity of a lakeside landscape with its storms or radiant calms'.[74]

But there is a second important window in the composition, and it might be thought of as the equal and opposite of the first, since its role is not to bring the outside in, but rather to hold the lakeside landscape at bay. Le Corbusier reasoned that if left unchecked, 'the ubiquitous landscape on all sides, omnipotent, becomes tiresome'.[75] So, he decided to 'limit it, dimension it', first of all by constructing a full-height garden wall along much of the lake-facing perimeter of the site, and then cutting a perfectly square opening into it at the height of a standard window, which is very much what the aperture appears to be. He installed a table below the hole-in-a-wall window, and pulled two chairs up to it, creating an intimate setting that the architect

himself in fact referred to as 'an interior'.[76] That is very much how the domestic-scaled setting appears in the photograph Lucien Hervé took of it, especially since the table is set as though for morning or afternoon tea.

The view that the 'window' frames of Lake Geneva and the majestic Alps rising above it is the same one that Appia took in at his drawing board and sublimated into his *Espaces rythmiques*, which are similarly framed on the picture plane of the page; Villa Le Lac, as Le Corbusier's lakeside house came to be known, is just a short stroll around the lakeshore from the medieval Château de Glérolles where Jean Mercier photographed the scenographer in his favourite *pull marin* gazing out towards the horizon where, in Le Corbusier's words, 'the spectacle arises – light, space – this water and these mountains ... That's all there is!'[77]

Just beyond those mountains where 'the spectacle arises' lies Italy, the home of opera, and that is where Appia turned all of his attention in the second half of 1923, having finally been presented with his long-awaited opportunity to stage one of Wagner's *Wort-Tondramen* along the lines of the settings he had first conceived in the 1890s.[78] The invitation to prepare the scenography for a production at the most famous opera house of all – Teatro alla Scala in Milan – came from none other than the famed conductor Arturo Toscanini, who was preparing a performance of the tragic love story *Tristan und Isolde*, which begins with the most famous single chord in the history of music – the 'Tristan Chord'. This first chord 'contains within itself not one but two dissonances, thus creating within the listener a double desire, agonising in its intensity, for resolution. The chord to which it then moves resolves one of these dissonances but not the other, thus providing resolution-but-not-resolution.'[79]

And it was dissonance that the conductor and scenographer were fully expecting; Teatro alla Scala was a bastion of conservatism within an Italian operatic establishment that was itself almost wholly innocent of the reformist scenographic ideas that had achieved a foothold in much of the rest of Europe by that time. Knowing the performance would be perceived as radical, Toscanini and Appia mounted a pre-emptive campaign to prepare the *pubblico*, organising an exhibition of Appia's drawings and translating several of his essays into Italian for publication in the Milanese papers.

As was only to be expected, Appia declined to make any public appearances in Milan, but he did write a lengthy exposition of his scenography for *Tristan und Isolde* that was published in the local press, and he discussed his ideas at length with his Italian collaborators during the course of three separate visits that he made to Milan at three-month intervals in the lead-up to the performance. Although he was seldom present himself during rehearsals, Appia was represented on the ground by his trusted friend Mercier. The arrangement suited them both; Mercier later recalled Appia saying to him at the time: 'I am the thought, and you are the action.'[80]

Appia knew exactly what he wanted to achieve emotionally, aesthetically and practically, and in the second half of 1923 he recounted all this to Mercier, who wrote down the scenographer's instructions in his beige-covered *Tristan und Isolde* notebook. In the end, this ran to some forty-four pages of detailed notes written out carefully in graphite pencil, with references to important parts of the musical score underlined in red. The notebook also holds four folded sheets of tracing paper on which Appia drew technical plans for the setting of the second act, indicating the specific locations of actors on the stage together with the passages of the musical score to which they relate.[81]

Regarding that setting for the second act, Appia told Mercier that when Isolde enters, she is only aware of two things – Tristan's absence, and the torch that powerfully symbolises this tragic fact. 'The warm summer night that vaults over the lofty trees of the castle courtyard does not register as factual reality for Isolde', he explained. So, as the curtain was raised at La Scala, all that the audience saw before them was the dimly lit stage with a single majestic torch mounted aloft at its centre, dazzling their eyes with its flickering flame so that only gradually did the outlines of the other objects on the stage appear – these being: a raised terrace in front of a mighty tower wall; an arched doorway cut into its heavy masonry; a flight of stairs wrapping around the wall and ascending out of sight behind it; and the faint outlines of darkly prodigious trees, formed by drapery. Appia was delighted with the effect during the eventual performance and wrote as much to his friend Oskar Wälterlin: 'Torch – admirable!! Immense flame, much larger than in my drawing!' And he was particularly impressed with the bravery of the stagehands: 'They defied the police.'[82]

Isolde extinguishes the torch in the second scene, thereby destroying the barrier between herself and Tristan, as Appia wrote to Wälterlin: 'Time, space, the echoes of the natural world surrounding her, the ominous torch, everything is swept away. Nothing exists – for now, Tristan is in Isolde's arms.'[83] Reunited, Tristan and Isolde dwell at first on the terrace and as they sing their parts they are silhouetted against the mighty wall of the castle. Slowly and together, they walk down a ramp to a platform and then down another ramp as the lights dim further, arriving finally at the lowest platform where a narrow stone bench awaits the two lovers. As they tenderly embrace, the outside world is rendered irrelevant to them, 'even the figures of the actors no longer have any clear definition', as Appia emphasised to Mercier, before going on to assert that the terrace, stairs, platforms and walls should all be neutral in colour, 'between soft green and warm grey, the lines of the stones picked out discreetly.' And as far as the proud, deeply rooted trees go, they were to be represented by large reddish-brown drapes highlighted with just a touch of green to suggest their foliage.

The entire setting was presented in chiaroscuro, with the lower left portion of the set bathed in a soft, violet light that appeared only slowly – first on the upper part of the set, before gliding down gradually to illuminate the lower platform: 'Slowly the dawn begins and the eye starts to make out the general forms of the setting, cold as bone; only one spot is veiled from the dawning day and remains soft and shadowy – the bench at the foot of the terrace.' The upper right portion of the stage – where King Mark enters – remained all the while expansive, ill-defined and foreboding.

The setting and lighting for the third act were likewise pared back to their essentials; the courtyard of Kurwenal's Castle was made up of a towering wall of ashlar masonry on the left-hand side of the stage that kinked around to become the rear wall, in which there was a half-round gateway in the centre, leading to the castle keep. In this way, the two sides of the large

Tristan und Isolde, Act 2, Scene 1, 48.0 × 63.0 cm, 1923

Tristan und Isolde, Act 2, Scene 2: The Garden in Front of Isolde's Chamber, 47.0 × 60.8 cm, 1923

Tristan und Isolde, Act 3: The Courtyard of Kurwenal's Castle, 48.1 × 62.1 cm, 1923

Tristan und Isolde, Act 3: The Courtyard of Kurwenal's Castle, 48.1×62.9 cm, 1923

Giuseppe Piermarini, Teatro alla Scala, Milan, 1778, viewed from Hotel Marino.

courtyard containing the massive trunk of a tree were framed. The third side of the courtyard, open at the front to face the audience – was formed by a full-height buttressed stub wall that stopped one third of the way back towards the front of the stage, turning into a low stone wall that framed a large portal open to the sky. It was through this opening that the stage was rendered visible by a light source that Appia said was to be at the same time diffuse and animate.

Appia had in fact come up with this composition in all its essentials back in 1896, and in preparation for the Milan production he pulled out the original drawings that in the intervening decades had been published every now and then, alongside his evolving ideas about the modern *mise-en-scène*. Appia went stepwise in the way of abstraction; this is what he wrote – in the third

person – about his original setting: 'If drawn again now, the author would simplify it further and remove the branches'; which is exactly what he did.[84] That passage in *L'Œuvre d'art vivant* is also notable for the fact that it reveals Appia thinking about the properly spatial possibilities of the stage in much the same way that an architect would think about the particular topographical conditions of their site: 'The bottom-left corner is a kind of geological slice, dark and neutral in colour, which allows the actor to be in the foreground yet without necessarily being on the horizontal floor of the stage', he wrote, adding, again in the third person, that 'the author often employs this technique'.[85]

At the beginning of the third act, Tristan stands on the left-hand side of the courtyard, by the gnarled old roots of the towering tree near the 'geological slice'. It is now the afternoon, and Appia wanted the lighting to start out 'diffuse, gentle and warm with a patch of stronger light in front of Tristan'. As the sun gradually descends in the sky, the light that it casts inches along the flagstones and comes to progressively illuminate Tristan – first just his feet, then his legs, his torso and, finally, his entire person – before fading fast as day turns to evening, then night. Of his intentions for this sequence, Appia told Mercier: 'Both the setting sun and the blood of his wound are symbols of Tristan's ecstasy – the courtyard of the castle must be drenched in red. Isolde, she who will forever heal his wound, nears, and he hears her voice, but then he falls lifeless into her arms. The beautiful radiant sky darkens as the sun sinks slowly into the sea, and its dying rays envelop Tristan and Isolde in a blood-red cloak.' According to Appia himself, the setting, music and dramatic performance at La Scala were so intimately related, and so well executed, that it was 'Irresistible – never before has Act 3 reached such formidable – almost shattering – intensity'.

The 1923 performance of *Tristan und Isolde* at Teatro all Scala, Milan.

On the whole, Appia felt that the staging of *Tristan und Isolde* at La Scala was true to his intentions, writing to his friend Paul Boepple that it was 'a hundred times superior to every other production'.[86] As was to be expected at La Scala, the operatic cast was outstanding, but what was less expected was the very keen attention paid to the technical details of the production, particularly in regard to the lighting. Appia later wrote that the standard procedure in Milan was to treat the setting as a 'last-minute improvisation, in accordance with the dictates of Italian theatrical tradition, which relies only on painted scenery', meaning that it is only the 'music itself and the gestures of the performers that are given proper care and attention, without comprehending how these might be organically united with the settings that are fabricated in workshops where little heed is paid to the musical score and libretto'.[87]

In order to overcome this aesthetic rift between the singers and their settings, Mercier installed himself in the royal box at the rear of the Teatro during rehearsals, turning it into a kind of command post from where he could coordinate the whole performance down below at a distance – ringing in the changes by telephone. Thankfully, Mercier was an adept intermediary between the orderly, exacting scenographer and his collaborators who were

The 1924 performance of the *Ring* in Basel. *Das Rheingold*, Scene 2: Valhalla landscape.

less so – Appia himself labelled his own limited dealings with the technicians responsible for stage management, costumes and lighting the 'agonies of Milan'.[88] His friend and fellow scenographer Craig wrote that 'Appia was badly helped. His assistants exclaimed "wonderful" and added the aside "unpractical" without attempting to aid him with whatever poor practicality they might possess. A large theatre like Teatro alla Scala is somewhat like an old-fashioned court – intrigue is despicable in such places, and paramount.'[89] Toscanini himself tried to encourage Appia to assert himself – 'speak up, Mr Appia'[90] – but his reserved disposition and natural disinclination for confrontation made that difficult for him to do.

Tristan und Isolde premiered on 20 December 1923 and, unsurprisingly, the shy scenographer failed to attend the opening, deciding rather to remain in his room at the Hotel Marino directly opposite the Teatro on Piazza della Scala, where he had by then been staying for a fortnight. So, Mercier was left by himself to supervise the performance, which he assured Appia was 'admirable'.[91] What is most remarkable is that Appia did not in fact attend one single performance that entire season – he quite literally could not bring himself to do it. The critics in the local press had no such difficulties in making their presence felt, and for the most part, it was the austere simplicity of the settings that riled them: 'Calvin arrives at La Scala' was the title of one review.[92] While some journalists underscored Appia's subtle and poetic use of light, they mostly criticised his settings for their lack of realism and their 'cubist' simplicity. One wrote that the setting for the second act 'resembled the backrooms of some tavern out in the countryside', and went on to assert that it was 'ridiculous, shameful, pretentious, oppressive to the eye ... so much squalor, so much dark grey desolation ... the lovers' duet to the tune of reinforced concrete'. The critic was no less sparing of the setting for the third act, which he dismissed contemptuously, comparing it to the ancient Roman sewage system – the Cloaca Maxima – 'that immense intestine, that dark ditch'. Out of the courtyard 'grows a giant brown mushroom, and Tristan is forced to die under it; black on grey, grey on black, with an ugly square of light in the reddish sky'.[93] It had in fact been just such a reaction to the performance of the third act of *Tristan und Isolde* that Wagner himself had prophesied while writing his *Wort-Tondrama*: 'This Tristan is turning into something *furchtbares* (dreadful). That final act!!! I am afraid that the opera will be *verboten* – unless the whole thing is turned into a parody by poor production. That is, only a mediocre performance can save me! A perfectly good one is bound to drive people mad – I cannot imagine what else could happen.'[94]

The 1924 performance of the *Ring* in Basel. *Das Rheingold*, Scene 3: Nibelheim's underground chasms.

While some critics were indeed driven mad by Appia's staging, others were not. Regarding that same setting for the third act, one critic wrote that it 'reveals Appia to be a poet of scenery, an artist of genius and vision ... revealing the ocean only through an opening in the castle's window is sheer genius

following spread
The 1924 performance of the *Ring* in Basel. *Die Walküre*, Act 3: On the Summit of a Rocky Mountain (Brünnhilde's Rock).

Louis Molina, *Parsifal*, Act 1: Clearing in the Forest, *c* 1920.

and reveals his delicate sensitivity. Silhouetted against the sky, the lovers acquire a new grandeur, and in the almost funereal circular enclosure their distress acquires a new and tragic dimension.'[95]

Appia's success in Milan was at best equivocal, but he remained open to opportunities to realise his ideas, and in 1924 he was finally given an opportunity to stage *Der Ring des Nibelungen*. The invitation came from Oskar Wälterlin, a young director at the Theater Basel.[96] But even if the operatic work was lavish, the conditions in Basel were anything but – the theatre only had two spotlights and two carbon-arc floodlights, and, in Wälterlin's words, the stage was 'a bit cramped'.[97] Nevertheless, encouraged by Wälterlin's enthusiasm, Appia, now sixty-two, was reinvigorated and quickly produced a set of new drawings, including one that reprised the monumental stage-set he drew in 1892 – rejected by Cosima Wagner – although this time it became darker, more sharply profiled, more rhythmic. Entirely symmetrical, the configuration takes in a steadily cadenced ascent towards the Valhalla landscape, which exhibits an ambiguity of scale not present in his earlier drawings. The distant mountainous dwelling place of the gods can also be read as a primitive altar in the middle ground, surmounted by a faint half-orb that might equally be the rising sun or the lustre of the Rheingold itself.

Some of the grandeur of Appia's drawing must have been lost in its modest staging, but the production was generally well received when it premiered on 21 November 1924. Predictably, Appia was too nervous to watch, choosing to sit out the performance in his hotel room. But shortly before the final curtain, Wälterlin persuaded Appia to join him on the stage.

Most critics were positive in their reviews, but the steadfastly conservative Wagner devotees were deeply offended, going so far as to rebuke the production as 'vandalism' and 'profanity'.[98] Appia was even personally attacked in the streets,[99] and the managing director of the theatre was forced to resign. In the days immediately afterwards, Appia wrote to a friend that the *Wagnerverein* 'used the foulest means ... this was their dreadful carnival, and they indulged themselves with complete impunity ... the poor man was hauled before a committee of fat-necked millionaires, as he told me grasping my arms and assuring me of his unmistakable loyalty. Everyone at the theatre did the same, outraged over this bourgeois tyranny.'[100]

While Appia retreated to Geneva to lick his wounds, others eagerly plundered his designs – though not those he made for the *Ring*, but rather the three that he had drawn back in 1896 for each of the three acts that make up Wagner's final work, *Parsifal*. Photographs of the settings that the Swiss scenographer Louis Molina (who was also born in Geneva, though ten years after Appia) prepared for Act 1: The Sacred Forest and Act 3: The Meadow in Bloom, show just how indebted he was to his forerunner, who was never gifted the opportunity to project his settings into the third dimension. If that opportunity had ever presented itself, the settings that Molina presented as his own would almost certainly have been the result – that's how 'faithful' they were to Appia's original vision.

Even more brazen for their fidelity were the drawings made by the scenographer and architect Joseph Urban, who was born within a year of Molina, though it was across the border in Austria. Urban's early professional life in fact mirrored that of his fellow scenographer Alfred Roller: he studied at the Akademie der bildenden Künste in Vienna and then went on to design sets for the Wiener Staatsoper. But then he travelled further afield, designing sets for the Théâtre des Champs-Elysées in Paris and at Covent Garden in London before emigrating to the United States in 1911 to take up the role of art director of the Boston Opera Company. In 1914 he moved on to New York City, which is where Arnold Genthe photographed him two years later, looking smug and rotund.

Louis Molina, *Parsifal*, Act 3: The Meadow in Bloom, *c* 1920.

One of the forty-seven productions for which Urban prepared the sets at the Metropolitan Opera was the 1920 staging of *Parsifal*. Rather than turning to Wagner's libretto for instruction or inspiration, Urban simply turned to Appia's 1896 drawings, and copied them. He must have thought nobody would ever find out – a justified presumption since Appia was little known, even back in the Old World, let alone in the New. Urban's drawing for Act 1: The Sacred Forest is practically identical to Appia's, except that the tree-columns have now become more obviously Gothic, and his drawing for Act 2: The Dungeon of Klingsor similarly emulates the original.

Following the agonies of Milan and the debacle of Basel, Appia himself turned his mind and hand once again to *Parsifal*, but unlike Molina and Urban, the settings he designed were thought afresh; they bear no resemblance to the ones that he had made thirty years prior, and in fact, although there are eight of them, they are all iterations of the one scene in Wagner's *Bühnenweihfestspiel* in which the sorcerer Klingsor's *Zauberschloß* (Enchanted Castle) – 'a dwelling place of abysmal darkness' according to Appia – collapses and the *Zaubergarten* (Enchanted Garden) rises up to take its place. The composition which Appia came up with, and drew again and again, concerns exactly that moment of transformation – the castle and garden are weighted equally. The castle occupies the top right-hand quarter of the page, and the wild vegetation that is rooted in the inclined ground plane off the garden extends over the left-hand side of the drawing and reaches across towards the castle. In three of the line drawings, it is the *Zauberschloß* that Appia focuses upon, in two of them he is concerned with the *Zaubergarten*, and in another two of them the castle and the garden are both given equal attention. Finally,

Das Rheingold, Scene 2: Valhalla Landscape, 47.2×54.7 cm, 1924

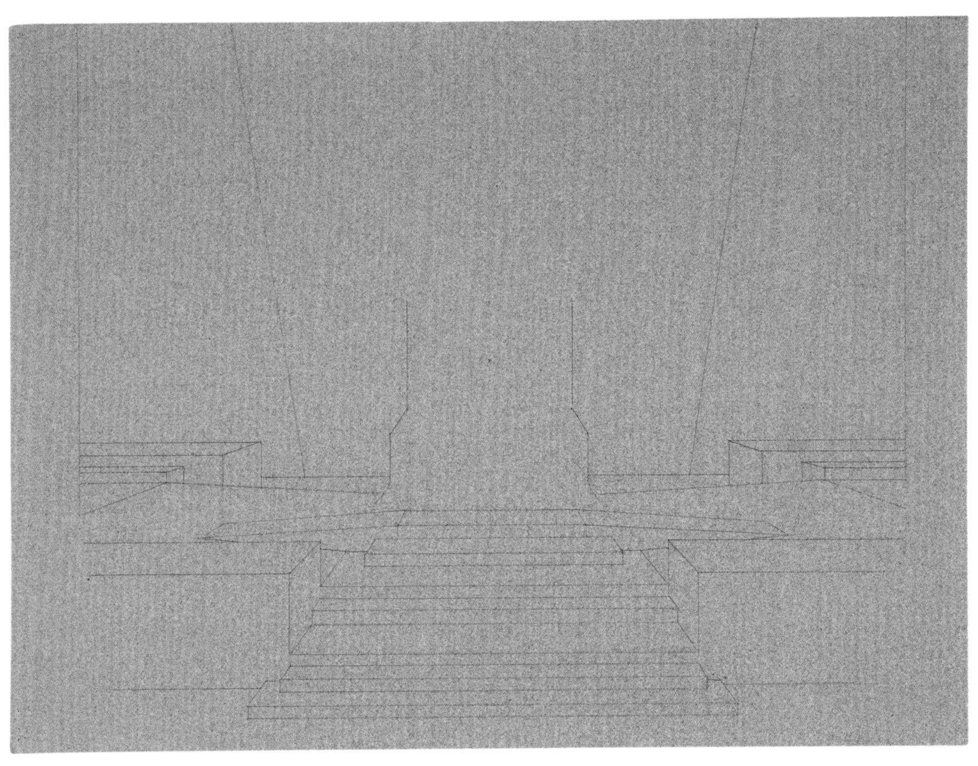

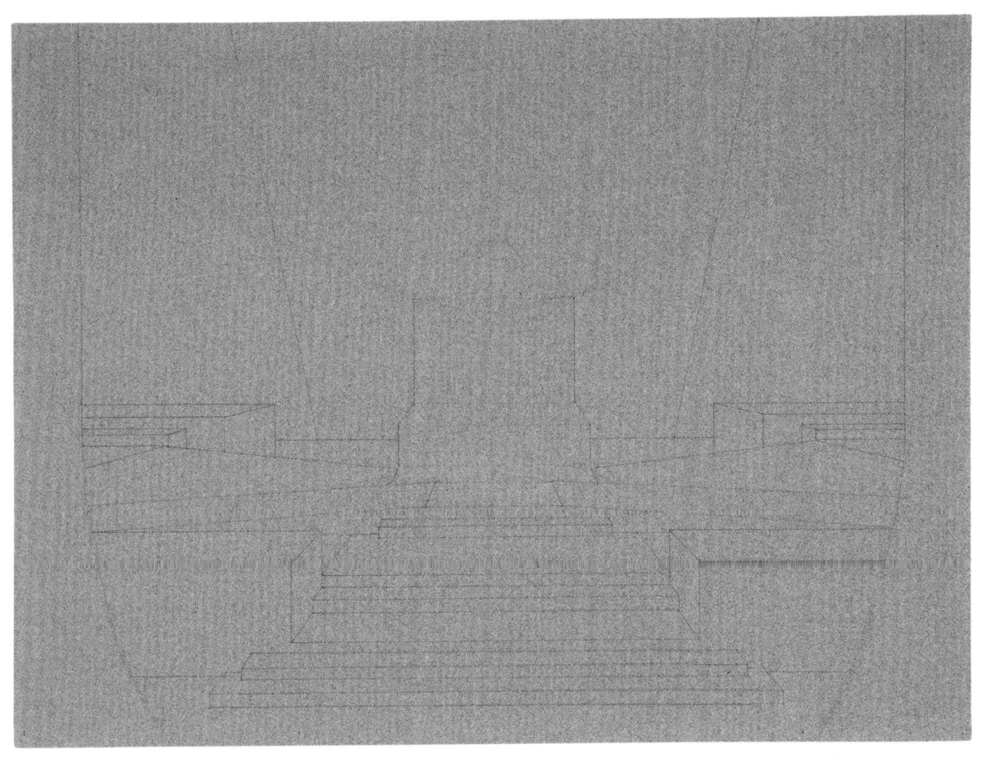

Das Rheingold, Scene 2: Valhalla Landscape, 48.1×62.8 cm and 47.9×63.0 cm, 1924

following spreads *Das Rheingold*: Scene 2: Valhalla Landscape, 46.6×62.0 cm, 1923;
Die Walküre, Act 1: Inside Hunding's House, 52.0×62.2 cm, 1924

Rheingold – Das Leuchten des Goldes. – I Scene. – (SKi

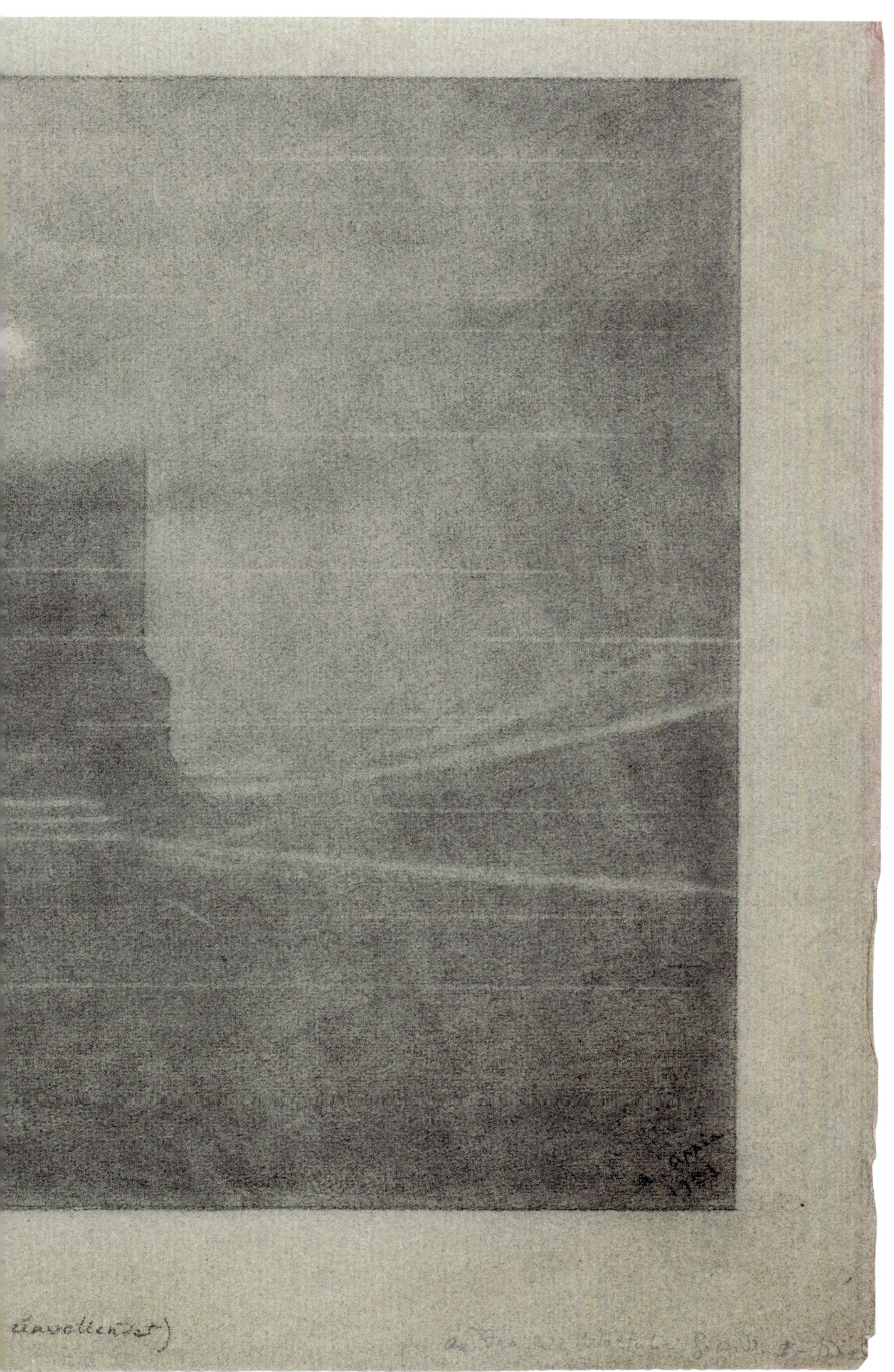

(Basel 1924). #15a

Walküre I, Ad. Appia 1924

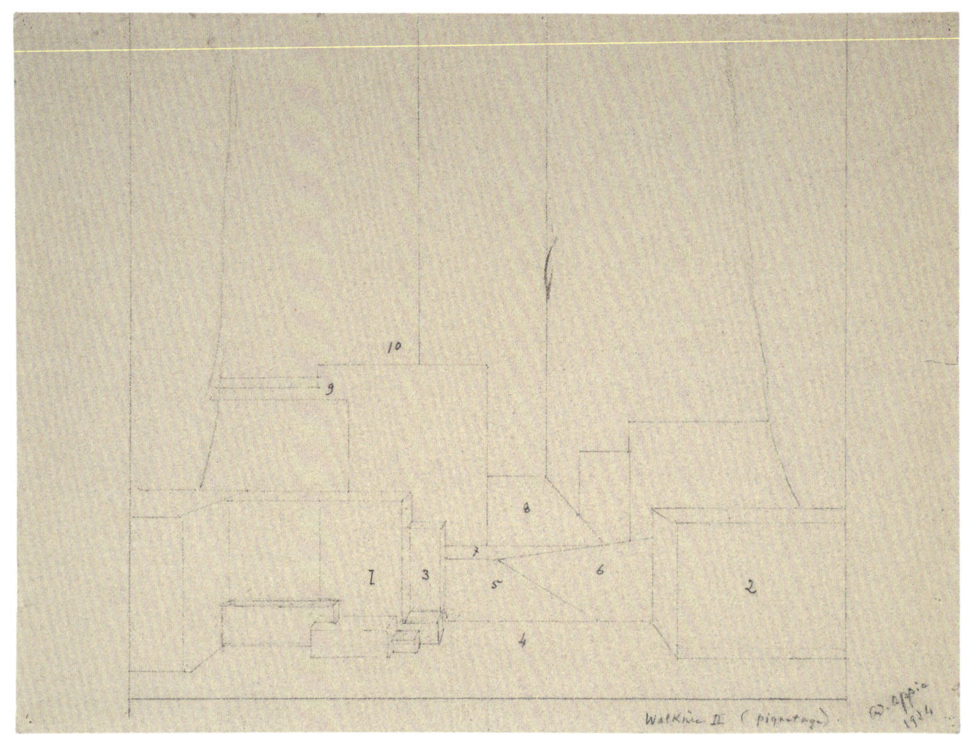

Die Walküre, Act 2: Wild Rocky Mountains, 48.0×63.0 cm; *Götterdämmerung*, Acts 1/2: Gunther's Royal Hall, 48.1×63.1 cm, 1924

Götterdämmerung, Acts 1/2: Gunther's Royal Hall, 48.1×63.0 cm, 1924

Götterdämmerung, Acts 1/2: Gunther's Royal Hall, 48.1×63.2 cm, 1924

Götterdämmerung, Acts 1/2: Gunther's Royal Hall, 47.4×62.7 cm, 1924

Appia made one fully rendered drawing of the scene that concludes with Parsifal 'gazing down into the garden in astonishment'.[101]

The chaste redeemer Parsifal fathered Lohengrin – 'However did he do it?' wondered Friedrich Nietzsche, cheekily[102] – and it was to the most Romantic of Wagner's operas that Appia turned for his final encounter with the *Meister*. *Lohengrin* would at first seem an unusual choice, given that its performance has always veered toward overt sentimentality. That is, until one reads what Appia had in mind for it: 'Of all of Wagner's works, *Lohengrin* is the only one that *must* be disrobed of its Romantic garb; the *mise-en-scène* must strive towards ultimate simplification, which will result in a dramatic-musical performance of unique intensity.'[103] And for Appia, it was not only the scenography for *Lohengrin* that needed to be updated, the musical performance did too: 'Unfortunately, the way that the music has traditionally

Joseph Urban, *Parsifal*, Act 1: Clearing in the Forest, Metropolitan Opera, New York, 1920.

been performed has accustomed our ears to an overflow of sentimentality. Therefore, it is in fact the musical interpretation that needs to be modified – it must become virile.'

Appia wrote out detailed staging notes, and he also made drawings for all three acts of the opera in 1926, beginning with the opening scene of the first act, which is set in a forest. He in fact made two versions of this drawing – one of them merely outlines the forms on the stage, whereas the other is fully rendered. He also made two other drawings for act one, but these are sequential. The first concerns the moment in the second scene when Lohengrin – a knight in shining armour – is first spotted in the distance, coming up the river in a boat being drawn by a swan. '*Seht, seht! Welch ein seltsam Wunder!*' (Behold! Behold! What strange and wondrous thing is this?) announce the disbelieving men in the scene all at once. And in the second drawing, Lohengrin has almost arrived, though his wondrous swan-drawn boat remains out of sight of the audience. *'Ein Wunder! Ein Wunder! Ein Wunder ist gekommen, ein unerhörtes, nie gesehenes Wunder!'* (A miracle! A miracle! A miracle has occurred, a miracle never before seen or heard!). Convention dictated that at this point in the performance the giant swan would sail into full view of the audience; its arrival was a highlight, one that was sacrosanct for traditional Wagnerites. But for Appia, the Romanticism of *Lohengrin* was sufficiently expressed in the musical score and the libretto, and there was no need for it to be reinforced in the performance. 'This holds especially true for the swan, which Wagner described with such insistent precision that to present it to the eyes would be a serious error, both from a dramatic point of view *and* an aesthetic point of view!'

Joseph Urban, *Parsifal*, Act 2: Klingsor's Dungeon, Metropolitan Opera, New York, 1920.

What Appia proposed to do instead of *showing* the swan was to announce Lohengrin's arrival via a 'miraculous light, one that is very white, silver even'.

This light would at first appear dimly, but would gradually intensify, becoming brightest at the moment when Lohengrin himself arrives on stage. 'When Lohengrin strides down from his barque and mingles with the characters, his unique light decreases little by little, and fades away.' Even Appia's strongest supporters were in two minds about this idea. One of them wrote: 'Appia's endeavours pointed the way, here and there, it is true, he went too far in his otherwise altogether justifiable desire to avoid all that was superfluous. When he proposed to eliminate even the swan in a stage setting for Wagner's "Lohengrin" he affected the inner "Romantic" life of the action, cutting it to the heart.'[104] It was not only the swan that Appia wanted to do away with: 'It goes without saying that the backdrop will be perfectly plain and, above all, will not represent any kind of landscape! The slightest indication would render the entire *mise-en-scène* void.' And rather than populating the stage with naturalistic forms, he proposed ranks of curtains that would frame

top to bottom, left to right *Parsifal*, Act 2: Klingsor's Enchanted Garden, 48.1×62.5 cm, 50.0×69.2 cm, 52.0×63.5 cm, 50.2×65.1 cm, 48.0×62.2 cm, and 47.3×63.3 cm, 1922

Parsifal, Act 2: Klingsor's Enchanted Garden, 48.2×63.2 cm, 1922

Lohengrin, Act 2, Scene 1: Opening, 48.0×63.1 cm, 1926

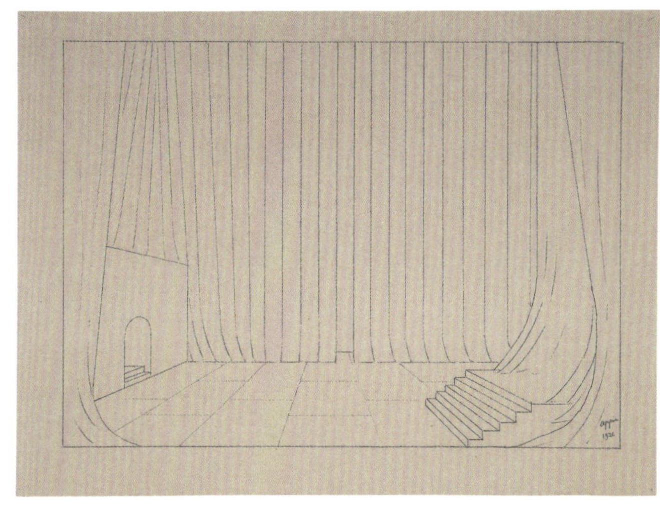

top to bottom, left to right *Lohengrin*, Act 1, Opening, 48.1×64.7 cm; Act 2, Scene 1: Opening, 48.0×63.1 cm; Act 1, Scene 1: The Arrival of Lohengrin 'Behold! Behold!', 48.1×63.3 cm; Act 2, Scene 3: Close: 'Make way for Elsa, our lady!', 48.1×63.0 cm; Act 1, Scene 1: 'A miracle! A miracle has happened', 48.3×63.3 cm; Act 3, Scene 1: Elsa's Bridal Chamber, 48.0×63.1 cm, 1926

spaces, and that 'on occasion will be moved by the performers themselves, and at other times – such as when Lohengrin appears – they will change formation invisibly. It is a matter of harmonising these two different kinds of movement – light will take care of the rest.'

The setting for the second act is the fortress at Antwerp, with the banqueting hall in the background, the women's quarters downstage left and the minster on the right. It is night, and Appia wrote that at the opening of the first scene, 'the curtains are to be very slightly ajar in the centre of the stage, letting in just a sliver of light that indicates the nocturnal celebration taking place inside.' And in regard to the setting itself, he wrote that the solid wall on the left of the stage and also the door in the centre of it (below the balcony) 'are not to be ornamented in any way at all – the impression they should give is one of solidity'. In his drawing – again the forms are only outlined, not rendered – Appia drew a couple of steps within the depth of the unadorned doorway; these are the ones that Elsa descends in order to make her entrance. The façade of the fortress is similarly unadorned; all it does is delimit the back of the stage, according to Appia. 'It is only the large door in the centre of the façade that has any sculptural element at all – its frame projects forward a little. No windows!' The arrangement of the curtains in this scene is much simpler than for those in the first act; except for the drapes at the rear of the balcony on the left, 'which the pages open themselves quite visibly, all the other curtains open invisibly, softly and musically. Again, the lighting takes care of the rest.'

Elsa appears on the balcony at the opening of the second scene, dressed all in white and 'the dim illumination increases gently but stops long before it becomes the absurd moonbeam that is still thought to be obligatory', wrote Appia. 'Ye heavens, so oft filled with my sad laments, now I must gratefully tell you of the happiness that is mine!' announces Elsa, whose gaiety is soon tempered by Ortrud, sowing seeds of doubt in her mind: 'Don't let him deceive you, that man for whom you have no name! Can you be sure he'll never leave you and disappear the way he came?' The two of them exit through the small door to the women's quarters, and maidservants close that door behind them.

It is the break of dawn when the third scene opens. 'Make way for Elsa, our lady! She is going in faith to the minster', the pages cry out. Our lady appears amongst the throng in a sumptuous wedding dress, and according to Appia, it is at this moment in the performance that 'the light attains its greatest intensity ... It would be lovely if it fell particularly brightly on Elsa as she reveals herself in front of the castle and descends the stairs.' The famous *Brautlied* (bridal song) follows, one that goes on for too long as far as Appia is concerned. However, 'it is very likely too well known for some of it to be left out without creating a scandal. And yet, that would be highly desirable! However, it might be possible to cut some bars from the reprise of the chorus; going from the fourth bar: "*bleibet zurück* (remain behind)" to the last bar: "*eint euch in treue* (join you in faith)". Either that or to "*Wo euch der Segen der Liebe bewahr* (where the blessing of love shall preserve you)!" a few lines earlier; this would usefully reduce by a good half this disagreeable reprise and would suffice to motivate Lohengrin's first lines in the following scene'. This following scene takes place in Elsa's bridal chamber and, according to Appia, it is important that the décor clearly conveys the fact that it is an intimate indoor setting, contrasting with the two preceding scenes that take place outdoors. 'The corner of the room on the right-hand side of the stage will be sufficient to give some solidity to the room that is otherwise framed by curtains', he wrote, showing what he meant in the drawing which he made for this final act and that is the final drawing of the set of eight that he made for *Lohengrin*. There is a window in Elsa's bridal chamber, which Appia noted should have a reveal 'deep enough to indicate the thickness of the wall, and to prevent the exterior landscape from being seen', and should be 'placed at the height which best suits Lohengrin as he sings "*Atmest du nicht mit mir die süssen Düfte?*" (Come, won't you share with me the night's sweet perfumes?), which is his attempt to divert Elsa from her entreaty to him to reveal his name now that they are alone together. Of the lighting of the scene, Appia wrote that the 'light emanating from the window should be soft – white or blue – in any case, different from the ambient light, which should be *warm* and diffuse'. Through that window, Elsa – though not the audience – sees the miraculous swan approach once more: 'Ah, no! Look there – the swan! The swan! He's gliding here across the silent water ... You've summoned him, he's coming to the shore!'[105]

According to Appia, the setting for the scene that follows is, in fact, the same as the first one, except that the rear curtains are to be drawn wide open, and also the lighting will be different: 'The dawn light emanates from above, and the backdrop (without landscape) is at first gently tinged in pink, but then quickly takes on the general colour of the outdoors.' All the while, 'during the beautiful prayer of Lohengrin', wrote Appia, 'it will be desirable for the miraculous light to fall brilliantly on him – and only on him'. Excitedly, the men and women exclaim as one: 'The swan! The swan! Look there, it has returned!' Lohengrin kisses Elsa goodbye: 'Farewell! Farewell! Farewell! My lovely wife!'[106] He then strides down to the riverbank and leaps into the barque which sails away, drawn now by a dove rather than the swan, which has returned to its human form – Gottfried, Elsa's brother, who will become the king and who now stands at her side. Elsa sinks lifeless to the ground, in Gottfried's arms. By now, Lohengrin has almost glided out of sight, and with him, according to Appia, 'the miraculous light dims and the curtain falls when the light has become so diminished and diffuse that it is no longer possible to distinguish the characters one from the other'.

With the departure of Lohengrin, Appia was finished with Wagner, though not with the medieval world that had so inspired the *Meister*; he turned his mind to the tragedies of the greatest playwright of all – William Shakespeare[107] – who wrote at a time of linguistic ferment, and frequently imported Latinisms into English, coining words such as *abstemious* and *addiction*, both relevant to Appia, the first because he wasn't, and the second because he was susceptible to it (alcohol and laudanum). It was to Shakespeare that Appia's thoughts should have turned long ago, according to Cosima Wagner, who many years before wrote the following to Appia's friend Hermann Graf Keyserling in an attempt to rid Bayreuth of the scenographer forever: 'I can think of a nice task for Herr Appia: scenography for Shakespeare. We know nothing of what he, the greatest of poets, intended in regard to the performance of his works; the incessant change of scenes presents a real problem to be solved – Lear in the heath, Macbeth with the witches – and so much

Appia, *Hamlet*, Act 1, Scene 5: A More Remote Part of the Platform, 1922.

else besides; now *that* offers the opportunity for free development by the great *Bühnengenie* (genius scenographer)!' She reminded Keyserling that 'just as the *Schöpfer* of our *Kunst* (namely her husband, Richard) constructed the stage at Bayreuth, he also definitively determined its scenography', and she signed off with the assertion that 'Shakespeare did not'.[108]

It was another determined female character – Jessica Davis Van Wyck – who ultimately convinced Appia to turn his attention to Shakespeare. The young American had taken a course on eurhythmics with Jaques-Dalcroze in Geneva and got it into her mind that not only would she like to meet Appia, but she would like to learn from him; in her own words, she 'begged

Mr Jaques-Dalcroze' to arrange for her to meet with Appia, in the hope that she might study with him. The inventor of eurhythmics said that he would 'try to do this, although he warned that Appia disliked intensely meeting strangers and that it was practically certain that he would refuse to teach anyone'.[109] Jaques-Dalcroze seemed well justified in his appraisal of the situation, given what Appia himself had written in a letter to his friend Edward Gordon Craig: 'My character and circumstances do not allow me so *active* a life as my artistic capabilities might seem to require. I only work well *alone*. That is a fate to which I have grown accustomed.'[110]

And yet, against all odds, Appia agreed. As Van Wyck later recalled in a brief article, 'Working with Appia', that she published in *Theatre Arts Monthly*, when she first met the scenographer, she was 'surprised at the extreme simplicity of this legendary character', describing him as a 'man about sixty years old, robust in stature and heavily bearded, with beetling black eyebrows over eyes that shone with kindness and spiritual vitality'. The outcome of that first meeting was that 'Mr Appia consented to accept a pupil, who for her part undertook to ask enough questions to keep the lessons going'.[111] Van Wyck wrote an account of these lessons that ultimately evolved into a collaboration in another brief, yet illuminating article entitled 'Designing Hamlet with Appia', for the fact that the 'Mad Prince of Denmark' had attracted most of their attention in the year that they spent working together, mostly via written

Appia, *Hamlet*, Act 3, Scene 1: A Room in the Castle, 1922.

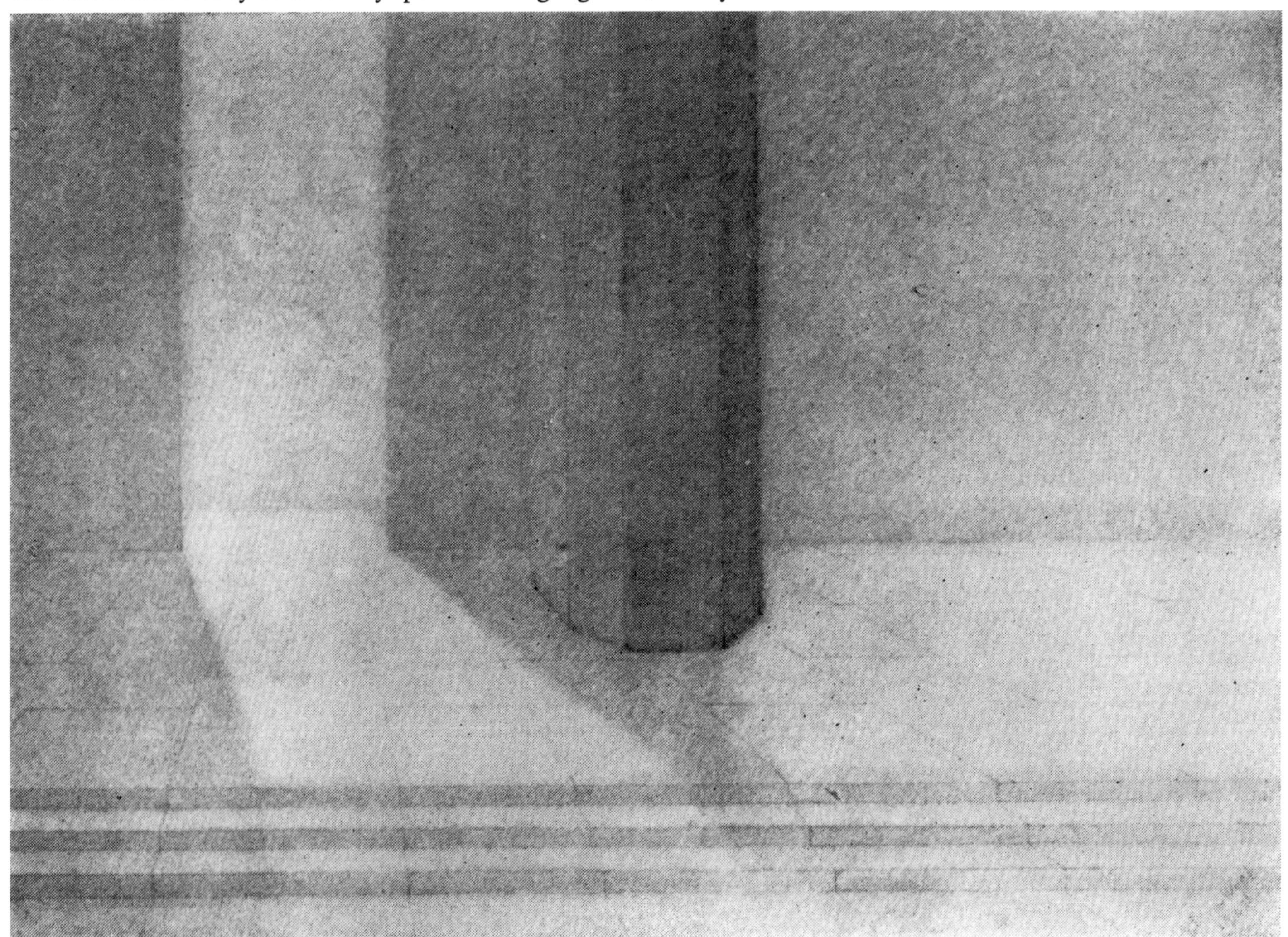

correspondence – Van Wyck was living in Florence, Appia in Geneva – but occasionally, they met to discuss their ideas in person.[112]

Just why it was to the tragedy of *Hamlet* that the pair devoted most of their shared endeavour is unknown, though one wonders whether Appia saw something of himself in the person of the prince – 'prototype of the enigmatic, sensitive and thoughtful young man, damaged by a corrupt society yet stimulated by everyone around him'.[113] There is also so very much material to work with, since *Hamlet* is Shakespeare's longest play – to speak every line of the full text, even at a gallop, takes about four hours.

The first scene in the play that Appia and Van Wyck prepared a setting for is Act 1, Scene 5: A More Remote Part of the Platform, which according to

Appia, *Hamlet*, Act 3, Scene 2: A Hall in the Castle, 1922.

Appia in the article 'Six Designs for Hamlet' must be a 'space both large and majestic', since this kind of meeting cannot take place in a 'hidden, mean corner'.[114] The meeting is between Prince Hamlet and the ghost of his recently deceased father King Hamlet, who in Appia's notes step out onto the stage together from behind a mighty wall on the right-hand side of the setting. 'I am thy father's spirit, doomed for a certain time to walk the night, and for the day confined to fast in fires, till the foul crimes done in my days of nature are burnt and purged away', announces the ghost, who then entreats his son to revenge his 'foul and most unnatural murder', which Hamlet swears to do, 'with wings as swift as meditation or the thoughts of love'.[115] In Appia's

notes, when the king's ghost says, 'adieu, adieu, adieu, remember me' and exits the scene, he does so by retiring up the stairs to the left that rise to a platform extending beyond view and that Appia describes as 'a parapet that dominates the precipice'. Hamlet does not follow him, but rather 'takes only one unconscious step, then stops, discouraged'. Of this scene as a whole, Appia writes that the movement 'is so slow as to be almost imperceptible' and the level of the stage lighting must 'illuminate perfectly the features of the two actors'. He further notes that the drawing accompanying his text depicts the illumination of the scene right at the end, when Hamlet's friend Horatio and the guard Marcellus arrive.[116] The drawing for this scene published in 'Six Designs for Hamlet' is fully rendered – though it is reproduced in greyscale

– and delivers the atmosphere that Appia intended. But the current whereabouts of that drawing, along with the other five that go along with it, is unknown. Having apparently vanished soon after publication, all six drawings in fact possess a spectral presence akin to that of the ghost of King Hamlet – they are in the world, but not entirely, disembodied as they are, and stripped of vital colour.

Act 3, Scene 1: A Room in the Castle is dominated by a large octangular pillar that has a double symbolism: 'Hamlet's body versus the pillar is Hamlet's soul versus the whips and scorns of time', Appia tells us, but at the same time 'by its support and towering protection, this pillar becomes an actor in the play, a kind of grim friend that lends strength to Hamlet'.[117] The light – which registers of course only in the published version of the drawing, not in the outline drawing that exists in the archive – 'comes from the left almost entirely, and is much stronger in the corridor. It is thrown forward through the opening of the curtains, making a path of light so that anyone standing in the opening casts a long shadow diagonally across the floor.'[118] Hamlet once again enters at the right, though this time singly, talking to himself. He says: 'To be, or not to be – that is the question; whether it is nobler in the mind to suffer the slings and arrows of outrageous fortune or to take arms against a sea of troubles and by opposing end them.'[119] For Appia, the pillar is a bulwark against Hamlet's 'sea of troubles'.[120]

The pillar reappears in the next scene in Act 3 – A Hall in the Castle, a hall that should be 'luxuriously laden with rugs, cushions and so forth, the colours rich and warm'.[121] To the left of the pillar, just in front of a large curtain that obscures the rear of that side of the stage, stands the dais with three royal chairs. It is the play-within-a-play scene that reveals Polonius to be King Hamlet's murderer; he cannot bear for the play to continue after the King in the play is killed via poison poured into his ear – 'Give o'er the play', 'lights, lights, lights!' he shouts.[122] Before the beginning of the 'dumb show' that Polonius cuts short, according to Appia, 'the lights in the proscenium should be dimmed slowly to the point of extinction'. In this way, the setting for the play will be seen in silhouette, while the 'dais will remain in the glare of fullest light'. This is to emphasise the all-important fact that actually the real play is the face of Polonius, which is so for Hamlet, says Appia, and 'so it should be for us, because we live this drama, only in so far as we are able to identify ourselves with Hamlet'. The players who enter from the left on the second level of the stage are to perform their play immediately above the steps, where the couch is indicated in the sketch, so that the audience, along with Hamlet, can 'watch the King watch the play'. The players are mere shadowy figures seen in profile; 'the King is the cynosure of all eyes'.[123]

Fortinbras, the King of Norway, arrives with his army in Act 4, Scene 4: A Plain in Denmark, a setting that Appia describes as 'sad but positive'. The soldiers descend the inclined plane between the border stones, and when the Norwegian King exhorts his captain to go – 'from me greet the Danish King. Tell him that by his licence Fortinbras craves the conveyance of a promised march over his kingdom' – the captain leaps over the edge of the ramp and comes forward. Appia notes that it is important that the border stones are sturdy elements, since they play an expressive role, and he describes the lighting of the scene as 'uniform, but definitely "open-air"'. It is a grey day, as in the

Appia, *Hamlet*, Act 4, Scene 4: A Plain in Denmark, 1922.

churchyard scene'. Appia concludes his brief notes on this scene with a very rare personal statement: 'I am particularly fond of this setting.'[124]

It is the churchyard scene in Act 5, Scene 1 that Appia turned to next, a scene that takes place under a 'sky of uniform grey; little light, as on an autumn day',[125] a setting that he describes as 'sad and a little mean' in keeping with what the priest says to Laertes, which is that the burial of his sister Ophelia, who died in doubtful circumstances, will be without ceremony: 'No more be done. We should profane the service of the dead to sing a requiem and such rest to her as to peace-departed souls.' To which Laertes responds, incensed: 'Lay her i'th' earth, and from her fair and unpolluted flesh may

violets spring! I tell thee, churlish priest, a ministering angel shall my sister be when thou liest howling.'[126] It is only then that Hamlet discovers that the burial which is taking place is that of Ophelia, and both he and Laertes leap into her grave, arguing and fighting until the King shouts, 'Pluck them asunder'. 'I loved Ophelia', announces Hamlet, 'Forty thousand brothers could not with all their quantity of love make up my sum.'[127]

The final *Hamlet* scene that Appia prepared notes and a drawing for is the one that concludes the play in most dramatic fashion, Act 5, Scene 2: A Hall in the Castle. Hamlet and Laertes agree to a duel, a final battle that Hamlet welcomes as his destiny whether he triumphs or not: 'There is special providence in the fall of a sparrow. If it be now, 'tis not to come. If it be not to come, it will be now. If it be not now, yet it will come. The readiness is all.'[128] Attendants enter with foils, daggers and gauntlets, followed by the King and Queen, and Laertes. One of the foils has a poisoned tip, and poisoned too is the wine that the King has set before him; wine that the Queen sups of first, unaware. 'It is the poisoned cup. It is too late', says the King, aside. Hamlet and Laertes trade thrusts of their blades, the former taunting the latter: 'Laertes. You do but dally. I pray you, pass with your best violence.'[129] In scuffling, they change rapiers and are both wounded with the weapon that only Laertes knows was poisoned: 'I am justly killed with mine own treachery', he says. And it is then that the dying Queen realises she has been poisoned and Hamlet is told by

Appia, *Hamlet*, Act 5, Scene 1: A Churchyard, 1922.

Laertes that he is too: 'Hamlet, thou art slain. No medicine in the world can do thee good.'[130] Realising now that the point of his rapier is 'envenomed', he stabs the King, and likewise forces him to drink the poisoned wine, after which the King dies, as does Laertes. Knowing now that his time too has come, Hamlet exhorts his loyal friend Horatio not to join with him in death, but rather 'to tell my story' to Fortinbras, whom they hear approaching in the distance with his army. 'The rest is silence' are Hamlet's famous final words, words that according to Appia 'contain potentially all that is to be expressed in the final scene. That silence must contain infinity!' The scene is to be illuminated by a 'pure, limpid, all-pervading light' that is 'not of the sun, or of the moon, but rather an idealised light, tinged with gold'.[131]

following spread
Appia, *Hamlet*, Act 5, Scene 2: A Hall in the Castle, 1922.

When Fortinbras arrives, 'a great sweep of open sky' suddenly flashes and spreads over the full width of the stage. The light in the foreground becomes dimmer and dimmer as Hamlet's lifeless body is borne by Fortinbras' soldiers on a shield up to the high platform, where he is left lying in profile to the audience. Appia writes that four torches have been placed in great iron rings that are attached below the four corners of the platform, 'so as not to interfere with its outline'. These torches that rise far above the level of the platform are lit, and 'Hamlet lies alone, high against the immense but friendly sky. The curtains come together very slowly, and the music ends when they have closed.'[132]

Now back working solo again – and feverishly so – Appia wrote in a letter to a friend that 'Macbeth has a hold on me, and I on him – exciting. I have an idea, and all that remains is to develop it.'[133] But unfortunately – at least based on what he left behind – three outline drawings and a few fragmentary notes – Appia failed to follow the tragedy of Macbeth through to the end. The first sparse drawing is for the scene with the three witches that opens the play. The First Witch, who Appia has entering from the left to join the other two who are already on the stage, asks: 'When shall we three meet again? In thunder, lightning, or in rain?' The Second Witch responds: 'When the hurly-burly's done, when the battle's lost and won.' And the third rounds out the opening lines: 'That will be ere the set of sun.'[134] And regarding the other two drawings, which are both castle settings, he wrote: 'The staircase is seen from the side, with a supporting wall or curtain on the other side. So, there is a lot of depth on the left-hand side of the stage. Perhaps a pillar should be embedded within it? A curtain closes off the rear of the stage.'[135] It is not clear which castles they are. One of them might be Inverness – Macbeth's castle, where he murders King Duncan – and the other Dunsinane Castle – where Macbeth himself is killed and beheaded by Macduff in the gruesome act that concludes the play.

At the same time that he was concerning himself with Shakespeare's great tragedies, Appia also prepared settings for dramatic works written closer to his own time, such as the Austrian dramatist Franz Grillparzer's mid-nineteenth-century retelling of the Greek myth of Hero and Leander, which he composed as a five-act tragedy and gave the name *Des Meeres und der Liebe Wellen* (The Waves of Sea and Love).[136] Hero was a priestess of Aphrodite – goddess of love, beauty, pleasure and passion – and she lived in a coastal tower on the European side of the Hellespont. Leander was a love-struck youth who lived on the other side; every night of one long warm summer he would swim across the strait just to be with her, piloted by the flickering light of a lamp that Hero held aloft for him. His carnal entreaty was that Aphrodite would scorn the worship of a virgin, and Hero consented. But on one stormy night late in that golden summer, the waves hurled Leander into the sea, and since the wind off the ocean extinguished Hero's lamp at that same time, Leander was set aimlessly adrift, and drowned. Aghast at the sight of her lover's lifeless body drifting towards the sandy shore, Hero flung herself over the edge of the tower to be reunited with him once and for all – in death. Appia made two drawings for *Des Meeres und der Liebe Wellen*, both very similar and at first sight unexceptional: mere outlines of a single sparse setting drawn in pencil on dark olive-coloured paper. The view is of three sides of a rectangular room that appears to have no spatial hierarchy; each side of the room is lined with steps that serve to focus attention on the patch of floor that they envelop. There is no distinction between stage and auditorium, which by extension means no distinction between actors and audience. This setting is, in fact, the most emphatic embodiment of an idea that Appia had been turning around in his mind for the better part of a decade – that of a 'theatre without spectators'. For example, in the preface that Appia wrote in October 1918 for the English edition of *Die Musik und die Inscenierung*,[137] he advocated for a 'free, vast, transformable space' in which the traditional breach between spectators and actors would be abolished; 'dramatic art will flourish – *with or without spectators*'.[138] And in a letter that he wrote to Craig on 30 November that same year, Appia specifically evoked *Des Meeres und der Liebe Wellen*: 'Two scenes only – the Sea as a friend; the Sea as an enemy, or said in another way – the friendly waves; the hostile waves. Virtually no words are to be spoken, and the music is to be very grand and simple (not symphonic). That is, there is to be almost nothing at all except the presence of human bodies. There is only a single setting; the public intermingles in everything.'[139] Generally counted among the two or three greatest works by Grillparzer, *Des Meeres und der Liebe Wellen* has been said to demonstrate 'a mastery of dramatic technique' that 'combines a ripeness of poetic expression with an insight into motive which suggests the modern psychological drama of (Henrik) Ibsen'.[140]

In his book *The Quintessence of Ibsenism*, George Bernard Shaw wrote of the great Norwegian playwright that 'he could see plainly the effect of Idealism as a social force on people quite unlike himself: that is to say, on everyday people in everyday life – on shipbuilders, bank managers, parsons, and doctors, as well as on saints, romantic adventurers, and emperors'.[141] Over time, Ibsen became less and less interested in writing 'tragedy for the sake of tears, or comedy for the sake of laughter', which meant that the critics 'soon declared that he had ceased to be an artist, but he, having something else to do with his talent than to fulfil critics' definitions, took no notice of them'.[142]

It was to one of Ibsen's psychological dramas that Appia turned next – *Lille Eyolf* (Little Eyolf) – which tells the story of the middle-class Allmers family, living on a property bordering the fjord outside Kristiania in Norway. At the outset of the play, the father of the family, Alfred, has just returned home after a trip into the sublime mountains that rise above the deep blue waters of the fjord, during which time he cleared his mind and resolved to focus on the care of his nine-year-old son Eyolf, rather than continuing to devote himself to the writing of his book *Human Responsibility*.

This is how Ibsen described the setting for the first act: 'A pretty and richly decorated garden-room, full of furniture, flowers, and plants. At the back, open glass doors, leading out to a veranda. An extensive view over the fjord. In the distance, wooded hillsides. A door in each of the side walls, the one on the right a folding door, placed far back. In front on the right, a sofa, with cushions and rugs. Besides the sofa, a small table, and chairs. In front, on the left, a larger table, with armchairs around it. On the table stands an open handbag. It is an early summer morning, with warm sunshine.'[143]

Appia made a drawing for this first setting and for the other two as well. He also wrote down his ideas for the *mise-en-scène* in a slim little blue notebook with twenty-four pages numbered 1–11 from the second sheet onwards – he only counted the right-hand pages. As usual, Appia wrote out his

following spread
King Lear, Acts 1 and 2, 48.1×63.2 cm, 1926.

appia
1926

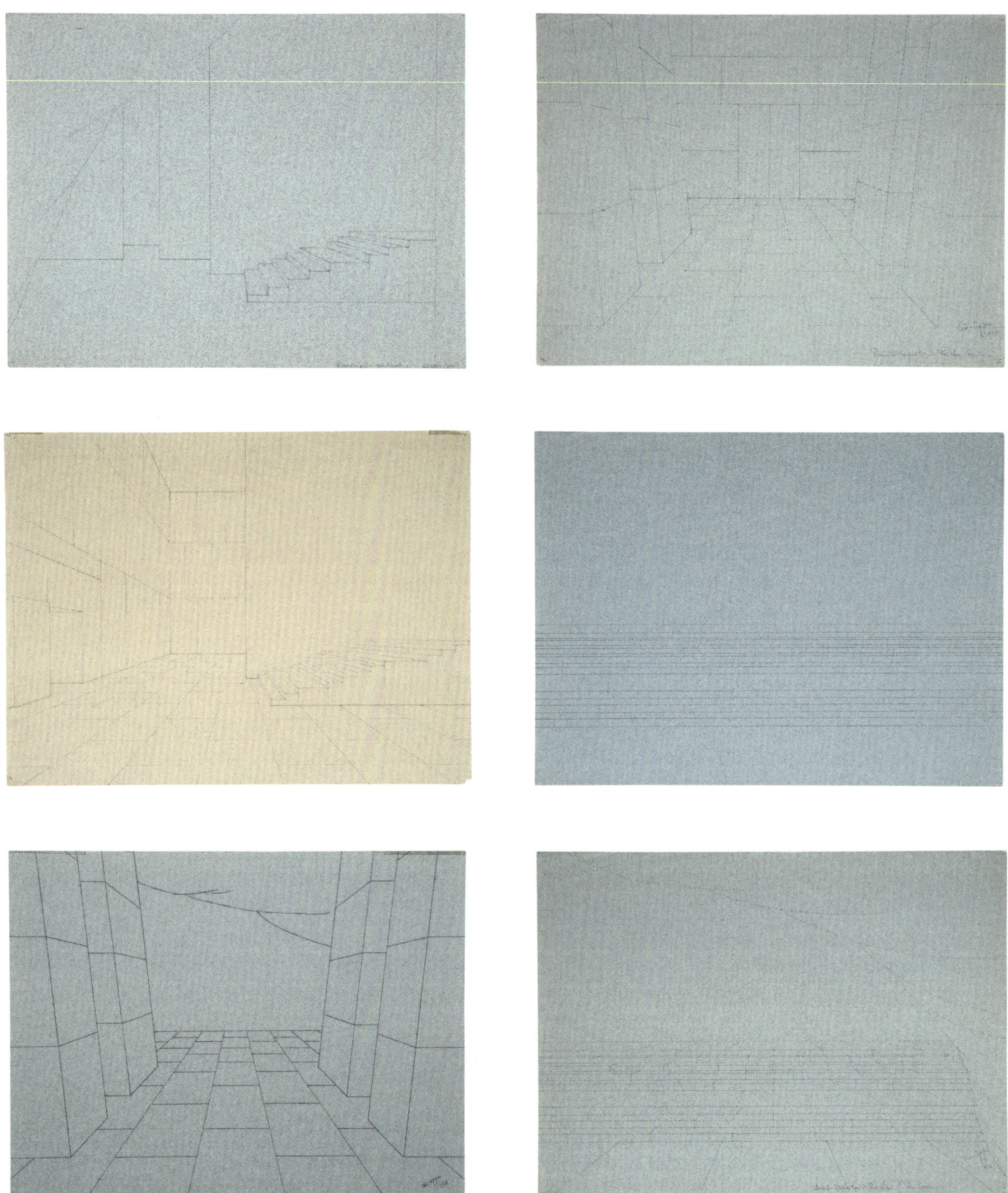

left column, top and centre *Macbeth*, 48.2×63.1 cm and 48.1×63.1 cm, 1926

top to bottom, left to right *King Lear*, Act 1: Scenes 3, 4 and 5; Act 2: Scenes 1, 2 and 4, 48.1×63.0 cm; Act 1, Basic Configuration, 48.5×64.7 cm; Basic Configuration of the Steps, 48.2×63.2 cm; Act 3, Scene 2, 48.5×64.9 cm, 1926

top to bottom, left to right *King Lear*, Act 3, Scene 1, 48.3×63.2 cm; Act 4, Scene 7, 48.1×63.1 cm; Act 3, Scene 7, 48.2×63.2 cm; Act 4, Scene 6, 48.2×63.3 cm; Act 4, Scene 7, 48.1×63.1 cm; Act 5, Basic Configuration, 48.2×63.2 cm, 1926

following spread *King Lear*, Act 3, Scene 2, 48.1×63.1 cm, 1926

Héro et Léandre (The Waves and the Sea of Love), 63.0×48.1 cm, 1922.

manuscript in pencil, bestowing upon it the title 'Stage direction / for Le Petit Eyolf / (Ibsen) / A Appia'.[144] No date is given, but Appia probably wrote it in the summer of 1924, which is also when he made the accompanying drawings that are dated to either 'April' or 'August' of that year.

As was his custom, Appia sought to strip away some of the naturalistic clutter of the conventional nineteenth-century stage. In the opening scene, he decided to 'omit the garden-room' entirely, indicating only the veranda, beyond which the garden itself extends. In the middle ground of that garden there are a couple of steps rising to a kind of narrow terrace fronted by a wooden balustrade from which an expansive view over the fjord opens up. According to Appia, the deep veranda is to be 'closed off at the sides by simple tarpaulin curtains that turn through right angles to frame the space'. And on the same line as the curtains there is a 'wooden frame representing the exterior entrance to the veranda; the two slim timber columns that are square and ornate stand out against the luminous background'.

In order to communicate the family's comfortable circumstances, Appia proposes that a run of elegant *cretonne* (a heavy cotton fabric, typically with a floral pattern) be hung along the heavy plain curtains up to mid-height, and he points out that all of the rattan furniture – chairs, tables and so forth – is to be in good taste, as are the cushions, flowers and mats on the ground. Regarding the terrace outside, Appia notes that the floor of it is to appear trampled, but it should not naturalistically represent grass, and there should certainly be no climbing vines, since 'they always look ridiculous on the stage'. Regarding the illumination of the scene, Appia wrote that the light in the veranda is to be diffuse, yet very clear, and the open air beyond is to be very bright. He notes that it is important to adjust the contrast between the two levels of illumination very carefully, so that it 'does not dazzle the eyes of the audience at all, and to allow the characters to be seen perfectly clearly'.

The curtains both left and right have a tall prised-open slit in them, allowing for the two entrances dictated by Ibsen, though they are not obviously doors. Appia notes that these openings 'are meant to lead into the interior of the house and will not let in exterior light. If this small detail is taken care of, the public will find the setting quite natural and will not be concerned by it.'

Turning now to the play itself, Alfred and Eyolf arrive on stage together by the entrance on the left, the former dressed in light summer clothes. Ibsen describes him as a 'slim, lightly built man of about thirty-six or thirty-seven, with gentle eyes and thin brown hair and beard. His expression is serious and thoughtful.' And his son Eyolf 'wears a suit that is cut like a uniform, with gold braid and gilt military buttons. He is lame and walks with a crutch under his left arm. His leg is shrunken, He is undersized and looks delicate, but has beautiful intelligent eyes.'[145] Eyolf lives a sheltered life; what he craves most is to do the things that other boys do – swim, hike, shoot arrows – but his father knows the impossibility of this, and intends to turn his son's mind toward lofty intellectual pursuits.

Héro et Léandre (The Waves and the Sea of Love), 63.0×48.1 cm, 1922.

Still in the first act of the play, the Allmers family is visited by a mysterious elderly woman – the 'Rat-Wife', who enters the stage softly and noiselessly by the door on the right. She is a 'thin little shrunk figure, old grey-haired, with keen, piercing eyes, dressed in an old-fashioned flowered gown, with a black hood and cloak'.[146] She has the power to enchant rodents into following her down to the fjord, and then out into the deep water where they drown, 'every blessed one', she says. Down below, 'all is as still, and soft and dark as their hearts can desire, the lovely little things. Down there they sleep a long, sweet sleep.'[147] The Rat-Wife takes her leave by the same door when she is told that her particular services are not required. But unbeknownst to his father and mother, Eyolf follows her. Once Eyolf has left the stage, Alfred speaks of his plans to be a better father to his son, plans at odds with those of his possessive wife, who wants Alfred all for herself. Their tense conversation is interrupted by 'confused cries and shrieks' that are heard in the distance, 'from the direction of the fjord'.[148] Eyolf followed the bewitching Rat-Wife out into the water and has drowned.

Alfred is disbelieving and disconsolate in the opening scene of the second act: 'I cannot grasp it. It seems so utterly impossible.' The setting is a narrow glen by the fjord in which Eyolf has drowned and which Alfred now gloomily gazes upon: 'How pitiless the fjord looks today, lying so heavy and drowsy – leaden-grey – with splashes of yellow – and reflecting the rain clouds.'[149] As described by Ibsen, Alfred is sitting on a bench at a table,

following spread
Little Eyolf, Act 2: Allmer's Forest, 48.3×63.2 cm, 1924.

Le petit Eyolf. II acte. Esquisse.

a. appia
1924

Little Eyolf, Act 1: The Garden Room, 48.2×63.0 cm, 1924

Little Eyolf, Act 3: In Allmer's Garden 48.1×63.0 cm, 1924

around which there are also a couple of chairs, 'all made of thin birch-staves'. Lofty old trees overarch this setting that is on the left of the stage. On the right-hand side there are also trees, but they are spread further apart, and the fjord is visible between them. A narrow brook flanked by a stepped path leaps down the slope from right to left and loses itself among the stones on the margin of the wood.

Appia describes his setting for the scene as relatively shallow, with a backdrop of drapes that are 'slit vertically here and there to represent the trunks of trees and to let in filtered light'. A staircase that is just wide enough for two people abreast stands in front of these drapes and descends from the right to left. And in front of the staircase on the right is another layer of drapes, but the openings in them are slightly wider than those that form the backdrop in order to vaguely reveal the characters as they walk down the path and enter the scene. The first to do so is Alfred's half-sister Asta, who set out some time ago to console him, but who only now has finally found her half-brother: 'I have been searching for you for such a long time', she says. 'Have you been sitting here long? All the time?'[150] Appia's setting differs here from the one described by Ibsen: 'There are no chairs; the bench and table appear to be made of a neutral-coloured stone that is a little greenish, reminiscent of the curtains.'

Alfred's wife Rita has been out searching for him, and she now arrives on the scene wearing a dark dress and black veil. 'Why do you come here?' asks Alfred. 'Only to look for you,' she says. Asta takes her leave and the husband and wife fall into a dark discussion that begins with Rita describing what the boys on the pier told her of their final sight of Eyolf, lying on the bottom of the fjord, deep down in the clear water. 'They said he was lying down on his back. And with great, open eyes.'[151] Alfred rises from the bench and moves close to her: 'Were they evil eyes that stared up? Up from the depths?' 'Alfred – !' she exclaims. 'Now things have come about – just as you wished, Rita.' Alfred accuses his wife of never having truly loved their child, a claim that she hurls back at him: 'Oh, the truth is that you never had any real love for him either.'[152] The terrible argument escalates and Alfred blames Rita for Eyolf's disability: 'It was your fault that he became – what he was! It was your fault that he could not save himself when he fell into the water.'[153] One day when Eyolf was a baby, Alfred had placed him on a cushion high up on a table, and he was sound asleep. 'But then you came – you, you, you – and lured me to you', to which Rita responds: 'Oh, better own at once that you forgot the child and everything else.' They eventually acknowledge equal responsibility for Eyolf's fall, but are despairing about the future, especially Rita, fearing that their gnawing guilt, sorrow and heartache will end in 'madness for both of us. For we can never – never make it good again.' Alfred gradually sees a way forward, but it will involve a transformation in their relationship: 'In what I now feel for you – in our common guilt and need of atonement – I seem to foresee a sort of resurrection ...'[154]

A canopy of trees overarches the spot where Alfred and Rita have been talking. Here the bench and table 'stand like neighbours', according to Appia. They are to be made from 'two sliced drapes that emerge from the far left and hang like branches; they flow towards the right and merge with the perpendicular drapes'. On the ground, the bottom of all the vertical drapes representing tree trunks gather sufficiently to appear as the roots of the trees. They are to be dark green-brown in colour and so is the ground, though here and there it has an earthy, green-tinged hue. Of the drapes that are used in this act, Appia wrote that they 'stand for all that is out in the open air, whereas the ordinary tarpaulins used in the other two acts represent either interiors or undefined locations'.

Regarding the lighting, Appia wrote that there should be two kinds, firstly 'that of the open air, which is golden and filters through the slitted drapes', and secondly a 'reflected bluish light emanating from the floor of the left wings, expressing the waters of the nearby fjord. This light that reflects off the fjord must colour the characters when they are exposed to it. Underneath the greenery the light is diffused yet clear.'[155] Ibsen concluded his own description of the scene with a summary of its atmosphere: 'It is a heavy, damp day, with driving mist-wreaths.'[156]

As drawn by Appia, the setting for the third act is almost identical to that of the first, except that it appears closer, as though the audience has taken four or five steps forward and is about to step out from the veranda and into the garden beyond. The stepped terrace now takes up more of the stage, and according to Appia, in this setting, 'we are better able to see the path that leads to the fjord and which turns left under the balustrade. The backdrop is similar to that of the first act, that is, uniformly blue and without a clearly defined landscape.'[157] As described by Ibsen, it is a 'late summer evening, with clear sky. Deepening twilight.'[158]

Alfred seems intent on leaving Rita, to live a life of solitude up in the mountains. Rita tells him what she intends to do: 'As soon as you are gone from me, I will go down to the beach, and bring all the poor neglected children home with me. All the mischievous boys ... from the day you leave me, they shall be here, all of them, as if they were mine.' Alfred is shocked: 'In our little Eyolf's place!' 'Yes, in our little Eyolf's place', confirms Rita. 'I want to make peace with the great, open eyes, you see.' 'Perhaps, I could join you in that? And help you, Rita?' 'But then you would have to remain here'. Alfred says softly: 'Let us try if it could not be so.'[159] Perhaps every now and then, he says to his wife, when peace descends, the spirits of those who have been lost may come to presence. 'Where shall we look for them, Alfred?' 'Upwards – towards the peaks. Towards the stars. And towards the great silence.'[160] In his own concluding lines, Appia wrote that the 'entire *mise-en-scène* of *Petit Eyolf* must attain such a great harmony that the audience no longer thinks about the story as it unfolds but rather focuses all of their attention on the characters alone ... *Petit Eyolf* is a drama of the purest intimacy.'[161]

Soon after Appia made his drawings for the three acts of *Little Eyolf* and completed the brief manuscript that accompanies them, he turned his attention to another three-act family drama of agonising intimacy that likewise has as its topic the death of a child and the fateful repercussions for the two anguished parents. But, this time it is not only the paired destiny of the father and mother that is at stake, but rather that of an entire people – the ancient Greeks.

Euripides' tragedy *Iphigenia at Aulis* opens with the mighty Greek army stalled at Aulis, increasingly impatient to set sail for the city of Troy which they intend to destroy as an act of retribution – Paris, the son of King Priam,

Iphigenia at Aulis, Act 3, Scene 2, 48.3×63.3 cm, 1926

Iphigenia at Aulis, Act 1, 48.1 × 63.0 cm, 1926

following spread *Iphigenia at Aulis*, Act 2, 48.0 × 63.2 cm, 1926

appia

has run away there with Helen, the wife of King Menelaeus of Sparta. The aggrieved king's brother Agamemnon, who is leading the great Greek coalition on their seabound quest for vengeance, summarises the current state of affairs: 'When the whole army had mustered here at Aulis, the wind died. Calm. We still cannot sail. There is only one hope of our going, according to Kalchas, the prophet. Iphigenia, my daughter, must be sacrificed to Artemis, the deity of this place. Then the wind will take us to Troy, and the city will fall to us.'[162] Agamemnon initially assents to the filicidal decree and sends for Iphigenia on the pretence of marrying her to the famed Greek warrior Achilles, but soon repents: 'What I have done is wrong, and I want to undo it.'[163] From now on, the audience experiences the play as an agonising effort to save the life of Iphigenia, and it becomes clear why Wagner once asserted that *Iphigenia at Aulis* 'delivers into our hands the broad idea of ancient Greek Tragedy, for it fills us with terror and pity in turn'.[164]

Agamemnon realises the plan must go ahead, in part because the brothers are not the only ones who know of it – so too does Odysseus: 'He is cunning, and it always turns out that he and the crowd are on the same side.'[165] Agamemnon knows that Odysseus will inflame discontent amongst the army, who are champing at the bit to embark for Troy: 'I have reached a point where circumstances leave me no choice. I shall be forced to shed her blood, to kill my daughter.'[166] Learning of her father's murderous intent, Iphigenia makes a tearful appeal: 'It is sweet to see the light. Do not make me look at what is under the earth.'[167] But Agamemnon sees no way out. He must indeed sacrifice his daughter, who in turn resigns herself to her fate: 'I must say goodbye to the light. I will not see the sun anymore.'[168] Leading the chorus in a hymn to the goddess Artemis, Iphigenia is willingly led away to her death: 'She goes to drench with her blood the altar of the divine goddess.'[169]

Appia made a drawing for the final bloody act of *Iphigenia at Aulis*, and it is in fact one of his most serene. The symmetrical composition, drawn on warm grey coloured paper, is anchored by the massive stone altar, attained by gradual ascent via a gentle sequence of stairs, platforms and landings that span the full width of the stage, as does the vast misty horizon beyond. The sacrifice of Iphigenia on this altar triggered a tragic sequence of events that began with the murder of Agamemnon by his wife Clytemnestra, who was incensed by the role he played in the killing of their daughter. Their son Orestes avenged his father in turn, murdering Clytemnestra. His sister Elektra was in on the matricidal plot, and her own story has taken on a life of its own, being continually reimagined. For example, Hugo von Hofmannsthal wrote the libretto for *Elektra*, an opera set to music by Richard Strauss. Roller prepared the settings, and in one of the drawings for the tragedy that unfolds inside the walls of Agamemnon's ancient palace in Mycenae, the rough-hewn masonry has been turned rose gold by the warming rays of the Mediterranean sun. The whole setting has a suitably foreboding air about it.

Elektra premiered in 1909, and amongst the audience was Jaques-Dalcroze, who was impressed, though not unequivocally so; in a short essay published in the journal *Le Rythme*, he wrote that there are certainly some artists who 'have an inborn knowledge of the rhythms of space; for example, Hugo von Hofmannsthal'. He then noted that the setting for *Elektra* featured a huge staircase, but unfortunately 'the actors, having little acquaintance with the most elementary notions of balance' roamed about on it with 'deplorable heaviness'.[170] The cast portraits of Marie Gutheil-Schoder as the vengeance-driven Elektra are notable not only for her crazed countenance but for the way that she makes active use of the heavy stone steps, terraces and platforms of Roller's three-dimensional setting. In one of them she is perched on a low platform with her head in her hands and her elbows on her knees, deep in thought – perhaps plotting the death of her mother Clytemnestra – while in another she stands tall atop that same platform with her arms raised up ecstatically to the evening sky, perhaps following the matricide that had ultimately been carried out by her brother Orestes, who is now 'wheeling in madness and pain', tormented as he is by the Furies.[171]

Performance of *Elektra*, *c* 1927.

It is here that the plot takes a twist. At the end of *Iphigenia at Aulis* a breathless messenger told of the miraculous event he witnessed when the priest took up his knife at the altar, looking for a place to plunge it: 'Everyone distinctly heard the knife striking, but no one could see the girl. She had vanished.' In her place was a deer that lay gasping, 'a large, beautiful animal, and its blood ran streaming over the altar of the goddess'.[172] He assumed that Iphigenia had been spirited away to heaven, but in fact she was transported to the barbarian land of the Taurians by the goddess Artemis, as Iphigenia herself recalls in the opening scene of Euripides' sequel, *Iphigenia among the Taurians*: 'Lifted high above the altar I was right on the verge of death when Artemis snatched me, put a deer in my place. Sent me clear through the air to the land of the Taurians: here!'[173] But her deliverance came with conditions. The goddess made

Marie Gutheil-Schoder as Elektra, Vienna State Opera, 1915.

Iphigenia a priestess at a temple in a sacred grove where she was to preside over the local ritual, 'beautiful in name only, that Artemis finds pleasing. By a law of the city older than me, I sacrifice any Greek man who comes here.'[174]

As fate would have it, the Furies have driven the Greek man Orestes toward the land of the Taurians, together with his sole true friend and possibly his lover, Pylades. As the curtain is drawn aside for the first act of *Iphigenia among the Taurians*, the scene is 'silent and empty, bathed in a warm light', according to Appia.[175] For him, the setting for this first act must 'strongly situate the drama – the ocean, light a little harsh, the sacred grove of Artemis with its sanctuary surrounded by trees'. The sea horizon and glimpse of open countryside are to appear on the backdrop, and the front of the stage is to be bound left and right by two successive wings of 'very dark drapes suggesting cypresses'.

Appia notes that particular care should be taken in the selection of these cypress-curtains, 'which are to be a beautiful deep colour and form large, heavy folds'. Regarding the physical elements on the stage, he wrote that about halfway back there is to be a low terrace up to which a few broad steps lead, leaving a short stretch of retaining wall on either side. In the centre of the terrace is a very simple block altar, 'such as the one in the first act of Orpheus'. Then, behind the altar, there are another couple of steps, narrower this time, leading up to the door of the temple. Appia pointed out that 'the whole area around the temple, on the terrace, is devoted exclusively to Iphigenia and the priestesses; no one else will set foot on it'. The temple itself is described as being of white marble that glistens in the light, and according to Appia it is to be of 'no particular style of architecture; the pediment cannot be seen; the lines in the stone are sober and *thin*'. The stairs and the walls of the temple are to be the same colour as the façade, and overall, as few colours as possible should be employed, since 'it is the play of light and shadow that will animate the scene'.

The silent and empty scene does not remain that way for long. Orestes and Pylades beach their boat and set foot on land, dressed according to Appia in such a simple manner that they come close to the Greek style of Iphigenia and her entourage – 'simple and uniform' – making them 'something of a hyphen' between the Taurians, who come across as 'jaunty and colourful', and the priestesses. The two men soon see the temple they sailed from Greece to find, and remark on the bloodstained altar with its gruesome wreath of human skulls – 'spoils from foreigners who died here'.

On the lighting for the final scene of this first act, Appia wrote that it should be dimmed almost imperceptibly in the foreground so that the attention of the audience is drawn to the sea horizon, the ground, the sanctuary, the terrace and the altar, all of which are bathed in a soft diffuse light that emanates from above, while 'chiaroscuro threatens from the front of the stage to the uppermost step of the first staircase'. Finally, of the setting as a whole, Appia wrote that it is to have a 'perpendicular character, which is favourable to the presence of the living human being'.

The two friends are apprehended and are escorted inside the temple with their hands tied, 'fresh victims for the goddess'.[176] It is inside the Temple of Artemis that an 'extreme style of hieratic simplicity' should be introduced, wrote Appia. The moody drawing that he made to illustrate what he meant does justice to the idea; it takes in a view towards the unyielding altar, seen from the side through a profoundly expectant ambient gloom. 'The lighting should be soft and diffuse. A mysterious light falls from above onto the altar and the steps that lead up to it.' Orestes and Iphigenia are siblings, but neither recognises the other, and it is the agonising possibility that the sister will kill her brother which drives the action that follows. The drapes framing this ominous 'space devoted to the crime should likely be dark red in colour, patternless, and with tight and hollow pleats, in order to accentuate the scene', wrote Appia. Iphigenia offers to spare one of the two friends on the condition that he carry a message for her back to her family in Greece, though she leaves it to the two men to decide who will live and who will die. And it is now that 'the real action, the essence of the drama' unfolds, according to Appia. For him, it is, in fact, the ensuing tussle for generosity between the two friends – 'drama at the highest level' – which is primary, 'even the plight of Iphigenia can be considered secondary to that of the two friends'.

Marie Gutheil-Schoder as Elektra, Vienna State Opera, 1915.

Orestes and Pylades each offer to die so that the other can be saved; Orestes says, for example, that it is 'utterly base to save oneself by sabotaging one's friends. This man is my friend and that's that. No less than myself, I want him to look upon the daylight.' Iphigenia is impressed: 'What nobility you were born from, what a true friend you are. I wish my one surviving brother were a man such as you – yes, I do have a brother, though I have never seen him.' 'Since it is your wish, we will send this fellow off with the message, and you shall die. A profound desire for this seems to possess you.' Orestes asks: 'Who will sacrifice me and bear the horror?' to which Iphigenia responds: 'I have this duty from the goddess.'[177]

Time is now running short, but Pylades retains some optimism that the death of his friend might be averted: 'The oracle has not yet destroyed you though you stand right next to death. And, you know it is the case – that extraordinary misfortune can call forth extraordinary reversals: all it takes is luck.'[178] Just in time, Orestes recognises the sister he thought long dead, standing before him: 'Beloved sister, I am stunned, but I embrace you with my disbelieving arms in open joy!'[179] Though Iphigenia does not believe her brother at once, he tells her of things that only he could know and is soon

following spreads *Iphigenia among the Taurians*, Act 1: The Sacred Grove of Artemis, 48.0×63.0 cm; Act 3: Iphigenia's Chamber, 47.8×62.5 cm, 1926.

Iphigenia among the Taurians, Act 1: The Sacred Grove of Artemis, 48.4×63.0 cm and 48.0×63.1 cm, 1926

Iphigenia among the Taurians, Act 2: Interior of the Temple of Artemis, 48.1×63.0 cm, 1926

Emil Pirchan, setting for Franz Grillparzer's *Medea*, performed at the Nationaltheater, Munich, 1919.

convinced, both overjoyed and relieved: 'You barely escaped an unholy death at my hands.'[180]

Athena appears and reveals that it was fated for Orestes to transport Iphigenia back to Greece, along with the cult statue of the goddess's own sister Artemis, for which he was to build a temple that would be named after the land of the Taurians whose shores the son of Agamemnon first beached his boat upon while 'wheeling in madness', tormented by the Furies. Loosed now from their ire, when Orestes finally made it back to Greece, his afflicted journeying was done.

The ancient Greek mythic-historical world to which *Iphigenia at Aulis*, *Iphigenia among the Taurians* and *Elektra* attest is the same one as that of *Medea*, originally written by Euripides but transposed to the modern stage by

Hofmannsthal's fellow Viennese dramatist Grillparzer. What the two modern interpretations of ancient tragic plays also have in common is the basic elements of their scenography, which in character if not outline can be traced back to Appia's drawings, particularly his orthogonal *Espaces rythmiques* with their arrangements of stairs, platforms, walls and columns, all standing before a distant watery horizon well beyond them. This genealogy can be clearly seen in the settings for *Medea* that the Czech scenographer and architect Emil Pirchan prepared for the Nationaltheater in Munich, and that one critic at the time praised for the way that they made 'the human and eternal in their tragic communion press forward, becoming detached from the time-bound and historical; the scenic architecture is laid entirely of ashlar masonry, delivering the strongest dramatic expression by encircling the action with three-dimensional space where in the past it was choked by imaginary perspectives painted on two-dimensional sets'. And he was impressed by the way that naturalism is entirely renounced, noting that 'colour, light and contour are all simplified in the tightest manner, presenting the audience with a setting that is unambiguous and profoundly poignant'.[181] While this description also held for Pirchan's other settings – including those that he prepared for Frank Wedekind's *Herakles* that clearly recall Appia's *Espace rythmique* drawing *Moonlight* – for this critic it is in the settings for *Medea* that Pirchan achieved his aesthetic crescendo, 'elevating the tragedy into the realm of the ethereal, and transporting antiquity into modern times'.[182]

Emil Pirchan, setting for Frank Wedekind's *Herakles*, performed at the Prinzregenten-Theater, Munich, 1919.

That statement equally applies to Appia and is in fact a neat summary of the aesthetic that he consistently projected over the course of his otherwise unsettled lifetime. In the later years of his life, Appia moved around restlessly,

lodging only ever temporarily, sometimes for weeks at a time and at others for months, sometimes voluntarily, such as when he stayed with friends or rented a room in a little *pension*, and other times at the behest of others, such as when he was wheeling in his own personal madness and was admitted to psychiatric institutions including the Waldau clinic in Bern. Each time he would gather his meagre bundle of belongings that amounted to no more than some books, letters, clothes and his drawing board, and move on. But eventually Appia too ceased his wandering. He moved into his final residence – a single room on the second floor of a small garden house in the grounds of the psychiatrist Dr Oscar Forel's clinic, La Métairie, near Nyon – in December 1925. In the sparse room – described by his friend Jacques Copeau as a monk's cell – were manuscripts and fresh drawings.[183] And there was also a pile of written correspondence, towards the top of which must have been some letters that

following spread
Faust Part 1, Scene 6: Faust's Study 3, 48.1×63.1 cm, 1927–28.

top to bottom, left to right *Faust* Part 1, Scene 1: Dedication, 48.2×63.3 cm; Scene 2: Prologue in Heaven, 48.1×63.1 cm; Scene 3: Faust's Study 1, 48.1×63.1 cm; Scene 4: Outside the City Gate 1, 48.1×63.2 cm; Scene 5: Outside the City Gate 1, 48.1×63.1 cm; Scene 6: Faust's Study 2, 48.1×63.2 cm, 1927–28

top to bottom, left to right *Faust* Part 1, Scene 8: Witch's Kitchen, 48.1×63.0 cm; Scene 9: A Street, 48.2×63.3 cm; Scene 10: Gretchen's Room 1 and 2, 48.1×63.1 cm; Scene 11: Martha's Room, 48.1×63.1 cm; Scene 12: In Martha's Garden, 48.2×63.3 cm; Scene 13: Forest and Cave, 48.1×63.2 cm, 1927–28

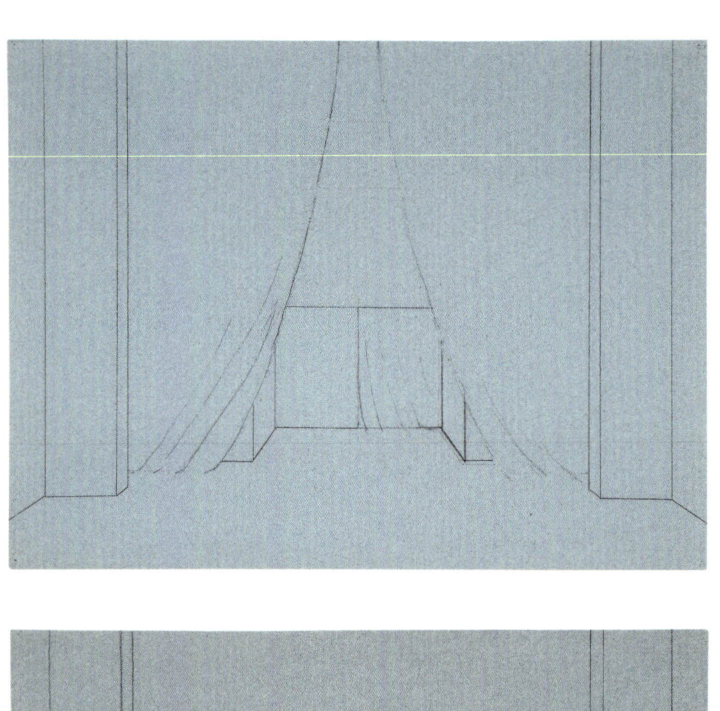

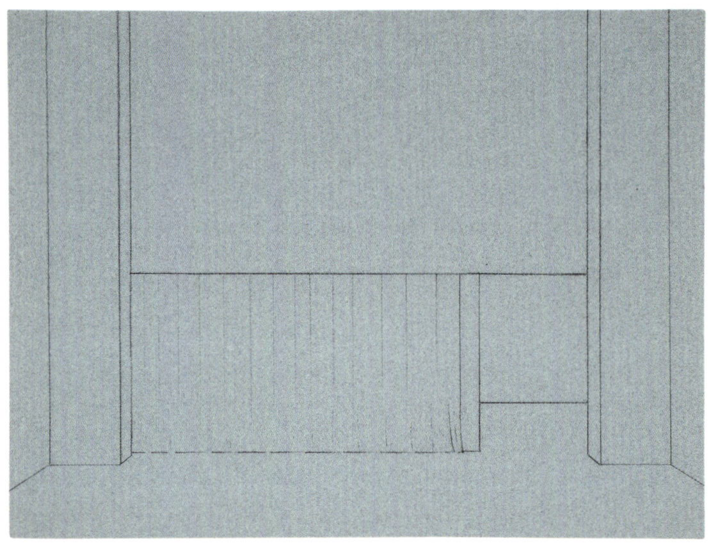

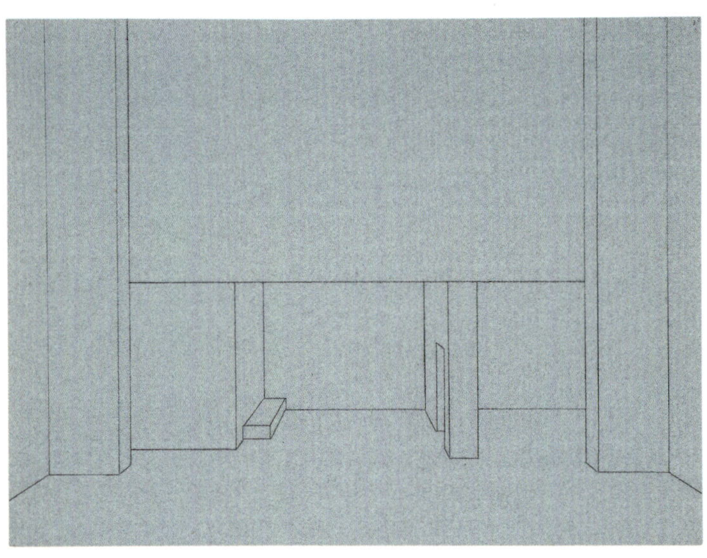

Faust Part 1, Scene 15: Cathedral Nave, 48.1×63.1 cm; Part 1, Scene 16: Prison 1, 48.2×63.2 cm; Part 1, Scene 17: Prison 2, 48.2×63.2 cm, 1927–28

Faust Part 1, Scene 17: Prison 2, 48.1×63.2 cm, 1927–28

Appia at age sixty-four in 1926.

had recently arrived from the German art historian and museum director Franz Rapp, who was then curating a major exhibition in Magdeburg on German theatre and was very keen to include a selection of Appia's drawings. Rapp had long been an admirer; five years earlier, in his *Das Deutsche Bühnenbild unserer Zeit* (German Scenography of Our Times), he had written: 'The fact cannot be overlooked that the roots of all that is contemporary go back to the Swiss scenographer Adolphe Appia, and he should not be forgotten in the history of modern stage design, particularly since he was first able to realise his ideas right in the centre of Germany – in Hellerau.'[184]

The letters that Appia sent to Rapp are revealing in a number of ways; firstly, on account of their timing (the very end of his working life) and purpose (a self-curated selection of drawings to summarise his contribution to twentieth-century German scenography), they present a kind of final self-assessment; secondly, they communicate his personal circumstances, idiosyncrasies, health and general disposition at the time. One letter that Appia sent to Rapp early on in 1926, while the two of them were still getting to know each other, begins with the line 'Please excuse the pencil. I do not write in ink.' And Appia informs Rapp that he is suffering from a 'malady of the heart', which is why he is currently residing with his friend Oscar Forel while he undergoes treatment. After signing-off 'adolphe appia' at the bottom of the second page, he pencilled a final line: 'I speak *Deutsch* in addition to *Französisch* and – when absolutely necessary – I can write it, but unfortunately with many mistakes!'[185]

As hesitant as Appia was about his facility with the German language, he was entirely confident about the quality of his drawings, particularly those that he had made in the thrall of the German *Meister* Richard Wagner. Appia was certain about which of his drawings should be shown, how they should hang in relation to each other, and even how they should be framed. Following some to-and-fro with Rapp about whether the original drawings should be sent (Appia was nervous that his drawings, which by now were very well travelled, might be further damaged), or whether photographic reproductions would suffice in their place, Appia agreed to terms, as set out in a letter that he posted to Rapp on 8 February 1927.

He appended a list of the original drawings that he would send to Magdeburg; these being three drawings each for *Das Rheingold*, *Die Walküre* and *Parsifal*, along with four *Espaces rythmiques*. And he would also send photographs of his drawings for *Orfeo ed Euridice*, *Tristan und Isolde*, *Lohengrin*, *King Lear* and *Little Eyolf*.[186] In the letter itself, Appia got down to brass tacks regarding the framing of his drawings: 'None of the frames are to be white, gold, black or coloured in any way, rather they must be natural timber. All the drawings and photographs are to be carefully mounted in their frames behind glass.' He was especially concerned for his *Parsifal* drawings, since by that time they had 'unfortunately suffered during the many journeys they have endured – particular care must be taken with them, and if possible, their frames should be slightly wider and also darker than those for the other original drawings.' Appia was just as particular about what should appear either inside or outside those frames: 'The labels that identify each of the original drawings are to be mounted *underneath* them. Under no circumstances are the catalogue numbers to appear within a frame – be it the original drawings or the ones that are being represented by photographs – rather, they are to be affixed to the wall *outside* of the frame.' And he concludes his letter with the stipulation that 'every original drawing is to be numbered individually according to the exhibition catalogue so that it is impossible to misidentify them'.[187]

The *German Theatre* exhibition ran from May to September 1927. Writing mid-show, Rapp was well pleased with the critical and popular reception that his exhibition was receiving, and he thanked Appia for his own contribution, going as far to say that 'for me, personally, the "Adolphe Appia" room is undoubtedly one of the best in the entire exhibition'. But Rapp then expressed his disappointment – though surely not surprise – that 'Herr Adolphe Appia did not visit the exhibition. You would have found that the room in which your work is on display accords in every way with your wishes – I followed your instructions to the letter when arranging the drawings.' He signed off with a knowing line: 'I hope that, somehow, your desires will soon be fulfilled. Yours with devotion, –R.'[188]

Notable by their absence from the selection of drawings that Appia sent to Magdeburg for the exhibition were the suite that he made for Goethe's *Faust*.[189] But that was not because Appia chose to omit them, rather because they were still on the drawing board in front of him: *Faust: Eine Tragödie* was his final project. And there is of course a poetic symmetry to the fact that *Faust* had been his initiation into the theatre, back in the Grand Théâtre de Genève half a century before. But that had been Charles Gounod's abridged version set to music.

This time, Appia steeled himself for his final dramatic confrontation with the genius polymath's *magnum opus*, which is sometimes considered to be nothing short of the greatest work in German literature, not for its breadth or length but rather for its depth; its central question is nothing less than is the price of one's soul. The demon Mephistopheles ventures a wager with God that he will be able to lure his favourite mortal man – Faust – away from his lofty, earnest intellectual strivings and downwards to those desires more passionate, carnal and fleeting – in short, more human.

Cosima had in fact recommended *Faust* as a challenge for Appia many years before: 'I would recommend Faust. A whole stage would have to be built for it – what an opportunity for discoveries, inventions, ideas! If Herr Appia succeeded in assisting the poet to achieve the fullest expression of his intentions (without distracting from him), then he would achieve something great – in fact, something everlasting.'[190] So, both the themes and the aesthetic stakes were high.

Appia studied his copy of *Faust* – the compact hardcover Kröner pocketbook edition – very closely and made copious margin-notes in pencil throughout.[191] Likewise in pencil, Appia prepared drawings for every one of the seventeen scenes in *Faust*, and they are all confidently delineated with that surety that comes with maturity; there is no evidence of hesitancy or of second thoughts, and there is no embellishment. Appia wrote an explanatory manuscript to go along with his drawings, and he in fact set greater store in his words than his depictions, stating: 'In what follows, I suggest that my description of the staging of Goethe's *Faust* is more important than the drawings that accompany it; by themselves, they offer nothing sufficiently resolved, let alone conclusive.'[192] And he does indeed articulate penetrating insights, particularly in regard to the way that the two actors who play Faust and Mephistopheles are to perform their roles. Appia realised that there is, in fact, only one character in the tragedy, and that is Faust himself; Mephistopheles is the devilish part of him. So, 'on stage there are two actors, two different bodies', and it is up to these actors to unite their characters 'like the two sides of a medallion'. They must assume 'similar postures, voice and movements. It is not a matter of mimicry, but rather of a kind of reciprocal parallelism – the audience must be taken aback when they see Mephistopheles and recognise gestures and inflections that bring Faust to mind, and vice versa.'[193] Appia then briefly addresses each scene in turn, interspersing key citations from Goethe's text with his own assertions as to how they should be staged. And his ideas are as fresh and sweeping as ever. For example, Appia proposed that for scene 15 – Cathedral Nave – rather than confining the *mise-en-scène* to the bounds of the stage, the auditorium itself should be lit in such

Deutsche Theater-Ausstellung in Magdeburg, 1927.

a way as to evoke the lofty vaulted interior of the cathedral, thereby producing an effect that would be both spatial and affecting; the audience would become worshippers in their pews, and would serve as witnesses to the tragedy of Faust as his fate unfolds before them.

As much as Appia was occupied with the fate of Faust, his mind at times turned to his own mortality, and he wrote his last will and testament, in which he stated: 'The death that delivers me must be respected', and 'my formal wish is to be cremated. If for some unforeseeable reason this is completely out of the question, I implore that whatever is medically imperative – bleeding-out or even autopsy – is carried out, to be certain that my death is final.'[194]

It is the blood of Faust that is spilled in one of the most arresting and consequential early scenes in the tragedy, one that takes place in Faust's study – his own monk's cell. Faust has been seduced by Mephistopheles' offer of unlimited knowledge and worldly pleasures in exchange for his soul after death, but wary of deceit, he calls for Mephistopheles to divulge his character. Mephistopheles responds: 'I am part of the darkness which brought forth the light, the proud light that now disputes the space ... and yet the struggle fails, since however much it strives, fettered to bodies it cleaves. It flows from the bodies that make it beautiful, by bodies is its course impeded. So, I hope that it will not take long – with the body it will perish.' Faust is ready to sign the pact – with his own blood. 'Done!' says the demon, 'And done again!' says Faust, well aware of the gravity of his commitment: 'It is I for whom the bell shall toll; you are free, your service done. For me the clock shall fail, to ruin run, and timeless night descend upon my soul.'[195] 'I'll sound the heights and depths that men can know; their very souls shall be with mine entwined. I'll load my bosom with their weal and woe, and share with them the shipwreck of mankind.'[196] Intriguingly, Appia in fact made a drawing for this scene which stands out from all of the others in the suite in that it is fully rendered with shadow and atmosphere – Faust's study seems to be slipping out of focus as the ambient light in the room fades, and one is reminded of the two final words that Goethe uttered before his heart finally failed him in his dimmed room in Weimar – 'more light!'[197]

Appia's own 'malady of the heart' claimed the scenographer at the age of sixty-five on 29 February 1928, and his funeral was staged in accordance with the quiet drama of his last will and testament: 'The ceremony that accompanies my burial must be simple, and it must flow silently: no gathering, no worship, no words and no music.'[198]

following page
Appia's death mask, 1928.

AFTER

Appia, *Espaces rythmiques* reproduced in the catalogue of the *International Exhibition of Theatre Art*, MOMA, New York, 1934.

In addition to setting out the terms for his silently flowing burial ceremony, Appia made provision in his will for the disbursement of his material possessions after his death: 'All of my personal effects; papers, letters, photographs, drawings, music, books and so forth are to be given to my friends Jean Mercier, Edouard Junod and Oscar Forel, who will dispose of these as they deem fit.'[1] After scattering Appia's ashes under a large cedar tree in the grounds of the Métairie clinic, the three custodians of the scenographer's artistic estate banded together and created La Fondation Adolphe Appia.[2] They then set about finding appropriate lodgings for Appia's 'personal effects ... drawings ... books and so forth', settling upon the Musée d'Art et d'Histoire in Geneva, which had offered them the following terms: '(a): The *héritage artistique* of Adolphe Appia ... will be deposited in the annexe of the museum at the Promenade du Pin. There will be provision for four panels measuring 97×97 cm, four panels measuring 107×55 cm and also a cabinet', and '(b): A room in the museum will be made available for a temporary exhibition running for between three weeks and a month'.[3]

The provisions were modest indeed, as the American scenographer and architect Lee Simonsen noted in his introduction to the catalogue accompanying the major *International Exhibition of Theatre Art* at the Museum of Modern Art (MOMA) in New York in 1934: 'Adolphe Appia's epoch-making designs are kept in a portfolio in the Musée d'Art et d'Histoire of his native city Geneva, in an annexe to the library where they can be seen only on request. It has seemingly never occurred to the curators of that institution, who show tiled stoves, helmets and halberds, that these drawings are worthy of wall space as part of a permanent exhibit open to the public.'[4] But Appia himself had once asserted that his suite of *Espaces rythmiques* were 'a point of departure, not a destination',[5] and the aesthetic the drawings projected and the ideas they embodied travelled far beyond the small room in the museum annexe – to Paris, for example, and the rooftop terrace of the penthouse apartment on 36 Avenue des Champs-Elysées that Le Corbusier completed for the flamboyant multi-millionaire art collector Charles de Beistegui in 1931, which is as much a piece of scenography as it is a work of architecture.[6]

The drama began for Beistegui's guests as soon as they stepped through the door to his penthouse and found themselves in an interior world set in motion by what Le Corbusier himself described as '*installations électrifiés*

Le Corbusier, rooftop of the Beistegui penthouse in Paris, 1931.

et méchaniques tres compliqués',[7] including doors that opened automatically and partition walls that slid out of the way, even a film projector that showed its flickering images on a screen that unfurled automatically as a chandelier was hoisted up on pulleys. Beistegui himself said that it was 'electricity, modern power' that activated the doors and moved the walls, but that his penthouse was illuminated solely by candlelight, 'the only kind that is a living light'.[8]

But it was when the party shifted gears and locations, moving from the candlelit interior to the set-piece of exterior terraces, that the Parisian *haute bohème* stepped out onto the stage which Le Corbusier – following Appia – had prepared for them. In her recent book *Inszenierung eine Mythos* (Staging a Myth), Turit Fröbe wrote that in a 'series of terraces and gardens over three different levels, connected by stairs that are nested in one another, a spatial sequence is created that artificially draws in the horizon, and together with the oversized paving tiles, gives the impression that the whole setting is, in fact, one of Appia's stage designs'.[9] And before her, Pierre Saddy frankly stated in his article 'Le Corbusier chez les riches' (Le Corbusier among the Rich) that the rooftop of the Beistegui penthouse was a 'reconstitution of the *Espaces rythmiques* created by Adolphe Appia at Hellerau'.[10]

Saddy's assertion could only ever be partly correct, since Hellerau was not yet in the picture when Appia made his drawings. But his point is well made insofar as the *Espaces rythmiques* that Appia drew with 'feverish determination' on his collapsible drawing board in the Château de Glérolles back in 1909 did indeed lead to his collaboration with Jaques-Dalcroze in Hellerau, a collaboration that, according to both the eyewitness accounts and the photographic evidence, attained its apotheosis in the pivotal scene in Act 2 of Gluck's opera *Orfeo ed Euridice* in which Orpheus descends into the underworld. The scene that follows that one, and concludes Act 2, is set in the Elysian Fields – an otherworldly place in which 'life glides in immortal ease for mortal man'.[11] That characterisation might also have held true for Charles de Beistegui as he was entertaining guests out on the rooftop of his penthouse apartment atop the Champs-Elysées – Paris's own Elysian Fields – and where, with the press of a button, the motorised hedges that bordered the stepped Appian terraces 'would move aside and down below, Paris would appear'.[12]

The Beistegui penthouse was one of a handful of projects by Le Corbusier that were showcased at the now-famed *Modern Architecture: International Exhibition* that Philip Johnson and Henry-Russell Hitchcock curated at MOMA in 1932,[13] the same venue as the *International Exhibition of Theatre Art*, held two years previously. The fact that 'Mr Charles de Beistegui' was one of the exhibition's patrons may go some way to explaining the inclusion of the apartment, arguably a curious selection. Regardless, it meant that Appia's aesthetic was projected to a large and appreciative audience (33,000 people visited the exhibition), even if his drawings and name were typically absent.

Mies van der Rohe was one of the other leading 'International Style' architects selected for inclusion in the MOMA exhibition: 'As a creator of space, he has no equal', wrote Johnson in the catalogue. His built projects, including the twin ground-bound brick houses that he designed for Josef Esters and Hermann Lange,[14] the two managing directors of a weaving mill, on adjoining levelled suburban sites in Krefeld just a short stroll from the Rhine, are altogether more sober affairs than Le Corbusier's Beistegui penthouse,

Interior perspective drawing by Mies van der Rohe for the Neue Wache Memorial competition, 1930.

leaving as they do 'an impression of austerity'.[15] However, these brick houses by the architect formerly known as Maria Ludwig Michael Mies – he too assumed a stage name just as Charles-Édouard Jeanneret had done, and at around the same time[16] – do possess some contrivances similar to those that animate the rooftop *machine à amuser*. These include *Senkfenster*, windows that can be made to disappear with the push of a button; they slide down slim channels and into the basement, opening up the white-walled interiors to the exterior sequences of courts, podia and terraces that eventually diminish into the meadowy landscape via runs of broad shallow steps that either span the full distance between a pair of low retaining walls or cascade and spill around them. The first scenario reminds one most of Appia's *Espace rythmique* entitled *Three Steps*, and the second of his drawing with the title *Steps in the Foreground*.

The two suburban redbrick houses were completed in 1930, the same year that Mies was invited to take part in a closed state-sponsored architectural competition for the design of a 'Memorial to the Fallen of the Great War' in the heart of Berlin. It was to be a reworking of Karl Friedrich Schinkel's neoclassical Neue Wache, the Prussian architect's small temple-like building that had fulfilled its purpose as a guard-house on Under den Linden during the nineteenth century, but had entered the twentieth emptied of function but filled with symbolism – as an important part of the Prussian *via triumphalis*. The competition brief called for a memorial that would use 'simple architectonic means to convey a solemn impression', in accord with the 'essence of the task and the seriousness of the times'.[17] In addition to Mies, those architects who were invited to respond to the brief were his former teacher Peter Behrens, who by that time was a professor at the Akademie der bildenden Künste in Vienna; Erich Blunck, editor of the *Deutsche Bauzeitung*; the Berlin architect Hans Grube; and finally Hans Poelzig and Heinrich Tessenow, both of whom had moved on from Dresden and were now professors at the Technische Hochschule Charlottenburg in Berlin. There were only two specific architectural demands for the project, the first of which was for the incorporation of some sort of commemorative symbol, and the second was for a central atrium that would open the building up to the sky.[18]

Mies delivered his proposal – which he had given the title *Raum* (space) – to the jury in July 1930. It did indeed include a central commemorative symbol – a low block of polished black granite that was to be received by a slight depression in the floor, and that would have DEN TOTEN (To the Dead) inscribed on its front face and the *Reichsadler* (German Imperial Eagle) etched into its top surface. The jury praised this device for its 'simple and great form' and its 'noble emotion' and 'strong symbolic power', but they were equivocal about other aspects of Mies's scheme, particularly his proposal to insert a set of tall double doors in the rear wall that would allow visitors to pass through the building – thus depriving it, in the words of the jury, of the 'tranquil harmony and balance' characteristic of a memorial, and investing it rather with the character of an 'anteroom'.[19] That was their primary objection, though it was not their only one; Mies had decided to ignore the requirement in the brief for an atrium, opting instead for a low, taut, flawless white ceiling that would contrast with the diaphanous marble walls in a dark green hue that he proposed to insert in front of the windows on the two flanks of the building, meaning that the interior would rely upon the light that made its way through these walls for its illumination, a provision the jury thought would be inadequate, turning the mood gloomy. And they furthermore thought that the emphasis on materiality – specifically the green marble – was somewhat 'exhibitionistic and affected', detracting from the formal strength of the building that Schinkel had designed. This said, Mies's proposal was a genuine contender, and in fact came second in the competition, attracting three votes from the nine-member jury.

Heinrich Tessenow, interior perspective drawing for the Neue Wache Memorial competition, 1930.

It was the scheme presented by Heinrich Tessenow that received the majority of votes – including the one cast by the architecture critic Karl Scheffler, who had been so impressed by the Bildungsanstalt in Hellerau that he imagined 'Schinkel would want to shake the architect's hand'.[20] Tessenow envisioned the atrium as an oculus through which both light and rain would fall into the unitary space below, landing on a black stone cube on the top of which would stand a golden oak wreath – 'the customary symbol for honouring the dead', as noted by the won-over jury, who repeatedly praised Tessenow's proposal for its simplicity and its 'commonly understood symbolism', along with its tranquillity: 'The quiet of the room and the ultimate simplicity of its form lend the memorial a solemnity that compels to silent worship or rapt attention', as they noted in their report.[21]

Tessenow had worked his way through many ideas in the design of his memorial, including one that involved the installation of an apparently infinitely deep pit in the centre of the square room, framed by a bronze cage-like grille inserted into a stepped recess in the floor. He said that a '*bodenloser Abgrund* (bottomless abyss) was the only appropriate architectural expression for war in a universal sense, and for all of those millions who have fallen victim to it'.[22]

But as finally proposed and then built, the abyss was replaced by its original opposite – a solid block of black granite that had the quality of a primitive altar or tomb, invoking thoughts of religious mourning for those soldiers

Heinrich Tessenow, Neue Wache Memorial, Berlin, 1931.

who had perished for the sake of the Reich. The wreath on top of the block-altar that bore the matter-of-fact inscription '1914–1918' was sculpted by Ludwig Gies, plated in gold and platinum. It was flanked and palely illuminated at dawn and dusk by two slender head-height candelabra, whose diffuse light served to blur the boundaries of the limestone panel-clad interior. The floor was laid with hand-cut basalt cobblestones, filled in between with lead. The night-black stones were all either square or rectangular, but of different sizes; they were set down in patches or fields, following an indiscernible logic that invested the ground with an oceanic quality which set it apart from the architectonic framing of the walls, and also from that other surface that bounded the space – the ceiling – which was all white and flawless. In its centre was a large, perfectly circular oculus open to the sky, which both permitted the passage of a shaft of light that registered the passing hours of the day and rendered the memorial vulnerable to the North German weather in all its moods.

The feuilletonist Siegfried Kracauer attended the inauguration of the Neue Wache Memorial on a damp early June morning in 1931, and then sat down at his desk in the afternoon to record his impressions for the evening edition of the *Frankfurter Zeitung*: 'When I visited the memorial this morning, steady rain fell down through the oculus, but this in no way disturbed the architecture – on the contrary, it consummated it. The water poured down onto the floor and the moisture darkened the stones, and it ran down the granite block in slender, pitch-black rivulets – it was as though the plinth was weeping.'[23]

And with that, the five out of the possible nine votes that were cast in favour of Tessenow were vindicated. Mies had accrued three of the others, leaving just one vote yet to be accounted for. Poelzig attracted that solitary vote, for his *Soldatengrab* (Grave of a Soldier), which made a much more literal allusion to a war cemetery, with a grave mound empty of a coffin but filled with the soil of a real battlefield, an idea that unfortunately most of the jury found to be 'disturbing'.[24]

At the same time that Poelzig was working on his disturbing *Soldatengrab* proposal, he was preparing an entry for a separate architectural competition which had an almost identical remit – a *Reichsehrenmal* (Reich Memorial) – except that it was to be sited far away from the metropolis, communing rather with the 'soil' of the fatherland in a wood just south of the small town of Bad Berka, itself a five-minute drive from Weimar. Poelzig imagined his project as an *Ehrenhain* (memorial grove), and in explaining the rationale behind his terraced architecture-landscape scheme, Poelzig said: 'Rather than a morbid edifice, I propose a park where German youths will be able to play war games.'[25] The project came to nought, but the drawings that Poelzig made for it were as compelling as ever, and it was in part for his drawing skills and his ability to pass these on to others that Poelzig had been employed as a professor at the Technische Hochschule Charlottenburg where, along with Tessenow, he was attracting eager architecture students from all over the Reich. One of them would go on to play a decisive role in the tragedy of the *Weltkrieg* that would soon follow, transforming the role of architecture in matters of war from one of solemn commemoration to chest-puffing incitement.

The son of an architect, just as his father was before him, Albert Speer first studied for a year at the Hochschule Karlsruhe and then another at the Technische Universität München before transferring to the Technische Hochschule Charlottenburg in 1925, the sole reason being that he wanted to study with Hans Poelzig; at least that is the only reason that he ever gave.[26] Poelzig himself had only just arrived in Berlin, but his reputation had preceded him, and since he only accepted ten students into his design seminars, it was difficult to score a seat. Poelzig set his eager prospective students a design task as a way of narrowing the field, and Speer failed to get through, reportedly due to his poor drawing skills. Much later, he wondered out aloud about the course that his life might have taken if he had managed to be taken in by Poelzig.[27] One does indeed wonder how things might have worked out differently. Speer wrote with respect to his entry into the Nazi party that the student body at Charlottenburg ruptured early on: the left-leaning students enrolled with Poelzig, while those with *völkisch* leanings enrolled with another recent arrival, Heinrich Tessenow.[28] Speer studied with the latter for four semesters before going on to become the architect's trusted assistant in 1927 – a high honour for an architect then only twenty-two and still a student. Later, Tessenow wrote a professional reference for Speer, stating: 'During his time as a student, Herr Speer was one of the most talented in my seminar, and his *Studienarbeiten* were often recognised with special accolades ... And as a teacher, he always stood by my side, in the best possible way. He liaised between myself and the students, with whom he enjoyed the best possible relationship.'[29] Speer in turn wrote the following about Tessenow: 'Outwardly he comes across as just as unimaginative and sober as me, and yet in his buildings there is something truly profound.'[30]

Heinrich Tessenow, interior of the Neue Wache Memorial, Berlin, 1931.

Speer graduated with his diploma at the age of twenty-three in 1928, but after a couple of fruitless years on the hunt for his own architectural

Hans Poelzig, exterior perspective drawing for the Reichs-Ehrenhain competition, Bad Berka, 1932.

commissions, he became restless: 'I was desperate to actually build something – in fact, that was my sole desire. I would have sold my soul like Faust for the opportunity to complete a large-scale building. And then, I found my Mephistopheles.'[31]

With a burning ambition to become a painter, architect or scenographer, Adolf Hitler had moved from the Austrian countryside to Vienna as an eighteen-year-old in 1907, hopeful of acceptance into the Akademie der bildenden Künste (Academy of Fine Arts), which involved a two-stage entrance examination. He negotiated the first hurdle, a preliminary assessment based on

a portfolio of drawings and paintings and, according to Hitler's own retelling of events, awaited the second, the live drawing exam, 'with a burning impatience, proudly confident of the result'.[32] His fate was the same that later befell Speer in his application to study with Poelzig: 'Adolf Hitler, born in Braunau am Inn, Upper Austria on 20 April 1889: Drawing exam unsatisfactory.'[33] Hitler had been so convinced that he would be accepted that the rejection struck him 'like a sudden blow from out of the blue. And yet, it was so.'[34]

But Hitler stayed on in Vienna, and in fact became ever more captivated by the world of the performing arts that had attracted him to the metropole in the first place. Standing head and shoulders above the rest was Richard

Wagner. 'My youthful enthusiasm for the Bayreuth *Meister* knew no bounds', Hitler wrote in *Mein Kampf* (My Struggle).[35] And, in one of his more private 'monologues', he said: 'We who stood with him were called Wagnerians, the others had no names.'[36] Hitler went to as many performances of Wagner's *Wort-Tondramen* as he could afford, enchanted by the singer-actors who roamed about in the majestic Germanic world that Alfred Roller, chief scenographer at the Vienna State Opera, conjured for them upon the stage.[37]

Roller had studied painting at the institution that had rejected Hitler, the Akademie der bildenden Künste, and he had become a professor of drawing at the Kunstgewerbeschule (School of Applied Arts) before taking up his position at the state opera, where in addition to preparing the staging for *Tristan und Isolde* he designed sets for all four acts of *Der Ring der Nibelungen*, though the productions were staged one per year rather than over the four successive evenings that Wagner had prescribed. That was all before 1907, the year in which Hitler failed his entrance exam, and also the year in which Roller began a short-lived correspondence with Appia. The letters they wrote to each other mostly concerned ideas for the staging of *Parsifal*, which Roller was yet to do. In fact, the two extant letters that Appia sent to Roller both concern Wagner's *Bühnenweihfestspiel*; the second of them is headed 'Justification

for the Three Settings (Parsifal: Clearing in the Forest; Klingsor's Dungeon; and The Meadow in Bloom)'. Running to sixteen pages, it is discursive, but also animated and precise.[38]

Keen to become part of that world of Wagnerian scenography, Hitler managed to obtain an invitation to meet Roller; his landlady helped him out by writing on his behalf to a friend who knew Roller to see whether he might meet with the aspiring artist, recommending Hitler as a 'serious, ambitious young man, more mature and settled than his age indicates, nice and sensible, from a perfectly decent family'.[39] Roller responded: 'Dear Madam, I will be happy to oblige you. Do tell young Hitler to call on me and to bring some of his works so that I can see how he is doing. I will surely advise him as best

Alfred Roller, drawing for *Parsifal*, Act 3, Scene 2: Interior of the Temple of the Holy Grail, 1913.

I can.'[40] Hitler was most grateful for the letter of introduction, and wrote a note of thanks: 'Herewith, dear Madam, my most sincere thanks for your good offices in obtaining for me admission to the great master of stage design, Professor Roller.'[41] But all of this penmanship came to nought – Hitler never mustered the courage to knock on the master scenographer's door.[42]

But another door soon yawned wide – war. Hitler was awarded the Iron Cross twice, as was Walter Gropius. However, at the conclusion of hostilities his thoughts went in the other direction to those of the founder of the Bauhaus – for him the old was *in*.

Hitler made his way back to Munich and quickly rose through the crowded ranks of right-wing rabble rousers – his vitriolic beer hall speeches attracting ever larger audiences – until eventually, in July 1921, the members of the Nationalsozialistische Deutsche Arbeiterpartei (Nazi party) granted him absolute power as party chairman, a vote he won 553 to 1. Later in that year, Hitler and his Sturmabteilung attempted their famed Bürgerbräu-Putsch – a failed coup that landed him in Landsberg prison in Bavaria for high treason. He was allowed regular visits from party comrades, and received gifts from well-wishers, including Hugo and Elsa Bruckmann, who on one occasion gave him records and a phonograph. Wagner's music resounded often in Landsberg, with Hitler listening lost in thought, as a comrade later recalled.[43]

Supporters, including Wagner's English-born daughter-in-law Winifred Wagner, also sent food parcels and letters. She reportedly also supplied some of the stationery on which Rudolf Hess transcribed the autobiography and political manifesto that Hitler dictated to him while they were both behind bars together – *Mein Kampf*. Winifred in fact brought up this rumour herself – neither confirming nor denying the truth of it – in Hans-Jürgen Syberberg's 1977 documentary film *The Confessions of Winifred Wagner*.[44] What is certain, however, is that she fell under Hitler's spell; on one occasion she told local Nazi party members that Hitler remained the 'coming man',[45] the one who would 'pull the sword from the German ash tree' just as Siegmund retrieves his father Wotan's sword Nothung in *Die Walküre*. Hitler himself used the Nothung metaphor in a letter he sent to Siegfried Wagner from Landsberg, describing Bayreuth as the place where 'first through the *Meister* and then through (Houston Stewart) Chamberlain was forged the spiritual sword with which we fight today'.[46]

Released and emboldened, and now with a manifesto in his hand, Hitler would become the Reichskanzler in January 1933. All the while, he was as theatrical as he was political, in part viewing the former as a means to success in the latter. And since the Germanic past that so captivated him was rather more mythical than historical, the works of the *Meister* Richard Wagner were constantly on the mind of the *Führer*, even when he had so much else with which to occupy it.

Speer himself recalled that on one occassion Hitler brought out a set of drawings that he had made for every one of the scenes in *Der Ring des Nibelungen*: 'Full of self-satisfaction, Hitler told us at our midday meal that he had been working on them night after night for three weeks, which was especially surprising to me since his calendar at that time was filled to the brim with visits, speeches, official inspections and other public events.' The architect added that 'although there was no doubt that Hitler's *Bühnenbildideen* (staging ideas) were not at all contemporary, they precisely reflected Richard Wagner's intentions'. And on another occasion, 'Hitler delivered from his bedroom in the Reich Chancellery finely drafted and coloured stage designs for every act of *Tristan und Isolde*.'[47]

By 1934, the tables had turned: 'Frau Winifred Wagner informed me on Saturday that *Der Kanzler*, or, as he is generally referred to in these parts, *Der Führer* (a title he also prefers himself), requests my presence in Berlin,'[48] recalled Roller. As two stiff *SS Soldaten* wheeled around and closed the enormous double doors to Hitler's office behind them, the scenographer found himself standing in a 'very large, long, almost empty hall with walls clad in red. At the other end of it stood a sizeable and weighty desk that was almost bare except for an enormous fabric-covered vase lamp. On the other side of the desk sat *Der Führer.*' Roller continues: 'He stood up briskly, shook my hand, and gestured for me to take a seat on the other side of the desk, opposite his.' Hitler then 'laughingly recalled the time he had wanted to show me his drawings and stage designs, and to this end had obtained a letter of introduction from a relative of his who had a connection to somebody in my family. But then, at the very last moment, he did not dare to speak with me.'

Hitler, no longer one for intimidation, except to exercise it, got down to business: 'When I went to Bayreuth, I saw that in many ways the scenery in Vienna was superior. That is why I have invited you here to Germany to design the settings for *Parsifal*.' And then he outlined the size of his ambitions: 'We want to be very generous and invite thousands of young Germans to Bayreuth to witness these performances. If Bayreuth is ever to become the German Olympia, then the production of *Parsifal* must be unique, inimitable.' 'I stood up and thanked Hitler briefly for his trust in me, and for his encouragement. He got up too, rounded his desk and extended his hand to me to bid farewell. But then rather than letting my hand go, he increased the pressure of his grip, staring all the while into my eyes, forcing me to return his gaze.' Stunned, Roller continues: 'Just how long this situation lasted I cannot say – I was entirely transfixed by the indomitable will that shone forth from those eyes. When he finally released me from his grip with one final firm shake of his hand, I had the feeling that I was now bound to Bayreuth under oath. He accompanied me the whole length of the hall, all the way to the door. There I was met once again by saluting SS soldiers, who escorted me out. I glanced at my watch on Wilhelmplatz, and to my surprise, I discovered that our whole encounter had lasted just twenty-five minutes.'

Winifred Wagner welcoming Hitler to the Bayreuth Festspielhaus in 1938.

Optionless, Roller went back to his drafting table and made new drawings for *Parsifal*, based closely on those that he had prepared three decades before. Though the drawings are compelling, the sets that were built based on them were less so, and Hitler reluctantly agreed with Winifred that they should be replaced by ones designed by her eldest son Wieland, himself a budding scenographer.

Wieland's sets were the ones that Hitler saw in 1938 when he attended the 25 July performance of *Parsifal* in Bayreuth,[49] where in a rare outing in civilian clothing, and bowing in deference to the bloodline, he was most enthusiastically greeted by Winifred, who had by that time taken over the running of the festival.[50] Hitler was a welcome and frequent visitor to Bayreuth, and in fact once said to Speer that he loved it there so much that he was considering 'living out his old age in that small city of high culture, which was suffused with Wagner's spirit'.[51] As much as the music and the myths, it was the notion of the *Gesamtkunstwerk* – a performance uniting all the arts, including music, theatre, dance and poetry, painting, sculpture and architecture – that captivated Hitler. In Wagner's formulation, art is a means to higher culture through the orchestration of a self-referential visual order of total aesthetic concordance under the control of the artist-conductor, to whom the audience is expected to submit.[52]

As Theodor Adorno wrote – and it might well have been about Hitler himself – 'Wagnerian gestures were from the outset translations onto the stage of the imagined reactions of the public; the murmurings of the people, applause, the triumph of self-confirmation, or waves of enthusiasm.'[53]

Less than two months after he saw *Parsifal* in Bayreuth, Hitler himself took centre-stage at the Nazi rally grounds in Nuremberg, as leader of the nation which – since Austria had been annexed earlier in the year – had been branded with the self-congratulatory title Großdeutschland. The Zeppelin Field in Nuremberg was the first major commission that Speer carried out for Hitler, who once said to his architect 'we must deliver illusions to the masses ... Illusions are not only required in the cinema and theatre!'[54] Speer listened, and contrived for his Mephistopheles a mighty example of what he would later call *Versammlungsarchitektur*, architecture for drawing people together. Encompassing an area the size of twelve football pitches, the Zeppelin Field carries the iconography of a large medieval fortification, including embankments and bastions that surround a vast levelled field on three sides and serve to direct the inward-looking gaze of the vast rows of rank and file toward the main tribune.

Albert Speer, *Lichtdom* (Cathedral of Light) at the Zeppelin Field, Nuremberg, 1938.

The interminable main elevation of this tribune is an unabated orthogonal affair of stairs, platforms and landings that in their rhythmic ascension are a summoning forth of those forces deemed to be immanent in the landscape, but that required the iron will of the rallying *Führer* to become manifest as architecture. In the stripped-back classicism of the tribune – which takes its cues from the Pergamon Altar, by that time residing in Berlin – there is an echo of ancient Greece, reaffirming the claimed Greco-German kinship that Cosima Wagner so admired in Arnold Böcklin's *Der heilige Hain* (The Sacred Grove), which for her was a 'mysteriously solemn yet celebratory painting in which the sanctity of the Germanic forest is consecrated at night with the beauty and spirit of ancient Greece ... a symbol of the way that the threads that bind peoples continue to be woven across time'.[55] What was 'consecrated at night' in Nuremberg was the cult of the Third Reich, presided over by the *Führer* shouting out from the rostrum that is the climax of the whole great affair of stairs, and which – of course – is only large enough for that one man to stand on.[56]

Hitler delivered his sermons to the Nazi masses inside the spectacular *Lichtdom* (Cathedral of Light) that Speer invented for him, involving 150

Wieland Wagner, settings for *Parsifal*, Act 3, Scene 2: Interior of the Gralstempel; Act 3, Scene 1: Good Friday, 1951.

searchlights streaming up heroically from the twenty-five bastions surrounding the Zeppelin Field into the dark Bavarian heavens above. In his introduction to the book *Neue deutsche Baukunst*, the publication of which Speer himself oversaw in 1941, his junior colleague Rudolf Wolters wrote a suitably glowing review: 'Right back at the beginning of his creative work, Albert Speer formed and shaped with light, and he has used it to an ever-greater extent ... It was at the Rally of Freedom in 1935 that the bundles of rays streaming from the searchlights enveloped the Zeppelin Field for the first time. These rays emanating sixteen kilometres up into the ether formed the Cathedral of Light, that tremendous spatial creation that is Speer's most original work.'[57] And later, in a reflective mood, Speer himself wrote: 'I am strangely moved by the thought that the most successful architectural creation of my life is a chimera; an immaterial phenomenon.'[58]

Speer wrote to his former teacher Tessenow in that same reflective mood on the occasion of the latter's sixty-fifth birthday in 1941, perhaps hoping for a kind word in regard to his own works of architecture that dominated the pages of *Neue deutsche Baukunst*: 'I would like to take this opportunity to warmly enquire whether it might be possible for the two of us to re-establish our former close relationship – me as your student and assistant – and you as my most highly esteemed teacher. Even if, in your eyes, my buildings do not follow along the lines of your teachings, I would like to declare that – in regard to the importance of clean *Grundrisse* (floor plans) and the logical development of building elevations – I could not possibly have wished for a better teacher than you, dear Professor Tessenow.'[59] If he ever wrote one, Professor Tessenow's response has gone unrecorded.

Following the war that annihilated his career along with many of his buildings and much of Europe, Speer was captured and then charged by the military tribunal in Nuremberg and sentenced to twenty years' imprisonment,[60] which he sat out in a tiny cell in Spandau prison on the outskirts of Berlin, the city where he had once been an eager student. With all the time in the world on his hands, Speer determined to chronicle the events of his life, and he furtively scribbled down notes on anything that he could find to write upon – including tobacco wrappers, toilet paper, calendar pages and cardboard packaging – and his thoughts often turned to architecture.[61] On 31 August 1947, it was his 'old teacher Tessenow' whom Speer was thinking of. 'His idea of modest and humane architecture has taken on a whole new meaning for me during this time.' But he was not only reminiscing: 'I foresee that it will be him, and not Gropius, Mies van der Rohe or Le Corbusier who will determine the future'.[62]

following spread Wieland Wagner, setting for *Das Rheingold*, Scene 4: Valhalla Landscape, Gods and Giants before Valhalla, 1955.

Twilight of the Gods: The Essential Wagner Collection: Six Track Sampler.

It was not easy for Speer to get his hands on books and journals that would help him with his deliberations on the future of architecture, but he occasionally managed to. In one of his diary entries, Speer records turning a page of a recent issue of the magazine *American Builder* and 'registering with astonishment the many German names: Gropius, Mendelssohn, Neutra, Breuer, Mies van der Rohe. Of course, I know them all; when I was studying in Berlin with Tessenow, many of them worked a couple of doors down the corridor, so to speak.'[63] Reflecting upon the path that he had chosen, he wrote: 'If I look afresh at my thoughts on architecture, what I desired to build in the 1930s essentially came back to my refusal to accept modernism, and it was that which attracted me to Tessenow. It can't be a coincidence that it wasn't Gropius or Mies van der Rohe who fascinated me as a young architect.'[64]

Though Speer refused to accept modernism, he shared interests and even convictions with some modern architects, Le Corbusier included. While he was interred at Spandau, Speer set a host of tasks for himself to ease the passage of time. One of these assignments was to write a book on the history of the window in architecture – *Die Geschichte des Fensters* was its working title. In one of his diary entries, Speer wrote: 'In order to break up the monotony, over the past two days I have written thirty pages of notes ... My thesis is that the ever-increasing desire for natural light in buildings is related to each epoch. At the outset, there does indeed seem to be some evidence pointing to a connection between the window-to-wall ratio and Rationalism'.[65] The fourth of Le Corbusier's Five Points concerned the *fenêtre en longueur* (ribbon window), and in his short and typically punchy text, he wrote: 'The entire history of architecture revolves around the window as a giver of light.'[66]

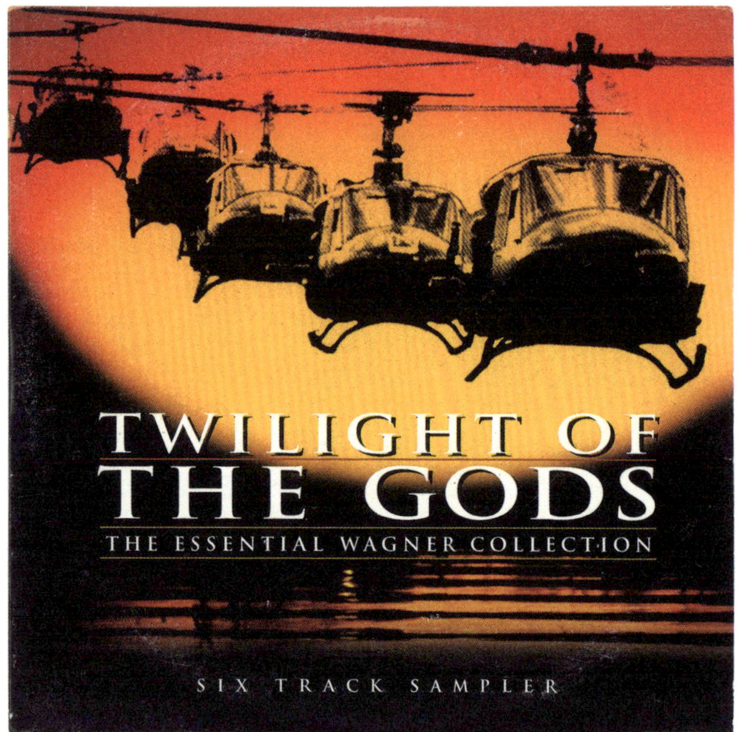

But ultimately, it was to the question of why he had made his Faustian pact with Hitler that Speer's mind kept returning: 'During the twenty years that I spent in Spandau prison, I often asked myself what I would have done if I had recognised Hitler's true face and the true nature of the regime that he had founded. The answer was simultaneously banal and depressing: my position as Hitler's architect had become indispensable to me.'[67]

Winifred Wagner provided a similar answer, long after the war and upon reflection, though without contrition: 'To have met him (Hitler)', she declared, 'is an experience I would not have missed'.[68] It was on account of her friendly relations with Hitler that Winifred was banned by a denazification court from ever again directing the Bayreuth Festival, so she handed over the reins to her two sons, Wieland and Wolfgang. Wieland, the elder of the two, had been photographed – obviously chuffed – with his 'Onkel Wolf' (Hitler) in the grounds of Wahnfried on the same day in 1938 that Hitler was in Bayreuth to see *Parsifal*; he had joined the Nazi party earlier in that year on the personal insistence of his Onkel Wolf, who later also insisted that he should never actually take up arms once the war began. Instead, Wieland held a sinecure at the Institut für physikalische Forschung founded by his brother-in-law, and spent his time there building model stage sets and developing new stage lighting systems. At his own denazification hearing in Bayreuth, Wieland was officially classified as a *Mitläufer* (passive follower), meaning that – officially – he was not as tainted by Nazism as his mother, and was free to make his own mark on Bayreuth.[69]

Wieland Wagner, setting for *Die Walküre*, Act 3, Scene 3: Magic Fire; the Grand Théâtre de Genève after it caught fire on 1 May 1951 during a rehearsal of *Die Walküre*, Act 3, Scene 3: Magic Fire.

Though Appia's book *Die Musik und die Inscenierung* had been banned from Bayreuth while Cosima was in charge,[70] it was held in the Wahnfried library by the time Wieland was on his way to becoming a scenographer, and he apparently read it very closely.[71] It seems that Wieland also had access to some of Appia's unpublished writings and even original drawings, hinting at them in a letter of thanks to a family friend for sending him some of the Swiss scenographer's works, which he had begun to study and was finding 'strange and interesting'.[72]

He was not the only one to imbibe Appia's ideas, which decades later were still fresh. The film-maker Syberberg (now turned interviewee, after interviewing Wieland's remorseless mother Winifred) said that he 'would so much like to be a student again, possessing Adolphe Appia's intellectual intensity, and studying his textbook of the modern theatre, modelled on the work of Richard Wagner; learning how Appia attempted to make the music embedded in a text manifest, through the translation of that text's inner rhythm into an intellectual-spiritual body of gesture and movement.'[73]

Wieland was less willing than Syberberg to recognise his aesthetic lineage, failing to publicly acknowledge his debt to Appia. In fact, in his essay 'Überlieferung und Neugestaltung' (On Inheritance and Designing Afresh) – which was part manifesto and part a plea for understanding – he at times seems to paraphrase the words that Appia had written in *Die Musik und die Inscenierung* half a century before.[74]

The settings that Wieland came up with for the 1951 production of *Parsifal* that opened the first post-war *Festspiele* were considered by many to be 'strange and interesting' themselves, since they were so very different to any that had

The Grand Théâtre de Genève after it was burnt out on 1 May 1951 during a rehearsal of *Die Walküre*, Act 3, Scene 3: Magic Fire.

appeared on the Bayreuth stage before, stripped as they were of all naturalism. That which Wieland had learned from Appia was there for all to see – for example in the spare, monumental simplicity of the interior of the *Gralstempel* that is all form and no ornament, or in the abstract, moody setting for the clearing in the forest in which Parsifal discovers that he is the Redeemer, and which brings to mind Appia's emphatic statement from 1904: 'I repeat, we shall no longer attempt to provide the illusion of a *forest*, but rather the illusion of a *person* in the atmosphere of a forest.'[75]

While Wieland could get away without acknowledging his debt to the ideas of Appia since they were not widely known at the time, the opposite held true for the wartime 'inheritance' that Wieland had to contend with – and never quite managed to shake off. 'Überlieferung und Neugestaltung' was published in the programme for the 1951 Bayreuth Festival, intended to be read by the audience in preparation for what they were about to see on the stage. The full-page opening illustration of the programme was a photograph of the severe bust of Richard Wagner made in 1939 by the sculptor Arno Breker, who had been anointed by Hitler as one of the *Gottbegnadeten* (divinely gifted artists).[76]

Though Appia was never held up in the same manner, he was not as unknown as Wieland thought; others had *also* studied Appia and were keen for his influence on the new Bayreuth aesthetic to be acknowledged. In his review of the 1951 festival, 'Tradition and Revolution at Bayreuth', the music critic Adolf Aber wrote: 'The simple truth is that the movement that seeks a new style of production and discards all the old "props" and paintings from the Wagnerian stage is much older than Wieland Wagner himself, and he is just as much responsible for it as he is for the rising of the sun over Bayreuth every morning. The artist who created the movement and whose name was mentioned by nobody in Bayreuth this summer is the ingenious Swiss stage designer Adolphe Appia.'[77]

Later in the same article, Aber wrote: 'I have not the slightest doubt that Wieland Wagner would have been much more successful in his commendable effort to bring Bayreuth up to date if he had studied Appia's first book (*Die Musik und die Inscenierung*) with the necessary care. He would then have realised that there must be something to make up for the clearing away of all objects that would blur the "style" of his kind of production. The whole aim of such a production is – as Appia points out – to get the actor, as the bearer of the drama, back into the centre of the spectator's attention, and this can only be done by means of the most subtle art of lighting on the stage.' Aber wrote that this 'elementary truth was neglected by Wieland Wagner to such an extent that even visitors who were for a long time quite willing to agree with him became dead tired, impatient and finally annoyed'.[78]

Perhaps now generally ill-disposed to performances that he was remembering from earlier in the year, Aber wrote of the *Ring*, which was the other work staged in that first post-war season, that 'when the curtain opened, and we were supposed to see something like the bottom of the Rhine and saw, in fact, nothing at all for some considerable time, we knew what we were in for'.[79] And he lamented the fact that in the 'Wild Rocky Mountains' setting for Act 2 of *Die Walküre* the 'mountains had been removed in favour of two giant curtains (or the like) giving more than anything else the impression of

Bombs dropped by the 446th Bombardment Group of the US Air Force descending on a German city in 1945.

a prison door closing on the actors', before signing off with the observation that 'only those who were privileged to sit in the higher seats saw the Rhine mercifully covering this whole sad business'.[80]

Certainly, on the basis of the striking photographs that were taken of the settings for *Parsifal* and the *Ring* in that first post-war season, Aber was at least a little unkind, and over the next few years the Wagner brothers continued to hone their aesthetic and technique, until the *new Bayreuth* was a style of its own. It was only then, seven years after his first post-war outing as the scenographer of Bayreuth, that Wieland was ready to offer fulsome recognition of Appia: 'It is part of the real tragedy of Wagner's work that Appia's ingenious aesthetic compulsion was at odds with the staging practices of his time' and 'Cosima Wagner's ban on Appia's book *Die Musik und die Inscenierung* made Bayreuth for decades the province of a long dead artistic style, thereby converting its once revolutionary role into exactly its opposite.'[81] His younger brother Wolfgang later attributed to Appia the fundamental shift at Bayreuth away from two-dimensional pictorial realism towards properly three-dimensional settings, and 'the replacement of *pictorial* scenography with *interpretive* scenography', which was the outcome of Appia's 'close reading of Wagner's works and the unique mythical worlds that they are set within'.[82] Wolfgang also speculated with confidence on where it was that his grandfather would find himself if he were alive in the twentieth century – Hollywood. 'If my grandfather were alive today, the one place we're absolutely certain he would work is Hollywood, for only Hollywood would understand the grandness of his dreams and his madnesses.'[83]

Wagner's music, according to the sleeve of the six-track sampler *Twilight of the Gods* is 'epic music – the original soundtrack of war and peace. Music embodying the most basic and powerful of human emotions: love, hate, fear, grief. Music telling stories made for Hollywood: tales of murder, greed, political intrigue, tragedy and ecstasy.'[84] While part of the attraction is the grand mythical content of particularly Wagner's late *Wort-Tondramen*, there is also the appeal of the leitmotif. As Adorno noted, the Wagnerian leitmotif 'leads directly to cinema music, where its sole function is to announce heroes or situations so as to allow the audience to orient itself more easily'.[85]

One of the most memorable leitmotifs in the *Ring* is that of the *Walküre*, the flock of swooping maidens in full battle armour who augured war, and when it was all over, carried valiant slain warriors from the battlefield to Valhalla. It is the most arresting version of this leitmotif – the *Walkürenritt*

(Ride of the Valkyries) – that helped Wagner's music live up to his grandson's prediction in most spectacular fashion. In Francis Ford Coppola's Vietnam War film, *Apocalypse Now*, a band of exultant yet apprehensive soldiers are on their helicopter-borne march toward enemy territory. Kilgore, the bare-chested surfboard-bearing leader of the airborne operation – and whose name might well be a reference to the sorcerer in *Parsifal*, Klingsor, who in Appia's words 'strives to drag humanity down to the irresolvable despair in which he himself is entangled'[86] – asks one of his young soldiers how he is feeling, to which Jimmy responds: '"Like a mean motherfucker, sir!"'[87] A bugler begins to bugle, and the helicopter takes off, 'rotors spinning, gas turbines belching fire from their jet pipes, sand and dust'. Twenty helicopters deploy into formation and move through the frame 'like a dance of dragonflies – magnificent in the sky as they split into two columns'. Full of bravado, Kilgore announces to another of his young charges that they will '"come in low out of the rising sun, and about a mile out, put on the music". "Music?" "Yeah, I use Wagner ... my boys love it". A hand switches on the tape deck. MUSIC COMES UP.' The Walküre, anticipating the arrival of their wrathful father Wotan, sing their piece *Heiaha! Heiaha! Hojotoho!* 'They make their descent into enemy territory.'[88]

Participants at the second Darmstadt symposium, *Mensch und Raum*, 1951, including Martin Heidegger and Rudolf Schwarz, seated next to each other.

The prodigious mythical world of *Der Ring des Nibelungen* invoked by Coppola, and that according to Wagner himself concerned no less than the 'genesis of the world and its *Untergang* (apocalypse)',[89] irrupted spectacularly into the world of the real in that same year in which the Wagner brothers staged their first post-war festival, though not in Bayreuth but rather in the building in Geneva where Appia had witnessed – and been bitterly disappointed by – his first theatrical performance many decades before. It had principally been the two-dimensional painted scenery on the stage that annoyed young Appia, who around that same time had built a cardboard model for a stage with a schoolfriend who insisted on furnishing it with conventional painted flats, which Appia simply could not stomach; so in order to restore the peace, the two boys 'solemnly burnt the whole thing down', as Appia recalled many years later, going on to express his prophetic wish that the 'same fate would befall the majority of our stages today'.[90]

It was during a midday rehearsal of the *Feuerzauber* (Magic Fire) finale to Act 3 of Wagner's *Die Walküre* on the first day of May in 1951 that an oxygen cylinder intended to feed the fire that protects Wotan's sleeping daughter Brünnhilde exploded, causing a fire that spread and grew, becoming an inferno that ultimately destroyed not only the stage, but also its proscenium arch and the fly tower up above, together with the gangways and the mechanical and electrical machinery. The seats for the orchestra went up in flames, as did those for the audience, up to the third tier. A huge crowd of speechless

onlookers gathered around, their gazes fanning up and down between the mighty fire itself and the tall column of smoke that issued into the skies above, dominating the city skyline well into the evening.

The Grand Théâtre de Genève was not the only building that would need to be rebuilt; Europe was still in tatters after the war, and the question of its reconstruction was a matter of debate both urgent and lively, particularly amongst architects. Less than a week after Wieland's post-war *Parsifal* production premiered at the end of July 1951, many of these architects convened for a three-day colloquium in the city of Darmstadt, a short distance from Bayreuth, where Haus Wahnfried itself now stood barely recognisable, having been bombed by the Allies along with most of the rest of the city right at the end of the war. A flotilla of B-17 and B-24 bombers – 'Liberators' – from the 446th Bombardment Group of the US Air Force had laid waste to the city of Wagner on 5 April 1945,[91] as drolly narrated by a veteran from that mission: 'Bayreuth, home of the Wagnerian music festivals, heard some hot licks not in the Nazi score when five planes of the Group got through some extremely bad weather to attack its marshalling yards on Mickey equipment.'[92] Liberated, the cities of Bayreuth and Darmstadt were now occupied – both of them lay within the American Occupation Zone.

The Darmstadt symposium, on the theme *Mensch und Raum* (Man and Space), got underway in the Civic Centre on the afternoon of Saturday, 4 August, alongside a carefully curated exhibition of architectural projects that were considered to be either exemplary of a past worthy of rememberance, or of a promising future lying in wait. Amongst the former were Tessenow's Bildungsanstalt in Hellerau and Neue Wache Memorial in Berlin, and Gropius's model factory at the Werkbund exhibition in Cologne and Bauhaus Building in Dessau. And notable amongst the latter was Le Corbusier's towering Unité d'habitation in Marseille, which was to be nothing less than a vertical city for 1,600 residents.[93]

The symposium was principally intended as a forum to propose and discuss strategies for the immediate urban and architectural regeneration of Europe's cadaverous post-war cities, but the keynote speakers were in no mind to offer readily implementable solutions. On the Sunday morning Martin Heidegger delivered his famously confounding talk *Bauen Wohnen Denken* (Building Dwelling Thinking) – 'only if we are capable of dwelling, only then can we build'[94] – following on from Rudolf Schwarz's more promisingly titled 'Das Anliegen der Baukunst' (The Primary Concerns of Architecture) the evening before. But Schwarz, too, looked towards the past as much as he did to the future, both on this particular occasion and in his life more generally, as he affirmed in a post-war letter to his friend Mies van der Rohe, who by that time was no longer residing in the Old World but in the New: 'As becomes ever more apparent to me, deep down I am a *stockkonservativer Mann* (dyed-in-the-wool conservative), one who finds it increasingly difficult to believe in the visions of some of our modern friends. So dreadfully much of that which developed through history has been brutally destroyed.'[95] And in another letter, Schwarz wrote: 'I feel that my very existence is at one with that of the West, as old-fashioned as that may sound. We only have a very short time to try and muster together that which can be saved, to permit a final glimmer of the old *untergehenden Lichtes* (final rays of the sun) to shine

Rudolf Schwarz, interior of St Fronleichnam (Corpus Christi Church), Aachen, 1930.

out over the world (our world that has become so small), so that the *alten Völker* (ancient peoples) can once again see what they have in common and carry this memory along with them into whatever lies ahead.'[96]

Schwarz's pre-war projects were displayed in the final room of the historical section of the *Mensch und Raum* exhibition – *Räume der Andacht* (Spaces of Devotion) – which was dedicated to 'those spaces that welcome gatherings of people when the private, social, intellectual and spiritual elements of their lives resonate'.[97] And though his words made him out to be an enemy of modernism, the Schwarz buildings shown in the exhibition revealed him to be a friend of sorts.[98] His Fronleichnamskirche (Corpus Christi Church) in Aachen has an interior as austere as those of Appia's late drawings, such as the one he made for Act 3 of *Iphigenia at Aulis*. The drawing comprises a rank of shallow stairs that span the scene and lead up to a middle-ground platform from which a second run of stairs ascends to the upper platform on which the bloodstained altar of Artemis awaits the sacrifice of a tearful Iphigenia, who has failed in her appeals to her father not to 'send me into death before my time. It is sweet to see the light. Do not make me look at what is under the earth.'[99] The aesthetic is remarkably like the one that prevails in Schwarz's church, which similarly derives from reflection upon what the architect later wrote about in *Vom Bau der Kirche* (The Church Incarnate) as the 'age-old struggle between man and earth. In it, man stands for buoyancy, lightness and clarity against heaviness, formlessness and darkness.'[100] For Schwarz, the age-old struggle was forever staged anew, which is why he was not interested in replicating the architecture of the past as a matter of style, but rather aimed to tap into a supra-historical essence of 'the sacred' that might be embodied by the contemporary *Zeitgeist*. It was for this conviction and the way that he articulated it in both words and diagrams in *The Church Incarnate* that Schwarz earned the high praise of Mies van der Rohe, who read the book avidly and was, in fact, closely involved in its translation into English,[101] declaring in his foreword that it 'throws light for the first time on the question of church building, and illuminates the whole question of architecture itself ... I have read it over and over again.'[102]

Soon after the publication of *The Church Incarnate*, Mies was delivered an opportunity to put some of its teachings into practice, receiving a commission to design what would turn out to be his sole ecclesiastical building – the Robert F Carr Memorial Chapel of St Savior at the Illinois Institute of Technology in Chicago.[103] As was to be expected, Mies's chapel takes minimalism further than Schwarz did, and the overall appearance of the interior of the spare rectangular chapel is one of bare, taut, ascetic precision. Long, uninterrupted side walls of squat buff-coloured bricks lead the eye towards the altar, which is backed by a lustrous, deeply pleated curtain dividing the congregation from the cloistered chambers behind.[104] The only furnishings are two low oak-veneer benches, and a gleaming stainless-steel altar rail and cross. The plan of the chapel is divided in two – a lay area given over to the earthly and an area allied to the sacred – and the threshold between them is orchestrated by the most minimal of means: the floor of the nave rises as a single very low step that reads more as a wrinkle in the earth than as an act of building. The solid travertine marble altar is the focus of the ascension, and it is where the very substantial chthonic content of the chapel is founded. And here the client for the building – Bishop Wallace E Conkling – shared, and perhaps even exceeded, Mies's own estimation of the importance of the altar to the chapel: 'My dear Mies ... Even though our funds be so limited, we *must* do the Altar right, above all else, for that is the thing for which we are building the Chapel.'[105] This time, it is Appia's drawing for the second act of *Iphigenia among the Taurians* that the chapel reminds one of most. This drawing takes in a side-on view towards the altar in the Temple of Artemis, and it marries primitive embodied experiences of spatiality and orientation with removed

Ludwig Mies van der Rohe, interior of the Chapel of St Savior, IIT, Chicago, 1952.

perspectival clarity and precision, which the chapel does as well. While the architecture itself is lucid, the words that Mies wrote about it are less so: 'I chose an intensive rather than an extensive form to express my conception, simply and honestly, of what a sacred building should be', and 'It was meant to be simple; and, in fact, it is simple. But in its simplicity it is not primitive, but noble, and in its smallness it is great – in fact, monumental.'[106]

While Mies was designing his simple-noble chapel of St Savior that sits aloof on the vast lawns of the IIT campus in Chicago that he himself had masterplanned – subjecting the entire site, an area equal to eight city blocks,

following spread
Le Corbusier, interior of Notre-Dame du Haut de Ronchamp, 1955.

Le Corbusier, exterior altar of Notre-Dame du Haut de Ronchamp, 1955.

to a relentless grid – Le Corbusier was toiling away on the design of what was likewise his first ecclesiastical commission. The site of the pilgrimage chapel of Notre-Dame du Haut de Ronchamp – atop a forested hill that stands 500 metres proud of its surroundings – could not possibly have been more different from the manicured campus lawns that Mies was designing his chapel for in Chicago. On his first visit to the site in the department of the Haute-Saône, northeastern France on 4 June 1950, Le Corbusier made a set of initial sketches in which it is clearly the spectacular landscape setting, the rolling hills and green woodlands, that mattered most, as he himself later wrote: 'On the hill, I meticulously drew the four horizons; it was they that unlocked the architecture – a visual echo in the realm of form.'[107]

The site was one with prospects that the ancient Romans had identified long ago; 'Ronchamp' probably derives from *Romanorum campus*, a Roman camp. Once that empire had crumbled, the site became a place of Christian pilgrimage in veneration of the Virgin. And the small stone chapel that was built there stood firm until the war that would soon be discussed at the *Mensch und Raum* symposium in Darmstadt exacted its toll. The initial intention of the group of parishioners who banded together to form the Association de l'œuvre Notre-Dame du Haut had been to reconstruct the original chapel, which was badly, though not irreparably, damaged; but they eventually abandoned that idea in favour of a brand-new building. Their first task was the selection of an architect, and they asked Canon Ledeur, Secretary of the Besançon Commission d'Art Sacré, for his opinion, to which the robed dignitary responded: Le Corbusier. For Ledeur, the fact that Le Corbusier was a professed disbeliever in organised religion was not grounds for disqualification. Father Marie-Alain Couturier, co-editor of the journal *L'Art sacré*, was similarly supportive. A man of the cloth who rejected reliance on rhetoric, Couturier trusted more to aesthetics, particularly poetry; 'anything else is spiritual academicism', he wrote.[108] His interest was in the furtherance of those with an 'instinct for the sacred', often 'masters from the outside' who had spiritual gifts purer and more exacting than 'many artists who profess the faith, and even – sad to say – in many members of the clergy. This fact may well be irritating, but at the present time it is undeniable. "The Spirit breatheth where the Spirit will".'[109]

Appia, *Iphigenia among the Taurians*, 1926.

But Canon Ledeur still had to plead his case with the spirited architect on behalf of the Association: 'It is true that we do not have much to offer you, but we do have this – a wonderful location and the possibility to really go all the way with the architecture. I am not sure whether you are interested in building churches, but, if you are ever going to build one, then the conditions offered by Ronchamp are ideal – you will be given free rein to create what you will.'[110] Yes, said Le Corbusier.

And so that is how the architect came to draw the four horizons that unlocked the architecture of Ronchamp, the sculptural whitewashed Roman Catholic chapel on the hill in which nigh a right angle is to be found. But this is not to say that measure is not present everywhere; the altar is the anchor that moors the shapes and forms that Le Corbusier placed in carefully tuned accord around it. 'If you go to Ronchamp', he wrote, 'you will see that the altar stands firm in its setting – it is a sacrificial stone'.[111] 'It is an altar like one of those that stood firm right back at the beginning of time, in front of which men stood – with the great Unknown as a witness – and sacrificed their children, killed them',[112] wrote Le Corbusier, thinking perhaps of ancient episodes in the tragedies of Homer or Euripides, such as the filicidal death of *Iphigenia at Aulis* on the command of her father Agamemnon, a gruesome fate that according to Euripides she met most stoically: 'She goes to drench with her blood the altar of the divine goddess Artemis.'[113]

But unlike the serene setting that Appia prepared for that bloody scene, and likewise dissimilar to the stripped-back modern interiors of the chapels by Schwarz and Mies that recall it, the ground plan of Ronchamp is not a symmetrical one. It does, however, have a definite centre of gravity, one much like that of a dancer or an athlete in motion, and unsurprisingly, it is this 'line of symmetry' that the altar – a solid block of white stone hewn from a quarry in Burgundy – balances upon. This pivotal east–west line that is clearly marked X - - - - - X on the plan drawing is similarly 'drafted' in the building itself, via a narrow strip of paving that runs the full length of the interior from the base of the west wall to the altar rail in the east.[114] But other than that, there is very little in the deftly sculpted interior of the chapel that is in obvious alignment, though everything resonates; in Le Corbusier's words, the effect is that of 'an acoustic phenomenon introduced into the realm of forms'. The tuning instrument that Le Corbusier used was the Modulor, a proportioning system which the architect had himself invented, one professedly in accord with the human body and its typical postures, whether standing tall or lying prone on the 'ancient altar', the one on which human sacrifices were made before the time of Christianity.

Appia in fact made one drawing of a pre-Christian altar on which a victim lies prone – a setting for the scene in the third act of *Iphigenia among the Taurians* in which Orestes is to be executed as a 'fresh victim for the goddess Artemis' by his unknowing sister Iphigenia. In Appia's dark drawing, Orestes is silhouetted together with the altar that he therefore appears to be at one with, while his sister stands robed and palely illuminated behind him, ready to carry out her sacrificial duty. The expansive ocean horizon can be glimpsed in the background, but the heavy walls are closing in on the scene, as they are too on the life of Orestes. He was saved, just in time, and Appia's drawing was rescued too, though only as an image, not as an artefact – the drawing itself is lost or destroyed, but a photograph of it remains.[115]

For Le Corbusier, the Christian altar recalls that ancient time of the House of Atreus, though the sacrifice has become symbolic. The 'drama that was atrocious and terrible', has been transformed into 'a very beautiful *signe*'.[116] Le Corbusier was keen to return to the origins of that *signe*, which for him had become obscured over time, since the Church had 'devalued its holy places by erecting all sorts of shenanigans – paintings, often awful stations of the cross and so forth, and altars crowded with formidable clutter'.[117] The altar at Ronchamp is 'simply a stone slab, and standing on it are only the ciborium and a tabernacle. And there are two small candles – that is enough', he said.[118]

But since Ronchamp is a pilgrimage chapel, and a small one at that, Le Corbusier designed an outdoor sanctuary for open-air ceremonies on those days in the liturgical calendar when throngs of worshippers would arrive, and as is the case inside the chapel, it is the altar around which everything else is ordered. According to the Abbé Ferry, from whom Le Corbusier received liturgical guidance, as the 'blue amphitheatre of sky and landscape unfurls in the distance, the altar is perceived as the fulcrum of a cosmic celebration'.[119]

At the consecration ceremony for Ronchamp on 25 June 1955, Le Corbusier declared to the Archbishop of Besançon and the other dignitaries who were assembled before a congregation of believers squinting in the early summer sunlight that 'some things are sacred, others are not, whether or not they are religious',[120] seemingly implying that he was, in fact, better qualified than the archbishop to recognise sacred things. Just how the architect's words were received on that day is unknown, but he himself was well pleased with the course of events, as he related to his mother in a letter that he wrote to her that very afternoon: 'Everything went off wonderfully at Ronchamp – all joy, beauty, and spiritual splendour. Your Corbu was in the place of honour, at the top. Well regarded, liked. Respected. This was a difficult game to play. It is the most revolutionary work of architecture for a long time.'[121]

Le Corbusier, exterior of Sainte-Marie de la Tourette, 1960.

Ronchamp was the first, but not the only, ecclesiastical commission that Le Corbusier – a man who in his own words had never experienced the miracle of faith – carried out. The man behind his second commission – Le Couvent Sainte-Marie de la Tourette, a Dominican monastery[122] – was the visionary Father Couturier, for whom talent trumped all else: 'It would, of course, be ideal if Christian art could be revived by men who are both geniuses and saints. However, if such men do not exist, we believe that it would be much

safer in the present circumstances to commission geniuses with no faith to bring about this renaissance – this resurrection – rather than believers with no talent.'[123] And in *L'Art sacré* he wrote: 'We used to say that not only did we believe that Le Corbusier was the greatest living architect, but also that his spontaneous perception of the sacral world was the strongest and most authentic of anyone we knew.'[124]

The agnostic man with talent first visited the site in L'Arbresle – a commune in the Rhône department, eastern France – on 4 May 1953. In a conversation that he later had with the monks for whom he built the monastery, Le Corbusier said: 'I came here and got out my sketchbook, as usual. I drew the horizons, I noted the course of the sun, and I got a feel for the lie of the land. I picked out the site, for this had not yet been done. In so doing, I was

Le Corbusier, interior of the church of Couvent Sainte-Marie de la Tourette, 1960.

performing an act either criminal or worthy. The first step is to choose.'[125] The site that Le Corbusier chose for himself is very different to the one that was preordained for him at Ronchamp. In fact, it might be thought of as its opposite. While Ronchamp sits proud atop a hill and commands its horizons,[126] La Tourette holds its ground on a steep hillside and establishes a horizon all of its own. Le Corbusier decided upon a site that was 'mobile, evasive, sloping and flowing'. So, rather than contending with the ground plane as given, he established his own datum, a kind of string line for the monastery that he would build *down* from, in his own words, 'a point of departure, reaching the ground as and when'.[127]

Having determined the fundamental horizon for the monastery of La Tourette – 'a silent dwelling place for one hundred bodies and one hundred

hearts'[128] – Le Corbusier set about designing the building itself, an undertaking too great for that one man alone.

Before he came to architecture, Iannis Xenakis studied engineering and music, and he brought the skills and techniques of both of those disciplines with him when he applied to work for Le Corbusier in his atelier in Paris. While accompanying Le Corbusier to the atelier at 35 rue de Sèvres one morning in 1953, the thirty-one-year-old Xenakis abruptly enquired of the architect whether he might work with him personally on a project. '"Yes", he said to me without hesitation, "I have a project that will suit you perfectly; it is pure geometry – a Dominican monastery".'[129]

Father Couturier, the client for the Dominican monastery of pure geometry, wrote that 'to be *true* today, a church should be no more than a flat roof on four walls. But their proportions – their volume, the distribution of light and shadow – could be so pure, so intense, that anyone coming in would feel the spiritual dignity and solemnity of the place',[130] a statement entirely in alignment with what Xenakis wrote after the monastery and its church were finished: 'To discover, to create a different, other architecture, unique and original in its essential nudity – that was our goal.'[131]

Le Corbusier, side chapels of the church of Couvent Sainte-Marie de la Tourette, 1960.

The essential nudity of the building is due in part to the material that Le Corbusier decided to construct it from: 'I used *béton brut*. The result: total fidelity to the model, a perfect reproduction of the mould. Concrete is a material that does not cheat; it replaces, it cuts out the need for that trickster – coating. *Béton brut* says: "I am concrete".'[132] However, it is not only the palette but also the components and composition – particularly of the church – that are pared back and bare, centring again on the altar, around which all else is ordered: 'The altar marks the centre of gravity and engenders a value, a hierarchy of things', wrote Le Corbusier. 'In music there is a key, a range, a chord; here it is the altar – the most sacred of all places that creates this note, and whose role it is to trigger the radiance of the *œuvre*. This is facilitated by proportions. Proportion is an ineffable thing.'[133]

But it took some time to settle on the final simple design of the altar, as the young bull Xenakis later recalled: 'I designed a high altar that was judged by the monks to be too abrupt, too high, too separative. In fact, I had conceived it a little like a place for terrible sacrifices. It was too dramatic – too Aztec.'[134] The revised version of the altar is still an affair of steps and platforms that rise up symmetrically within an austere rectilinear volume – 'no more than a flat roof on four walls' – and which for its formal composition and distribution of light and shadow has invited comparison with Appia's drawings, chief among them his *Espaces rythmiques*, but also others such as those that he made for the Valhalla landscape scene in *Das Rheingold*, particularly the final version – now lost – that he prepared for the ill-fated 1924 staging of the *Ring* in Basel, in which sharply profiled steps and platforms make up the foreground of the setting. It is this final version that Giuliano Gresleri brought into visual dialogue with Le Corbusier's own setting for the interior of the church at La Tourette, facing the two of them off across the spine in a double-page spread in his book on the architect's youthful journey to the East, *Viaggio in Oriente*.[135]

Appia, *Das Rheingold*, Scene 2: Valhalla Landscape, 1924.

And the two images do indeed resonate, in part due to their shared aesthetic – both are rhythmic symmetrical compositions of steps and platforms set within stark, monochromatic settings – but it is for the fact that they both invoke the chthonic powers of the earth that they belong together. One of the consequences of Le Corbusier's decision to build *down* from a string line up in the sky rather than *up* from a levelled site on the ground is that the further he went in the direction of building the monastery, the deeper his excavations into the 'evasive, sloping' hillside would be. And those elements of the building that dig down deepest are the church and its flanking side chapels – seven of them in all – each centred on a stone altar, like 'those that stood firm right back at the beginning of time', and each one is set a step lower down than the one that came before it.

The scene for which Appia prepared his setting is, in fact, the only one in the *Ring* in which the Germanic earth goddess Erda – the 'eternal world's primal seeress', in Wagner's own words – appears. Her arrival in the second scene of *Das Rheingold* is darkly portentous, emerging as she does from 'out of a chasm in the rocks' that stands on one side of the stage: 'Erda suddenly becomes visible, rising up out of the deep'. She embodies the fecund powers of the earth – the receptacle for all that has come into being, and all that in time will pass away: 'All that was – I know; all that is, all that will be – I see that too.' And what Erda now foresees is nothing less than the *Weltuntergang*, the end of the world: 'All that is, – will end! A dark day is dawning for the gods',[136] Erda announces to Wotan before descending out of sight once again, while the light on the stage dies away to nothingness. In Appia's setting, and in his own words, it is the 'cavern on the left out of which the apparition of Erda arises',[137] while the matching cavern on the right leads down to Nibelheim's underground chasms, which in Wagner's staging instructions must be designed in such a way as to give the impression that 'the stage is constantly sinking downwards into the earth'.[138]

Beyond the twin caverns that provide passage to the world of the subterranean flows the mighty River Rhine, on the far shore of which is a vast spreading plain. Rising above this potent landscape, in Appia's words, is Valhalla, 'mighty, rocky, artificial',[139] erected while Wotan was asleep and made visible as the light of breaking day falls with growing splendour. 'Accomplished – the immortal work! Fortress of the gods, crown of the mountain – the superb swagger of the tremendous building!', Wotan avows on waking. 'I carried it in my dreams, and as my will revealed it, strong and fine, it stands there for all to see – a noble, magnificent edifice.'[140]

A mountain of a building, the Unité d'habitation also swaggers superbly, standing there for all to see. If La Tourette is to be understood as a descent, then the Unité is undoubtedly an *ascent*, rising from the double row of fifteen pilotis that hoist the torso of the mighty building up onto their shoulders, allowing the semi-natural landscape of the ancient port city of Marseille to flow by uninterrupted down below. These mighty pilotis are like the trunks of trees in that not only are they structural, they gather and dispense the systems of supply and waste that course through the building above, systems that are usually buried in the ground beneath a city, but that in the Unité – a vertical city – are tended in a raised artificial ground. This *sol artificiel* is made up of a strong, hollow grid of girders standing directly atop the pilotis, receiv-

Le Corbusier, Unité d'habitation Marseille, 1953.

ing and then carrying within itself myriad shafts, ducts and pipes that heat the building in winter and cool it in summer, and relieve it of wastewater and rubbish all the year around.

The vertical city that rises from this artificial ground has streets, as do ordinary cities, but in the Unité they are *rues intérieures*, interior streets, which run the full length of the building north to south. They are low in height but are generously wide; the shiny black floor casts up a reflection of the white ceiling, and of the apartment doors that, one after the other after the other, are a polyphony of colour. But as in other cities, each street has its own identity, delivered here by the individual colour dedicated to each of them, applied to the delivery boxes of each apartment, and that considered together register an ascent; the first is sea-blue, the second is green, the third yellow, the fourth orange, the fifth red, the sixth violet and the uppermost seventh street is sky-blue. That there are fewer *rues intérieures* than there are floor levels in the Unité is owing to the fact that each of them services three floors; the apartments – more than 300 of them – are split-level and slot into each other top to toe, one is 'top-down', and the other is 'bottom-up'. In addition to these streets of housing, as it were, there is a double-storey street that Le Corbusier conceived as the vertical city's retail quarter, including a butcher, fishmonger, greengrocer, laundry, newsagent, boulangerie and hairdresser.

Arriving at the Unité from the side of the sunny Mediterranean, residents and visitors alike step into the *hall d'entrée* – a low-ceilinged hypostyle foyer – and move through it to the vestibule at the rear, which contains the four large elevators that might be thought of as the four-lane highway of the building, rising up through the Unité to either stop at, or pass right by, each of its *rues intérieures* – | Sea-Blue | Green | Yellow | Orange | Red | Violet | Sky-Blue – before reaching its final destination | Rooftop.

Lucien Hervé, photographs of the roof terrace of the Unité d'habitation Marseille, 1957.

The architectural tableau of this rooftop includes a nursery, kindergarten, paddling pool and gymnasium, two solaria, artificial mountains sculpted in concrete, plus tall ventilation stacks cast in that same raw material, all circumscribed by a 300-metre running track that Le Corbusier termed the 'esplanade of physical culture'.[141] The scenic ensemble reads as a concerted attempt to embody the architect's own earlier definition of architecture as the 'masterly, correct and magnificent play of forms brought together in light',[142] or in other words of his – this time in direct reference to the Unité rooftop itself – a '*symphonie plastique*'.[143]

At the northernmost extremity of the sculptural rooftop symphony, Le Corbusier composed an elemental open-air theatre in coarsely shuttered cast concrete, where festivals could be held in summer 'without any *mise-en-scène* or expense'.[144] Primitive in character, the theatre is at once a celebration of ancient cultural origins that he hoped to recuperate and a monochromatic architectural composition of perspectival clarity.[145]

The whole setting is deeply redolent of Appia's drawings, particularly when composed and stripped of colour, as in the 1957 series of photographs shot by Lucien Hervé.[146] Clearly briefed by Le Corbusier regarding the thematic significance of the horizon, Hervé held his Rolleiflex medium-format camera at exactly the height of the parapet (also the height of the stage) that bounds the rooftop.[147] Some photographs seem to have been taken quickly while others were carefully staged, but the overall setup is very much like that of a perspective drawing. The rectangular space of the open-air theatre is paced with a rectangular grid impressed into the slab – a 'ruled surface'[148] – and the perspective-like setup is further emphasised by the long, closely grouped shuttering lines of the flanking wall as they converge towards the vanishing point on the horizon.

Hervé affixed his monochromatic prints onto stiff sheets of coloured card – pastel-hued yellow, green, blue, purple or orange – generally twelve images at a time. These compositions have generally been referred to as contact sheets, though that is not at all what they are. Rather than straightforward reproductions of photographs taken sequentially on a single roll of film, each sheet is an exercise in the composition of a series of photographs that might belong together since they were shot one after the other, or on a single day, but their belonging might just as well be thematic – all, say, of the *sol artificiel* or the interior of an apartment, taken days or even years apart.[149] That is, Hervé's carefully composed sheets should be thought of as the staging – the *scenography* – of the Unité, abstracting from the full, lived plenitude of the mountain-building that stands within a sea's-breeze of the Mediterranean a carefully constructed image of it, seen through the eye of the photographer, like the way the creator of a perspective drawing sets out the viewpoint for the observer on the picture plane of the page.

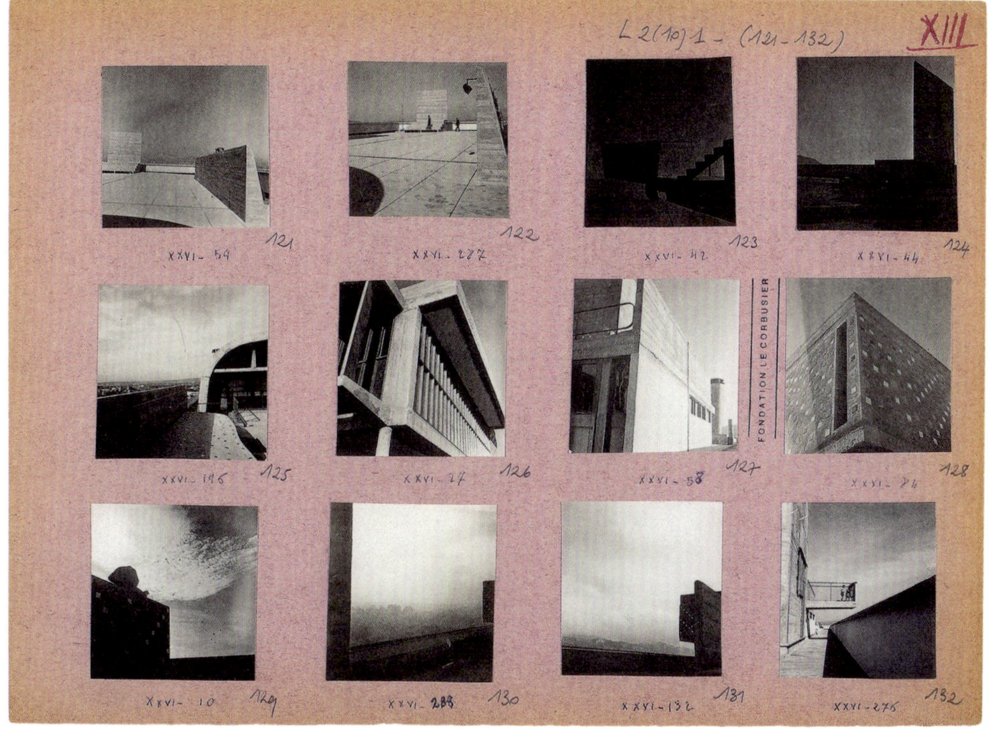

Lucien Hervé, photographs of the roof terrace of the Unité d'habitation Marseille, 1957.

following spread
Lucien Hervé, photographs of the open-air theatre on the roof terrace of the Unité d'habitation Marseille, 1957.

Hervé carefully chose the colour of each backing card on which he composed his black and white prints in order to impart a certain mood or atmosphere.[150] So, the photographer's palette resembled Appia's, insofar as the scenographer similarly only ever worked in monochrome – making his drawings with charcoal, graphite and white pastel. And he did so on those Ingres papers made by Canson & Montgolfier – mostly in hues of pale blue, green, beige or amber – which imbued each drawing with a distinctive ambient undertone.

Appia, the scenographer who was always distant yet also always enigmatically present, might himself be thought of the same way. The *Espaces rythmiques* that he drew and erased into being on the collapsible drawing board in front of him not only brought to realisation the *Raumstil* for eurhythmics, as he claimed, but also visualised a profoundly modern sensibility that wanted things both ways: cultural rebirth and continuity with the depths of tradition.

Avril 1957- Marseille
L-II-166
457
L-II-256
458
L-II-143
460
L-II-24
461
L-II-17
464
L-II-30
467
L-II-31
468

L2(12) 1 - (457- 470)

L-II 139 459

L-II-143 460

L-II-20 462

L-II-19 463

-25 465

FONDATION LE CORBUSIER

L-II-26 466

L-II-116 469

L-II-127 470

OLPH

PPIA

CODA

Le Corbusier's Unité d'habitation was inaugurated in Marseille in 1952 and in that same year Appia's *heritage artistique* was exhumed by his nephew Edmond Appia from the cabinet in the annexe of the Musée d'art et d'histoire in Geneva, where his work had lain undisturbed for a quarter of a century. Most likely Edmond's interest had been piqued by the success of Wieland Wagner's 'new' Bayreuth productions which, depending on one's point of view, either honoured or plundered Appia's aesthetic.[1] He tested the waters amongst his friends and colleagues and found that they, in fact, held Appia in what amounted to a presentiment of esteem since there was so very little to go by. Edmond set about correcting this state of affairs, establishing, for example, a rapport with André Veinstein in France, who published some of Appia's previously unknown texts.[2] And then in 1961, the director of the Collection Suisse du Theâtre, Edmund Stadler, offered to rehouse the entire Musée d'Art et d'Histoire collection in a basement room of the Swiss National Library in Bern – a location scarcely more salubrious than that of the museum annexe, but the institutional setting would in time prove to be decisively so.

With only meagre financial means at his disposal, but both emboldened by the fact that he had now become the sole director of the Fondation Adolphe Appia and weighed down with the responsibility that came along with it, Stadler poured his energy into curating a major travelling exhibition that would commence its journey at the font in Bern in 1962 – the centenary of Appia's birth. Lucia Moholy, famed of course for the photographs she took at the Bauhaus,[3] wrote a lengthy, insightful review of the 'rare kind of exhibition' which began: 'Adolphe Appia (1862–1928) was honoured by a memorial display of sketches, manuscripts, typescripts, catalogues, notes and other documentary material relating to his ideas and projects in the field of stage design ... he was one of the first and, also, one of the main instigators of modern ideas in theatrical history'.[4] She first mentioned Appia's early Wagnerian settings that showed the 'more Romantic mood of his younger years', and then wrote at greater length about the *Espaces rythmiques* that, in her words, 'made up an appreciable part of the display' and that derived from his fertile exchange of ideas with Jaques-Dalcroze, some of which later materialised in the 1912 and 1913 productions of Gluck's *Orfeo ed Euridice* in Hellerau: 'This performance impressed the whole of Europe, soon to be forgotten again ... The human figure being an integral part of the design, he felt that freedom of movement was only compatible with a stage of the utmost simplicity, the austere dignity of the scene acting as a challenge to living gesture. Guided by this principle, he reduced stage design to its bare elements, using the horizontal, the perpendicular, the diagonal, the slant, the slope, the stairs, and very little else.'[5] She was very impressed by the exhibition itself, but not by the fact that there was nothing material to take away from it: 'A catalogue was, unfortunately, not available.'[6]

From Bern, the exhibition travelled to Florence, Venice and Milan, then to Geneva – the city of Appia's birth – before being shipped over to the Victoria & Albert Museum in London, though that iteration was 'slightly reduced in size through lack of space', according to Stadler.[7] One hundred and seven images were included in the exhibition, which had now been given the name *Appia and the New Approach to Stage Design*. Mostly, these were of course Appia's own atmospheric drawings, but there were also some images that provided

preceding left page
Cover of 'Adolphe Appia, 1er Septembre 1862–29 Février 1928'.

Poster for the *Adolphe Appia 1862–1928: Darsteller–Raum–Licht* exhibition held at the Austrian Theatre Museum in Vienna, 13 June–6 October 1980.

context for them, including a photograph of one of Max Brückner's Wagnerian settings at Bayreuth and another of the *Orfeo ed Euridice* setting in the Festsaal at Hellerau. This time a catalogue was indeed made available, but it was only a slim stapled-together booklet of twenty-six pages of excerpts of text (all of which Stadler had written himself) and fifteen pages of illustrations – twenty-four plates of Appia's drawings, all stripped of colour.

Eight years later, in 1978, the entire collection of the Société Suisse du Théâtre was donated to a newly founded institution, the Schweizerische Theatersammlung, which had four member organisations: the Swiss Confederation, the Canton of Bern, the City of Bern and the Société Suisse du Théâtre. And then the year after that, the Swiss Arts Council, Pro Helvetia, commissioned Denis Bablet (Head of Research at the Centre National de la Recherché Scientifique in Paris) and Marie-Louise Bablet to curate another exhibition that would be included in *Pariser Espaces* '79.

That exhibition, *Adolphe Appia 1862–1928: acteur–espace–lumière* (the catalogue, again a small book of ninety-six pages, was published in French, German and English)[8] became *Adolphe Appia 1862–1928: Darsteller–Raum–Licht* when it returned to Switzerland and was first shown at the *Helmhaus* in Zurich in the winter of 1980. From 1982, the show went on tour, making its way all the way up to Helsinki and Tampere in Finland, then back down to Germany, jagging between East and West – taking in the cities of Rostock, Berlin, Erfurt, Halle, Düsseldorf and Bonn – before setting sail for Rio de Janeiro. The monochrome poster on beige paper advertising the exhibition remained the same everywhere since the batch had been printed back in Switzerland in advance – the lower three quarters taken up by a cropped reproduction of Appia's *Espace rythmique: Steps in the Foreground* while the scenographer's name was printed in bold in large letters running along the top edge. The space between Appia's name at the top and his drawing down below was empty – that was where the poster was customised with information relevant to the exhibition's current showing, such as its location in the city, its opening and closing dates and patronage: the Ausstellungszentrum am Fernsehturm Berlin, 7. Juli–25. Juli 1989, Zentrum für Kunstausstellungen der DDR – in the case of East Berlin in the year that its wall came down.

By that time, Appia's drawings had been on the road for seven years and were showing signs of wear. But demand for the exhibition was undiminished, so Pro Helvetia decided to 'multiply' the exhibition by making 1:1 facsimile copies of twenty of the drawings, and found a printing company in

Geneva that happened to have in stock precisely those Canson & Montgolfier papers that Appia himself had always used. Pro Helvetia printed as many copies of the facsimiles as the stash of fortuitously available papers allowed, and once demand for the exhibition finally abated, they donated the remaining sets of reproductions to the Schweizerische Theatersammlung in Bern, which published 300 numbered copies of them as *Adolphe Appia (1862–1928): Zwanzig Faksimilies aus seinem bühnenbildnerischen Entwurfswerk* (Twenty Facsimiles of His Stage Designs) in 1993.[9]

Poster for the *Adolphe Appia 1862–1928: Darsteller–Raum–Licht* exhibition held at the Helmhaus in Zurich, 12 January–17 February 1980.

Marie-Louise Bablet was also preparing Appia's *Œuvres complètes*, which would appear in four volumes published in 1983, 1986, 1991 and 1998 by the Société Suisse du Théâtre and L'Age d'Homme in Lausanne with the generous support of the Schweizerischer Nationalfonds.[10] Collectively, these volumes are a remarkably rich repository of biographical facts and listings of primary and secondary documents, and each of them runs to around 500 pages. But they are scantly illustrated and are not tied together by any narrative other than bare chronology. Only one edition of the *Œuvres complètes* has ever been printed, and even then, only in a small run. And of course, since they are written in French their contents are denied to an English-language audience. A fifth and final volume was originally planned – a complete illustrated catalogue of Appia's drawings – but it never materialised.

As for the original drawings that would have appeared in the fifth volume had it come to fruition, they had been carefully returned to storage back in 1985 in the SAPA Foundation, Swiss Archive of the Performing Arts – a modest cultural-philanthropic operation inconspicuously lodged in a repurposed corner of a car park under the Bern courthouse.[11] Having double-checked the address and opening times – Wednesday and Thursday afternoons – on an information board under the kind of triple-vaulted glaucomic fibreglass awning produced for suburban bus stops in the 1980s, you step inside the archive and find that the reading room ceilings are low, the walls windowless, and the furniture is *sachlich* but comfortable; it feels like a small-town library. The staff are eager, capable and affable, and they are well supported by enthusiast-volunteers and interns working away quietly on the grey laminate-topped tables in the reading room.

Roused from their resting place in the large plan-drawers in the room next door, Appia's drawings are delivered for viewing one at a time. Up close, they are revelatory; shimmering with those qualities that would have come to life through dramatic performance – through music, lighting, costumes and bodies, of both actors and audience.

But when we turn over these pale-hued sheets of Canson & Montgolfier paper, we are presented with an altogether different kind of graphic: a set of apparently *ad hoc* markings (mostly single words and numbers) made at different times and for different reasons, but which turn out to be as informative as they are intriguing when considered all together. For example, the German Theatre Museum in Munich – one of only a couple of other institutions that hold original works by Appia – has an 1892 drawing for the third act of *Die Walküre* (On the Summit of a Rocky Mountain, Awaiting the Arrival of Wotan), which depicts a flock of expectant Valkyries with spears held high, perched before an ominous darkly gathering storm. On the rear of the drawing are six inscriptions of various kinds. Written in graphite pencil are: the title of the drawing, 'Vor der Antritt Wotan', in the middle-centre of the page; 'Rivaz' (the town Appia was living in when he made the drawing), up in the top-left corner; and located left-centre, 'X'. In red pencil, and then scribbled out in graphite pencil, is a number, '25'. There is also an ink stamp reading 'THEATERMUSEUM' and noting the inventory number that the drawing still holds today: 'IV6571' (the ink must have been running dry on the day of acquisition, since in addition to the imprint on which the inventory number is noted are three other patchy attempts). Finally, there is a large white label with a decorative dark blue border pasted down on the bottom-right of the page, also bearing an inventory number, but one much more detailed and now redundant – '319,241,3d,Th.M'. On the back of another drawing, this time an *Espace rythmique* called *The Steps*, there are ten inscriptions. Written in graphite pencil are: the title of the drawing, *Escalier en face*, in the middle-centre of the page; identification of the series to which this drawing belongs, 'projet d'espace', bottom-right; a number, '3', bottom-left; another number, '194', middle-centre; and another notation, located left-centre, 'XIV'. In red pencil, and then scribbled out in graphite pencil, are two numbers: '14' and '37'. Again, there is a white label, this time affixed sideways and slightly askew in the top left, with a printed title – 'stedelijk van abbe-museum eindhoven' (Van Abbemuseum for Modern and Contemporary Art, Eindhoven) – and other information written in black pen: 'kunstenaar: A Appia, titel: Le trap cat 16, eigenaar: Theater Museum München, exposite tot: 22.11'.64'. And finally, there is a single ink stamp reading 'THEATERMUSEUM' and noting its current inventory number: 'IV749'.

Poster for the *Adolphe Appia 1862–1928: Actor–Space–Light* exhibition held at the City of Edinburgh Art Centre, 9 February–9 March 1985.

The German Theatre Museum, founded in 1910 and now housed at Galeriestraße 4a in Munich, holds four drawings in its graphics collection (donated by Appia after they were shown at the exhibition in Magdeburg in

1927), while its photo collection has eleven prints of the ill-fated 1924 performance of *Der Ring des Nibelungen* in Basel. It also owns exemplars of the two folios, *Adolphe Appia, 1er septembre 1862–29 février 1928*[12] and *Adolphe Appia (1862–1928): Zwanzig Faksimilies aus seinem bühnenbildnerischen Entwurfswerk*. The Musée d'Art et d'Histoire in Geneva holds eighteen of Appia's drawings: thirteen that had belonged to Émile Jaques-Dalcroze and which the museum progressively acquired from the music pedagogue's son Gabriel between 1979 and 1982, and five of them in 1993. Then there are two drawings in the collection of the Institute of Theatre Studies at Cologne University, which Appia gifted to the institute's head, Carl Niessen, following the Basel performance of *Der Ring des Nibelungen*. And finally, there are two collections in the Beinecke Rare Book and Manuscript Library at Yale University that hold archival material relating to Appia. One of them is the Donald Oenslager Collection of Adolphe Appia (GEN MSS 81), which contains two original Appia drawings that Oenslager (who taught in the Yale School of Drama) acquired from Henri Bonifas' family, correspondence, typescript manuscripts, articles and miscellaneous papers. The other is the Walther Volbach Collection on Adolphe Appia (GEN MSS 1014), an extensive seven-box collection comprising personal correspondence between Volbach and individuals who knew Appia personally, including the scenographer's nephew Edmond and his long-time friend Jean Mercier; journal articles, newspaper clippings and research notes; a couple of letters that Appia sent to Houston Stewart Chamberlain; and also full and partial English translations of some of Appia's writings.

Poster for the *Scene Designs by Adolphe Appia 1862–1928* exhibition held at Reed College in Portland, Oregon, 25 February–3 March 1985.

The German émigré Volbach was, in fact, introduced to Appia as a topic of research by Oenslager, who had begun his career as a stage actor in the 1920s before moving behind the scenes, working as a scenographer on Broadway productions from the 1930s to the 1950s. He was also on the Faculty of the Yale School of Drama, teaching design there for half a century, during which time he amassed an extensive collection of materials on and by Appia, including many untranslated and unpublished essays. He also knew the scenographer's violinist nephew, Edmond.[13] This is what Volbach wrote about his propitious encounter with Oenslager: 'I had a fair knowledge of his (Appia's) writings, but I did not know their scope until Donald Oenslager, the distinguished designer, showed me his treasure of unknown Appia essays. Through him, I got in touch with Edmond Appia, a nephew of Adolphe and the director of the Fondation Adolphe Appia in Geneva. Mr Appia, an internationally known musician and conductor, was agreeable to my project and authorised me to publish all of Appia's writings in English and French.'

Volbach first wrote a couple of articles on Appia for *Educational Theatre Journal*: 'Appia's Productions and Contemporary Reaction' in 1961 and then, two years later, his first biographical sketch, 'A Profile of Adolphe Appia'.[14] He eventually produced the first book-length biography of the scenographer, *Adolphe Appia: Prophet of the Modern Theatre*, a knowledgeable and cogently written, easily digestible account of Appia's life and work, published by Wesleyan University Press in 1968.[15] The illustrations are all black and white, and there are not many of them, although some were archival and previously unpublished, including some photographs of Appia that have in turn been republished here, together with Volbach's instructions to the printer regarding orientation (always portrait) and cropping.

Volbach also co-edited a publication of translations of a selection of Appia's writings – *Adolphe Appia: Essays and Scenarios and Designs*[16] – together with Richard Beacham, who was also associated with theatre studies at Yale University before he moved to the United Kingdom in 1974, first to the University of Warwick, where he co-founded its School of Theatre Studies, and then to King's College London. Beacham wrote the next lengthy work on Appia – *Adolphe Appia: Theatre Artist* – which was published by Cambridge University Press in 1987. He expanded and reworked it to become *Adolphe Appia: Artist and Visionary of the Modern Theatre*, published in 1994 by Harwood Academic as volume six in their 'Contemporary Theatre Studies' series.[17] Beacham's is the most thorough book on Appia to date, and it is principally though not entirely due to this work that he is now generally recognised as the international authority on Appia within the discipline of theatre studies, which is where Beacham's terms of reference reside. *Adolphe Appia: Artist and Visionary of the Modern Theatre* was translated into German and published as *Adolphe Appia: Künstler und Visionär des modernen Theaters* by Alexander Verlag in 2006, and unlike the scantly illustrated English-language version, this one is fulsomely illustrated, with several pages of high-quality colour plates.[18]

It was around the time that Beacham first started writing on Appia's place in theatre studies that others began to come alive to the scenographer's impact in the field of architecture, beginning with the Italian architect and historian Manfredo Tafuri, who wrote about the 'hallucinating bareness of Appia's scenes' in his seminal 1987 book *The Sphere and the Labyrinth*[19] while discussing the desire of the European avant-garde for the theatre and the city to dissolve, the goal always the same, to 'drag the spectator into the centre of scenic events'.[20] And around the same time that Tafuri was writing, Marco De Michelis began to publish on that architect who had designed the theatre where Appia's very ambition to drag the spectator into the centre of scenic events was embodied – Heinrich Tessenow. In 1990 De Michelis wrote his article 'Modernity and Reform: Heinrich Tessenow and the Institut Dalcroze at Hellerau' for a special issue of *Perspecta* on 'Theatre, Theatricality and Architecture',[21] and in the following year published his major work, *Heinrich Tessenow 1876–1959: Das architektonische Gesamtwerk*.[22]

K Michael Hays found the 'lucid reduction to essentials' most striking in Tessenow's architecture, as he wrote in 'Tessenow's Architecture as National Allegory: Critique of Capitalism or Protofascism?' in *Assemblage* in 1989. 'Only in the single, complete object can his compositional procedure manifest itself', continued Hays.[23] That description could also apply to Appia, who was not mentioned by name then, though he was in another article that Hays wrote for *Assemblage* in 1999, ten years after the first, this time on the Italian 'paper architect' Lauretta Vinciarelli, whose drawings 'engage the viewer not only through their perspective but also through their almost haunting sense of impending occupation', recognising that 'many of the spaces are almost theaterlike (think of Adolf (sic) Appia), awaiting actors and audiences on their daises, steps, and in their wings'.[24] The Australian-German architect Peter Wilson made similarly perceptive notes on Appia in one of his sketchbooks, but just like Hays he misspelled the scenographer's name, this time as 'Adolph'. These two slip-ups are illuminating insofar as they attest to Appia's current status in architectural theory and practice more generally – there is a fairly broadly held belief that he is of significance, but just where this significance resides is rather more sensed than known. Daniel Libeskind, an architect who like Appia first made his name with his radical drawings, proposes that Appia 'shook the world, and created not just modern staging, modern choreography, modern theatre, modern lighting, but also a new relationship between the different arts – through *architecture*'.[25]

Peter Carl has also identified and outlined Appia's role in the development of modern architectural 'space', which, as he wrote in an essay for *AA Files*, 'accepts everything, but requires any particular thing to account for itself at all levels. Analogy becomes an infinite field, and architecture becomes the medium in which to hold the references together by reverting to the primitive arrangements of matter and light first discovered by Adolphe Appia'.[26] And he had earlier written that since the advent of 'space' the 'principal reference to continuity has been "ground" or "earth". Although anticipated by monumental topographies, this ground seems to have been definitively consolidated in the profiled earth and light of Adolphe Appia ... manifest as stairs, terraces, recesses and mounds, the eye guided toward a (generally) luminous sky through empty contoured surfaces by stepped profiles, re-iterated horizons of the fragmentary remains, or anticipation, of *Kultur*.'[27]

I first sighted one of Appia's drawings during one of Peter's lectures, at around 9:45am on Wednesday, 5 May 2000.[28] I know it was then because I still have the five unbound pages of handwritten lecture notes I made that morning in the Department of Architecture at the University of Cambridge.[29] All reclaimed brick and off-form concrete, the darkened lecture theatre felt more like a cave than a room, illuminated only by the images that materialised before our eyes, cast – as in Plato's own cave – by an unseen source of light behind us. The Kodak carousel clicked forward by one, and Appia's drawing *The Diver* appeared on the screen – a spare chthonic setting that in its architectural register seemed to look both backwards and forwards in time. I made a quick sketch and noted down next to it: 'Adolphe Appia ... *Espaces rythmiques* ... earth + sky ... basis of modernity'.

following spread
Richard Peduzzi, setting for *Das Rheingold*, Prelude and Scene 1: In the Depths of the Rhine, 1976.

Prelude

1 Adolphe Appia to Karl Reyle, 26 September 1926.

2 Sabina Loriga, 'The Role of the Individual in History: Biographical and Historical Writing in the Nineteenth and Twentieth Century', in *Theoretical Discussions of Biography: Approaches from History, Microhistory, and Life Writing*, ed Binne de Haan and Hans Renders (New York: Edwin Mellen, 2013), 134.

3 Siegfried Kracauer, *History: The Last Things Before the Last* (New York: Oxford University Press, 1969), 123.

4 Hayden White, 'The Question of Narrative in Contemporary Historical Theory', *History and Theory* 23, no 1 (February 1984), 30. See also White's book *The Content of the Form: Narrative Discourse and Historical Representation* (Baltimore: John Hopkins University Press, 1987). For more on narrative history, see Louis Mink, 'Narrative Form as a Cognitive Instrument', in *The Writing of History: Literary Form and Historical Understanding*, ed Robert Canary and Henry Kozicki (Madison: University of Wisconsin Press, 1978), 143–44; Paul Ricoeur, 'Narrative Time', *Critical Inquiry* 7, no 1 (1980), 169–90; and Ricoeur, *Time and Narrative*, trans Kathleen McLaughlin and David Pellauer (Chicago: University of Chicago Press, 1984).

5 Appia's drawings are held in three key archives: the Swiss Archive of Performing Arts (SAPA) in Bern, the Deutsches Theatermuseum (DTM) in Munich, and the Musée d'art et d'histoire (MAH) de Genève in Geneva. There are also a handful of drawings in the Beinecke Rare Book and Manuscript Library (BRBML) at Yale University. Each of these institutions has been remarkably generous, going to the extent of scanning Appia's drawings anew for the purpose of this book.

6 On the Via Appia, see Robert Kaster, *The Appian Way: Ghost Road, Queen of Roads* (Chicago: University of Chicago Press, 2012); and Ivana Della Portella, ed, *The Appian Way from its Foundation to the Middle Ages* (Verona: Arsenale Editrice, 2004).

7 Publius Papinius Statius, *Silvae*, ed and trans D R Shackleton Bailey, Loeb Classical Library 206 (Cambridge, MA: Harvard University Press, 2015), 103 (Book 2.2.12). The name Via Appia derived from the censor Appius Claudius Caecus, who initiated the road's construction in 312 BCE.

8 Kaster, *The Appian Way*, 44.

9 Johann Wolfgang von Goethe, diary entry for 11 November 1786. Cited in Goethe, *Italienische Reise*, vol 1 (Leipzig: Insel, 1913), 142.

10 See Giovanni Battista Piranesi, *Le antichità romane*, vol 2 (Rome: Angelo Rotili, 1756). On Goethe's collection of prints, see Johannes Grave, *Der 'Ideale Kunstkörper': Johann Wolfgang von Goethe als Sammler von Druckgraphiken und Zeichnungen* (Göttingen: Vandenhoeck & Ruprecht, 2006), 17. For an essay focusing particularly on Piranesi's etchings, see Victor Plahte Tschudi, 'Goethe in the Hall and His Journeys in Printed Rome', *Architectural Histories* 3, no 1 (2015): 1–17. And for an extended study on Piranesi in the modern era, see Tschudi, *Piranesi and the Modern Age* (Cambridge, MA: MIT Press, 2022).

Early

1 Note that late in his life, Appia wrote a brief article on the cathedral: 'En écoutant l'orgue à Saint-Pierre', *Journal de Genève*, no 276 (October 1914).

2 'Ein ehrwürdiges Stück Tuch: Dr Appias Armbinde', *Du: kulturelle Monatsschrift* 2, no 8 (1942), 3.

3 Appia to Karl Reyle, 26 September 1926.

4 Adolphe Appia, 'Expériences de théâtre et recherches personelles' (1922). This is a fifty-three-page unpublished and unpaginated manuscript, typed on unlined paper. It is signed: 'Ad. Appia / (November–December 1921).' The text is reproduced in *Adolphe Appia: Œuvres complètes*, ed Marie-Louise Bablet, vol 4, 1921–1928 (Lausanne: L'Âge d'Homme, 1991), 36–56.

5 Dr Dumur, Director of the *Collège de la ville de Vevey* to Louis Appia, 19 June 1877. Cited in *Adolphe Appia: Œuvres complètes*, ed Marie-Louise Bablet, vol 1, 1880–1894 (Lausanne: L'Âge d'Homme, 1983), 56.

6 Appia's school grades, rated on a scale of 1 to 10, ranged between 5 and 10: in the subject of French, his grades oscillated between 7 and 8; in German from 5 to 9; his performance in industrial draughtsmanship consistently landed within the range of 7 to 8, while in the domain of fine arts drawing, his scores consistently ranged from 9 to 10. In music, his grades varied from 6 to 10. For a more detailed account of Appia's schooling, refer to *Adolphe Appia: Œuvres complètes*, 1: 55–58.

7 Appia, 'Expériences de théâtre et recherches personelles' (1922).

8 Thomas Mann, 'The Making of The Magic Mountain', *The Atlantic*, January 1953, 41.

9 Mann, 'The Making of The Magic Mountain', 42.

10 Nicholas Vazsonyi, 'Reading Right from Left: Hans Mayer and Postwar Wagner Reception', *Opera Quarterly* 30, no 2 (2014), 232.

11 Friedrich Nietzsche, *Der Fall Wagner: Ein Musikanten-Problem* (Leipzig: C G Naumann, 1888), preface.

12 Friedrich Nietzsche, 'Richard Wagner in Bayreuth', in *Nietzsche Werke*, ed Giorgio Colli and Mazzino Montinari, vol 4 (Berlin: De Gruyter, 1967), 59.

13 Wagner, *Collected Prose Works*, trans William Ashton Ellis, vol 1, *The Artwork of the Future and Other Works* (London: Kegan Paul, Trench, Trübner, 1892), 19.

14 A photograph of the arrest warrants for Wagner and Semper, both printed on the same page, is archived in the *Deutsche Fotothek* in Dresden (DF Hauptkatalog 0053880).

15 Gottfried Semper to Heinrich Hübsch, January 1852. Regarding Semper's architectural theories, see *Die vier Elemente der Baukunst* (Braunschweig: Friedrich Vieweg und Sohn, 1851); and Harry Francis Mallgrave, *Gottfried Semper: Architect of the Nineteenth Century* (New Haven: Yale University Press, 1996). Semper was born in Hamburg, which is

where he attended the Gelehrtenschule des Johanneums before starting his university education as a student of history and mathematics in Göttingen. He then turned to architecture and studied at the Ludwig-Maximilians-Universität in Munich, after which he obtained a post as Professor of Architecture at the Königliche Akademie der bildenden Künste (Royal Academy of Fine Arts) in Dresden. The flourishing of the city during the years that followed provided the young architect with considerable opportunities to both teach and build – for example the Dresden Synagogue, a building noted for its rather expressive Moorish Revival interior that included a silver lamp of eternal light, which caught the fancy of Richard and Cosima Wagner, who then apparently went to great lengths to get their hands on a reproduction of it. Wagner also eventually got his hands on a baton that Semper designed especially for him in 1858, and on which were inscribed the names of his compositions up to that time: 'Nibelungen, Rheingold, Walküre, Siegfried, Tristan und Isolde'. For more on Wagner and Semper, see Hermann Sturm, *Alltag & Kult: Gottfried Semper, Richard Wagner, Friedrich Theodor Vischer, Gottfried Keller* (Basel: Birkhäuser, 2003); and *Cosima Wagner's Diaries*, ed Martin Gregor-Dellin and Dietrich Mack, trans Geoffrey Skelton, vol 1, *1869–1877* (London: Collins, 1978), 138–49, 878, 1018.

16 Wagner to Franz Liszt, June 1849. Cited in Richard Wagner, *Selected Letters of Richard Wagner*, trans Stewart Spencer and Barry Millington (London: Dent, 1987), 171.

17 Although Wagner was not the first to theoretically formulate the notion of the *Gesamtkunstwerk* – which is attributed to the German writer and philosopher Eusebius Trahndorff (1782–1863) – he emerged as the pre-eminent advocate of its vision. Wagner's first use of the term was in 1849 and it remains uncertain whether he was aware of Trahndorff's earlier essay, *Ästhetik, oder Lehre von der Weltanschauung und Kunst* (Berlin: Maurer, 1827).

18 Wagner, *Die Kunst und die Revolution* (Leipzig: Otto Wigand, 1849); and Wagner, *Das Kunstwerk der Zukunft* (Leipzig: Otto Wigand, 1850).

19 Wagner, *Das Kunstwerk der Zukunft*, 187–89.

20 Richard Wagner, 'A Communication to My Friends', in *Collected Prose Works*, vol 1, *The Artwork of the Future and Other Works*, trans William Ashton Ellis (New York: Broude Bros, 1966), 391. In his treatise *Oper und Drama* (1851), Wagner further articulated the aesthetics of his new kind of drama that attained its fullest realisation in *Der Ring des Nibelungen*.

21 Wagner, *My Life*, ed Mary Whittall, trans Andrew Gray (Cambridge: Cambridge University Press, 1983), 260. Note that Wagner kept a copy of Jacob Grimm's *Deutsche Mythologie* (Göttingen: Dieterich, 1835) in his library in Dresden. Additionally, he referenced the collection of narrative poems authored by anonymous writers collectively known as the Poetic Edda, as well as the Volsung Saga, which informed his concept for the Wälsungen lineage, descending from Wotan. To substantiate Wagner's familiarity with the Prose Edda, see Cosima Wagner's diaries in which, for example, she wrote: 'In the evening R read me a passage from the Edda'. *Cosima Wagner's Diaries*, 419.

22 The cornerstone of the Bayreuth Festspielhaus was ceremoniously set on 22 May 1872, Wagner's fifty-ninth birthday. 'It was a nasty, rainy day.' Thomas Kelly, *First Nights at the Opera* (New Haven: Yale University Press, 2004), 239.

23 Wagner, *Das Kunstwerk der Zukunft*, 96. (Wagner's emphasis.)

24 Richard Wagner, *Das Bühnenfestspielhaus zu Bayreuth* (Leipzig: E W Fritzsch, 1873), 21. The full title of Wagner's essay is 'Das Bühnenfestspielhaus zu Bayreuth nebst einem Berichte über die Grundsteinlegung desselben. Mit sechs architectonischen Plänen'.

25 Wagner, *Das Bühnenfestspielhaus zu Bayreuth*, 22.

26 Wagner, *Das Bühnenfestspielhaus zu Bayreuth*, 23. Regarding the 'mystical abyss' in the Bayreuth Festspielhaus, see Beat Wyss and Denise Bratton, 'Ragnarök of Illusion: Richard Wagner's "Mystical Abyss" at Bayreuth', *October* 54 (1990), 57–78.

27 Wagner, *Das Bühnenfestspielhaus zu Bayreuth*, 23.

28 Wagner, *Das Bühnenfestspielhaus zu Bayreuth*, 23–25.

29 Wagner, *Das Bühnenfestspielhaus zu Bayreuth*, 26. Note that Cosima claimed that the idea to visually express the bulk of the stage tower was in fact hers: 'Brückwald, the architect, comes in the morning and many things are discussed. I advise letting the stage tower rise boldly above the whole building as its main feature and not concealing it, but rather keeping the auditorium as low as possible, as a sort of low entry hall to the stage'. Cosima Wagner, diary entry for 25 May 1872.

30 Wagner, *Das Bühnenfestspielhaus zu Bayreuth*, 26, 27.

31 Wagner, *Das Bühnenfestspielhaus zu Bayreuth*, 27, 29–30.

32 Otto Brückwald, 'Das Bühnenfestspielhaus zu Bayreuth', *Deutsche Bauzeitung* 9, no 1 (1875), 1–5. See also Ned A Bowman, 'Investing a Theatrical Ideal: Wagner's Bayreuth "Festspielhaus",' *Educational Theatre Journal* 18, no 4 (December 1966), 429–38.

33 Wagner to Josef Hoffmann, 28 July 1872. Cited in Albert Franz Seligman, 'Josef Hoffmann und Richard Wagner', *Neue Freie Presse, Wien*, 4 October 1906. On Josef Hoffmann's designs for the first performance of *Der Ring* in 1876, see Oswald Georg Bauer, *Josef Hoffmann: Der Bühnenbildner der ersten Bayreuther Festspiele* (Munich: Deutscher Kunstverlag, 2008).

34 Wagner to King Ludwig II, 1 October 1874. Cited in Otto Strobel, ed, *Königsbriefe: König Ludwig II und Richard Wagner Briefwechsel*, vol 3 (Karlsruhe: G Braun, 1936), 40.

35 Cited in Hartmut Säuberlich, 'Richard Wagner und die Probleme des Bühnenbildes seiner Werke im 19. Jahrhundert', PhD thesis (University of Kiel, 1966), 242.

36 Cosima approached Böcklin again in March 1878, hopeful that she might convince him to design the settings and costumes for *Parsifal*, but he declined once more. Both Wagners made one final entreaty to Böcklin in July 1880 when the three of them met in the Villa d'Angri on the rocky peninsula of Posilippo near Naples, but the Wagners were once again rebuffed. Cosima's recollection of Böcklin from that meeting was of a man with a 'peculiar, pithy nature', one who had been 'made bitter by experience'. Cited in Susanne Bürger, ed, *Arnold Böcklin (1827–1901): Gemälde, Zeichnungen, Plastiken* (Basel: Kunsthalle Basel und Basler Kunstverein, 1977), 19. For more

on Wagner and Böcklin, see Niemann, *Richard Wagner und Arnold Böcklin, oder über das Wesen von Landschaft und Musik.* (Leipzig: J Zeitler, 1904).

37 Wagner to Josef Hoffmann, 28 July 1872. Cited in Seligman, 'Josef Hoffmann und Richard Wagner'.

38 Josef Hoffmann to Wagner, 2 August 1872. Cited in Dietrich Mack, *Der Bayreuther Inszenierungsstil, 1876–1976* (Munich: Prestel, 1976), 72. Cosima concluded from Hoffmann's 'good letter' that he 'seemed to comprehend his duty'. Cosima Wagner, diary entry for 15 August 1872.

39 Cosima Wagner, diary entry for 13 October 1872.

40 Wagner to Carl Brandt, 22 October 1872. Cited in Wagner, *Bayreuther Briefe Richard Wagners, 1871–1883*, ed Carl Friedrich Glasenapp (Berlin: Schuster & Loeffler, 1907), 104.

41 Wagner to Carl Brandt, 22 October 1872. Cited in Wagner, *Bayreuther Briefe*, 104.

42 Wagner to Josef Hoffmann, 22 October 1872. Cited in Wagner, *Bayreuther Briefe*, 105.

43 Brückwald, 'Das Bühnenfestspielhaus zu Bayreuth', 2.

44 Cosima Wagner, diary entry for 28 November 1873.

45 Cosima Wagner, diary entry for 29 November 1873.

46 Richard Wagner, *Sämtliche Schriften und Dichtungen*, vol 4 (Leipzig: Volksausgabe, 1911), 64.

47 Cosima Wagner, diary entry for 30 November 1873.

48 Max and Gotthold Brückner to Josef Hoffmann, 19 December 1873 (RWM, Hs 93/r54).

49 Ludwig II financed the construction of Haus Wahnfried, designed by the Berlin-based architect Wilhelm Neumann. Wagner had the following inscription placed above the entrance portal: 'Hier wo mein Wähnen Frieden fand – Wahnfried – sei dieses Haus von mir benannt' (Here, delusions have found peace, may this residence be named Wahnfried).

50 Cosima Wagner, diary entry for 28 April 1874.

51 Josef Hoffmann to Friedrich Feustel, 3 August 1874 (Post stamp: Darmstadt) (RWM, Hs 80/Vii-2).

52 Cosima Wagner, diary entry for 24 August 1874.

53 Cosima Wagner, diary entry for 26 August 1874.

54 Cited in Maja Loehr, 'Der Wiener Maler Josef Hoffmann als Mitgestalter der ersten Bayreuther Festspiele', *Theater einst und jetzt 1* (1947), 9.

55 Loehr, 'Der Wiener Maler Josef Hoffmann', 8.

56 Loehr, 'Der Wiener Maler Josef Hoffmann', 8.

57 Cosima Wagner, diary entry for 13 September 1874.

58 Loehr, 'Der Wiener Maler Josef Hoffmann', 9.

59 Cosima Wagner, diary entry for 1 October 1874.

60 Cosima Wagner, diary entry for 12 October 1874.

61 Wagner to Josef Hoffmann, 12 October 1874. Cited in Wagner, *Bayreuther Briefe*, 182.

62 Cosima Wagner, diary entry for 15 October 1874.

63 Cosima Wagner, diary entry for 3 December 1874.

64 Kelly, *First Nights at the Opera*, 250.

65 Richard Wagner, *Das Rheingold, Vorspiel zu der Trilogie: Der Ring des Nibelungen von Richard Wagner* (Mainz: Schott's Söhne, 1876), 5.

66 Alex Ross, *Wagnerism: Art and Politics in the Shadow of Music* (London: 4th Estate, 2021), 17.

67 Ross, *Wagnerism*, 17. Cosima recorded Wagner's own description of the beginning of *Das Rheingold*: 'It is, so to speak, the world's lullaby'. Cosima Wagner, diary entry for 17 July 1869.

68 Wagner's first draft of the *Partitur* for *Das Rheingold, Vorspiel und erste Scene (auf dem Grund des Rheins)* is dated and signed 'Zurich, 1 Febr. 54, RW'. It is held in the Richard Wagner Museum in Bayreuth (NA A III a2).

69 Wagner, *Das Rheingold*, 5.

70 Richard Fricke, *Wagner in Rehearsal: The Diaries of Richard Fricke, 1875–1876*, ed James Deaville and Evan Baker, trans George Fricke (New York: Pendragon, 1998), 64–65.

71 Cited in Fricke, *Wagner in Rehearsal*, 68.

72 Cosima recorded Wagner's upset at the tardiness of the Brückner brothers, who were busy completing other commissions: 'R is terribly worn out and annoyed by how behind many things are, above all the decorations of the Brückner brothers, who in the meantime have painted fourteen decorations for the Duke of Meiningen.' Cosima Wagner, diary entry for 6 June 1876.

73 Carl Emil Doepler, *A Memoir of Bayreuth: 1876*, trans Peter Cook (London: Staples St Albans, 1979). Cited in Kelly, *First Nights at the Opera*, 255.

74 Cited in Kelly, *First Nights at the Opera*, 258. Wagner's nephew Clemens Brockhaus reported that 'the three *Rheintöchter* have just managed to make their midday meal, one of them getting sausages, another bread, and the third beer'. Cited in Robert Hartford, *Bayreuth, The Early Years: An Account of the Early Decades of the Wagner Festival as Seen by the Celebrated Visitors & Participants* (London: V Gollancz, 1980), 86.

75 Cited in Hartford, *Bayreuth, The Early Years*, 66.

76 Virginia Woolf, 'Impressions at Bayreuth', in *The Essays of Virginia Woolf*, vol 1, *1904–1912*, ed Andrew McNellie and Stuart N Clarke (New York: Harcourt Brace, 1967), 290. For another brief account of the 1909 Festival, see Ida Wilczek, 'Die Festspieltage in Bayreuth', *Wissen und Leben* 4 (1909), 141–44.

77 Woolf, 'Impressions at Bayreuth', 290.

78 Woolf, 'Impressions at Bayreuth', 290.

79 Nietzsche, *Der Fall Wagner*, 4. For more on Wagner and modernity, the music critic Alex Ross recently wrote in *Wagnerism*: 'The words "modern" and "modernism" are slippery ones, prone to endless disputation. By and large, they indicate a body of work that cuts against prevailing modes of representation, broaches transgressive themes, threatens zones of bourgeois comfort'. And also that 'Wagner was modern; he was decadent; and he was dangerous'. Ross, *Wagnerism*, 356, 71.

80 Cited in Walther R Volbach, *Adolphe Appia: Prophet of the Modern Theatre* (Middletown: Wesleyan University Press, 1968), 45.

81 The director of the Collège de la ville de Vevey, 12 September 1881.

82 Appia, 'Expériences de théâtre et recherches personelles' (1922).

83 Appia, 'Expériences de théâtre et recherches personelles' (1922).

84 Appia, 'Expériences de théâtre et recherches personelles' (1922).

85 Adolphe Appia, 'Introduction à mes notes personelles' (1905). This 30×20 cm notebook is bound in hard grey cardboard and is made up of only twelve yellowing lined pages, each numbered in pencil (1–12). The title page bears the following inscription,

written in pencil in Appia's neat looping hand: 'Introduction to my personal notes / 1905'. It is held at SAPA. A transcription is published in *Adolphe Appia: Œuvres complètes*, ed Marie-Louise Bablet, vol 2, 1895–1905 (Lausanne: L'Âge d'Homme, 1986), 409–14.

86 The term 'homosexuality' was coined in 1869 by the Austrian *litterateur* Karl Maria Kertbeny, who was opposed to sodomy laws. Homophobic reaction brought down several high-profile figures in the first years of the twentieth century, the most prominent of them Philipp Eulenburg, a confidant of both the Kaiser and Cosima Wagner.

87 Appia's ties with the Symbolists and the Wagnerian Circle in Paris are documented in Mazzocchi Doglio, *Il teatro simbolista in Francia (1890–1896)* (Rome: Edizioni Abete, 1978). See particularly chapter 3: 'Il mito di Wagner', 25–37, and chapter 12: 'La scenografica symbolista', 189–220.

88 Appia struggled with addiction to alcohol and laudanum for much of his adult life and spent substantial periods of time in sanatoria and psychiatric clinics attempting to detoxify. In the years 1921 and 1922 he resided for a total of seven months in the Waldau clinic on the outskirts of Bern. For a vivid, informative account of the pleasure, pains and addictive power of laudanum (a solution of opium dissolved in alcohol), see Thomas De Quincey, *Confessions of an English Opium-Eater* (London: Taylor and Hessey, 1823). On page 4, in the opening passage, De Quincey wrote: 'If opium-eating be a sensual pleasure, and if I am bound to confess that I have indulged in it to an excess, not yet recorded of any other man, it is no less true, that I have struggled against this fascinating enthralment with a religious zeal, and have, at length, accomplished what I never yet heard attributed to any other man – have untwisted, almost to its final links, the accursed chain which fettered me.'

89 *Adolphe Appia: Œuvres complètes*, 1: 62.

90 Agénor Boissier to Chamberlain, 28 July 1901. Cited in *Adolphe Appia: Œuvres complètes*, 1: 64.

91 Regarding Appia's musical compositions, see *Adolphe Appia: Œuvres complètes*, 1: xx.

92 In 1889/90 Appia worked in Dresden as an informal apprentice to Hugo Bähr – 'the father of light' – whose lighting experiments had already been influential in the German theatre, and whose innovations had been employed with considerable success at Bayreuth as far back as 1876. Bähr developed and used a variety of carbon-arc devices, projections and other lighting effects, and it was under his guidance that Appia learned many of the techniques he later employed in his own work. Marie L Bablet-Hahn provides a full account of Bähr's work and its significance for Appia in *Adolphe Appia: Œuvres complètes*, 1: 72, 355–65 and 376–80.

93 'Mr Kietz is ready to start with you on the morning of 22 April'. Chamberlain to Appia, 6 April 1889. Cited in Ernst Newman, *The Life of Richard Wagner*, vol 1, *1813–1848* (New York: Alfred Knopf, 1933), 272. The Leipzig-born German painter Benedikt Kietz studied at the Kunstakademie in Dresden, which is where he came to know Richard Wagner, who in fact dedicated his *Klavierstück* in E-major, *Lied ohne Worte* (Song Without Words) to the painter in 1840, two years before Kietz painted the composer's portrait.

94 Newman, *The Life of Richard Wagner*, 272.

95 Cosima Wagner to Chamberlain, 23 October 1888. Cited in Cosima Wagner, *Das zweite Leben: Briefe und Aufzeichnungen, 1883–1930*, ed Dietrich Mack (Munich: R Piper, 1980), 163. Note also that Wagner's earliest known mention of his ambition to construct a Festspielhaus – for a performance of *Siegfried's Tod*, the original title for *Der Ring* – is in a letter that he sent to Kietz, dated 14 September 1850. See also Wagner, *Cosima Wagner's Diaries*, 226.

96 Mann, 'The Making of The Magic Mountain', 41.

97 Mann, 'The Making of The Magic Mountain', 41.

98 Ross, *Wagnerism*, 35.

99 Mann, 'The Making of The Magic Mountain', 44.

100 Appia, 'Expériences de théâtre et recherches personelles' (1922). Appia stayed first at Gennersbrunn, and then in 1893 settled at Bière, in the countryside a few miles north of Lake Geneva, where he was to make his home until 1900.

101 Appia's original handwritten manuscript for 'Notes des mise en scène für den Ring des Nibelungen' (1891) is now lost, but there are two copies of it. One of them was written out by somebody other than Appia (SAPA: B1), though he himself signed and dated it on the title page – 'Adolphe Appia 91–92'. The other (SAPA: C1) is made up of ten typed pages, with some handwritten corrections by Appia. It is reproduced in *Adolphe Appia: Œuvres complètes*, 1: 109–254.

102 Appia, 'Expériences de théâtre et recherches personelles' (1922).

103 Appia, 'Expériences de théâtre et recherches personelles' (1922).

104 SAPA: E2.

105 The following quotations from the libretto for *Der Ring des Nibelungen* refer to the original four-volume edition published by Schott's Söhne in Mainz in 1876, which Appia owned. Rather than citing the individual page number for each quotation, I have provided the enclosing page numbers for each scene (in the case of *Das Rheingold*) or act (in the case of *Die Walküre*, *Siegfried* and *Götterdämmerung*) at first mention in the text. Unless otherwise noted, the quotations are in the order in which they appear in Wagner's libretto.

106 Appia, 'Expériences de théâtre et recherches personelles' (1922).

107 Appia, 'Expériences de théâtre et recherches personelles' (1922). The musical score for *Das Rheingold* that Appia owned, and is here referring to, is the one that Karl Klindworth had arranged for piano: Richard Wagner, *Das Rheingold: Vollstandiger Klavierauszug von Karl Klindworth* (Mainz: Schott's Söhne, 1861). A gifted pianist, Klindworth was a star pupil of Franz Liszt and later became close friends with Richard Wagner. He founded his own conservatory, the Klindworth-Musikschule, in Berlin and became well known as a teacher. But he regarded his transcription for piano of *Der Ring des Nibelungen* as his true life's work. Late in his life, Klindworth and his wife Henriette, both in their seventies, adopted a nine-year-old English orphan, Winifred Marjorie Williams, who at the age of seventeen met and fell in love with Wagner's son Siegfried. At the age of eighteen, Winifred Marjorie Williams became Winifred Wagner. She took over the running of the Bayreuth Festival in 1933 following the death of her husband, becoming close friends with Hitler in the lead-up to the Second World War, before being

banned from the directorship of the festival in its wake. See 'An Orphan from Sussex (1897–1915)'; 'The Newlyweds (1915–22)'; 'Winifred, the New Boss of Bayreuth (1930–33)'; and 'The Long Ending (1943–45), in Brigitte Hamann, *Winifred Wagner: A Life at the Heart of Hitler's Bayreuth*, trans Alan Bance (London: Granta, 2005), 1–20, 21–50, 147–80 and 355–401.

108 Wagner, 'Erste Scene: Auf dem Grunde der Rheins', in *Das Rheingold, Vorspiel zu der Trilogie*, 5–18.

109 Wagner, 'Zweite Scene: Freie Gegend auf Bergeshöhen', in *Das Rheingold*, 19–39.

110 Appia later described Valhalla as a 'criminal edifice', one that was 'piled onto the world through a crude manoeuvre'. Adolphe Appia, *L'Œuvre d'art vivant* (Geneva: Atar, 1921), unpaginated.

111 Adolphe Appia, *La Mise en scène du drame Wagnérien* (Paris: Léon Chailley, 1895), 36.

112 Appia, *La Mise en scène du drame Wagnérien*, 36.

113 Adolphe Appia, 'Drei Dekorationen für "Parsifal", Walhall-Landschaft und Walkürenfels', *Wissen und Leben* 4 (1909), 248.

114 Wagner, *Das Rheingold*, 37.

115 Wagner, *Das Rheingold*, 40.

116 Wagner, 'Dritte Scene: Unterirdische Kluft', in *Das Rheingold*, 40–75.

117 Appia, *La Mise en scène du drame Wagnérien*, 36.

118 Appia, *La Mise en scène du drame Wagnérien*, 36.

119 Wagner, 'Erster Aufzug: Das Innere eines Wohnraumes', in *Die Walküre. Erster Tag aus der Trilogie: Der Ring des Nibelungen von Richard Wagner* (Mainz: Schott's Söhne, 1876), 5–26.

120 Appia, 'Notes des mise en scène für den Ring des Nibelungen' (1891).

121 Appia, 'Notes des mise en scène für den Ring des Nibelungen' (1891).

122 Appia, 'Notes des mise en scène für den Ring des Nibelungen' (1891).

123 Appia, 'Notes des mise en scène für den Ring des Nibelungen' (1891).

124 Appia, 'Notes des mise en scène für den Ring des Nibelungen' (1891).

125 Wagner, 'Zweiter Aufzug: Wildes Felsengebirg', in *Die Walküre*, 26–57.

126 Appia, 'Notes des mise en scène für den Ring des Nibelungen' (1891).

127 Appia, 'Notes des mise en scène für den Ring des Nibelungen' (1891).

128 Appia, 'Notes des mise en scène für den Ring des Nibelungen' (1891).

129 Appia, 'Notes des mise en scène für den Ring des Nibelungen' (1891).

130 According to Wagner's staging instructions, the setting for the third act of *Die Walküre* is bordered by a pine forest. On the left-hand side of the stage there is an entrance to a cave above which a rocky cliff rises. The background stands wide open, and a few wispy clouds skirt the cliff, as though driven there by a storm. Wagner, 'Dritter Aufzug: Auf dem Gipfel eines Felsberges', in *Die Walküre*, 57–84.

131 Appia, *L'Œuvre d'art vivant*, unpaginated.

132 Ross, *Wagnerism*, 565.

133 Ross, *Wagnerism*, 565.

134 Appia, 'Notes des mise en scène für den Ring des Nibelungen' (1891).

135 Wagner, 'Erster Aufzug: Wald', in *Siegfried, Zweiter Tag aus der Trilogie: Der Ring des Nibelungen von Richard Wagner* (Mainz: Schott's Söhne, 1876), 5–42.

136 Appia, 'Notes des mise en scène für den Ring des Nibelungen' (1891).

137 Wagner, 'Zweiter Aufzug: Wald', in *Siegfried*, 43–72.

138 Wagner, 'Dritter Aufzug: Wilde Gegend', in *Siegfried*, 73–98.

139 Wagner, 'Vorspiel: Auf dem Walkürenfelsen', in *Götterdämmerung, Dritter Tag aus der Trilogie: Der Ring des Nibelungen von Richard Wagner* (Mainz: Schott's Söhne, 1876), 5–14.

140 Wagner, 'Zweiter Aufzug: Uferraum', in *Götterdämmerung*, 38–62.

141 Wagner, 'Dritter Aufzug: Wildes Wald- und Felsenthal', in *Götterdämmerung*, 63–86.

142 Appia to Chamberlain, 21 August 1893.

143 Édouard Schuré also wrote on Wagner and his works. See, for example, Édouard Schuré, 'Le drame musical et l'œuvre de Monsieur Richard Wagner', *Revue des deux mondes* 80, no 4 (April 1869), 948–91.

144 Appia, *La Mise en scène du drame Wagnérien*.

145 Georges Humbert, 'Littérature wagnérienne, 1894–1895: Adolphe Appia, La mise en scène du drame Wagnérien', *Gazette musicale de la Suisse romande*, May 1895, 155. See also Hans von Wolzogen, 'Literarische Anzeigen: Adolphe Appia, La mise-en-scène du drame wagnérien', *Bayreuther Blätter* 18, no 4–5 (1895). According to Appia, the only 'interesting response' he received was from Stéphane Mallarmé, though the poet's words are unrecorded. Appia to Houston Stewart Chamberlain, 6 March 1895.

146 Appia, *La mise en scène du drame Wagnérien*, 29.

147 Wagner, *Parsifal: Ein Bühnenweihfestspiel* (Mainz: Schott's Söhne, 1877). Elsewhere Wagner wrote: 'One might say that where religion becomes aesthetic, it is the responsibility of art to preserve the core of religion'. Wagner, 'Religion und Kunst (1880)', in *Sämtliche Schriften und Dichtungen*, vol 10 (Leipzig: Breitkopf & Härtel, 1911), 211. See also Sue Zemka, 'Wagner's Opera of Redemption: "Parsifal" at Bayreuth', *Criticism* 27, no 3 (1985), 263–82; and Ryan Minor, 'Wagner's Last Chorus: Consecrating Space and Spectatorship in "Parsifal",' *Cambridge Opera Journal* 17, no 1 (March 2005), 1–36.

148 Parsifal premiered on 26 July 1882. After the sixteenth and final performance that year, on 29 August, Wagner and Cosima travelled to Venice to see out the winter. And that is where Wagner suffered a heart attack and died in the sixteenth-century palazzo Ca' Vendramin Calergi on 13 February 1883, at the age of sixty-nine. A gondolier rowed his body across the waters of the Grand Canal to the Stazione di Venezia Santa Lucia, and from there he was transported by train to Bayreuth, where he was buried in the grounds of Wahnfried, as Cosima later would be too.

149 Appia, *Richard Wagner et la mise en scène* (1925). This eight-page typed manuscript held at SAPA is signed and dated 'Adolphe Appia / Genève, mars 1925'. A transcription is published in *Adolphe Appia: Œuvres complètes*, 4: 469–71.

150 Appia, 'Parsifal. mise en scène' (1896) is a five-page manuscript typed on white, unlined paper, without any handwritten corrections. A transcription is published in *Adolphe Appia: Œuvres complètes*, ed Marie-Louise Bablet, vol 2, 1895–1905 (Lausanne: L'Âge d'Homme, 1986), 276–82. Appia prepared a second manuscript, 'Trois projets de décors pour Parsifal' (1908), which he used as the basis for two publications: 'Entwürfe zu Parsifal-Dekorationen', *Dekorative Kunst, illustrierte Zeitschrift für angewandte Kunst* 16 (Munich, 1908), 278–80 and 'Drei Dekorationen für "Parsifal", Walhall-Landschaft und Walkürenfels', *Wissen und Leben* 4 (1909), 240–52.

Finally, he prepared '(Notes sur la) Mise en scène de Parsifal' (1912), a seven-page manuscript typed on white, unlined paper. The title page is unpaginated, while the rest are numbered. There are a small number of corrections in pencil. Appia signed and dated his manuscript on the final page and wrote 'Destiné à la tradition allemande / pour une revue Der Thürmer'. It was translated into German, and published as Appia and Karl Storck, 'Die Inszenierung des Parsifal', *Der Türmer: Monatsschrift für Gemüt und Geist* 16, no 5 (February 1914), 806–14.

151 Wagner, *Parsifal: Ein Bühnenweihfestspiel*, 5.

152 Appia reportedly once said 'I design with my eraser.' Jean Mercier to Walter Volbach, 28 November 1960.

153 Appia, 'Drei Dekorationen für "Parsifal", Walhall-Landschaft und Walkürenfels', 242.

154 Appia, *L'Œuvre d'art vivant*, unpaginated.

155 Appia, *L'Œuvre d'art vivant*, unpaginated.

156 Wagner, *Parsifal*, trans Graham Salter (Richmond, Surrey: Overture, 2011), 157.

157 Appia, 'Trois projets de décors pour Parsifal' (1908).

158 Wagner, *Parsifal*, 157.

159 Appia, *L'Œuvre d'art vivant*, unpaginated.

160 Appia, *L'Œuvre d'art vivant*, unpaginated.

161 Appia, *L'Œuvre d'art vivant*, unpaginated.

162 Wagner, *Parsifal*, 165.

163 Wagner, *Parsifal*, 209.

164 Appia, *L'Œuvre d'art vivant*, unpaginated.

165 Wagner, *Parsifal*, 209.

166 Appia, *L'Œuvre d'art vivant*, unpaginated.

167 Adolphe Appia, 'Notes sur le théâtre', *La vie musicale* 1, no 16 (April 1908), 280.

168 Appia, 'Notes sur le théâtre', 280.

169 Appia to Chamberlain, 6 January 1896. Note that in their letters, Appia addressed Chamberlain as 'Wotan', and that Chamberlain in turn addressed Appia as 'Romeo'.

170 Houston Stewart Chamberlain, *Richard Wagner* (Munich: Verlagsanstalt für Kunst und Wissenschaft, 1896).

171 Appia, *Die Musik und die Inscenierung* (Munich: Bruckmann, 1899), preface.

172 Appia to Chamberlain, 16 August 1896.

173 Chamberlain to Appia, 28 November 1896.

174 Chamberlain to Appia, 28 November 1896.

175 Appia, *Die Musik und die Inscenierung*, 93.

176 Appia, *Die Musik und die Inscenierung*, 88.

177 Appia, *Die Musik und die Inscenierung*, 87.

178 Appia, *Die Musik und die Inscenierung*, 85.

179 Appia to Chamberlain, 15 April 1896.

180 In his preface to *Die Musik und die Inscenierung*, Appia paid tribute to Cantacuzène, referring to her as his collaborator: 'I would here like to express my deep gratitude to Princess Elsa Cantacuzène whose high sympathy and subtle and persevering intuition allow me today to present my French manuscript to the public for which it was intended. My translator has, through her dedication, become my collaborator. Perhaps in this capacity she would like to share with me the fate of this present volume.' Appia, *Die Musik und die Inscenierung*, x.

181 Collotype is a gelatine-based photographic printing process that faithfully reproduces images across a diverse spectrum of tones, obviating the requirement for halftone screens. It was invented in 1855 by Alphonse Poitevin, a French chemist characterised as one of the 'great unheralded figures in photography'. Martin Parr and Gerry Badger, *The Photobook: A History*, vol 1 (London: Phaidon, 2004), 19.

182 Appia to Chamberlain, 2 April 1897.

183 Appia to Chamberlain, 18 April 1898.

184 Adolphe Appia, 'Tristan et Isolde: Mise en scène' (1896) is an eleven-page manuscript typed on white unlined paper. It is enclosed in a green cardboard cover with a pencil inscription (not in Appia's hand): 'Tristan / 1923'. Appia revised his staging notes in 1923 for the staging of *Tristan und Isolde*: 'Introduction aux représentations de Tristan et Isolde à la Scala de Milan' (1923).

185 Appia, *Die Musik und die Inscenierung*, 274.

186 Cited in *Adolphe Appia: Œuvres complètes*, 1:39.

187 Appia to Chamberlain, 24 May 1899.

188 Cosima Wagner to Appia, 31 March 1899.

189 Alfred Dufour, 'Musique: La musique et la mise en scène', *Journal de Genève*, 6 July 1899, cited in *Adolphe Appia*, 2: 214.

190 Appia to Chamberlain, 6 January 1896.

191 Appia to Chamberlain, 26 December 1899.

192 Friedrich Nietzsche, *Why I Am So Clever*, trans R J Hollingdale (London: Penguin, 2016), 7. The German philosopher was mightily impressed by Cosima, writing for example: 'Frau Cosima Wagner is by far the noblest nature; and, so that I shouldn't say one word too few, I say that Richard Wagner was by far the most closely related man to me ... The rest is silence.' (Note that this is a quotation from Hamlet – the prince's final words. Act 5, Scene 2). *Why I Am So Clever*, 7; and: 'The few instances of high culture I have encountered in Germany have all been of French origin, above all Frau Cosima Wagner, by far the first voice I have heard in questions of taste.' *Ecce Homo: Wie man wird, was man ist* (Leipzig: Insel, 1908), 37. And of direct relevance here, Nietzsche once wrote: 'Music demands her equal sister, gymnastics, for her necessary embodiment in the real world of the visible.' 'Richard Wagner in Bayreuth', 376.

193 Ross, *Wagnerism*, 249.

194 Born in Munich in 1863, the German publisher Hugo Bruckmann was the younger of two sons of Friedrich Bruckmann, who had founded the publishing house and gave it its name. When his father died in 1898 Hugo and his elder brother took over the reins at F Bruckmann KAG. But their interest was not only in books. Hugo and his wife Elsa were amongst the earliest and most influential promoters of the then rabble-rouser Adolf Hitler, and they assisted the *Führer* in gaining access to, and acceptance within, upper-class circles in Munich. Othmar Plöckinger, *Geschichte eines Buches: Adolf Hitlers Mein Kampf, 1922–1945* (Munich: Oldenbourg, 2011), 40, 159. Bruckmann published Hitler's *Mein Kampf*: from 1930 he was a board member of the *Kampfbund* for German culture, founded by Alfred Rosenberg, and from 1932 until his death in 1941 he was a Nazi member of the Reichstag.

195 James Forman, *Nazism* (New York: F Watts, 1978), 14.

196 Houston Stewart Chamberlain, *Die Grundlagen des neunzehnten Jahrhunderts* (Munich: Bruckmann, 1899), 8.

197 Raymond Penel to Walther Volbach, 18 February 1961. Cited in Walther R Volbach, 'Adolphe Appia und Houston Stewart Chamberlain', *Die Musikforschung* 18, no 4 (October/December 1965), 388.

198 Chamberlain to Appia, 13 November 1894.

199 Chamberlain to Appia, 24 November 1894.

200 Cosima Wagner to Hermann Graf Keyserling, 11 April 1903. Cited in Mack, *Cosima Wagner*, 630.

201 Loehr, 'Der Wiener Maler Josef Hoffmann', 8.

202 Cited in Edmund Stadler, 'Adolphe Appia and Richard Wagner', in *Adolphe Appia*, ed John Pope-Hennessy (London: V&A Museum, 1970), 12.

203 Appia, 'Expériences de théâtre et recherches personelles' (1922).

204 Max Brückner, *Der Ring des Nibelungen von Richard Wagner: Dekorationsentwürfe von Prof. Max Brückner in Coburg zur Aufführung in Bayreuth im Jahre 1896* (Bayreuth: Heinrich Heuschmann, 1896), Introduction. Having certainly met with the approval of both Richard and Cosima Wagner, Gebrüder Brückner designed and constructed the sets for every Wagner opera between 1882 and 1911.

205 Cosima Wagner to Max Brückner, Bayreuth, 18 January 1894. Cited in Mack, *Cosima Wagner*, 367–68.

206 Cosima Wagner to Chamberlain, 23 October 1888. Cited in *Das zweite Leben*, 166. Cosima wrote directly to Appia only once, from Haus Riedberg in the small Bavarian city of Partenkirchen in the autumn of 1902, letting him know that although his drawings were 'remarkable' they were 'too architectural'. Cosima Wagner to Appia, 4 September 1902.

207 Appia to his sister Hélène, 15 February 1899.

208 Appia to Elsa Cantacuzene-Bruckmann, 28 March 1904. Cited in *Adolphe Appia: Œuvres complètes*, 1: 41.

209 Appia, 'Introduction à mes notes personelles' (1905).

Middle

1 For some key writings by Émile Jaques-Dalcroze on the method of eurhythmics that he invented and developed, see, in order of their publication: *Méthode Jaques-Dalcroze pour le développement de l'instinct rythmique, du sens auditif et du sentiment tonal* (Paris: Sandoz, Jobin, 1906), an eight-volume set of textbooks outlining lessons on eurhythmics which were to be mastered in turn; 'L'Education par le rythme', Le *Rhythme*, 1909, 63–70; 'Was die Rhythmische Gymnastik Ihnen gibt und was sie von Ihnen fordert', in *Der Rhythmus: Ein Jahrbuch*, vol 1 (Jena: Eugen Diederichs, 1911), 32–56; *La Rythmique* (Lausanne: Jobin, 1916); and *Rhythm, Music and Education*, trans Harald Rubinstein (London: Chatto and Windus, 1921) 'Dedicated to my Friend Adolphe Appia'. Appia wrote his own account of the origin of eurhythmics, published in French as 'L'Origine et les débuts de la gymnastique rythmique', *Les Feuillets: Revue mensuelle de culture suisse* 1, no 11 (November 1911), 393–403, and in German as 'Über Ursprung und Anfang der Rhythmischen Gymnastik', in *Der Rhythmus: Ein Jahrbuch*, 1: 20–31. For an account of the significance of eurhythmics written at the time of Hellerau, see Karl Storck, *E Jaques-Dalcroze. Seine Stellung und Aufgabe in unserer Zeit* (Stuttgart: Greiner und Pfeiffer, 1912), and for an excellent summary account see Claire-Lise Dutoit-Carlier, 'Jaques-Dalcroze, créateur de la rythmique', in *Émile Jaques-Dalcroze. L'Homme, le compositeur, le créateur de la rythmique* (Neuchâtel: Editions de la Baconnière, 1965), 305–412.

2 Margaret Naumburg, 'The Dalcroze Idea and What It Means', *The Outlook*, 17 January 1914, 127.

3 Note that 1892 was the year in which Appia made his first drawings for *Der Ring des Nibelungen*, at which time he was thirty years old.

4 Jaques-Dalcroze, 'Rhythm as a Factor in Education', in *The Eurhythmics of Jaques-Dalcroze*, ed Michael Ernest Sadler (Boston: Small Maynard, 1915), 5.

5 Jaques-Dalcroze, 'Rhythm as a Factor in Education', 5.

6 Ethel Ingham, 'Lessons at Hellerau', in *The Eurhythmics of Jaques-Dalcroze* (London: Constable, 1912), 31.

7 Jaques-Dalcroze, 'Rhythm as a Factor in Education', 8.

8 Jaques-Dalcroze, *Eurhythmics, Art and Education*, trans Frederick Rothwell (London: Chatto and Windus, 1930), 58. Elsewhere, Jaques-Dalcroze wrote: 'In the principles of artistic education, they – the Ancient Greeks – are still our masters.' Jaques-Dalcroze, *Rhythm, Music and Education*, v.

9 On the Boissonnas dynasty of photographers, see Nicolas Bouvier, *Boissonnas: Une dynastie de photographes, 1864–1983* (Lausanne: Editions Payot, 1983). See also Daniel Girardin, 'Frédéric Boissonnas: Between Tradition and Modernity', *History of Photography* 22, no 3 (2015), 281–83.

10 For Boissonnas's own account of the invention of the Téléphot, see 'Un nouveau télé-objectif: La téléphot rapide Vautier-Dufour et Schaer', *Revue suisse de photographie* 15 (1903), 10–21. See also Alfred Gradenwitz, 'The "Telephot": A Novel Apparatus for Photographing at Great Distances', *Scientific American* 88, no 26 (June 1903), 406; and Ernest Sauser, 'Le Téléphot', *Revue suisse de photographie* 18 (1906), 269–72.

11 Le Corbusier, *New World of Space* (New York: Reynal & Hitchcock, 1948), 66.

12 Georg Fuchs, *Der Tanz* (Stuttgart: von Streker & Schröder, 1906), 24. Note that Fuchs wrote the following about Appia in his book *Die Schaubühne der Zukunft* (Berlin: Schuster & Loeffler, 1905), 28: 'Adolf Appia proposed an abstracted setting for the purpose of *Musikdrama* in his work *Die Musik und die Inscenierung*, translated by Prinzessin Elsa Cantacuzene, Munich. Published by Bruckmann, 1899.'

13 Émile Magnin, *L'Art et l'hypnose: Interprétation plastique d'oeuvres littéraires et musicales* (Geneva: Atar, 1906).

14 Regarding the exhibition *Greece: Famous Sites and Forgotten Corners*, see Céline Eidenbenz, 'Hypnosis at the Parthenon: Magdeleine G photographed by Fred Boissonnas', *Études Photographiques* 28 (November 2011), 200–04.

15 Daniel Baud-Bovy was curator of the Musée Rath from 1905 to 1913 and director of the École Supérieure des Beaux-Arts in Geneva from 1909 to 1919. He was President of the Commission fédérale des beaux-arts from 1916 to 1938 and was a member of the Pro Helvetia foundation. He and his friend

Boissonnas completed the first known ascent of Mount Olympus, in 1913.

16 Baud-Bovy and Boissonnas, *En Grèce par monts et par vaux* (Geneva, 1910).

17 Homer, *The Odyssey*, trans Robert Fagles (London: Penguin, 2006), 272.

18 Victor Bérard and Boissonnas, *Dans le sillage d'Ulysse: Album odysséen* (Paris: Librairie Armand Colin, 1933). See also Armand Bérard, 'Victor Bérard et les "Navigations d'Ulysse",' *La Nouvelle Revue des Deux Mondes*, April 1972, 50–59; and Estelle Sohier, 'L'Odyssée: Du mythe à la photographie' (Bibliothèque de Genève, 2017), particularly regarding the dates of the maritime journeys.

19 Appia, 'Expériences de théâtre et recherches personelles' (1922). A transcription is published in *Adolphe Appia: Œuvres complètes*, ed Marie-Louise Bablet, vol 4, 1921–1928 (Lausanne: L'Âge d'Homme, 1991), 36–56.

20 See Suzanne Perrottet and Giorgio Wolfensberger, *Suzanne Perrottet, ein bewegtes Leben* (Bern: Benteli, 1989), excerpts from which are published as Perrottet, 'Dalcroze' Lieblingschülerin erinnert sich', in *Hellerau leuchtete: Zeitzeugenberichte und Erinnerungen*, ed Erhardt Heinold and Günther Großer (Dresden: Verlag der Kunst, 2007), 141–53.

21 The men in the photograph are Joan Llongueras; Appia (third from left); Ostraga; Glowacki; Edouard Combe; Jean D'Udine; and Paul André.

22 Edmund Stadler, 'Jaques-Dalcroze et Adolphe Appia', in *Émile Jaques-Dalcroze: L'homme, le compositeur, le créateur de la rythmique* (Neuchâtel: Editions de la Baconnière, 1965), 459.

23 Appia, 'Expériences de théâtre et recherches personelles' (1922).

24 On the history of the Château de Glérolles see Philip Jamin, 'Les châteaux vaudois: le château de Glérolles', *Le conteur vaudois: Journal de la Suisse romande* 54, no 32 (1916), 2. The Château de Glérolles is a thirty-room guesthouse nestled upon the northern shoreline of Lake Geneva. Its construction seems to have begun around 1150, initiated by the ecclesiastical prelate who presided over the episcopal seat of Lausanne. The château served purposes both civil and military: historical records bear witness to the capture and subsequent execution of several gangs of brigands in the vicinity of Glérolles. On the first floor, there was a device called *la cage aux sorcières* (the witches' cage), a curious apparatus resembling a large chest made of thick planks reinforced both inside and outside with iron. It incorporated a grille, permitting those confined within it only the minimum of air and light. In 1803, Napoleon established the Swiss Confederation, under which Vaud was elevated to the status of a canton. It was then that the château was acquired as a private estate by the Ruchonnet family, a tenure that persisted through numerous generations until the year 1977. In response to an enquiry I made to Patricia Rey, the current proprietor of the château, concerning the specific location of Appia's rooms, she wrote the following on 13 June 2017: 'According to the description you provided, it must have been the original tower built in 1150, situated on the western wing of the château. In the two photographs that I have attached you will see that the two small windows on the right afford views into the courtyard of the château, while the large, rounded arch window with the balcony overlooks the lake, facing out to the mountains beyond. Hence, it is highly likely that it was indeed in this tower that Mr Adolphe Appia resided.'

25 Appia in fact stayed at the château as far back as 1901, as attested by the dedication he wrote to Paul Bonifas on the cover page of the copy of *Die Musik und die Inscenierung* that Appia gifted to him. (Walther Volbach collection on Adolphe Appia, GEN MSS 1014, Box 6, Object ID: 10552146.)

26 Walther R Volbach, 'Jacques Copeau, Appia's Finest Disciple', *Educational Theatre Journal* 17, no 3 (October 1965), 206–14.

27 Jacques Copeau, 'Adolphe Appia et l'art scénique', *La Nación*, April 1928. Cited in *Adolphe Appia: Œuvres complètes*, ed Marie-Louise Bablet, vol 3, 1906–1921 (Lausanne: L'Âge d'Homme, 1988), 61–69.

28 Denis Bablet asserts that Appia found inspiration for his *Espaces rythmiques* in his direct surroundings: 'This artificial nature lived up to the real nature that Appia was intimate with, the one he was accustomed to see in its bare lines and primary elements: water, sky, walls, and light – the horizontality of the water of Lake Geneva, the verticality of a cypress tree, the play of verticals and horizontals in the vineyards.' Denis Bablet and Marie-Louise Bablet, eds, *Adolphe Appia 1862–1928: Darsteller–Raum–Licht* (Zurich: Pro Helvetia, 1982), 13.

29 Jean Mercier to Walter Volbach, 28 November 1960 (Walter Volbach Collection on Adolphe Appia, BRBML). The Swiss stage director first met Appia by chance in 1909 in the sanatorium of the wine-growing village of Chexbres. When Appia took up residence in his modest lodgings at the Château de Glérolles Mercier visited him there frequently, and it was apparently in the course of their long conversations that Mercier's interest in the theatre intensified. Many years later, Mercier served as an adviser to Appia on his book *L'Œuvre d'art vivant*, and helped to secure a publisher for the manuscript. See the discussion in Walther R Volbach, *Adolphe Appia: Prophet of the Modern Theatre* (Middletown: Wesleyan University Press, 1968), 131–32.

30 Mercier, cited in Volbach, *Adolphe Appia*, 120.

31 Friedrich Schiller, 'Über die ästhetische Erziehung des Menschen in einer reyhe von Briefen', *Die Horen* 1 (1795), Letter 9. Another one of the lines Schiller wrote, this time in Letter 22, is: 'When music reaches its noblest power, it becomes form.' Appia used this quotation as his epigraph for Appia, *Die Musik und die Inscenierung*.

32 Appia himself remarked that his drawing *The Steps* was made with Hellerau in mind: 'Bühnenbild für rhythmische Gymnastik v. Jaques-Dalcroze, von Hellerau (1909)'. Appia, 'Die Musik und das Bühnenbild', in *Theaterkunst Ausstellung im Kunstgewerbemuseum Zurich* (Zurich, 1914), 21.

33 Appia, *L'Œuvre d'art vivant*, unpaginated.

34 Appia, *L'Œuvre d'art vivant*, unpaginated.

35 The work for which Henri Odier is best known is 'Essai d'analyse psychologique du mécanisme du langage dans la compréhension' (Essay on the Psychological Analysis of the Mechanism of Language in Comprehension), PhD thesis (Université de Berne, 1904).

36 In a letter that he sent to Odier on 21 April 1911, Appia wrote that he was dissatisfied with this drawing, partly owing to its format, which he thought was 'awkward'.

37 Appia, *Notes sur le théâtre* (1908). A transcription is published in *Adolphe Appia: Œuvres complètes*, ed Marie-Louise Bablet, vol 3, 1906–1921 (Lausanne: L'Âge d'Homme, 1988), 61–69.
38 Appia, *L'Œuvre d'art vivant*, 42.
39 Serge Wolkonsky, 'Адольф Аппиа (Adolphe Appia)', Аполлон: литературный альманах (*Apollo: A Literary Almanac*) 6 (1912), 25–31, cited in Bablet and Bablet, eds, *Adolphe Appia 1862–1928: Darsteller–Raum–Licht*, 27. Prince Serge Wolkonsky, who came to be heavily involved in the Hellerau scene, was born in Estonia in 1860. His royalty derived from his mother, Princess Elizaveta Grigorievna Volkonskaya.
40 Prints of Böcklin's painting *Die Toteninsel* were very popular in Central Europe in the early twentieth century. Vladimir Nabokov observed that they could be 'found in every Berlin home'. *Despair* (London: John Long, 1937), 56. The Swiss Symbolist produced several different versions of this mysterious painting between 1880 and 1901 – the third of which he painted in 1883. This is the one that the ardent Böcklin admirer, Adolf Hitler, acquired fifty years later. Hitler hung it first at his Berghof in Obersalzberg and then in the Neue Reichskanzlei in Berlin. For more on *Die Toteninsel*, see Franz Zelger, *Arnold Böcklin: Die Toteninsel: Selbstheroisierung und Abgesang der abendländischen Kultur* (Frankfurt am Main: Fischer, 1991).
41 Appia, *L'Œuvre d'art vivant*, unpaginated.
42 Wolkonsky, 'Адольф Аппиа (Adolphe Appia)', 26.
43 Friedrich Schiller, 'Der Taucher', in *Musen-Almanach für das Jahr 1798* (Tübingen: J G Cotta, 1798), 121.
44 Schiller, 'Der Taucher', 126.
45 Schiller, 'Der Taucher', 130.
46 For an expanded discussion of the one-point perspective drawings by Gilly, Sartoris and Appia, including an analysis of their perspectival setup, alongside Alberti's original theoretical formulation, see my essay 'Of Lines Terrestrial and Occult: Friedrich Gilly, Alberto Sartoris, Adolphe Appia, and the Matter of Perspective', *DMJournal-Architecture and Representation* 2: Drawing Instruments/Instrumental Drawings (October 2023), 178–94.
47 Leon Battista Alberti, *On Painting*, trans John Spencer (New Haven: Yale University Press, 1966). For a compact treatment of Alberti's perspectival method, see Alfonso Procaccini, 'Alberti and the "Framing" of Perspective', *Journal of Aesthetics and Art Criticism* 40, no 1 (1981), 29–39.
48 Alberti, *On Painting*, 56.
49 Alberti, *On Painting*, 177.
50 Timothy Kitao, 'Prejudice in Perspective: A Study of Vignola's Perspective Treatise', *Art Bulletin* 44, no 3 (September 1962), 178. See also Cecil Grayson, 'L B Alberti's "Costruzione Legittima",' *Italian Studies* 19, no 1 (1964), 14–27.
51 For a list of all the books on perspective drawing that Gilly held in his library, see *Friedrich Gilly: Essays on Architecture 1796–1799*, trans David Britt (Santa Monica: Getty Center, 1994), 99.
52 Jean Dubreuil, *The Practice of Perspective*, trans Ephraim Chambers, 4th ed (London: John Bowles, 1765).
53 The term that Alberti used for what came to be known as the 'principal ray' in a perspective drawing was a 'centric ray', and for him it was above all an optical phenomenon: 'The centric ray is the most active and the strongest of all the rays. ... We could say many things about this ray, but this will be enough – tightly encircled by the other rays, it is the last to abandon the thing seen, from which it merits the name, prince of rays.' Alberti, *On Painting*, 48.
54 James Hodgson, 'The Theory of Perspective', in *The Practice of Perspective: Or, An Easy Method of Representing Natural Objects According to the Rules of Art*, trans Ephraim Chambers (London: John Bowles, 1765), ii.
55 Hodgson, 'The Theory of Perspective', iii.
56 *Sebastiano Serlio: On Architecture. Books I–V of 'Tutte l'opere d'architettura et Prospetiva'*, vol 1, trans Vaughan Hart and Peter Hicks (New Haven: Yale University Press, 1996), Book 2, folio 25r.
57 Cited in Mario Zadow, *Karl Friedrich Schinkel: Ein Sohn der Spätaufklärung* (Stuttgart: Axel Menges, 2001), 148. On Gilly as a teacher see 'Friedrich Gilly als Lehrer: Die Privatgesellschaft junger Architekten', in Carlheinz Feye and Jürgen Nottmeyer, eds, *Friedrich Gilly, 1772–1800, und die Privatgesellschaft junger Architekten* (Berlin: Willmuth Arenhövel, 1987), 174–78. The (probably apocryphal) story goes that Schinkel saw Gilly's perspective drawing, *Friedrich der Große Denkmal*, as a sixteen-year-old schoolboy in 1797 and decided then and there to become an architect. What is certain, however, is that the impression it made on the future *Baumeister* was an enduring one. Many years later, Schinkel hung it in the meeting room of the Bauakademie he designed. Barry Bergdoll has gone so far as to say that this single drawing 'might be said to have stamped Schinkel's entire career'. Bergdoll, 'A Postponed Architectural Career: Schinkel's Vision for Architecture', in *Karl Friedrich Schinkel: An Architect for Prussia* (New York: Rizzoli, 1994), 10.
58 On Schinkel as a scenographer, see Hans-Georg von Arburg, 'Modern Architecture Takes the Stage: Karl Friedrich Schinkel's Architectural Spectacles', in *Performing Knowledge, 1750–1850*, ed Mary Helen Dupree and Sean B Franzel (Berlin: De Gruyter, 2015), 165–90; Kurt Forster, 'Only Things That Stir the Imagination', in *Karl Friedrich Schinkel: The Drama of Architecture*, ed John Zukowsky (Berlin: Wasmuth, 1994), 18–35; Emma Letizia Jones, 'The Wanderer'. *AA Files*, no 72 (2016), 152–60.; and Anna Marie Pfäfflin, 'Bühnenbild und inszenierter Raum: Zum Konzept des Theatralischen im Werk von Karl Friedrich Schinkel', *Jahrbuch der Berliner-Museen* 56 (2014), 111–21.
59 Sartoris became best-known for his oblique parallel projection drawings, for which he generally adopted the paradigmatic 45/45-degree angle of axonometry, a prominent example of which appears on the cover of Kenneth Frampton's seminal book, *Modern Architecture: A Critical History* (New York: Rizzoli, 1981). Since there is no convergence towards a vanishing point in parallel projection, there is no privileged point of view as there is in perspective drawings, and one is never closer or further away from one part of the drawing than another, which is what gives them their 'floating' quality. That scale measurement is possible along all three axes is a property of axonometric projection highly valued in science and engineering, and in the project of rationalist architecture.
60 *Sebastiano Serlio*, 72. On the theme of steps in architecture, see Jacques Gubler, 'Des pieds nus gravissant un

escalier', in *Adolphe Appia ou le renouveau de l'esthétique théâtrale: Dessins et esquisses de décors*, ed Jörg Zutter (Lausanne: Éditions Payot, 1992), 93–108; and Pier Vittorio Aureli and Martino Tattara, *Platforms: Architecture and the Use of the Ground* (Milan: Black Square, 2021).

61 Joseph Leo Koerner, *Caspar David Friedrich and the Subject of Landscape* (London: Reaktion Books, 1990), 20.

62 Koerner, *Caspar David Friedrich and the Subject of Landscape*, 20, 93.

63 See Kristina Mösl and Philipp Demandt, eds, *Der Mönch ist zurück: Die Restaurierung von Caspar David Friedrichs Mönch am Meer und Abtei im Eichwald* (Berlin: Staatliche Museen zu Berlin–Nationalgalerie, 2016), 7, 27.

64 Koerner, *Caspar David Friedrich and the Subject of Landscape*, 93.

65 Hodgson, 'The Theory of Perspective', iii.

66 Appia, 'Expériences de théâtre et recherches personnelles' (1922).

67 Appia, 'Expériences de théâtre et recherches personnelles' (1922). See the following text by Jaques-Dalcroze for confirmation that it was Appia who gave him the idea of using stairs, platforms and so forth as part of his teaching of eurhythmics: 'Rhythm and Gesture in Music Drama and Criticism', in *Rhythm, Music and Education*, trans Harald Rubinstein (London: Chatto and Windus, 1921), 152.

68 Wolf Dohrn, 'Die Aufgabe der Bildungsanstalt Jaques-Dalcroze', in *Der Rhythmus: Ein Jahrbuch*, vol 1 (Jena: Eugen Diederichs, 1911), 2. 'The foundation stone was laid in Hellerau in wonderful weather ...' wrote Marie Adama van Scheltema in 'Charakterbild des Meisters', in *Hellerau leuchtete: Zeitzeugenberichte und Erinnerungen*, ed Erhardt Heinold and Günther Großer (Dresden: Verlag der Kunst, 2007), 136. Note that in the Centre d'iconographie collection in the Bibliothèque de Gèneve there is a photograph of van Scheltema at the laying of the foundation stone ceremony, standing alongside Jaques-Dalcroze and Suzanne Perrottet.

69 Dohrn, 'Die Aufgabe der Bildungsanstalt Jaques-Dalcroze', 19.

70 'Strictly speaking, the whole arrangement was called the Bildungsanstalt für rhythmische Gymnastik, or Bildungsanstalt for short. But we children simply referred to it as Die Anstalt.' Peter de Mendelssohn, *Hellerau: Mein unverlierbares Europa* (Dresden: Hellerau Verlag, 1993), 51.

71 Darius Milhaud, *Notes Without Music* (New York: Alfred A Knopf, 1953), 54.

72 Alfred Günther, 'Hellerau, eine Kunstbewegung', in *Hellerau leuchtete*, 395–96.

73 Elfride Feudel, 'Schule der Rhythmischen Erziehung', in *Hellerau leuchtete*, 154–55.

74 Ebenezer Howard, *Garden Cities of To-morrow* (London: Swan Sonnenschein, 1898) was published in German as *Gartenstädte in Sicht*, trans Maria Wallroth-Unterlip (Jena: Eugen Diederichs, 1907).

75 Howard, 'Leserbrief', *Dresdner Anzeige*, September 1912, republished as 'Der erste Eindruck' in *Hellerau leuchtete*, 229.

76 Karl Bücher, *Arbeit und Rhythmus* (Leipzig: Hirzel, 1896).

77 Mendelssohn, *Hellerau*, 49–50.

78 Mendelssohn, *Hellerau*, 51.

79 On the history of the Deutsche Werkstätten and Hellerau, see Klaus-Peter Arnold, *Vom Sofakissen zum Städtebau: Die Geschichte der Deutschen Werkstätten und der Gartenstadt Hellerau* (Dresden: Verlag der Kunst, 1993).

80 'It was the witty Berliner L F Schulz who invented the nickname "Holz-Goethe" for his Dresden friend Schmidt, who was generally humourless. Schmidt laughed out aloud when he heard the name, recognising that deep down there was some truth to it.' Theodor Heuss, 'Werkbund Beginn', in *Hellerau leuchtete*, 31.

81 Karl Schmidt, 'Die Gründung von Hellerau', in *Hellerau leuchtete*, 22.

82 Mendelssohn, *Hellerau*, 50.

83 Wolkonsky, 'Meine Erinnerungen', in *In Memoriam Hellerau*, ed E Feudel (Freiburg im Breisgau: Rombach, 1960), 49.

84 Wolkonsky, 'Meine Erinnerungen', 49.

85 Mendelssohn, *Hellerau*, 51.

86 Mendelssohn, *Hellerau*, 51.

87 Karl Scheffler, 'Heinrich Tessenow', *Kunst und Künstler* 11, no 1 (1913), 48.

88 Scheffler, 'Heinrich Tessenow', 46.

89 Scheffler, 'Heinrich Tessenow', 50. Further on Tessenow's architecture, see Marco De Michelis and Vicki Bilenker, 'Modernity and Reform: Heinrich Tessenow and the Institut Dalcroze at Hellerau', *Perspecta* 26, Theatre, Theatricality and Architecture (1990), 143–70; and De Michelis, *Heinrich Tessenow 1876–1950: Das architektonische Gesamtwerk* (Milan: Electa, 1991). Note that Scheffler was later a member on the nine-person jury for the *Ehrenmal Neue Wache* competition, and that he voted for Tessenow. Scheffler penned his autobiography and published it as *Die fetten und die mageren Jahre* (Munich: P List, 1946).

90 Theodor Fischer, 'Was ich bauen möchte', *Hohe Warte* 3 (1906), 327.

91 On the collaboration between Jaques-Dalcroze and Appia at Hellerau, see Richard Beacham, 'Appia, Jaques-Dalcroze, and Hellerau, Part One: "Music Made Visible",' *New Theatre Quarterly* 1, no 2 (May 1985), 154–64; and 'Appia, Jaques-Dalcroze, and Hellerau, Part Two: "Poetry in Motion",' *New Theatre Quarterly* 1, no 3 (August 1985), 245–61.

92 Jaques-Dalcroze to Appia, 3 June 1910. Cited in Edmund Stadler, 'Émile Jaques-Dalcroze et Adolphe Appia', in *Émile Jaques-Dalcroze: L'homme, le compositeur, le créateur de la rythmique* (Neuchâtel: Editions de la Baconnière, 1965), 439.

93 Some authors have been strident in their assertion that Appia's role in the design of the performance space, if not the Festspielhaus itself, was in fact decisive rather than participatory. See for example Mary Elizabeth Tallon, 'Appia's Theatre at Hellerau', *Theatre Journal* 36, no 4 (December 1984), 495–504.

94 Appia to Jaques-Dalcroze, cited in Karl Storck, *E Jaques-Dalcroze. Seine Stellung und Aufgabe in unserer Zeit* (Stuttgart: Greiner und Pfeiffer, 1912), 89. Note that Storck reproduced four of Appia's 1909 *Espaces rythmiques* in his book as plates inserted between pages 32 and 33: *Oblique Shadow*; *Terrace with Three Columns*; *The Shadow of the Cypress*; and *Clearing in the Forest* (which in fact seems never to have been published anywhere else).

95 Margaret Naumburg, 'The Dalcroze Idea and What It Means', *The Outlook*, 17 January 1914, 127.

96 The following are excerpts from Salzmann's patent for an auditorium lighting system based on the 'luminous organ' of the Festsaal: 'Method of illumination by means of diffused light generated by strategically placed electric light bulbs that are uniformly distributed between two walls, one of which reflects light, and one that

diffuses it evenly into the space that is to be illuminated ... The light bulbs are precisely positioned at the midpoint between the two walls. It was observed that this configuration allows the front fabric panels to evenly disperse and diffuse the light from the bulbs, resulting in a uniform illumination without discernible halos or shadows between the individual sources of light. The effect resembles diffuse daylight. This system is adaptable to all spatial conditions.' *Kaiserliches Patentamt*, Patent no 280509 Class 4b, Group 22, *Bühnenbeleuchtung* (stage lighting), patented in the Deutsches Reich on 24 October 1913. Further on the conception and design of the Festsaal lighting apparatus, see Claire Kuschnig, 'Beleuchtungskonzept von Alexander von Salzmann', in *Rekonstruktion der Zukunft: Raum, Licht, Bewegung, Utopie*, ed Dieter Jaenicke and Ralph Lindner (Leipzig: Spector, 2017), 103–07.

97 Alexander von Salzmann, 'Licht, Belichtung und Beleuchtung', in *Claudel-Programmbuch* (Hellerau: Hellerau Verlag, 1913), 89–90. See also Appia's 1912 essay 'La gymnastique rythmique et la lumière', *Le Rythme* 34 (December 1932), 15–17, in which he wrote: 'To be form-giving or plastic, light must exist in an atmosphere, a luminous atmosphere. Therefore a harmonious and endlessly changeable balance between illumination and creative or plastic light will engender ... *luminous sound*, the precise coordination of luminous vibrations in space to those of the music.'

98 Salzmann, 'Licht, Belichtung und Beleuchtung', 90.

99 George Bernard Shaw to Stella Patrick Campbell, 30 June 1913. Cited in George Bernard Shaw, 'Kulturfrühling in Hellerau', in *Hellerau leuchtete*, 264. For further correspondence between Shaw and Campbell see Alan Dent, ed, *Bernard Shaw and Mrs Patrick Campbell: Their Correspondence* (London: Victor Gollancz, 1952), 124–27.

100 Franz Werfel, 'Die Bühne von Hellerau', *Die neue Rundschau* 25 (November 1913), 1624.

101 Appia, 'Über Ursprung und Anfang der Rhythmischen Gymnastik', in *Der Rhythmus: Ein Jahrbuch*, 1: 20–31, 64.

102 Adolphe Appia, *L'Œuvre d'art vivant* (Geneva: Atar, 1921), 14.

103 Appia, cited in Stadler, 'Émile Jaques-Dalcroze et Adolphe Appia', 440.

104 Wolf Dohrn, Preface to 'Jahresbericht der Bildungsanstalt Jaques-Dalcroze für das Unterrichtsjahr 1910/11', in *Der Rhythmus: Ein Jahrbuch*, 1: 65–81.

105 Jaques-Dalcroze, *Eurhythmics, Art and Education*, 61.

106 Karl Scheffler, 'Das Haus', in *Der Rhythmus: Ein Jahrbuch*, vol 2 (Jena: Eugen Diederichs, 1912), 2–13.

107 Mendelssohn, *Hellerau*, 52.

108 The letters and postcards that Inga and Ragna Jacobi sent to their parents from Hellerau were mostly written in German, though some are in Norwegian, and occasionally both languages are used in the same letter. The correspondence is published in Petra Kabus, *Innenansichten: Zwei norwegische Schülerinnen der Bildungsanstalt Jaques-Dalcroze in Hellerau* (Dresden: Deutscher Werkbund Sachsen, 2009).

109 Ragna Jacobi to her parents, 23 April 1912.

110 'Der Unterrichtsplan' in 'Jahresbericht der Bildungsanstalt Jaques-Dalcroze für das Unterrichtsjahr 1910/11', 80–81.

111 Ethel Ingham, 'Lessons at Hellerau', in *The Eurhythmics of Jaques-Dalcroze* (London: Constable, 1912), 49.

112 Inga Jacobi to her sister Ragna Jacobi, 23 May 1911.

113 Ragna Jacobi to her parents, 28 October 1911.

114 Jaques-Dalcroze, 'From the Lectures of Émile Jaques-Dalcroze: Leipzig, 10 December 1911', in *The Eurhythmics of Jaques-Dalcroze*, 26–27.

115 Jaques-Dalcroze, 'Address to the Dresden Teachers' Association: 28 May 1912', in *The Eurhythmics of Jaques-Dalcroze*, 27.

116 The other three women in the photograph are Annie Beck, Marie Adama van Scheltema and Mitzi Steinwender.

117 'Nachrichten über den Neubau des Instituts und die Unterrichtskurse 1911/12', in *Der Rhythmus: Ein Jahrbuch*, 1: 72–79.

118 Ludwig Glaeser interview with Mary Wigman, Berlin, 13 September 1972, (Mies van der Rohe Archive, MoMA). Note that the house which Bruhn shared with Wigman stood on 'the gently curving, stately main street Am grünen Zipfel' which leads up from the Waldschänke to the marketplace. Erich Haenel, 'Die Gartenstadt Hellerau', *Dekorative Kunst, illustrierte Zeitschrift für angewandte Kunst* 14, no 7 (April 1911), 320. For more on Mies in Hellerau, see Lutz Robbers, 'Modern Architecture in the Age of Cinema: Mies van der Rohe and the Moving Image,' PhD thesis (Princeton University, 2012), chapter 4; and Robbers, '1912 – Hellerau as Spielraum', in *Participation in Art and Architecture*, ed Martino Stierli and Mechtild Widrich (London: I B Tauris, 2015), 197–226. Barry Bergdoll also mentions Mies's connection with Hellerau, arguing for example that the garden of the Werner House (1912–13) recalls 'both Schinkel's staging of a portico and trellis in the landscape at the Charlottenhof and Adolphe Appia's contemporary stage designs for Heinrich Tessenow's Festsaal at Hellerau'. Bergdoll, 'The Nature of Mies's Space', in *Mies in Berlin*, ed Bergdoll and Terence Riley (New York: Museum of Modern Art, 2001), 78.

119 Franz Schulze, *Mies van der Rohe: A Critical Biography* (Chicago: Chicago University Press, 1985), 70.

120 While employed as a tax inspector at the time of his daughter Ada's birth, Friedrich Wilhelm Gustav subsequently transitioned into a role as a manufacturer of small motors. Remarkably, he can be credited with the invention of the taxi meter, thus contributing to the coinage of the term 'taxi'. He was evidently inventive and industrious, and it is conceivable that he discerned a semblance of these traits in the young architect who had begun to court his daughter.

121 Schulze, *Mies van der Rohe*, 71.

122 Schulze, *Mies van der Rohe*, 71.

123 Alois Riehl died on 21 November 1924, at home in the house that Mies built for him. The architect also designed the neo-Kantian philosopher's tombstone. See Fritz Neumeyer, 'Mies's First Project: Revisiting the Atmosphere at Klösterli', in *Mies in Berlin*, ed Bergdoll and Riley (New York: Museum of Modern Art, 2001), 309–17; and Bergdoll, 'The Nature of Mies's Space', 67–105.

124 It is possible that a shared sense of the meaning of 'space' played a part: 'The theme of space is the artistic "idea" of the work, which gives rise to its formal content and to which the substance of the work is subordinate',

the philosopher wrote in Alois Riehl, 'Bemerkungen zum Problem der Form in der Dichtkunst', *Vierteljahrsschrift für wissenschaftliche Philosophie* 21 (1897).

125 Anton Jaumann, 'Vom künstlerischen Nachwuchs', *Innendekoration* 21, no 7 (July 1910), 272. This article published in the summer of 1910 was the first one in the professional literature in which the Riehl House appeared. It is worth noting that in the same year, Hermann Muthesius featured it prominently in a double-page spread in the second edition of *Landhaus und Garten*, a book that served as a declaration of principles for the garden reform movement. Hermann Muthesius, *Landhaus und Garten: Beispiel neuzeitlicher Landhäuser nebst Grundrissen, Innenräumen und Gärten*, 2nd ed (Munich: Bruckmann, 1910), 50–51.

126 Bergdoll, 'The Nature of Mies's Space', 72.

127 Cited in Neumeyer, 'Mies's First Project', 314.

128 Ragna Jacobi to her parents, 1 March 1912.

129 Inga Jacobi to her parents, 13 January 1912.

130 Shaw to Stella Patrick Campbell, 30 June 1913. Cited in Shaw, 'Kulturfrühling in Hellerau', 264–65.

131 Ragna Jacobi to her parents, 19 March 1912.

132 Ethel Ingham studied with Jaques-Dalcroze in Hellerau and later played a pivotal role in co-founding the London School of Dalcroze Eurhythmics in 1913. She penned an account of the daily routine of the resident students at the Großes Pensionshaus, which began with 'the striking of a gong at seven o'clock; the house is immediately alive'. The day unfolds, and activities typically conclude shortly after supper: 'Late hours are not encouraged at the Hostel – indeed, everybody is glad to retire early, for the work is absorbing and demands plenty of energy.' Ingham, 'Lessons at Hellerau', 56, 58. For architectural plans of the Großes Pensionshaus see the 'Jahresbericht der Bildungsanstalt Jaques-Dalcroze für das Unterrichtsjahr 1910/11', 71. And there are additional descriptions on pages 91–92. Refer also to 'Die Bildungsanstalt Dalcroze in Hellerau bei Dresden', *Blätter für Architektur und Kunsthandwerk* 26, no 5 (May 1913), 17–20.

133 'Jahresbericht der Bildungsanstalt Jaques-Dalcroze für das Unterrichtsjahr 1910/11', 91.

134 Milhaud, *Notes Without Music*, 55.

135 Walther R Volbach, *Adolphe Appia: Prophet of the Modern Theatre* (Middletown: Wesleyan University Press, 1968), 85.

136 Ernst Ansermet, 'La Gymnastique Rythmique a Hellerau', SIM 9, no 7 (July 1913), 58.

137 Appia, 'Über Ursprung und Anfang der Rhythmischen Gymnastik', 61.

138 Wolkonsky, 'Die Wende in meinem Leben', in *Hellerau leuchtete*, 200.

139 Appia, 'Über Ursprung und Anfang der Rhythmischen Gymnastik', 64.

140 On this episode, see Stadler, 'Jaques-Dalcroze et Adolphe Appia', 443–45.

141 Émile Jaques-Dalcroze to Appia, 3 June 1911.

142 Perrottet, 'Dalcroze' Lieblingschülerin erinnert sich', 152.

143 Appia, *L'Œuvre d'art vivant*, unpaginated.

144 Homer, *The Odyssey*, trans Robert Fagles (London: Penguin, 2006), 142.

145 Appia, *L'Œuvre d'art vivant*, unpaginated.

146 On this setting for the Elysian Fields, see Upton Sinclair, 'Music Made Visible', in *World's End* (London: T Werner Laurie, 1948), 11–24, in which he wrote on page 14: 'The mountain of motion burst forth into silent song. The denizens of Hell were transformed into the shades of the Elysian Fields, and showers of blessings fell upon them out of the music ... It was music made visible; and when the curtain had fallen upon the bliss of Orpheus and his bride, a storm of applause shook the auditorium. Men and women stood shouting their delight at the revelation of a new form of art.'

147 Wolkonsky, 'Meine Erinnerungen', 25–26.

148 Wolkonsky, 'Meine Erinnerungen', 25–26. For two of the few overwhelmingly negative critical accounts of the Festspiele, see F A Geissler 'Die Dalcroze-Schulfeste in Hellerau', *Die Musik: Illustrierte Halbmonatsschrift* 11, no 4 (1912), 154–57; and Ulrich Rauscher, 'Hellerau', *Die Schaubühne* 9, no 42 (1913), 1003–06. 'When the chorus sings (which they should refrain from doing, given their inadequate vocal training), they mostly use the Italian solemnisation, without any text. This "do-re-mi" singing conveys an impression of desperation, a deliberate renunciation of what Wagner set as the ideal, namely the birth of music from poetry – the higher unity of sound and word ... But the audience liked it. People pay, want to get something for their money, and the power of suggestion is as great as the fear of appearing outmoded. The old profound tale of the emperor's new clothes becomes the truth over and over again', wrote Geissler on pages 156–57 of his essay, which is mostly critical of the musical aspect of the performances. And Rauscher wrote more generally of the artistic endeavour of Hellerau on the opening page of his essay: 'What most characterises the artists of Hellerau is their lack of consistency. If the concept of relentlessness – an iron will – is associated with true artists, those at Hellerau are driven by an irresponsible desire to initiate, to "test out", both characteristics of the dilettante. They intend to reform dance, clothing, housing and the theatre: the artist must focus on only one. They have ideas but they lack the drive; they have education but not a vocation.'

149 Wolkonsky, 'Meine Erinnerungen', 25–26.

150 Shaw to Stella Patrick Campbell, 30 June 1913. Published in Shaw, 'Kulturfrühling in Hellerau', 265. Further regarding Shaw's presence in Hellerau, Mendelssohn wrote: 'I do remember a tall gentleman with a beard and a curiously confused look who walked past our garden gate and looked in at us children on the lawn with interest. My father said it was Mr Bernard Shaw of England, and that we had nothing to fear from him.' Mendelssohn, *Hellerau*, 52. See also Sinclair, 'Music Made Visible', 12–13.

151 Günther, 'Hellerau, eine Kunstbewegung', 396.

152 Friedrich Schnack, 'Mein Hellerauer Zeit war zu Ende', in *Hellerau leuchtete*, 416.

153 Haenel, 'Die Gartenstadt Hellerau', 320.

154 Franz Kafka, diary entry for 30 June 1914. Cited in Franz Kafka, *Tagebücher 1910–1923*, ed Max Brod (Frankfurt am Main: Fischer, 1951), 406.

155 Le Corbusier, *Journey to the East*, trans Ivan Žaknić (Cambridge, MA: MIT Press, 2007). The Swiss musician and composer Albert Jeanneret was born in

La Chaux-de-Fonds in 1886, one year before his famous brother Charles-Édouard. Jeanneret, a skilled violinist, embarked upon his formal musical education at the prestigious Berlin Hochschule für Musik and further honed his talents at the Conservatoire de musique de Genève. Subsequently, he assumed a faculty position at the Bildungsanstalt in Hellerau.

156 *Le Corbusier correspondance: Lettres à la famille*, vol 1, 1900–1925 (Paris: Infolio, 2011), 339. Note the transcription on the back of a historical postcard: 'Waldschänke Hellerau. Strassenbahnlinie 7, Haltestelle Waldschänke 3 Minuten'.

157 On Le Corbusier as a photographer see Tim Benton, *Le Corbusier: Secret Photographer* (Zurich: Lars Müller, 2013).

158 Le Corbusier, *Étude sur le mouvement d'art décoratif en Allemagne* (La Chaux-de-Fonds: École de l'Art, 1912), 42, 49.

159 Le Corbusier, unpublished notes signed *Hellerau, ce 1er juillet 1913. Ch(arles)-E(Edouard) Jeanneret, architecte*, cited in *Adolphe Appia: Œuvres complètes*, ed Marie-Louise Bablet, vol 3, 1906–1921 (Lausanne: L'Âge d'Homme, 1988), 205.

160 Albert Jeanneret to Appia, 14 April 1913.

161 *Le Corbusier correspondance: Lettres à la famille*, 1: 326.

162 *Le Corbusier correspondance: Lettres à la famille*, 1: 340.

163 Le Corbusier, *Journey to the East*, 216. Further on Le Corbusier and the Acropolis, see Turit Fröbe, *Die Inszenierung eines Mythos: Le Corbusier und die Akropolis* (Basel: Birkhäuser, 2017); and Richard A Etlin, 'Le Corbusier, Choisy, and French Hellenism: The Search for a New Architecture', *Art Bulletin* 69, no 2 (June 1987), 264–78.

164 Ernest Renan, *Prière sur l'Acropole* (Paris: Édouard Pelletan, 1899).

165 Charles-Édouard Jeanneret to William Ritter, 1 March 1911 (Box 357, Archives Litteraires Suisses, Bibliothèque Nationale de Berne, Fonds William Ritter). Note that Ritter wrote a review of Appia's *La Mise en scène du drame Wagnérien* (Paris: Léon Chailley, 1895). See *Adolphe Appia: Œuvres complètes*, 1: 292–93.

166 Sigfried Giedeon, *The Eternal Present: A Contribution on Constancy and Change* (New York: Pantheon, 1962), 10.

167 Le Corbusier made this sketch on page 147 of his Carnet 3 in early October 1911. He later reproduced it, along with the annotation, in *Une maison, un palais* (Paris: G Crès, 1928), 15. For a facsimile of the original, see Le Corbusier, *Carnet 3: Voyage d'Orient* (New York: Rizzoli, 1988).

168 Appia to Houston Stuart Chamberlain (SAPA, within the ranges: Ja1 15 1–11; or Ja1 16 1–16). Cited in Stadler, 'Jaques-Dalcroze et Adolphe Appia', 449. See also Alfred Berchtold, 'Émile Jaques-Dalcroze et son temps', in *Émile Jaques-Dalcroze: L'homme, le compositeur, le créateur de la rythmique* (Neuchâtel: Éditions de la Baconnière, 1965), 103–08; and *Adolphe Appia: Œuvres complètes*, 3: 266–72.

169 See Frédéric Boissonnas, Paul-Edmond Martin, and Horace Micheli, *Les Fêtes de Juin 1914: Album du Centenaire genevois* (Geneva: Editions d'art Boissonnas, 1922).

170 Paul Bonifas to Walther Volbach, 1960, cited in Richard Beacham, '"Anonymity Is the Essence": In Search of Adolphe Appia', *New Theatre Quarterly* 28, no 2 (May 2012), 147. Note that Appia in fact resided with the French actor for a time, evidenced by a letter that Chamberlain sent to him at Bonifas' address on 6 March 1917.

171 Mendelssohn, *Hellerau*, 52.

172 Ulrich Becker-Glauch, 'Abschied von der Bildungsanstalt und von Wolf Dohrn', in *Hellerau leuchtete*, 318.

173 Becker-Glauch, 'Abschied von der Bildungsanstalt und von Wolf Dohrn', 317.

174 Friedrich Naumann, 'Trauerrede zum Gedächtnis von Wolf Dohrn', in *Hellerau leuchtete*, 327.

175 Naumann, 'Trauerrede zum Gedächtnis von Wolf Dohrn', 332.

176 Naumann, 'Trauerrede zum Gedächtnis von Wolf Dohrn', 334.

177 On Jaques-Dalcroze's involvement in the protest against the German bombing of Reims and the circumstances that led to his subsequent dismissal from Hellerau, see Berchtold, 'Émile Jaques-Dalcroze et son temps', 103–12; Robert Winckelmann, *Der Genfer Protest und J-D Ausschuss zur Gründung eine Vereins zur Erhaltung der methode J-D in Deutschland: Die Tatsachen über die Lostrennung der Bildungsanstalt von ihrem bisherigen Leiter J-D* (Berlin, 1914); and Karl Lorenz, 'Der Untergang Helleraus 1914: Bericht aus Genf zum 60. Jahrestag des "Genfer Protestes",' in *Rhythmik in der Erziehung* (Seelze-Velber: Kallmeyer, 1974). And for the protest letter itself see 'Protestation contre le bombardement de Reims', *L'image de la guerre* 1, no 2 (1914), which is a reprint of the original article published in *Journal de Genève*.

178 Carl von Clausewitz, *Vom Kriege* (Berlin: Ferdinand Dümmler, 1832), vol 2, book 5, chapter 2.

179 Feudel, 'Schule der Rhythmischen Erziehung', 154–55.

180 Schnack, 'Mein Hellerauer Zeit war zu Ende', 423.

Late

1 See Appia, 'Die Musik und das Bühnenbild', in *Theaterkunst Ausstellung im Kunstgewerbemuseum Zurich* (Zurich, 1914), 15–20, which includes the text authored by Appia for the catalogue of the *Theaterkunst* exhibition. Additionally, see Heinrich Schlosser, 'Die Zürcher Theaterkunstausstellung', *Das Werk: Architektur und Kunst* 1, no 3 (1914), 13–16, which precedes Appia's text in the catalogue. Appia's drawings were shown at the following exhibitions that took place during his lifetime: Darmstadt, 1909; *Moderne Szenenkunst*, Mannheim, 1913; *Theaterkunstausstellung*, Kunstgewerbemuseum Zurich, 6 February–30 April 1914; *Deutsche Werkbundausstellung*, Cologne, May–October 1914; *Institut Jaques-Dalcroze*, Geneva, 1918; *Internationale Theater Tentoonstellung* (International Theatre Exhibition), Amsterdam, January–February 1922; International Theatre Design Exhibition, V&A, London, 3 June–16 July 1922; *Teatro alla Scala*, Milan, 1923; Stockholm, 1924; *Raumbilder für die Bühne von Adolphe Appia, Gewerbemuseum*, Basel, October 1924; Zurich, April 1925; Leipzig, June 1925; and the *Deutsche Theater-Ausstellung*, Magdeburg, 1927.

2 Denis Bablet, 'Craig and Appia', in *The Theatre of Edward Gordon Craig*, trans Daphne Woodward (London: Eyre Methuen, 1981), 175.

3 Cited in Bablet, 'Craig and Appia', 176.

4 Gordon Craig, *On the Art of the Theatre* (London: Heinemann, 1911), footnote on page vii.

5 See Denis Bablet, 'The School', in *The Theatre of Edward Gordon Craig*, trans Daphne Woodward (London: Eyre Methuen, 1981), 161–73.

6 Craig to Appia, 4 May 1914. The written correspondence between Appia and Craig amounts to no fewer than forty-six pencil-written letters and postcards in Appia's hand, and forty in ink by Craig, all post-stamped between 4 April 1914 and 13 January 1924 (Craig sent the first, Appia the last). Those sent by Craig to Appia are held at SAPA in Bern, and those from Appia to Craig are held in the Fonds E G Craig in the Bibliothèque Nationale in Paris. For two accounts by Richard Beacham of the relationship between Appia and Craig, based upon their written correspondence, see "'Brothers in Suffering and Joy': The Appia-Craig Correspondence', *New Theatre Quarterly* 4, no 15 (August 1988), 268–88; and 'Adolphe Appia und Edward Gordon Craig: Treffpunkt in Elysium', in *Rekonstruktion der Zukunft: Raum, Licht, Bewegung, Utopie*, ed Dieter Jaenicke and Ralph Lindner (Leipzig: Spector, 2017), 53–58.

7 Appia to Craig, 24 November 1921.

8 Jaques-Dalcroze, cited in Edmund Stadler, 'Jaques-Dalcroze et Adolphe Appia', in *Émile Jaques-Dalcroze: L'homme, le compositeur, le créateur de la rythmique* (Neuchâtel: Editions de la Baconnière, 1965), 441. On Craig's settings for *Hamlet*, see Denis Bablet, 'The Moscow Hamlet', in *The Theatre of Edward Gordon Craig*, trans Daphne Woodward (London: Eyre Methuen, 1981), 133–60; *In My Mind's Eye: Edward Gordon Craig and Hamlet: An Exhibition of Prints & Books, Mainly from the Personal Archives of Gordon Craig and His Family from the Collection of Jason Buzas* (London: Sophie Schneideman Rare Books, 2009); and Jacques Rouché, *L'Art théâtral moderne* (Paris: Edouard Cornély, 1910). Regarding Craig more generally, see Jeffrey Akard, *Edward Gordon Craig* (Cambridge: Cambridge University Press, 1983).

9 Matei Roussou, 'L'Exposition internationale de théâtre d'Amsterdam', *Le Monde illustré*, 18 March 1922, 193.

10 Roussou, 'L'Exposition internationale de théâtre d'Amsterdam', 193. Further on the 1922 Amsterdam exhibition, see Hendrik Wijdeveld, ed, 'Internationale Theater Tentoonstellung Amsterdam 1922', *Wendingen* 4, no 9–10 (1921) which, in addition to describing the exhibition, includes Appia's essay 'Art vivant ou nature morte'; photographs of the room in which his drawings were hung (some Wagnerian settings, but also *Espaces rythmiques*); and also a floor plan of the exhibition that clearly reveals the importance placed on Appia's work, insofar as his drawings are the first ones that visitors to the exhibition were guided towards.

11 Carl Van Vechten, 'Adolphe Appia and Gordon Craig', *Forum* 17, no 10 (1915): 483–87. This article is published in full as Van Vechten, 'Adolphe Appia and Gordon Craig', in *Music After the Great War, and Other Studies* (New York: G Schirmer, 1915), 159–68.

12 Craig to Appia, 23 November 1915.

13 Appia to Craig, 24 November 1915.

14 Appia to Van Vechten, 8 February 1916.

15 Appia to Craig, 8 February 1916.

16 On the 1914 Werkbund exhibition, see Carl Rehorst, ed, *Offizieller Katalog der Deutschen Werkbund-Ausstellung: Cöln 1914, Mai–Oktober* (Cologne: Rudolf Mosse, 1914); Fritz Hellwag, 'Der Deutsche Werkbund und seine Ausstellung Köln 1914', *Kunstgewerbeblatt* 3 (1915): 41–54; and Robert Breuer, 'Die Cölner Werkbund-Ausstellung, Mai–Oktober 1914', *Deutsche Kunst und Dekoration* 12, no 3 (1914): 416–36. Note that the co-founder of Hellerau, Wolf Dohrn, was in fact the first secretary of the Deutscher Werkbund.

17 Maurice Browne, *Too Late to Lament* (Bloomington: Indiana University Press, 1955), 166.

18 Appia to Franz Rapp, 6 December 1926. 'While only two pages are devoted to the topic of the theatre in the official catalogue of the Cologne Werkbund exhibition, it is worthwhile reading the short unsigned text that precedes the list of exhibited works, since it is not only illustrative of the ideas that animated the Werkbund, it is also symptomatic of the fact that the "reform" that Appia demanded in 1899 in his book *Die Musik und die Inscenierung* was starting to be realised, even if the name of the instigator was carefully omitted.' *Adolphe Appia: Œuvres complètes*, ed Marie-Louise Bablet, vol 3, 1906–1921 (Lausanne: L'Âge d'Homme, 1988), 184.

19 Craig to Appia, 4 May 1914.

20 Appia to Craig, 8 May 1914.

21 Walter Gropius to his mother Manon Auguste Pauline Gropius, 21 October 1907. Cited in Reginald R Isaacs, *Walter Gropius: Der Mensch und sein Werk*, vol 1 (Berlin: Gebr. Mann, 1983), 91.

22 Some of the other significant Werkbund exhibition buildings were the Festive Hall by Peter Behrens, the Austrian Pavilion by Josef Hoffmann, the Farbenschau Pavilion by Hermann Muthesius and the Werkbund Theatre by Henry van de Velde.

23 Hellwag, 'Der Deutsche Werkbund und seine Ausstellung Köln 1914', 44. Appia was worried about the drawings he had sent for the exhibition, not knowing how and when they would be returned to him. But Alfred Altherr, who had curated the theatre art exhibition at the Museum of Applied Arts in Zurich earlier in the year, and who had become friends with Appia, arranged for their safe dispatch back to Switzerland.

24 On Gropius's wartime years, see Reginald R Isaacs, *Walter Gropius: An Illustrated Biography of the Creator of the Bauhaus* (Boston: Bullfinch Press, 1991), 38–58.

25 Cited in Franz Schulze, *Mies van der Rohe: A Critical Biography* (Chicago: Chicago University Press, 1985), 81.

26 Gropius, cited in Isaacs, *Walter Gropius*, 62.

27 Gropius to Tomas Maldonado, 24 November 1963.

28 Gropius, *Programm und Manifest des Staatlichen Bauhauses* (Weimar, 1919).

29 Appia, 'Acteur, Espace, Lumière, Peinture (1910)', cited in Appia, 'Darsteller, Raum, Licht, Malerei (1919)', in *Texte zur Theorie des Raums*, ed Stephan Günzel (Stuttgart: Reclam, 2013), 121.

30 Adolphe Appia, *L'Œuvre d'art vivant* (Geneva: Atar, 1921), 101.

31 See Gropius, *Bauhausbücher 12: Bauhausbauten Dessau* (Munich: Albert Langen, 1930), 15.

32 See Melissa Trimmingham, *The Theatre of the Bauhaus: The Modern and Postmodern Stage of Oskar Schlemmer* (New York: Routledge, 2011); Noam Elcott,

'Spaceless Play: Oskar Schlemmer's Dance Against Enlightenment', in *Artificial Darkness: An Obscure History of Modern Art and Media* (Chicago: University of Chicago Press, 2016), 165–228; and finally, Tut Schlemmer, *The Letters and Diaries of Oskar Schlemmer. Selected and Edited by Tut Schlemmer*, trans Krishna Winton (Evanston: Northwestern University Press, 1972).

33 Appia to Albert Burger, undated.

34 Oskar Schlemmer, 'Mensch und Kunstfigur', in *Bauhausbücher 4: Die Bühne im Bauhaus*, ed Gropius and L Moholy-Nagy (Munich: Albert Langen, 1924), 13.

35 László Moholy-Nagy, 'Theater, Zirkus, Varieté', in *Bauhausbücher 4: Die Bühne im Bauhaus,* 52.

36 Moholy-Nagy, 'Theater, Zirkus, Varieté', 44, 54.

37 Oskar Schlemmer, 'Bühne', *Bauhaus: Zeitschrift für Bau und Gestaltung* 1, no 3 (July 1927), unpaginated.

38 See Adolphe Appia, 'Plantation. Praticables (extraits). A propos d'éclairage' (1895), cited in *Adolphe Appia: Œuvres complètes*, ed Marie-Louise Bablet, vol 2, 1895–1905 (Lausanne: L'Âge d'Homme, 1986), 241–42.

39 Charles-Édouard Jeanneret, Amédée Ozenfant and Paul Dermée, 'L'Esprit nouveau', *L'Esprit nouveau*, no 1 (1920), 3–5.

40 Note that Adolf Loos wrote the following in his essay 'Ornament and Crime', and that the sentence was italicised in the original: 'The evolution of culture is synonymous with the removal of ornamentation from objects of everyday use.' Loos, 'Ornament et Crime', *L'Esprit nouveau*, no 2 (1920), 160.

41 BGE: FBB P Ryth 019, top left.

42 Albert Jeanneret, 'La Rythmique 1', *L'Esprit nouveau*, no 2 (1920), 183. On the relationship between Albert Jeanneret, Le Corbusier and Amédée Ozenfant, see Judi Loach, 'Architecture, Science and Purity', in *Being Modern: The Cultural Impact of Science in the Early Twentieth Century* (London: UCL Press, 2018), 207–44.

43 Jeanneret, 'La Rythmique 1', 186.

44 Albert Jeanneret, 'La Rythmique 2', *L'Esprit nouveau*, no 3 (1920), 332–33.

45 Jeanneret, 'La Rythmique 2', 333.

46 Jeanneret, 'La Rythmique 2', 338. Jaques-Dalcroze himself was high in praise for Albert Jeanneret's two-part *L'Esprit nouveau* essay: 'You cannot fathom the immense pleasure I derive from reading your work, the solace that these youthful, vibrant essays provide me! ... In your *L'Esprit nouveau* texts, I expel a sigh of contentment, for I feel the authenticity that prevails in them, and the eagerness to explore new solutions to the timeless questions that plague humanity. May this spirit of truth and simplicity that pervades your magazine remain unaltered, I implore!' Jaques-Dalcroze to Albert Jeanneret, cited in Alfred Berchtold, 'Émile Jaques-Dalcroze et son temps', in *Émile Jaques-Dalcroze: L'homme, le compositeur, le créateur de la rythmique* (Neuchâtel: Editions de la Baconnière, 1965), 130.

47 'L'architecture est le jeu savant, correct et magnifique des volumes assemblés sous la lumière.' Le Corbusier-Saugnier, 'Trois rappels à MM. Les Architectes', *L'Esprit nouveau*, no 1 (1920), 91–96.

48 Le Corbusier-Saugnier, 'Architecture III: Pure création de l'esprit', *L'Esprit nouveau*, no 16 (1922), 1917.

49 Le Corbusier, *New World of Space* (New York: Reynal & Hitchcock, 1948), 66.

50 Boissonnas's original signed, labelled but undated photograph, *L'Acropole vue du Pnyx*, is actually made up of two large side-by-side gelatin silver prints mounted on dark green cardboard, measuring a sizeable 113×39 cm in total. One of the hefty folios in which it was stitched is held in the graphics collection of the Musées d'Art et d'Histoire in Geneva.

51 Le Corbusier-Saugnier, 'Architecture III: Pure création de l'esprit'. See Maxime Collignon, *Le Parthénon: L'histoire l'architecture et la sculpture* (Paris: Libraire Hachette, 1914); and Boissonnas, *L'Acropole d'Athènes* (Paris: Albert Morancé, 1910).

52 Le Corbusier-Saugnier, 'Architecture III', 1916, 1919.

53 Le Corbusier-Saugnier, 'Vers une architecture', *L'Esprit nouveau*, no 18 (1923), unpaginated.

54 Le Corbusier mailed Jaques-Dalcroze a copy of *Vers une architecture* on 12 January 1924.

55 Boissonnas to Le Corbusier, 5 November 1923.

56 Appia, *L'Œuvre d'art vivant*, 24.

57 Pierre Saddy and Claude Malécot, eds, *Le Corbusier: Le passé à réaction poétique* (Paris: Caisse Nationale des Monuments Historiques et des Sites/Ministère de la Culture et de la Communication, 1988), 209.

58 Appia commenced the writing of *L'Œuvre d'art vivant* in 1918, and by the autumn of 1919 he was editing it. He completed the final typed version in October 1920, though the manuscript no longer exists. *Adolphe Appia: Œuvres complètes*, 3: 354.

59 'There are no books or articles by or about Adolphe Appia in Le Corbusier's library, nor in the archive', Isabelle Godineau (Head of Archives and Collections, Fondation Le Corbusier) to the author, 19 April 2022.

60 Appia, *L'Œuvre d'art vivant*, 24.

61 Friedrich Schiller, 'Über die ästhetische Erziehung des Menschen in einer Reyhe von Briefen', *Die Horen* 6 (1795), Letter 22. Note that Appia had used this quotation as his epigraph for *Die Musik und die Inscenierung*.

62 Appia, *L'Œuvre d'art vivant*, 32–33.

63 Le Corbusier-Saugnier, 'Architecture III', 1904.

64 Appia, *L'Œuvre d'art vivant*, 106.

65 Le Corbusier-Saugnier, 'Vers une architecture', unpaginated.

66 Le Corbusier and Pierre Jeanneret, *The Complete Architectural Works*, vol 1, *1910–1929* (London: Thames & Hudson, 1964), 74. The publication in which Le Corbusier first made the statement 'The house is a machine for living in' is Le Corbusier-Saugnier, 'Vers une architecture', ix.

67 In 1939, Albert Jeanneret made his return to Switzerland and initially took up residence in Vevey. However, he later relocated to Villa Le Lac, the diminutive house on the shores of Lake Geneva that his brother Le Corbusier had designed for their parents, Georges-Edouard Jeanneret and Marie Charlotte Amélie Jeanneret-Perret. Their father passed away a little over a year after the completion of the house. However, their mother continued to live there for more than half a century, before she died a centenarian in 1960. Jeanneret then assumed residence of the villa, where he lived until his own death in 1973.

68 Le Corbusier, *Une petite maison, 1923* (Zurich: Girsberger, 1954), 7.

69 Le Corbusier, *Une petite maison, 1923*, 30. The *fenêtre en longueur* was number four of the Five Points of a New Architecture that Le Corbusier and Pierre Jeanneret typed out and co-signed on 24 July

1927. It was published in that same year in Alfred Roth, *Zwei Wohnhäuser von Le Corbusier und Pierre Jeanneret; Fünf Punkte zu einer neuen Architektur von Le Corbusier und Pierre Jeanneret* (Stuttgart: F Wedekind, 1927).

70 Le Corbusier, lecture notes, Lausanne, 18 February 1924. Published in Tim Benton, *The Rhetoric of Modernism: Le Corbusier as a Lecturer* (Basel: Birkhäuser, 2009), 86.

71 Corbusier, *Une petite maison, 1923*, 7.

72 Le Corbusier, *Une petite maison, 1923*, 9. On Le Corbusier's appreciation of the setting of Lake Geneva, see Benton, *The Rhetoric of Modernism*, 82–86, which includes sketches that Le Corbusier made of the terraced landscape around Rivaz.

73 Le Corbusier, *Precisions on the Present State of Architecture and City*, trans Edith Schreiber Aujame (Cambridge, MA: MIT Press, 1991), 130.

74 Le Corbusier, *Precisions*, 130.

75 Le Corbusier, *Une petite maison, 1923*, 22.

76 Le Corbusier, *Une petite maison, 1923*, 24. Le Corbusier wrote elsewhere that the garden of the *petite maison*, 'surrounded by walls', is 'used as a summer living room'. Le Corbusier, *Precisions*, 128–30. He often asserted his conviction that 'an exterior is always an interior', for example, in the sub-section of his *L'esprit nouveau* essay 'Architecture II' entitled 'The Outside is Always an Inside'. For the original, see Le Corbusier-Saugnier, 'Architecture II: L'illusion des plans', *L'Esprit nouveau*, 1922, 1775–78, and for its publication as part of a recent English-language edition of *Vers une architecture*, see 'Architecture II: The Illusion of the Plan', in *Toward an Architecture*, trans John Goodman (Los Angeles: Getty Research Institute, 2007), 224–27. See also Sylvain Malfroy, 'Der Aussenraum ist immer ein Innenraum', *Werk, Bauen + Wohnen* 81, no 6 (1994), 36–41. Further on the vacillating sense of scale in Le Corbusier's *petite maison*, note that in a letter to his fiancée Yvonne Gallis he described the house as 'an ancient temple at the water's edge'. Le Corbusier to Yvonne Gallis, 11 September 1924, cited in Bruno Reichlin, 'My Father Lived One Year in This House. The Scenery Fascinated Him', in *Le Corbusier: An Atlas of Modern Landscapes*, ed Jean-Louis Cohen (New York: Museum of Modern Art, 2012), 71.

77 Corbusier, *Une petite maison, 1923*, 23, 27.

78 *Tristan und Isolde* was based on the Arthurian love story *Tristan and Iseult*, and Wagner referred to his own retelling of it not as an opera, but rather *eine Handlung* (literally, a drama, a plot, or an action). Note that Appia had seen the 1886 performance of *Tristan und Isolde* at Bayreuth, the production of which had been overseen by Cosima Wagner.

79 Brian Magee, *The Tristan Chord: Wagner and Philosophy* (New York: Metropolitan Books, 2002), 208.

80 Jean Mercier to Walter Volbach, 11 March 1961.

81 Appia, 'Cahier de Jean Mercier pour Tristan et Isolde' (1923). Some excerpts from the notebook are published in *Adolphe Appia: Œuvres complètes*, ed Marie-Louise Bablet, vol 4, 1921–1928 (Lausanne: L'Âge d'Homme, 1991), 243–46. See also Appia's 'Tristan et Iseult: Brève analyse du drame' (1923); 'Introduction aux représentations de Tristan et Isolde à la Scala de Milan' (1923); and the two articles 'Tristano e Isotta à la Scala', *La Semaine littéraire* 22 (January 1924), 17–18; and 'La préparation de Tristan à la Scala', *Journal de Genève* 20 (January 1924), 5, both of which are transcribed in *Adolphe Appia: Œuvres complètes*, 4: 247–49.

82 Appia to Oskar Wälterlin, 12 January 1924.

83 Appia to Oskar Wälterlin, 12 January 1924.

84 Appia, *L'Œuvre d'art vivant*, unpaginated.

85 Appia, *L'Œuvre d'art vivant*, unpaginated.

86 Appia to Paul Boepple, December 1923.

87 Appia, 'La préparation de Tristan à la Scala', 5.

88 Appia to Oskar Wälterlin, 12 January 1924.

89 Edward Gordon Craig, *Fourteen Notes* (Seattle: University of Washington Book Store, 1931), 11.

90 Appia to Oskar Wälterlin, 12 January 1924.

91 Appia sent Oskar Wälterlin a letter from the Hotel Marino in Florence on 5 December 1923.

92 Ugo Ojetti, 'Calvino alla Scala', *L'Avanti*, December 1923.

93 Ojetti, 'Calvino alla Scala'.

94 Wagner to his friend, lover and confidant Mathilde Wesendonck, April 1859. Cited in Elliot Zuckerman, *The First Hundred Years of Wagner's Tristan* (New York: Columbia University Press, 1964), 33.

95 Enrico Corradini, 'Una lettera ad Adolfo Appia', 1924.

96 On the working relationship between Appia and Wälterlin, see Peter Loeffler, *Oskar Wälterlin: Ein Profil* (Basel: Birkhäuser, 1979), 57–82, and also Wälterlin's own account, 'Adolphe Appia und die Inszenierung von Wagners "Ring",' in *Bekenntnis zum Theater* (Zurich: Opprecht, 1955), 12–26.

97 Oskar Wälterlin to Walther Volbach, 11 April 1960.

98 Adolf Zinsstag, 'Zur neu-Inszenierung des Nibelungenringes', *Rundschau Bürgerzeitung*, January 1925. See also Zinsstag, 'Die Prostitution eines Kunstwerkes am Basler Stadttheater', *Rundschau Bürgerzeitung*, 6 February 1925; Zinsstag, 'Via Appia', *Rundschau Bürgerzeitung*, 27 February 1925; and Zinsstag, 'Kunstfeindliches aus Basel', *Rundschau Bürgerzeitung*, 9 April 1925. Zinsstag, a musician and goldsmith, was the most avid Wagner admirer. When he constructed his family residence, Zinsstag christened it *zum Rheingold.* Over time, Zinsstag cultivated a friendship with Wagner's son Siegfried, and spent much of his own savings on the purchase of the original handwritten score of the *Siegfried-Idylls*, a symphonic poem for chamber orchestra that Wagner had composed as a birthday gift for his wife, Cosima.

99 Appia to Paul Boepple, 11 March 1925.

100 Appia to Jacques Copeau, 25 March 1925. Cited in *Adolphe Appia: Œuvres complètes*, 4: 276. For a carefully documented account of the circumstances of the Basel scandal, see Karl Reyle, 'Als der "Appia Ring" zersprang', *National Zeitung*, 18 November 1961, 26.

101 Wagner, *Parsifal*, trans Graham Salter (Richmond, Surrey: Overture, 2011), 107.

102 Friedrich Nietzsche, *Der Fall Wagner: Ein Musikanten-Problem* (Leipzig: C G Naumann, 1888), 32.

103 Appia's original manuscript for 'Lohengrin (Wagner). (Scénario abrégé)' (1923) no longer exists, but a nineteen-page typed version that he signed – 'Ad. Appia / 1926' – is held in the Swiss Archive of Performing Arts (SAPA: 46a–c). A transcription is published in *Adolphe Appia: Œuvres complètes*, 4: 449–58.

104 Paul Alfred Merbach, 'Modern German Theatre Art', in *International Exhibition of Theatre Arts* (New York: Museum of Modern Art, 1934), 31.
105 Richard Wagner, *Lohengrin*, trans Amanda Holden (London: John Calder, 1993), 86.
106 Wagner, *Lohengrin*, 92.
107 William Shakespeare was a popular playwright during his time, committed to the theatre and the live performance of his plays, a commitment shared by Appia. This devotion is exemplified by the fact that only approximately half of Shakespeare's plays were published during his lifetime, and these publications took the form of slender paperback volumes known as quartos. They earned this name because they were made from printed sheets folded twice to produce four leaves, equivalent to eight pages. Notably, none of these quartos provide any indication of Shakespeare's involvement in their publication. For Shakespeare, the primary avenue of 'publication' was through performance. And it was for the Globe, London's famous Elizabethan playhouse, that he wrote his plays – a wooden, more or less circular, structure, open to the elements. It featured a thrust stage crowned by a canopy, extending into the area where audience members paying a single penny would stand. Surrounding this standing area were galleries where patrons could be seated by paying an additional penny. It is worth noting that while certain props like cauldrons, stocks, artificial trees or beds were used to suggest particular settings, there was no representational scenery as we know it today.
108 Cosima Wagner to Hermann Graf Keyserling, 11 April 1903. Cited in Cosima Wagner, *Das zweite Leben: Briefe und Aufzeichnungen, 1883–1930*, ed Dietrich Mack (Munich: R Piper, 1980), 631–32. Refer also to the following letters between Appia and Keyserling: SAPA: Ja5 1–19 and Jb6 132–3.
109 Jessica Davis Van Wyck, 'Working with Appia', *Theatre Arts Monthly* 8, no 12 (December 1924), 817.
110 Appia to Craig, 31 January 1919.
111 Van Wyck, 'Working with Appia', 817.
112 Jessica Davis Van Wyck, 'Designing Hamlet with Appia', *Theatre Arts Monthly* 9, no 1 (January 1925), 17.
113 Paul Prescott, *Introduction to William Shakespeare, Hamlet* (London: Penguin Classics, 1980), xxii.
114 Appia and Van Wyck, 'Six Designs for Hamlet', *Theatre Arts Monthly* 9, no 1 (January 1925), 21.
115 Shakespeare, *Hamlet*, 32.
116 Appia and Van Wyck, 'Six Designs for Hamlet', 21.
117 Appia and Van Wyck, 'Six Designs for Hamlet', 23. 'The final drawing is signed "D Van Wyck / 1922", while the preliminary drawing is by Appia; it was "copied" by Jessica, who then attributed the authorship to herself!' *Adolphe Appia: Œuvres complètes*, 4: 405.
118 Appia and Van Wyck, 'Six Designs for Hamlet', 23.
119 Shakespeare, *Hamlet*, 66.
120 Appia and Van Wyck, 'Six Designs for Hamlet', 23.
121 Appia and Van Wyck, 'Six Designs for Hamlet', 24.
122 Shakespeare, *Hamlet*, 80.
123 Appia and Van Wyck, 'Six Designs for Hamlet', 24.
124 Appia and Van Wyck, 'Six Designs for Hamlet', 27.
125 Appia and Van Wyck, 'Six Designs for Hamlet', 28.
126 Shakespeare, *Hamlet*, 128.
127 Shakespeare, *Hamlet*, 129.
128 Shakespeare, *Hamlet*, 137.
129 Shakespeare, *Hamlet*, 141
130 Shakespeare, *Hamlet*, 142
131 Appia and Van Wyck, 'Six Designs for Hamlet', 31.
132 Appia and Van Wyck, 'Six Designs for Hamlet', 31. Note that this drawing was published in John Pope-Hennessy, *Adolphe Appia* (London: V&A Museum, 1970), 40, plate 19, with the caption '*Hamlet*, 1922. Act V'.
133 Within correspondence sent to Jean Binet, dated 4 September 1927, Appia alluded to his proposed settings for *Macbeth*. However, these notes are fragmentary and undated, spread over two separate loose sheets of paper. On the opening page, he made the statement: 'Macbeth / 4 drawings, but no definitive remarks regarding the staging'. A transcription of Adolphe Appia, 'Macbeth' (1926) is published in *Adolphe Appia: Œuvres complètes*, 3: 417–18.
134 Shakespeare, 'Macbeth', in *Four Tragedies* (London: Penguin, 1994), 843.
135 Appia, 'Macbeth'.
136 Franz Grillparzer, *Des Meeres und der Liebe Wellen* (Vienna: F B Wallishausser, 1840). On the relationship between the lead female characters in Shakespeare's *Romeo and Juliet* and Grillparzer's *Des Meares und der Liebe Wellen*, see Douglas Yates, 'Grillparzer's Hero and Shakespeare's Juliet', *Modern Language Review* 21, no 4 (October 1926), 419–25.
137 Appia wrote out two copies of his preface to the English edition of *Die Musik und die Inscenierung*, both times in pencil; the first is a draft made up of thirteen greying unlined sheets of paper that Appia numbered and then signed on the last page: 'Adolphe Appia / octobre 1918 / Rivaz. Suisse'; and the second is the final version, written on sixteen sheets of yellowing paper, signed and dated on the final page: 'Adolphe Appia / octobre 1918 / Chexbres. Suisse'. Both copies are inserted in a larger sheet of paper folded in half, on which Appia wrote in haste: 'Preface Ed. English', on both sides. A transcription of the second manuscript is published in *Adolphe Appia: Œuvres complètes*, 3: 331–34.
138 Appia, *La musique et la mise en scène (1892–1897)*, ed Edmund Stadler (Bern: Theaterkultur-Verlag, 1963), preface, xiii. Cited in *Adolphe Appia: Œuvres complètes*, 3: 334. Appia's emphasis.
139 Appia to Edward Gordon Craig, 30 November 1918.
140 See Douglas Yates, *Franz Grillparzer: A Critical Biography* (Oxford: B Blackwell, 1946).
141 George Bernard Shaw, *The Quintessence of Ibsenism* (London: Walter Scott, 1891), 72.
142 Shaw, *The Quintessence of Ibsenism*, 72–73.
143 Henrik Ibsen, *Little Eyolf*, trans William Archer, *The Collected Works of Henrik Ibsen*, vol 11 (London: William Heinemann, 1907), 3.
144 A transcription of Adolphe Appia, 'Mise en scène du Petit Eyolf' (1924) is published in *Adolphe Appia: Œuvres complètes*, 4: 414–16.
145 Ibsen, *Little Eyolf*, 9, 10.
146 Ibsen, *Little Eyolf*, 9–10.
147 Ibsen, *Little Eyolf*, 25.
148 Ibsen, *Little Eyolf*, 59.
149 Ibsen, *Little Eyolf*, 64, 65.
150 Ibsen, *Little Eyolf*, 64.
151 Ibsen, *Little Eyolf*, 86.
152 Ibsen, *Little Eyolf*, 91.
153 Ibsen, *Little Eyolf*, 93.
154 Ibsen, *Little Eyolf*, 95, 101.
155 Appia, 'Mise en scène du Petit Eyolf' (1924).

156 Ibsen, *Little Eyolf*, 63.

157 Appia, 'Mise en scène du Petit Eyolf' (1924).

158 Ibsen, *Little Eyolf*, 113.

159 Ibsen, *Little Eyolf*, 145, 149.

160 Ibsen, *Little Eyolf*, 151.

161 Appia, 'Mise en scène du Petit Eyolf' (1924).

162 Euripides, *Iphigenia at Aulis*, 28.

163 Euripides, *Iphigenia at Aulis*, 29.

164 Richard Wagner, 'Über die Ouvertüre (1841)', in *Sämtliche Schriften und Dichtungen*, vol 1 (Leipzig: Breitkopf & Härtel, 1911), 203. Note that Wagner composed two musical pieces for *Iphigenia at Aulis*: the first an arrangement for the entire opera (WWV 77), and the second a *Konzertschluß* to the Overture (WWV 87).

165 Euripides, *Iphigenia at Aulis*, 46.

166 Euripides, *Iphigenia at Aulis*, 45.

167 Euripides, *Iphigenia at Aulis*, 77.

168 Euripides, *Iphigenia at Aulis*, 80.

169 Euripides, *Iphigenia at Aulis*, 91.

170 Jaques-Dalcroze, 'Rhythm as a Factor in Education', in *The Eurhythmics of Jaques-Dalcroze*, ed Michael Ernest Sadler (Boston: Small Maynard, 1915), 11, first published as Émile Jaques-Dalcroze, 'L'Education par le rythme', *Le Rhythme*, 1909, 63–70. It is worth noting that the sets which Roller designed for the 1909 production of Richard Strauss's *Elektra* at the Vienna State Opera were used all the way up to 1937.

171 Euripides, *Iphigenia among the Taurians*, 10.

172 Euripides, *Iphigenia at Aulis*, 94.

173 Euripides, *Iphigenia among the Taurians*, 8.

174 Euripides, *Iphigenia among the Taurians*, 8–9.

175 Appia made drawings for all four acts of *Iphigenia among the Taurians* and wrote out some notes on the staging of the first two of them in a little beige-coloured oilcloth notebook that he left undated, though given that he signed and dated his drawings as having been made in 1926 and also wrote in a letter to Karl Reyle that same year that he was 'working on both Iphigenias', the sixteen pages of notes likely also date from that same time. A transcription of Adolphe Appia, 'Iphigénie en Tauride. Scénario. Considérations générales' (1926) is published in *Adolphe Appia: Œuvres complètes*, 4: 442–44.

176 Euripides, *Iphigenia among the Taurians*, 10.

177 Euripides, *Iphigenia among the Taurians*, 29.

178 Euripides, *Iphigenia among the Taurians*, 34.

179 Euripides, *Iphigenia among the Taurians*, 38.

180 Euripides, *Iphigenia among the Taurians*, 41.

181 Curt Moreck, 'Bühnenbilder von Emil Pirchan', *Innen-Dekoration* 31, no 4 (April 1920), 133. Emil Pirchan, an architect, scenographer and graphic artist, was born in Brno in the year 1884. He was one of Otto Wagner's students in Vienna from 1903 to 1906, before relocating to Munich in 1908 and founding his own art school focusing on scenography and graphic design. He assumed the role of stage design director at the Bavarian State Opera in 1918 and, in 1921, transferred to the Prussian State Opera in Berlin, where he continued his work in the same capacity. In 1932 Pirchan moved to Prague, where he took up the position of head of set design at the New German Theatre. Finally, in 1936, he took up the position of professor at the Akademie der bildenden Künste in Vienna and simultaneously assumed the directorship of the Meisterschule für Bühnenbildkunst und Festgestaltung (Master School for Stage Design). For more on Pirchan's life and work, refer to Beat Steffan, *Emil Pirchan: Universal Artist* (Wädenswil: NIMBUS Kunst und Bücher, 2018).

182 Moreck, 'Bühnenbilder von Emil Pirchan', 133.

183 Jacques Copeau, 'Adolphe Appia et l'art de la scène', *Cahiers de la Compagnie Madelaine Renaud et Jean-Louis Barrault* 13, no 10 (1955), 92–97. On Appia and Copeau, see Walther R Volbach, 'Jacques Copeau, Appia's Finest Disciple', *Educational Theatre Journal* 17, no 3 (October 1965), 206–14.

184 Franz Rapp, 'Das deutsche Bühnenbild unserer Zeit', *Die Form: Monatsschrift für gestaltende Arbeit* 1, no 3 (1922), 11. Most of the written correspondence between Appia and Rapp is archived in the Deutsches Theatermuseum (DTM) in Munich: 'Briefwechsel–Adolphe Appia–Franz Rapp'. The letters span the dates 11 January 1926 to 10 September 1927. The final letter is from Appia, sent just four months before he died. There are also some letters from Rapp to Appia in SAPA, spanning from 1 December 1926 to 29 November 1927.

185 Appia to Rapp, 12 November 1926. (DTM–Briefwechsel Appia–Franz Rapp).

186 Appia to Rapp, 8 February 1927. There is another letter in the collection that is particularly significant insofar as it is Appia's own listing of the exhibitions of his drawings up to the time, and also because he notes how many drawings were shown at each exhibition, and which ones they were. Appia to Rapp, 6 December 1926.

187 Appia to Rapp, 8 February 1927.

188 Rapp to Appia, 4 July 1927, addressed: 'c/o Dr Oscar Forel, La Métairie Psychiatric Clinic, Nyon, Canton Vaud'.

189 Johann Wolfgang von Goethe, *Faust: Eine Tragödie* (Tübingen: Cotta, 1808), published in English as Johann Wolfgang von Goethe, *Faust: Part One*, trans Philip Wane (London: Penguin, 1949), 87. Note that Wagner in fact also composed pieces for *Faust Part 1*; firstly, *Seven Compositions on Goethe's Faust* in 1831, and then in 1840 his first version of a *Faust Overture* that was conceived as the first movement to a *Faust Symphony*.

190 Cosima Wagner to Hermann Graf Keyserling, Bayreuth, 11 April 1903. Cited in *Das zweite Leben*, 631–32.

191 Goethe, *Goethes Faust Erster und zweiter Teil* (Leipzig: Alfred Kröner, undated).

192 The original fifty-five-page manuscript of *Goethes Faust: Erster Teil, als Dichtung dargestellt*, handwritten by Appia in pencil, is held at SAPA. Concerning the timeline of when Appia composed the manuscript and made his drawings, there is a letter from Appia to Jean Binet dated 1 June 1927 in which he mentions that he is actively 'working on Faust Part 1' and that 'the drawings are finished, now I am moving on to the writing'. And then, on 11 July, he wrote to Roda Mahert: 'I am getting close to finishing my manuscript and hope to be able to deliver it in August.' *Goethes Faust: Erster Teil, als Dichtung dargestellt* was eventually published in 1929 – after Appia's death – by Fritz Klopp Verlag in Bonn. This publication was edited by Carl Niessen, who was concurrently preparing the exhibition titled *Faust auf der Bühne, Faust in der bildenden Kunst* in Braunschweig and initially intended to showcase Appia's drawings. See Frederick Lehner, 'Goethes Faust auf der Bühne', *German Quarterly* 25, no 2 (March 1952), 95–102.

193 Appia, *Goethes Faust: Erster Teil, als Dichtung dargestellt*, 11.

194 Adolphe Appia, 'Testament' (January 1927), cited in *Adolphe Appia: Œuvres complètes*, 4: 24.

195 Goethe, *Faust*, 87.

196 Goethe, *Faust*, 90.

197 Carl Vogel, 'Die letzte Krankheit Goethes, beschrieben und nebst einigen andern Bemerkungen über denselben', *Journal der practischen Heilkunde* 76 (1833), 17. A cast made of Goethe's head is often described as a death mask, but that is incorrect in that it was made in 1807 while the poet, novelist, playwright, philosopher, diplomat, lawyer, civil servant and scientist was still very much alive; it was made at the request of Franz Joseph Gall, the inventor of phrenology. For an extended critical essay on life and death masks that addresses both the techniques involved in their making and also their status as cultural and aesthetic artefacts, see Marcia Pointon, 'Casts, Imprints and the Deathliness of Things: Artifacts at the Edge', *Art Bulletin* 96, no 2 (June 2014), 170–95. On page 172, Pointon writes: 'Recognising the betwixt and between of the death mask after death prior to burial we might see its function as an attempt to hold on to the person. This liminality is registered also in the fact that "the mask of death" may refer not to a death mask but metaphorically to the frozen features of the dead face: a face that is also not a face. Moreover, the death mask is on the cusp also in the sense that it occupies a disputed space that is neither private nor public and, belongs neither to the original nor to the copy.'

198 Appia, 'Testament' (January 1927).

After

1 *Adolphe Appia: Œuvres complètes*, ed Marie-Louise Bablet, vol 4, 1921–1928 (Lausanne: L'Âge d'Homme, 1991), 24.

2 Jean Mercier, Edouard Junod and Oscar Forel jointly signed the *acte de partage* (deed of partition) of La Fondation Adolphe Appia on 15 August 1928.

3 Oscar Forel to Hélène Appia, 6 August 1929.

4 Lee Simonsen, 'The Designer and the Theatre', in *International Exhibition of Theatre Art* (New York: Museum of Modern Art, 1934), 14.

5 Adolphe Appia, *L'Œuvre d'art vivant* (Geneva: Atar, 1921), unpaginated.

6 On the Beistegui penthouse, see *The Le Corbusier Archive*, vol 8, *Appartement de Beistegui, Cité Univérsitaire – Pavillon Suisse, Ville Radieuse, and Other Buildings and Projects*, 1930, ed H Allen Brooks (New York: Garland and Fondation Le Corbusier, 1982); 'Sur les toits de Paris: Le jardin enchanté de Monsieur Charles de Beistegui', photographs by George Buffotot, *Vogue* (France), October 1932, 54–55; Paolo Melis, 'Il "cadavere squisito" di Le Corbusier: Pierre Jeanneret e Charles Beistegui', *Controspazio* 9, no 3 (1977), 36–37; Pierre Saddy, 'Le Corbusier chez les riches: l'appartement Charles de Beistegui', *Architecture, mouvement, continuité*, 49 (1979): 57–70; Manfredo Tafuri, 'The City in the Work of Le Corbusier', in *Le Corbusier*, ed H Allen Brooks (Princeton: Princeton University Press, 1987), 203–18; Van den Bergh, 'Charles Beistegui: Autobiography and Patronage', OASE 83: *Commissioning Architecture* (December 2010): 17–40; Anthony Vidler, 'Beistegui Apartment, or Horizons Deferred', in *Le Corbusier: An Atlas of Modern Landscapes*, ed Jean-Louis Cohen (New York: Museum of Modern Art, 2013), 274–79; Van den Bergh, *Beistegui avant Le Corbusier* (Paris: Éditions B2, 2015); Ross Anderson, 'All of Paris, Darkly: Le Corbusier's Beistegui Apartment, 1929–1931', in *Proceedings of the International Congress Le Corbusier, 50 Years Later*, ed J Torres Cueco (Valencia: Universitat Politècnica de Valencia, 2015), 113–27; and, most substantially, Van den Bergh, *Machine à Amuser: The Life and Death of the Beistegui Penthouse Apartment* (Cambridge, MA: MIT Press, 2024).

7 *Le Corbusier et Pierre Jeanneret: Œuvre complète de 1929–1934*, ed Willy Boesiger (Basel: Birkhäuser, 1935), 53.

8 Charles de Beistegui interviewed by Roger Baschet, published as 'Les demeures parisiennes: À la recherche d'un décor', *Plaisir de France*, March 1936, 26–29. Cited in Saddy, 'Le Corbusier chez les riches: l'appartement Charles de Beistegui', 70. Note that the Beistegui penthouse received more attention in fashion magazines – *Plaisir de France* and *Vogue*, for example – than it did in architectural journals.

9 Turit Fröbe, *Die Inszenierung eines Mythos: Le Corbusier und die Akropolis* (Basel: Birkhäuser, 2017), 116. Further on Appia and Le Corbusier, see Fröbe's sub-chapter 'Volumen in Licht – der Einfluss Henri Provensals und des Instituts Jaques-Dalcroze in Hellerau', 104–16. She includes two *Espaces rythmiques* – *The Alleyway* and *The Diver*. And further on Le Corbusier and the Parthenon, see Julio Bermudez, 'Le Corbusier at the Parthenon', in *Transcending Architecture* (Washington: Catholic University of America Press, 2015), 88–110.

10 Saddy, 'Le Corbusier chez les riches', 59.

11 Homer, *The Odyssey*, trans Robert Fagles (London: Penguin, 2006), 142.

12 Pierre Saddy, 'Le Corbusier e l'Arlecchino', *Rassegna* 3 (July 1980), 25–32.

13 See *Modern Architecture: International Exhibition* (New York: Museum of Modern Art, 1932), 89.

14 On Haus Josef Esters and Haus Lange, see Barry Bergdoll and Terence Riley, *Mies in Berlin* (New York: Museum of Modern Art, 2001), 89–90, 220–21.

15 Franz Schulze, *Mies van der Rohe: A Critical Biography* (Chicago: Chicago University Press, 1985), 144.

16 Mies made the decision to adopt Mies van der Rohe as a professional alias, although the exact moment when he did so remains uncertain, since he never bothered to formalise his name change through legal means. He probably adopted his pseudonym around 1921, although its first documented appearance in print occurred in a May 1922 edition of the journal *Die Bauwelt*. In any case, what Mies did was couple his father's surname with his mother's maiden name using the artificial connector 'van der'. It appears that he dared not adopt the title of genuine German nobility 'von', but instead

the 'van der' borrowed from his Dutch neighbours had a subtly elegant ring to the German ear. See Schulze, *Mies van der Rohe*, 104. On Charles-Édouard Jeanneret's transformation into Le Corbusier, refer to Fröbe, 'Aus Jeanneret wird Le Corbusier 1918–1923' in Fröbe, *Die Inszenierung eines Mythos: Le Corbusier und die Akropolis*, 117–44.

17 *Wettbewerbsprogramm* (Bundesarchiv Koblenz R32/358, 65–67), cited in Christoph Stölzl, *Die Neue Wache Unter den Linden: Ein Deutsches Denkmal im Wandel der Geschichte* (Berlin: Koehler & Amelang, 1993), 28. For more on the architectural competition, see Walter Curt Behrendt, 'Eine Gedächtnisstätte für die Gefallenen des Weltkrieges: Zum Umbau der Neuen Wache in Berlin', *Zentrallblatt der Bauverwaltung* 50, no 29 (1930), and for a recent critical appraisal see Sean Forner, 'War Commemoration and the Republic in Crisis: Weimar Germany and the Neue Wache', *Central European History* 35, no 4 (2002), 513–49.

18 'Wettbewerbsprogramm' (Bundesarchiv Koblenz R32/358).

19 Behrendt, 'Eine Gedächtnisstätte für die Gefallenen des Weltkrieges'.

20 Karl Scheffler, 'Heinrich Tessenow', *Kunst und Künstler* 11, no 1 (1913), 46. For Scheffler's review of Tessenow's memorial, see 'Das Ehrenmal', *Kunst und Künstler* 29, no 10 (1931), 399.

21 'Niederschrift der Sitzung des Begutachtungsausschusses', 15 July 1930 (BA R32/358).

22 Heinrich Tessenow, cited in Schlichter, *Erinnerungen zum Ehrenmal*, undated, unpublished two-page manuscript (SMB–Kunstbibliothek, NL-HT). Note that after the jury voted in favour of Tessenow's design, the Neue Wache was renamed the 'Gedächtnisstätte fur die Gefallenen des Weltkrieges' (Memorial Site for the Fallen of the Great War).

23 Siegfried Kracauer, 'Zur Einweihung des Berliner Ehrenmals', *Frankfurter Zeitung*, 2 June 1931. See also Kracauer, 'Tessenow baut das Berliner Ehrenmal', *Frankfurter Zeitung*, 22 July 1930.

24 Cited in Forner, 'War Commemoration and the Republic in Crisis', 527.

25 Andreas Frenzel, 'Daß das Reichsehrenmal eine würdige Stätte finde bei Höxter', *Westfälische Zeitschrift* 150 (2000), 369. For more on Poelzig, see Julius Posener and Kristin Feireiss, *Hans Poelzig: Reflections on His Life and Work* (Cambridge, MA: MIT Press, 1992).

26 Albert Speer, *Erinnerungen* (Frankfurt am Main: Ullstein, 1969), 27.

27 Gitta Sereny, *Albert Speer: His Battle with Truth* (London: Macmillan, 1995), 89.

28 Speer, *Erinnerungen*, 31.

29 Heinrich Tessenow, architectural reference for Albert Speer, 12 May 1932.

30 Speer, *Erinnerungen*, 27.

31 Speer, *Erinnerungen*, 44.

32 Adolf Hitler, *Mein Kampf: Eine kritische Edition*, ed Christian Hartmann et al. (Munich: Institut für Zeitgeschichte, 2016), 17.

33 Cited in Brigitte Hamann, *Hitler's Vienna: A Dictator's Apprenticeship* (New York: Oxford University Press, 1999), 32.

34 Hitler, *Mein Kampf*, 18.

35 Hitler, *Mein Kampf*, 14.

36 Adolf Hitler, *Monologe im Führer-Hauptquartier, 1941–1944: Die Aufzeichnungen Heinrich Heims*, ed Werner Jochmann (Hamburg: Albrecht Knaus, 1980), 224.

37 See August Kubizek, *Adolf Hitler, mein Jugendfreund* (Graz: Leopold Stocker, 1953), chapter 15: 'In der Hofoper', 216–25. On Alfred Roller's work as a scenographer at the Wiener Staatsoper, with particular reference to his collaboration with Gustav Mahler, see Patrick Carnegy, *Wagner and the Art of the Theatre* (New Haven: Yale University Press, 2006), 162–74. Roller designed the settings for the following productions of *Der Ring des Nibelungen* at the *Staatsoper*: *Das Rheingold* (1905); *Die Walküre* (1907); *Siegfried* (1908); and *Götterdämmerung* (1909). And he also prepared the staging for *Tristan und Isolde* (1903); *Lohengrin, Act 1* (1904); and *Lohengrin, Acts 1 and 2* (1906). Note that Appia had undertaken an unofficial apprenticeship at the Staatsoper (then called the Wiener Hofoper, Vienna Court Opera) in 1890.

38 Appia to Alfred Roller, 10 June and 27 June 1907.

39 Cited in Hamann, *Hitler's Vienna*, 39.

40 Cited in Hamann, *Hitler's Vienna*, 39.

41 Cited in Hamann, *Hitler's Vienna*, 40.

42 This is how Hitler remembered the episode with Roller: 'It is not possible to get anywhere in Austria without a personal recommendation. When I went to Vienna, I had a recommendation for Roller, but I didn't make use of it. If I had, he would have taken me on immediately. I don't know whether that road would have been better, but in any case, it would have been much easier for me!' Hitler, as recorded on 15 January 1942 by Martin Bormann's adjutant Heinrich Heim, who had been charged with the task of making a written record of Hitler's Monologues. Hitler, *Monologe im Führer-Hauptquartier*, 200.

43 Karl Fiehler, in *Quellen und Dokumente zur Geschichte von 'Mein Kampf', 1924–1945* (Stuttgart: Franz Steiner, 2016), 112.

44 *Winifred Wagner und die Geschichte des Hauses Wahnfried, 1914–1975*, directed by Hans-Jürgen Syberberg (Bayerischer Rundfunk, 1975).

45 Brigitte Hamann, *Winifred Wagner oder Hitlers Bayreuth* (Munich: Piper, 2002), 91.

46 Adolf Hitler, *Sämtliche Aufzeichnungen: 1905–1924* (Stuttgart: Deutsche Verlags-Anstalt, 1980), 1232. Note that by this time Appia's former friend Chamberlain had become firmly ensconced in the Wagner family, having married Richard and Cosima Wagner's daughter Eva von Bülow in 1908.

47 Speer, diary entry for 11 May 1948. Unless otherwise noted, the quotations from Speer's diary are from his *Spandauer Tagebücher* (Berlin: Ullstein, 2005). Note here that it was in fact a performance of *Tristan und Isolde* that Hitler had seen during his very first visit to Vienna in 1906, the settings for which Roller had designed. Hitler to August Kubizek, 7 May 1906. Cited in Hamann, *Hitler's Vienna*, 26.

48 Roller himself recorded this episode with Hitler in a seven-page handwritten document that is now lost. Oskar Pausch, then director of the *Österreichischen Theatermuseum* made a transcription from a copy of the original, published as 'Der Besuch Alfred Rollers bei Adolf Hitler 1934: Ein verschollenes Dokument', ÖZG 2, no 2 (2012), 237–44.

49 In the 1938 season alone, Hitler attended the opening performance (*Tristan und Isolde*); *Parsifal* (25 July); *Rheingold* (27 July); *Walküre* (28 July); and *Götterdämmerung* (1 August). See *Völkischer Beobachter* (25–28 July inclusive and 3 August 1938).

50 Winifred began running the Bayreuth Festival when her husband Siegfried died in 1930. Her last season was 1945. See Brigitte Hamann, *Winifred Wagner: A Life at the Heart of Hitler's Bayreuth*, trans Alan Bance (London: Granta, 2005).

51 Speer, diary entry for 11 May 1948.

52 Refer to Richard Wagner's two long essays, *Die Kunst und die Revolution* (Leipzig: Otto Wigand, 1849) and *Das Kunstwerk der Zukunft* (Leipzig: Otto Wigand, 1850). Cosima herself wrote in her diary on 6 January 1872 that Wagner's music was 'not just to be listened to; the true sense of it is gained only by those who are swept along inside it'. *Cosima Wagner's Diaries*, ed Martin Gregor-Dellin and Dietrich Mack, trans Geoffrey Skelton, vol 1, *1869–1877* (London: Collins, 1978), 447.

53 Theodor Adorno, *Versuch über Wagner* (Berlin: Suhrkamp, 1952), 40.

54 Speer, diary entry for 11 May 1948.

55 Cosima Wagner to Bodo von dem Knesebeck, 3 January 1897. Cited in Cosima Wagner, *Das zweite Leben: Briefe und Aufzeichnungen 1883–1930*, ed Dietrich Mack (Munich: R Piper, 1980), 438. 'Dear esteemed Baron, I can scarcely describe to you my astonishment at sighting (a print of) *Hain der Vestalinnen* (The Sacred Grove of the Vestal Virgins) waiting for me on my *Weihnachtstisch!* (Christmas table). I saw this painting for the first time three years ago at the Kunstmuseum Basel, and it made a greater impression on me than any other Böcklin ever had! Yes, it has in fact become a symbol of my inner life, as it were, in that it comes into my mind practically every time that I think with longing for a common refuge in a *Heiligtum* (sanctuary)! ... This mysteriously solemn yet celebratory painting, in which the sanctity of the Germanic forest is consecrated at night with the beauty and spirit of ancient Greece, has become for me a dear symbol of the way that the threads that bind peoples continue to be woven across time, and that consoles me!'

56 Contrary to the way he presented himself on the occasion, this is what Hitler later said about the Nazi party rallies: 'Nuremberg requires a dreadful exertion on my behalf – it is the worst time of the year! The reason we have stretched the rally out to ten days is so that I don't have to say everything all in one speech. And also, now the proclamation is read out by somebody else. I just can't speak that much anymore! And I want to get up and leave when I realise that it is difficult for me to go through with the old-style rally. The most exhausting part is when I have to stand for hour upon hour for the march past. I have gotten dizzy a few times; you have no idea how excruciating it is to have to stand with your knees locked for so long. And I need some more protection from the sun. I made it easier for myself to salute with outstretched arm last time, but I am used to looking at everyone in turn – all the men are looking at me ... perhaps it will be possible to have the columns march past in rows of sixteen rather than twelve. Then five hours would become four hours, which would be quite something.' Hitler, *Monologe im Führer-Hauptquartier*, 225.

57 Rudolf Wolters, introduction to Albert Speer, *Neue deutsche Baukunst* (Berlin: Volk und Reich, 1941), 15.

58 Speer, *Spandauer Tagebücher* (1975), 381. Further on the *Lichtdom* at the Zeppelin Field, see Anne Krauter, 'Die Schriften Paul Scheerbarts und der Lichtdom von Albert Speer: "Das grosse Licht",' PhD thesis (University of Heidelberg, 1997). And on Speer's architecture, see Léon Krier, Robert A M Stern and Albert Speer, *Albert Speer Architecture 1932–1942* (Brussels: Archives d'Architecture Moderne, 1985); and Sebastian Tesch, *Albert Speer (1905–1981)* (Vienna: Böhlau, 2016).

59 Albert Speer to Heinrich Tessenow, 3 April 1941.

60 A transcript of the military tribunal's charges and findings against Speer have been published as 'Die Urteilsprechung gegen Albert Speer' in Adelbert Reif, *Albert Speer: Kontroversen um ein deutsches Phänomen* (Munich: Bernard & Graefe, 1978), 218–22.

61 After his release on 1 October 1966, Speer collected all his notes – which by that time numbered around 25,000 – from his fellow architect and former colleague Rudolf Wolters, who had stashed them all away safely for him in a suitcase. They were then collated, ordered and edited for publication as *Spandauer Tagebücher*. For a compact critical appraisal of Speer's diaries see Eberhard Schulz, 'Albert Speers Gefängnisbuch', in *Albert Speer: Kontroversen um ein deutsches Phänomen*, 473–79.

62 Speer, diary entry for 31 August 1947.

63 Speer, diary entry for 7 May 1955.

64 Speer, diary entry for 22 November 1949.

65 Speer, diary entry for 29 January 1958.

66 Alfred Roth, *Zwei Wohnhäuser von Le Corbusier und Pierre Jeanneret; Fünf Punkte zu einer neuen Architektur von Le Corbusier und Pierre Jeanneret* (Stuttgart: F Wedekind, 1927). See also Werner Oechslin, 'Les Cinq Points d'une Architecture Nouvelle', trans Wilfried Wang, *Assemblage* 4 (October 1987), 82–93.

67 Speer, *Erinnerungen*, 45.

68 Syberberg, 'The Confessions of Winifred Wagner'.

69 See Ingrid Kapsamer, *Wieland Wagner: Wegbereiter und Weltwirkung* (Vienna: Styria, 2010); the introduction to *Wieland Wagner inszeniert Richard Wagner* (Constance: Rosgarten, 1960); Walter Erich Schäfer, *Wieland Wagner: Persönlichkeit und Leistung* (Tübingen: Wunderlich, 1970); Antoine Goléa, *Entretiens avec Wieland Wagner* (Paris: Pierre Belfond, 1967); and Dominique Jameux, 'Wieland Wagner et le nouveau Bayreuth', *Musical* 8: Opéra et mise en scène (January 1989), 101–17.

70 Wieland Wagner, 'Denkmalschutz für Wagner?' *Österreichische Musikzeitschrift* 13, no 9 (September 1958), 359.

71 Geoffrey Skelton, *Wieland Wagner: The Positive Sceptic* (London: Gollancz, 1971), 72.

72 'Ich bin gerade dabei, das merkwürdige und interessante Werk zu studieren.' Wieland Wagner to Willy Krienitz, 15 May 1943. Cited in Kapsamer, *Wieland Wagner: Wegbereiter und Weltwirkung*, 110.

73 Bert Cardullo, '"Adolphe Appia and Me": A Discussion with Hans-Jürgen Syberberg', *Literature/Film Quarterly* 38, no 1 (2010), 9.

74 Wieland Wagner, 'Überlieferung und Neugestaltung', *Maske und Kothurn* 1, no 3–4 (1955), 214–18.

75 Adolphe Appia, 'Comment reformer notre mise-en-scène' (1904). A transcription is published in *Adolphe Appia: Œuvres complètes*, ed Marie-Louise Bablet, vol 2, 1895–1905 (Lausanne: L'Âge d'Homme, 1986), 347–52. The best illustration of this idea amongst Appia's drawings is his *Espace rythmique: The Clearing*.

76 *Das Bayreuther Festspielbuch*, edited by Bayreuth Festspielleitung (Bayreuth: Wagner-Buchhandlung Georg Niehrenheim, 1951), title page.

77 Adolf Aber, 'Tradition and Revolution at Bayreuth', *Musical Times* 92 (October 1951), 456. Note further that Appia and Aber wrote to each other between 1926

and 1928. There are seven letters from Aber in the Swiss Archive of Performing Arts (SAPA: Jb6 42-Jb6 48).

78 Aber, 'Tradition and Revolution at Bayreuth', 456. Aber further wrote: 'His (Appia's) first book design with the subject appeared in 1899 (!). Its title is *Die Musik und die Inscenierung*, its publisher F Bruckmann A-G in Munich. … A second book, entitled *L'Œuvre d'art vivant*, followed in 1921. I am quoting these two works with such great care because they are both illustrated, and if Wieland Wagner finds a copy of the first-quoted book in his late uncle's library he will – probably to his great surprise – discover a drawing of the rock of the Valkyries which resembles his own conception of 1951 as one egg resembles another.'

79 Aber, 'Tradition and Revolution at Bayreuth', 456.

80 Aber, 'Tradition and Revolution at Bayreuth', 457.

81 Wagner, 'Denkmalschutz für Wagner?' 359. On the relationship between Appia's aesthetics and those of Wieland Wagner, see Schäfer, *Wieland Wagner: Persönlichkeit und Leistung*.

82 Wolfgang Wagner, foreword to Oswald Georg Bauer, *Richard Wagner: Die Bühnenwerke von der Uraufführung bis heute* (Frankfurt am Main: Propyläen, 1982), 8.

83 Wolfgang Wagner in an interview with the British filmmaker Tony Palmer, cited in Palmer's foreword to Jeonwong Joe and Sander Gilman, eds, *Wagner and Cinema* (Indianapolis: Indiana University Press, 2010), x–xi. Note additionally that Max Steiner, composer of *King Kong* and *Casablanca*, declared: 'If Wagner had lived in this century, he would have been the Number One film composer.' Émile Vuillermoz, 'La Musique des images' in *L'art cinématographique* (Paris: Felix Alcan, 1927), 56. And the film producer Sam Goldwyn once reportedly commanded one of his composers to 'write music like Wagner, only louder'.

84 Wagner, *Twilight of the Gods: The Essential Wagner Collection: Six Track Sampler* (Deutsche Grammophon, 1998), compact disc, back cover description.

85 Adorno, *Versuch über Wagner*, 54.

86 Adolphe Appia, 'Trois projets de décors pour Parsifal' (1908). A transcription is published in *Adolphe Appia: Œuvres complètes*, 2: 286–88.

87 John Milius and Francis Ford Coppola, *Apocalypse Now Redux: An Original Screenplay* (New York: Miramax Books, 2001).

88 Milius and Coppola, *Apocalypse Now Redux*.

89 Wagner to Franz Liszt, 11 February 1853. Cited in Richard Wagner, *Selected Letters of Richard Wagner*, trans Stewart Spencer and Barry Millington (London: Dent, 1987). This letter accompanied the very first private edition of the libretto for *Der Ring des Nibelungen*, which Wagner posted to Liszt.

90 Adolphe Appia, 'Expériences de théâtre et recherches personelles' (1922). A transcription is reproduced in *Adolphe Appia: Œuvres complètes*, 4: 36–56.

91 Edward H Castens, ed, *The Story of the 446th Bomb Group* (San Angelo: Newsphoto Publishing Company, 1946), 28.

92 Albert F Pishioneri, *Me, Mom and WWII* (Bloomington: AuthorHouse, 2008), 370.

93 See Ulrich Conrads and Peter Neitzke, eds, *Mensch und Raum: Das Darmstädter Gespräch 1951* (Braunschweig: Vieweg, 1991).

94 Martin Heidegger, 'Bauen Wohnen Denken', in *Mensch und Raum*, 100.

95 Rudolf Schwarz to Ludwig Mies van der Rohe, 9 October 1948 (Library of Congress, Ludwig Mies van der Rohe Papers, Container 53). I would like to thank Kathleen James-Chakraborty for making available to me her transcribed excerpts from some of the letters held in the Library of Congress.

96 Schwarz to Mies van der Rohe, 21 May 1947. (Library of Congress, Ludwig Mies van der Rohe Papers, Container 53).

97 Conrads and Neitzke, *Mensch und Raum*, 58.

98 Three churches by Schwarz were included in the *Mensch und Raum* exhibition: St Fronleichnam (Corpus Christi), Aachen, 1930; St Albertus Magnus Chapel, Leversbach, 1932; and Kalk Chapel, Cologne, 1950. Further on Schwarz's relationship to modernism, see Helen Thomas, 'Rudolf Schwarz and Another Kind of Modernism', *AA Files*, no 73 (2016), 163–82.

99 Euripides, *Iphigenia at Aulis*, trans W S Merwin and George E Dimock (Oxford: Oxford University Press, 1978), 77.

100 Rudolf Schwarz, *The Church Incarnate: The Sacred Function of Christian Architecture*, trans Cynthia Harris (Chicago: Henry Regnery, 1958), 100. See also Schwarz's *Von der Bebauung der Erde* (Salzburg: Verlag Anton Pustet, 1949); and *Kirchenbau: Welt vor der Schwelle* (Heidelberg: F H Kerle, 1960), in which he articulates the continuity of building from geological stratification to architecture as the final layer of earth-building. Note that Mies sent Schwarz 'care packages' from America during World War II. For a publication on Schwarz's architecture that includes excellent photographs and line drawings, see Adam Caruso and Helen Thomas, *Rudolf Schwarz and the Monumental Order of Things* (Zurich: gta, 2016). The architect's own drawings are held in the Historisches Archiv des Erzbistums Köln.

101 'Mies helped very much with the translation – that is, he helped Cynthia Harris to understand Schwarz's ideas.' Werner Blaser, *Mies van der Rohe: The Art of Structure* (Basel: Birkhäuser, 1993), 231.

102 Mies van der Rohe, unpaginated foreword to Schwarz, *The Church Incarnate*. Further on the relationship between the architecture of Schwarz and Mies van der Rohe, see Thomas H Beeby, 'Rudolf Schwarz and Mies van der Rohe: The Form of Spirit', in *Constructing the Ineffable: Contemporary Sacred Architecture*, ed Karla Cavarra Britton (New Haven Yale University Press, 2010), 82–95.

103 Mies received the brief for the Chapel of St Savior on 18 March 1949. Since the chapel was completed in 1952, it is possible that this was one of the buildings Speer came across while leafing through the pages of *American Builder* in his Spandau prison cell in 1955.

104 For a close reading of the IIT chapel, see my chapters 'Minimal Ritual: Mies van der Rohe's Chapel of St. Savior, 1952', in *Modernism and American Mid-20th Century Sacred Architecture*, ed Anat Geva (New York: Routledge, 2019), 15–30; and 'Revelatory Earth: Adolphe Appia and the Prospect of a Modern Sacred', in *Modern Architecture and the Sacred: Religious Legacies and Spiritual Renewal*, ed Ross Anderson and Maximilian Sternberg (London: Bloomsbury Academic, 2021), 181–95. I would like to thank Paul Galloway, the Architecture and Design Study Center Supervisor,

for his generous expert assistance in navigating the Ludwig Mies van der Rohe Archive. In addition to retrieving the drawings for the chapel, he made available rare original photographs and a large amount of written correspondence. For a large selection of Mies's drawings, see Arthur Drexler, ed, *The Mies van der Rohe Archive: Illustrated Catalogue of the Mies van der Rohe Drawings in the Museum of Modern Art*, vol 5, *Robert F Carr Memorial of Saint Savior, S R Crown Hall and Other Buildings and Projects* (New York: Garland Publishing, 1986).

105 Wallace E Conkling to Mies van der Rohe, 22 December 1951. The word 'must' is underlined in Conkling's original letter. The solid travertine altar measures 244 cm long × 81 cm deep × 99 cm high, and weighs 7.6 tonnes.

106 Mies van der Rohe, 'A Chapel', *Arts and Architecture* 70, no 1 (January 1953), 19. Unsurprisingly for the taciturn architect to whom the statement 'build, don't talk' is attributed, the real arena for his struggle was architecture as an embodied practice – on the drawing board, and with an eye to the construction site – rather than the discourses surrounding building, where he was ill at ease.

107 Le Corbusier, *Textes et dessins pour Ronchamp* (Paris: Les Cahiers Forces Vives, 1965). Published in English as Le Corbusier, *Texts and Sketches for Ronchamp* (Ronchamp: Association œuvre de Notre-Dame du Haut, 1982), unpaginated.

108 Marie-Alain Couturier, *Sacred Art*, trans Granger Ryan (Austin: University of Texas Press, 1989), 10.

109 Couturier, *Sacred Art*, 154.

110 Canon Ledeur to Danièle Pauly, March 1974.

111 Jean Petit, *Le Corbusier lui-même* (Geneva: Panoramas Forces Vives, 1970), 184.

112 Petit, *Le Corbusier lui-même*, 184.

113 Euripides, *Iphigenia at Aulis*, 91.

114 For a reconstruction of the geometric figure undergirding the plan of Ronchamp, see Peter Carl, 'Ornament and Time: A Prolegomena, Part 2', AA *Files*, no 23 (1992), 55. Further on the chapel itself, see *Le Corbusier: Œuvre complète de 1952–1957*, ed Willy Boesiger (Basel: Birkhäuser, 1957), 16–41; *The Le Corbusier Archive*, vol 20, *Ronchamp, Maison Jaoul, and Other Buildings and Projects, 1951*–1952, ed H Allen Brooks (New York: Garland and Fondation Le Corbusier, 1983); Le Corbusier, *Ronchamp: Les carnets de la recherche patiente*, trans Jacqueline Cullen (Stuttgart: Gerd Hatje, 1957); and Danièle Pauly, *Le Corbusier: The Chapel at Ronchamp*, trans Sarah Parsons (Basel: Birkhäuser, 2008).

115 The photograph of the drawing is reproduced in *Adolphe Appia: Œuvres complètes*, 4: 445. The caption reads: 'Iphigenia among the Taurians, unpublished photograph of a lost sketch, undated (1926?). Roquette Collection, Geneva. The sacrifice of Orestes? …'

116 Petit, *Le Corbusier lui-même*, 184.

117 Petit, *Le Corbusier lui-même*, 184.

118 Petit, *Le Corbusier lui-même*, 184.

119 Abbé Ferry, cited in Jean Petit, *Le livre de Ronchamp* (Paris: Les Cahiers Forces Vives, 1961), 67.

120 Le Corbusier, *Ronchamp: Les carnets de la recherche patiente*, 25.

121 Le Corbusier to his mother Marie, 25 June 1955.

122 A key source here is Giuliano Gresleri, *Viaggio in Oriente: Charles Edouard Jeanneret fotografo e scrittore* (Venice: Marsilio, 1984). See particularly pages 51–55. And refer also to David Leatherbarrow and Richard Wesley, 'Alone-Together Naturally', in *Three Cultural Ecologies* (New York: Routledge, 2018), 115–48; *Le Corbusier: Œuvre complète de 1952–1957*, 42–49; Le Corbusier, 'Le Couvent Sainte-Marie de La Tourette construct par Le Corbusier', *L'Art sacré* 14, no 7–8 (March 1960), 5; and Philipe Potié, *Le Corbusier: Le Couvent Sainte-Marie de la Tourette* (Basel: Birkhäuser, 2001).

123 Couturier, cited in Potié, *Le Corbusier: Le Couvent Sainte-Marie de la Tourette*, 60.

124 Couturier, 'Le Corbusier', *L'Art sacré* 14, no 7–8 (March–April 1954), 9–10.

125 Le Corbusier, interviewed by the Dominican monks in October 1960, published as Le Corbusier, 'Le Couvent Sainte-Marie de La Tourette construit par Le Corbusier'.

126 'To the West, it (Ronchamp) commands the valley of the Saône, to the East the chain of the Vosges; two small valleys to the north and south. These landscapes with four horizons are a presence; they are your hosts. To these four horizons the Chapel addresses itself …' Le Corbusier, *Modulor 2: Let the User Speak Next*, trans Peter de Francia and Anna Bostock (London: Faber and Faber, 1958), 252–53.

127 Le Corbusier, 'Le Couvent Sainte-Marie de la Tourette construit par Le Corbusier'. Elsewhere, Le Corbusier wrote: 'The building was designed from the top down … from the horizontal summit, the building defines its organism as a descent', cited in Jean Petit, *Un couvent de Le Corbusier* (Paris: Forces Vives, 1961), 20. Further on the 'horizon' of La Tourette, see Hubert Damisch and Julie Rose, 'Against the Slope', *Log* 4 (2005): 29–48.

128 Couturier, cited in Potié, *Le Corbusier: Le Couvent Sainte-Marie de la Tourette*, 7.

129 Iannis Xenakis, 'The Monastery of La Tourette', in *Le Corbusier*, ed H Allen Brooks, 143.

130 Couturier, 'Au régime de la pauverté' (1950), reproduced in Couturier, *Sacred Art*, 42.

131 Xenakis, 'The Monastery of La Tourette', 143.

132 *Wieland Wagner inszeniert Richard Wagner*, 50.

133 Le Corbusier, 'Le Couvent Sainte-Marie de La Tourette construit par Le Corbusier'.

134 Xenakis, 'The Monastery of La Tourette', 146.

135 Gresleri, *Viaggio in Oriente* 54–55. Note that on the page on which Appia's Valhalla landscape drawing is reproduced, Gresleri also placed Appia's *Espace rythmique: Der Taucher*, plus a photograph of the setting for *Orfeo ed Euridice* in the Festspielhaus at Hellerau.

136 Wagner, *Das Rheingold: Vorspiel zu der Trilogie: Der Ring des Nibelungen von Richard Wagner* (Mainz: Schott's Söhne, 1876), 67–68. On the Erda episode in Scene 4 of *Das Rheingold*, see Warren Darcy, '"Everything That Is, Ends!": The Genesis and Meaning of the Erda Episode in "Das Rheingold",' *Musical Times* 129, no 1747 (September 1988), 443–47.

137 Adolphe Appia, *Die Musik und die Inscenierung* (Munich: Bruckmann, 1899), 275.

138 Wagner, *Das Rheingold: Vorspiel zu der Trilogie*, 40.

139 Appia, *Die Musik und die Inscenierung*, unpaginated.

140 Wagner, *Das Rheingold: Vorspiel zu der Trilogie*, 19.

141 *Le Corbusier: Œuvre complète de 1946–1952*, ed Willy Boesiger (Basel: Birkhäuser,

1953), 222. Further on the Unité rooftop, see Tim Benton, 'Marseille: Unité d'habitation, or "The Company of Clouds, the Sky, or the Stars",' in *Le Corbusier: An Atlas of Modern Landscapes*, ed Jean-Louis Cohen (New York: Museum of Modern Art, 2012), 201–05; and Jacques Sbriglio, *L'Unité d'habitation de Marseille* (Basel: Birkhäuser, 2004).

142 Le Corbusier, *Vers une Architecture* (Paris: G Crès, 1923), 16.

143 *Le Corbusier: Œuvre complète de 1946–1952*, 218. Note that Le Corbusier once described the Unité rooftop as 'a veritable Acropolis open to a Homeric landscape'. Le Corbusier to Mr Tenudji, 2 August 1952. Cited in Roberto Gargiani and Anna Rosellini, *Le Corbusier Béton Brut and Ineffable Space, 1940–1965: Surface, Materials and Psychophysiology of Vision* (Lausanne: EPFL Press, 2011), 11.

144 *Le Corbusier: Œuvre complète de 1946–1952*, 222.

145 In one of the productions on the rooftop stage, a young girl performed alone and barefoot on the stage before a jostling audience, wearing a coarse animal skin tied around her waist by a length of cord. Le Corbusier published a full-page reproduction of a photograph of this performance in his book *The Nursery Schools* and paired it with a photograph of two children – a boy and a girl, both around six years old – sitting quietly and facing each other on a large, felled tree lying on a patch of stony ground dotted around by shrubs and cypresses. A fragment of the Unité nestles surprising well into the background. Le Corbusier, *The Nursery Schools*, trans Eleanor Levieux (New York: Orion, 1968), 82–83.

146 Le Corbusier first met Lucien Hervé in 1949, having been greatly impressed by a batch of some of the more than six hundred photographs of the Unité that the photographer shot over the course of a single day: 'I have examined the large set of photographs that you took of the Unité d'habitation. I wish to convey my most sincere congratulations for your exceptional work. You have the soul of an architect.' Le Corbusier to Hervé, 15 December 1949. He invited Hervé to his atelier, as the photographer later recalled in an interview: 'We spoke to each other over the telephone, and he invited me to his painter's studio the following Monday morning, where he usually spent the first part of the day painting. We talked a lot about painting and Le Corbusier was delighted to discover my genuine passion for it. We also talked a lot about music, and he frequently mentioned his brother Albert Jeanneret, a violinist and teacher. I had the impression I was setting out on an exceptional intellectual adventure.' Giampiero Bosoni, 'Lucien Hervé fotografo di Le Corbusier', *Abitare*, no 309 (1992), 206. The two worked together right up until Le Corbusier's death on 27 August 1965. On their working relationship, see Marco Iuliano, 'Lucien Hervé and Le Corbusier: Pair or Peers?' *Journal of Architecture* 21, no 7 (2016), 1100–26.

147 Later, in addition to his Rolleiflex, Hervé used a Bronica, a Japanese copy of a Hasselblad, plus two German-made cameras – a Plaubel and a Linhof.

148 *Le Corbusier: Œuvre complète de 1946–1952*, 221.

149 A representative selection of Hervé's sheets of photographs mounted on coloured sheets of *carton* are published in Jacques Sbriglio, *Le Corbusier & Lucien Hervé: A Dialogue Between Architect and Photographer* (Los Angeles: Getty Publications, 2011), 27–87. Note that Hervé freely cropped his prints of individual photographs as part of the process of composition, once referring to himself as a 'photographer with scissors'. Hans Ulrich Obrist, *Lucien Hervé* (Paris: Manuella, 2011), 10–11.

150 Of his decision to use coloured backing sheets for his photographs of Le Corbusier's buildings, Hervé said in an interview: 'At first the photos were in black and white, but then I realised that colour was essential to the representation of his work, which came somewhere between painting and architecture'. Bosoni, 'Lucien Hervé fotografo di Le Corbusier', 206.

Coda

1 'Unfortunately, nothing at all was done with the collection either in Zurich or in Geneva – the collection lay dormant until 1952 – which is the year when, probably following the success of the first "*nouveau style*" in Bayreuth, Appia's nephew Edmond Appia "exhumed" the collection (the word is not too strong).' *Adolphe Appia: Œuvres complètes*, ed Marie-Louise Bablet, vol 1, 1880–1894 (Lausanne: L'Âge d'Homme, 1983), ix.

2 See for example Adolphe Appia, 'Notes de mise-en-scène pour L'Anneau de Nibelungen (1891–1892)', *Revue d'histoire du théâtre* 21 (1954), 46–59, for which Veinstein wrote an introductory text. And see also Veinstein's 'Redécouvrons Adolphe Appia', *Cahiers de la Compagnie Madeleine Renaud – Jean-Louis Barrault* 3, no 10 (1955).

3 Lucia Moholy, who had studied philosophy, philology and art history at the University of Prague, met László Moholy-Nagy in 1920 and they married in January of the following year. Many years later she published *Marginal Notes* (Krefeld: Scherpe, 1972) in which she both discussed her collaboration with Moholy-Nagy at the Bauhaus and sought to reclaim artistic credit for her photographs, which were at the time experimental and are now iconic. See also Robin Schuldenfrei, 'Images in Exile: Lucia Moholy's Bauhaus Negatives and the Construction of the Bauhaus Legacy', *History of Photography* 37, no 2 (May 2013), 182–203.

4 Lucia Moholy, 'Switzerland', *Burlington Magazine* 104, no 717 (December 1962), 566.

5 Moholy, 'Switzerland', 566–67.

6 Moholy, 'Switzerland', 567.

7 Edmund Stadler, 'Epilogue' in John Pope-Hennessy, *Adolphe Appia* (London: V&A Museum, 1970), 26.

8 Denis Bablet and Marie-Louise Bablet, eds, *Adolphe Appia 1862–1928: acteur–espace–lumière* (Zurich: Pro Helvetia, 1981). See also Denis Bablet, 'The Actor, Space and Lighting', in *The Revolutions of Stage Design in the 20th Century* (Paris: Leon Amiel, 1977), 40–50; and Misolette Bablet, 'Adolphe Appia: L'architecte du sensible', Musical 8: Opéra et mise en scène (January 1989), 78–99.

9 Martin Dreier, *Adolphe Appia (1862–1928): Zwanzig Faksimilies aus seinem bühnenbildnerischen Entwurfswerk* (Bern: Stiftung Schweizerische Theatersammlung, 1993).

10 *Adolphe Appia: Œuvres complètes*, ed Marie-Louise Bablet, 4 vols (Lausanne: L'Âge d'Homme, 1983–91).

11 Compare the remarkable modestness of Appia's archive with those of Le Corbusier and Mies. The significance of these two archives to the consolidation of the reputations of the two canonical architects to whom they are devoted cannot be overstated. For example, in the opening line of the acknowledgements in his widely read critical biography of Mies, Franz Schulze writes: 'The greatest boon to Miesian scholarship in the past forty years has been the establishment in 1968 of the Mies van der Rohe Archive at the Museum of Modern Art', *Mies van der Rohe: A Critical Biography* (Chicago: Chicago University Press, 1985), xiii. Likewise, the Fondation Le Corbusier is generously funded and comfortably accommodated in conjoined UNESCO World Heritage villas of the architect's own design, and there is every indication that it will be an institution of 'unlimited duration' (as per its statutes, approved by Le Corbusier on 11 June 1965).

12 Adolphe Appia, *Adolphe Appia, 1er septembre 1862–29 février 1928* (Zurich: Orell Füssli, 1929).

13 Appia's musical nephew Edmond was born in Turin on 7 May 1894. He became a violinist, studying firstly at the conservatory in Geneva, then in Paris, after which he joined the Royal Conservatory of Music in Brussels. He was decorated with the *Légion d'honneur* in 1952 and died in 1961.

14 Walther R Volbach, 'Appia's Productions and Contemporary Reaction', *Educational Theatre Journal* 13, no 1 (March 1961), 1–10; 'A Profile of Adolphe Appia', *Educational Theatre Journal* 15, no 1 (March 1963), 7–14.

15 Volbach, *Adolphe Appia: Prophet of the Modern Theatre* (Middletown: Wesleyan University Press, 1968).

16 Richard Beacham and Walther R Volbach, eds, *Adolphe Appia: Essays, Scenarios and Designs*, trans Walther Volbach (London: UMI, 1989).

17 Richard Beacham, *Adolphe Appia: Artist and Visionary of the Modern Theatre* (Reading: Harwood Academic, 1994).

18 Further regarding the scholarship on Appia that is available in German, the most substantial piece of research is Gernot Giertz's PhD thesis, which he completed at Ludwig-Maximilians-Universität in Munich and subsequently published as *Kultus ohne Götter: Emile Jacques-Dalcroze und Adolphe Appia: Der Versuch einer Theaterreform auf der Grundlage der Rhythmischen Gymnastik* (Munich: Kitzinger, 1975). It is a thorough study that focuses particularly on the collaboration between Appia and Jaques-Dalcroze at Hellerau. Only a small number of copies of the book were published and even in German libraries it is difficult to obtain today. See also Nina Sonntag, *Raumtheater: Adolphe Appias theaterästhetische Konzeption in Hellerau* (Essen: Klartext, 2011).

19 Manfredo Tafuri, *The Sphere and the Labyrinth: Avant-Gardes and Architecture from Piranesi to the 1970s* (Cambridge, MA: MIT Press, 1987), 98.

20 Tafuri, *The Sphere and the Labyrinth*, 98, 109.

21 Marco De Michelis and Vicki Bilenker, 'Modernity and Reform: Heinrich Tessenow and the Institut Dalcroze at Hellerau', *Perspecta* 26: *Theatre, Theatricality and Architecture* (1990): 143–70. See also De Michelis, 'L'Institut Jaques-Dalcroze à Hellerau', in *Adolphe Appia ou le renouveau de l'esthétique théâtrale* (Lausanne: Éditions Payot, 1992), 21–47.

22 Marco De Michelis, *Heinrich Tessenow 1876–1950: Das architektonische Gesamtwerk* (Milan: Electa, 1991).

23 K Michael Hays, 'Tessenow's Architecture as National Allegory: Critique of Capitalism or Protofascism?', *Assemblage* 8 (February 1989), 110.

24 K Michael Hays, 'Not Architecture but Evidence that It Exists: A Note on Lauretta Vinciarelli's Watercolors', *Assemblage* 38 (April 1999), 52. Further on Vinciarelli, see Rebecca Siefert, 'Lauretta Vinciarelli Illuminated', *AA Files*, no 75 (2017), 71–85.

25 Daniel Libeskind, 'Die Zukunft aus der Vergangenheit rekonstruieren', keynote lecture (Festspielhaus Hellerau, October 2017).

26 Peter Carl and Irena Murray, 'Geometry and Analogy: Le Corbusier's Baghdad Veils', *AA Files*, no 67 (2013), 51.

27 Peter Carl, 'On Depth: Particular and Universal, Fragment and Field', in *Fragments: Architecture and the Unfinished: Essays Presented to Robin Middleton*, ed Barry Bergdoll and Werner Oechslin (New York: Thames & Hudson, 2006), 26.

28 I undertook both my MPhil (History and Philosophy of Architecture) and PhD at the University of Cambridge, supervised by Peter. I am grateful to him for the revelation of Appia and for our ongoing exchange of ideas that informed my essay, 'The Appian Way', *AA Files*, no 75 (December 2017), 163–82, which in turn led to this book.

29 Colin St John Wilson designed the extension to the Department of Architecture at Scroope Terrace, Cambridge. Le Corbusier and Henry Moore spoke at the inauguration in 1959, making sketches for the audience on large lengths of unfurled paper as they did so. The extension is a rigorously proportioned, decidedly unadorned building constructed from reclaimed bricks and off-form concrete, of which the lecture theatre occupies the west half of the first floor. Particular care was given to the means of modulating both natural and artificial light during lectures: 'The sculpted projection platform is a concrete shelf cantilevered out of the mass of the core. The lecture room podium is diagonally opposite. Light control is manual where accessible (the window to the right of the lecturer is a series of connected vertical timber louvres) and motorised where not. The roof to the first floor comprises glazed strips between fair-faced concrete beams. These are blacked out by horizontally pivoted plywood blades connected by a continuous spindle. Artificial lighting cantilevers from the beams.' Roger Stonehouse, *Colin St John Wilson* (London: Black Dog, 2007), 194.

Appia's Writings

Notes des mise en scène für den Ring des Nibelungen (1891–1892)
Manuscript: SAPA A1, B1, C1a-c
'Notes des mise en scène für den Ring des Nibelungen (1891–1892)', *Revue d'histoire du théâtre* 6, nos 1–2 (1954), 46–59
Walküre (1891)
Manuscript: SAPA C2a-b
Siegfried (1892)
Manuscript: SAPA C3a-c
Götterdämmerung (1891)
Manuscript: SAPA: C4a-c
Maîtres-Chanteurs. Mise en scène (1892)
Manuscript: SAPA A1, C5a-c
La Musique et la mise en scène (1892)
Manuscript: SAPA A4, C8
Die Musik und die Inscenierung. Munich: Bruckmann, 1899
Music and the Art of the Theatre, edited by Barnard Hewitt, translated by Robert W Corrigan and Mary Douglas Dirks, Coral Gables, FL: University of Miami Press, 1962
La musique et la mise en scène (1892–1897), edited by Edmund Stadler, Bern: Theaterkultur-Verlag, 1963
La Mise en scène du drame Wagnérien (1895)
La Mise en scène du drame Wagnérien, Paris: Léon Chailley, 1895
Staging Wagnerian Drama, translated by Peter Loeffler, Basel: Birkhäuser, 1988
Plantation. Praticables (extraits), À propos d'éclairage (1895)
Manuscript: Fonds Rouché, Bibliothèque de l'Opera, Paris
Tristan et Isolde, Mise en scène (1896)
Manuscript: SAPA C6a-b
Parsifal, Mise en scène (1896)
Manuscript: SAPA C7a-b
Comment réformer notre mise en scène (1900)
Manuscript: SAPA C9a-c
Der Saal des Prinzregenten-Theaters (1901)
'Der Saal des Prinzregenten-Theaters: Eine technische Betrachtung von Adolphe Appia', *Die Gesellschaft* 18, no 3 (1902), 198–204
Un nouveau matériel artistique (1902)
Manuscript: Bruckmannianna, Bayrische Staatsbibliothek, Munich
Comment reformer notre mise-en-scène (1904)
Manuscript: BRBML Collection Donald Oenslager
'Comment reformer notre mise-en-scène', *La revue des revues* 1, no 9 (June 1904), 342–49
Ébauches d'un drame en musique (1904)
Manuscript: Collection Roquette, Genève
Introduction à mes notes personelles (1905)
Manuscript: SAPA A6, C55
Retour à la musique (1906)
Manuscript: SAPA C10a-b
'Retour à la musique', *Journal de Genève*, August 1906
Notes sur le théâtre (1908)
Manuscript: SAPA C11a-b
'Notes sur le théâtre', *La vie musicale* 1, no 15 (April 1908), 233–38
'Notes sur le théâtre', *La vie musicale* 1, no 16 (April 1908), 253–56
Trois projets de décors pour Parsifal (1908)
Manuscript: Bruckmannianna, Bayrische Staatsbibliothek, Munich
'Entwürfe zu Parsifal-Dekorationen', *Dekorative Kunst, illustrierte Zeitschrift für angewandte Kunst* 16 (Munich, 1908), 278–80
'Drei Dekorationen für 'Parsifal', Walhall-Landschaft und Walkürenfels'. *Wissen und Leben* 4 (1909), 240–52
Réponse au questionnaire 'Notre consultation sur le théâtre' (1908)
'Réponse au questionnaire 'Notre consultation sur le théâtre', *L'Essor social, moral, religieux: Journal romand paraissant le Samedi* 3, no 28 (July 1908)
Style et solidarité (1909)
Manuscript: SAPA C12a-c
'Style et solidarité', *Le Rythme* 1, no 6 (1909), 49–52
'Stil und Solidarität', *Der Rhythmus* 1, no 6 (September 1909), 49–53
Quelques Pensées et citations (1909)
'Quelques Pensées et citations', *Le Rythme* 37 (August 1934), 31–32
Acteur, espace, lumière, peinture (1910)
Manuscript: SAPA C50a-b
'Acteur, éspace, lumière, peinture', *Théâtre populaire* 5 (January–February 1954), 37–42
L'Origine et les débuts de la gymnastique rythmique (1911)
Manuscript: SAPA C13a-d
'L'Origine et les débuts de la gymnastique rythmique', *Les Feuillets: Revue mensuelle de culture suisse* 1, no 11 (November 1911), 393–403
'Über Ursprung und Anfang der Rhythmischen Gymnastik', In *Der Rhythmus: Ein Jahrbuch herausgegeben von der Bildunsgsanstalt Jaques-Dalcroze, Dresden-Hellerau*, 1: 20–31 Jena: Eugen Diederichs, 1911
Du costume pour la gymnastique rythmique (1912)
Manuscript: SAPA C14a-c
'Über die Kostumfrage für die rhythmische Gymnastik, in *Der Rhythmus: Ein Jahrbuch herausgegeben von der Bildunsgsanstalt Jaques-Dalcroze, Dresden-Hellerau*, 2: 56–64, Jena: Eugen Diederichs, 1912
La Gymnastique rythmique et la lumière (1912)
Manuscript: SAPA B5, C15
La gymnastique rythmique et la lumière', *Le Rythme* 34 (December 1932), 15–17
The Origin and First-beginning of Rhythmical Gymnastics (1912)
Manuscript: SAPA C16a-e
Rhythmical Gymnastics and the Theatre (1912)
Manuscript: SAPA C17a-c
(Notes sur la) Mise en scène de Parsifal (1912)
Manuscript: SAPA A3, C18
'Die Inszenierung des Parsifal', *Der Türmer* 16, no 5 (February 1914), 806–14
Gutachten und Ratschläge zu den Schulfesten (1912)
'Gutachten und Ratschläge zu den Schulfesten', in *Der Rhythmus*, 2: 83, Jena: Eugen Diederichs, 1912
La gymnastique rythmique et le théâtre (1912)
Manuscript: SAPA A8, C52a-b
'Die rhythmische Gymnastik und das Theater', in *Der Rhythmus*: Jaques-Dalcroze, 1: 57–64 Jena: Eugen Diederichs, 1911
'La Gymnastique rythmique et le théâtre', *Les Feuillets: Revue mensuelle de culture suisse*, no 14 (February 1912), 49–56

Die Musik und das Bühnenbild (1914)
'Die Musik und das Bühnenbild', *Das Werk: Architektur und Kunst* 3 (1914), 17–26
'Die Musik und das Bühnenbild', in *Theaterkunst Ausstellung im Kunstgewerbemuseum Zurich*, 15–20, Zurich, 1914
En écoutant l'orgue à Saint-Pierre (1914)
'En écoutant l'orgue à Saint-Pierre', *Journal de Genève*, no 276 (October 1914)
Au spectateur (1917)
'Au spectateur', *Fêtes de l'institut Jaques-Dalcroze*, 1917
Préface à l'édition anglaise de 'Musik und Inscenierung' (1918)
Manuscript: SAPA A9a-b, C19a-d
Seconde Préface à 'Musik und Inscenierung' (1918)
Manuscript: SAPA C51
L'Œuvre d'art vivant (1918)
L'Œuvre d'art vivant, Geneva: Atar, 1921
The Work of Living Art and Man is the Measure of All Things, edited by Barnard Hewitt, translated by H D Albright, Books of the Theatre 2, Coral Gables, FL: University of Miami Press, 1960
L'Art est une attitude (1920)
Manuscript: SAPA A10, C20
'L'Art est une attitude', *Aujourd'hui* 3, no 17 (May 1958), 6–7
Après une lecture de Port-Royal (1921)
Manuscript: SAPA C21a-b
La mise en scène et son avenir (1921)
Manuscript: SAPA C22a-c
'La messa in scena e il suo avvenire', *Il Convegno* 4, no 10 (October 1923), 483–510
'The Future of Production', *Theatre Arts Monthly*, August 1932, 649–66
'La mise en scène et son avenir', *Cahiers de la Compagnie Madelaine Renaud et Jean-Louis Barrault* 13, no 10 (1955), 98–115
L'Ancienne attitude (1921)
Manuscript: SAPA A17
Essai sur un problème dangereux (1921)
Manuscript: SAPA C23a-b
Formes nouvelles. Conte (1921)
Manuscript: SAPA C24a-c
Le Geste de l'art (1921)
Manuscript: SAPA A11, C25
Art Vivant ou Nature Morte (1921)
Manuscript: SAPA C26a-d
'Art vivant ou nature morte?' *Wendingen* 4, no 9–10 (1921), 7–15
'Living Art or Frozen Nature', translated by Marvin Carlson, *Players Magazine* 33, no 4 (1962)
Expériences de théâtre et recherches personelles (1922)
Manuscript: SAPA A12, C38a-b
Monumentalité (1922)
Manuscript: SAPA C27
'Monumentalité', *La Revue d'Esthetique*, October 1953, 349–68
Mécanisation (1922)
Manuscript: SAPA C35a-b
Pittoresque (1922)
Manuscript: SAPA C36a-b
Le sujet (1922)
Manuscript: SAPA C28a-b
L'intermédiare (1922)
Manuscript: SAPA C29a-c
Réflexions sur l'Espace et le Temps (1922)
Manuscript: SAPA C30a-b
'Réflexions sur l'Espace et le Temps'. *Aujourd'hui* 3, no 17 (1958), 6
Fiction (1922)
Manuscript: SAPA A18
L'Enfant et l'art dramatique (1922)
'L'Enfant et l'art dramatique: À propos de l'Enfant et de l'Art dramatique', *Pour l'Ere Nouvelle* 5–6 (1923)
Carmen IIIe acte (1923)
Manuscript: SAPA A15, C31
Tristan et Iseult. Brève analyse du drame (1923)
Manuscript: SAPA A13, C32
'Tristano e Isotta à la Scala', *La Semaine littéraire* 22 (January 1924), 17–18
L'Homme est la mesure de toutes choses (Protagoras) (1923)
Manuscript: SAPA C33
'L'Homme est la mesure de toutes choses', *La Revue théâtrale* 25 (1953), 7–15
Introduction aux représentations de Tristan et Isolde à la Scala de Milan (1923)
Manuscript: SAPA C34
Lohengrin (Wagner), (Scénario abregé) (1923)
Manuscript: SAPA C46a-c
Drammatizzazione/ à Jean Mercier (1923)
'Drammatizzazione / à Jean Mercier', *Il Convegno* 5, no 8 (August 1924), 425–37
L'arte vivente nel teatro / A Jean Mercier (1923)
'L'arte vivente nel teatro / à Jean Mercier'. *Il Convegno* 6, nos 2–3 (February 1925), 118–31
Avertissement pour l'édition des mes 'Essais' en 1 volume (1923)
Manuscript: SAPA A28, C44a-b
La Réforme et le théâtre de Bâle (1924)
Manuscript: C37
'A propos d'art scénique: La Réforme et le théâtre de Bâle', *Gazette de Lausanne*, May 1925
La préparation de Tristan à la Scala (1924)
'La préparation de Tristan à la Scala', *Journal de Genève* 20 (January 1924), 5
Rheingold (1924)
Manuscript: SAPA A20
Walküre, esquisse de scenario (1924)
Manuscript: SAPA A21
Siegfried (1924)
Manuscript: SAPA C53
Götterdämmerung (1924)
Manuscript: SAPA A22, C42
Mise en scène du Petit Eyolf (1924)
À propos d'art scénique (1925)
Manuscript: SAPA C39a-b
'À propos d'art scénique'. *Gazette de Lausanne*, 3 May 1925
Richard Wagner et la mise en scène (1925)
Manuscript: SAPA A25, C40
'Das Problem der Stilbühne bei den Werken Richard Wagners. Mitreferat', in *Bericht über den 1, Musikwissenschaftlichen Kongreß der Deutschen Musikgesellschaft in Leipzig, vom 4, bis 8, Juni 1925*, 314–17, Leipzig: Breitkopf und Haertel, 1926
'Richard Wagner et la mise en scène', October 1956, 392–93
Conférence pour Zurich (L'Art dramatique vivant) (1925)
Manuscript: SAPA A23, C41a-b
Götterdämmerung (Wagner). Mise en scène (1925)
Manuscript: SAPA C42a-b
Prométhée d'Eschyle. Mise en scène (1925)
Manuscript: SAPA C43
Iphigénie en Tauride. Scénario, Considérations générales (1926)
Manuscript: SAPA A26, C45
Conférence américaine (1926)
Manuscript: SAPA A27
Macbeth (1926–1927)
Manuscript: SAPA A29
Curriculum vitae (1927)
Manuscript: SAPA A30, C47
Goethes Faust: Erster Teil, als Dichtung dargestellt (1927–1928)
Manuscript: SAPA A31, C48, C49-c
Goethes Faust: Erster Teil, als Dichtung dargestellt, Bonn: Fritz Klopp, 1929

Bibliography

Aber, Adolf, 'Tradition and Revolution at Bayreuth', *Musical Times* 92 (October 1951), 453–57

Adolphe Appia: Œuvres complètes, edited by Marie-Louise Bablet, 4 vols, Lausanne: L'Âge d'Homme, 1983–1991

Adorno, Theodor, *Versuch über Wagner*, Berlin: Suhrkamp, 1952

Akard, Jeffrey, *Edward Gordon Craig*, Cambridge: Cambridge University Press, 1983

Alberti, Leon Battista, *On Painting*, translated by John Spencer, New Haven: Yale University Press, 1966

Anderson, Ross, 'All of Paris, Darkly: Le Corbusier's Beistegui Apartment, 1929–1931', in *Proceedings of the International Congress Le Corbusier, 50 Years Later*, edited by J Torres Cueco, 113–27, Valencia: Universitat Politècnica de Valencia, 2015

'Minimal Ritual: Mies van der Rohe's Chapel of St Savior, 1952', in *Modernism and American Mid-20th Century Sacred Architecture*, edited by Anat Geva, 15–30, New York: Routledge, 2019

'Of Lines Terrestrial and Occult: Friedrich Gilly, Alberto Sartoris, Adolphe Appia, and the Matter of Perspective', *DMJournal–Architecture and Representation* 2: Drawing Instruments/Instrumental Drawings (October 2023), 178–94

'Revelatory Earth: Adolphe Appia and the Prospect of a Modern Sacred', in *Modern Architecture and the Sacred: Religious Legacies and Spiritual Renewal*, edited by Ross Anderson and Maximilian Sternberg, 181–95, London: Bloomsbury Academic, 2021

'The Appian Way', *AA Files* 75 (2017), 163–82

Ansermet, Ernst, 'La Gymnastique rythmique à Hellerau', *SIM* 9, nos 7–8 (July 1913), 57–59

Appia, Adolphe, and Jessica Davis Van Wyck, 'Six Designs for Hamlet', *Theatre Arts Monthly* 9, no 1 (January 1925), 20–31

Arburg, Hans-Georg von, 'Modern Architecture Takes the Stage: Karl Friedrich Schinkel's Architectural Spectacles', in *Performing Knowledge, 1750–1850*, edited by Mary Helen Dupree and Sean B Franzel, 165–90, Berlin: De Gruyter, 2015

Arnold, Klaus-Peter, *Vom Sofakissen zum Städtebau: Die Geschichte der Deutschen Werkstätten und der Gartenstadt Hellerau*, Dresden: Verlag der Kunst, 1993

Aureli, Pier Vittorio, and Martino Tattara, *Platforms: Architecture and the Use of the Ground*, Milan: Black Square, 2021

Bablet, Denis, 'Craig and Appia', in *The Theatre of Edward Gordon Craig*, translated by Daphne Woodward, 174–81, London: Eyre Methuen, 1981

'The Actor, Space and Lighting', in *The Revolutions of Stage Design in the 20th Century*, 40–50, Paris: Leon Amiel, 1977

'The Moscow Hamlet', in *The Theatre of Edward Gordon Craig*, translated by Daphne Woodward, 133–60, London: Eyre Methuen, 1981

Bablet, Denis, and Marie-Louise Bablet, eds, *Adolphe Appia 1862–1928: acteur–espace–lumière*, Zurich: Pro Helvetia, 1981

Adolphe Appia 1862–1928: Actor–Space–Light, translated by Burton Melnick, Zurich: Pro Helvetia, 1982

Adolphe Appia 1862–1928: Darsteller–Raum–Licht, Zurich: Pro Helvetia, 1982

Bablet, Misolette, 'Adolphe Appia: L'architecte du sensible', *Musical* 8: Opéra et mise en scène (January 1989), 78–99

Bauer, Oswald Georg, *Josef Hoffmann: Der Bühnenbildner der ersten Bayreuther Festspiele*, Munich: Deutscher Kunstverlag, 2008,

Richard Wagner: Die Bühnenwerke von der Uraufführung bis heute, Frankfurt am Main: Propyläen, 1982

Beacham, Richard, 'Adolphe Appia und Edward Gordon Craig: Treffpunkt in Elysium', in *Rekonstruktion der Zukunft: Raum, Licht, Bewegung, Utopie*, edited by Dieter Jaenicke and Ralph Lindner, 53–58, Leipzig: Spector, 2017

Adolphe Appia: Artist and Visionary of the Modern Theatre, Reading: Harwood Academic, 1994

'"Anonymity Is the Essence": In Search of Adolphe Appia', *New Theatre Quarterly* 28, no 2 (May 2012), 143–62

'Appia, Jaques-Dalcroze, and Hellerau, Part One: "Music Made Visible",' *New Theatre Quarterly* 1, no 2 (May 1985), 154–64

'Appia, Jaques-Dalcroze, and Hellerau, Part Two: "Poetry in Motion",' *New Theatre Quarterly* 1, no 3 (August 1985), 245–61

'"Brothers in Suffering and Joy": The Appia-Craig Correspondence', *New Theatre Quarterly* 4, no 15 (August 1988), 268–88

Beacham, Richard and Walther R Volbach, eds, *Adolphe Appia: Essays, Scenarios and Designs*, translated by Walther R Volbach, London: UMI, 1989

Beeby, Thomas H 'Rudolf Schwarz and Mies van der Rohe: The Form of the Spirit', in *Constructing the Ineffable: Contemporary Sacred Architecture*, edited by Karla Cavarra Britton, 82–95, New Haven: Yale University Press, 2010.

Behrendt, Walter Curt, 'Eine Gedächtnisstätte für die Gefallenen des Weltkrieges: Zum Umbau der Neuen Wache in Berlin', *Zentralblatt der Bauverwaltung* 50, no 29 (1930)

Benton, Tim. *Le Corbusier: Secret Photographer*, Zurich: Lars Müller, 2013

'Marseille: Unité d'habitation, or "The Company of Clouds, the Sky, or the Stars",' in *Le Corbusier: An Atlas of Modern Landscapes*, edited by Jean-Louis Cohen, 201–05, New York: Museum of Modern Art, 2012

The Rhetoric of Modernism: Le Corbusier as a Lecturer, Basel: Birkhäuser, 2009

Bérard, Armand, 'Victor Bérard et les "Navigations d'Ulysse",' *La Nouvelle Revue des Deux Mondes*, April 1972, 50–59

Bérard, Victor, and Frédéric Boissonnas, *Dans le sillage d'Ulysse: Album odysséen*, Paris: Librairie Armand Colin, 1933

Berchtold, Alfred, 'Émile Jaques-Dalcroze et son temps', in *Émile Jaques-Dalcroze: L'homme, le compositeur, le créateur de la rythmique*,

27–158, Neuchâtel: Editions de la Baconnière, 1965
Bergdoll, Barry, *Karl Friedrich Schinkel: An Architect for Prussia*, New York: Rizzoli, 1994
'The Nature of Mies's Space', in *Mies in Berlin*, edited by Barry Bergdoll and Terence Riley, 67–105, New York: Museum of Modern Art, 2001
Bergdoll, Barry, and Terence Riley, *Mies in Berlin*, New York: Museum of Modern Art, 2001
Bergh, Wim van den, *Beistegui avant Le Corbusier*, Paris: Éditions B2, 2015
'Charles Beistegui: Autobiography and Patronage', OASE 83: *Commissioning Architecture* (December 2010), 17–40
Machine à Amuser: The Life and Death of the Beistegui Penthouse Apartment, Cambridge, MA: MIT Press, 2024
Bermudez, Julio, 'Le Corbusier at the Parthenon', in *Transcending Architecture*, 88–110, Washington: Catholic University of America Press, 2015
Blaser, Werner, *Mies van der Rohe: The Art of Structure*, Basel: Birkhäuser, 1993
Boissonnas, Frédéric, *L'Acropole d'Athènes*, Paris: Albert Morancé, 1910
'Un nouveau télé-objectif: la téléphot rapide Vautier-Dufour et Schaer', *Revue suisse de photographie* 15 (1903), 10–21
Boissonnas, Frédéric, Paul-Edmond Martin and Horace Micheli, *Les Fêtes de Juin 1914: Album du Centenaire genevois*, Geneva: Editions d'art Boissonnas, 1922
Bosoni, Giampiero, 'Lucien Hervé fotografo di Le Corbusier', *Abitare* 309 (1992), 166–71
Bouvier, Nicolas, *Boissonnas: Une dynastie de photographes, 1864–1983*, Lausanne: Editions Payot, 1983
Bowman, Ned A, 'Investing a Theatrical Ideal: Wagner's Bayreuth "Festspielhaus",' *Educational Theatre Journal* 18, no 4 (December 1966), 429–38
Breuer, Robert, 'Die Cölner Werkbund-Ausstellung, Mai-Oktober 1914', *Deutsche Kunst und Dekoration* 12, no 3 (1914), 416–36
Browne, Maurice, *Too Late to Lament*, Bloomington: Indiana University Press, 1955
Brückner, Max, *Der Ring Des Nibelungen von Richard Wagner: Dekorationsentwürfe von Prof Max Brückner in Coburg zur Aufführung in Bayreuth im Jahre 1896*, Bayreuth: Heinrich Heuschmann, 1896
Brückwald, Otto, 'Das Bühnenfestspielhaus zu Bayreuth', *Deutsche Bauzeitung* 9, no 1 (1875), 1–5
Bücher, Karl, *Arbeit und Rhythmus*, Leipzig: Hirzel, 1896
Bürger, Susanne, ed, *Arnold Böcklin (1827–1901): Gemälde, Zeichnungen, Plastiken*, Basel: Kunsthalle Basel und Basler Kunstverein, 1977
Cardullo, Bert, '"Adolphe Appia and Me": A Discussion with Hans-Jürgen Syberberg', *Literature/Film Quarterly* 38, no 1 (2010), 5–15
Carl, Peter, 'On Depth: Particular and Universal, Fragment and Field', in *Fragments: Architecture and the Unfinished: Essays Presented to Robin Middleton*, edited by Barry Bergdoll and Werner Oechslin, 23–42, New York: Thames & Hudson, 2006
'Ornament and Time: A Prolegomena, Part 2', *AA Files* 23 (1992), 49–64
Carl, Peter, and Irena Murray, 'Geometry and Analogy: Le Corbusier's Baghdad Veils'. *AA Files* 67 (2013), 49–60
Carnegy, Patrick, *Wagner and the Art of the Theatre*, New Haven: Yale University Press, 2006
Caruso, Adam, and Helen Thomas, *Rudolf Schwarz and the Monumental Order of Things*, Zurich: gta, 2016
Castens, Edward H, ed, *The Story of the 446th Bomb Group*, San Angelo: Newsphoto Publishing Company, 1946
Chamberlain, Houston Stewart, *Die Grundlagen des neunzehnten Jahrhunderts*, Munich: Bruckmann, 1899
Richard Wagner, Munich: Verlagsanstalt für Kunst und Wissenschaft, 1896
Clausewitz, Carl von, *Vom Kriege*, Berlin: Ferdinand Dümmler, 1832
Collignon, Maxime, *Le Parthénon: L'histoire, l'architecture et la sculpture*, Paris: Libraire Hachette, 1914
Conrads, Ulrich, and Peter Neitzke, *Mensch und Raum: Das Darmstädter Gespräch 1951*, Braunschweig: Vieweg, 1991
Copeau, Jacques, 'Adolphe Appia et l'art de la scène', *Cahiers de la Compagnie Madelaine Renaud et Jean-Louis Barrault* 13, no 10 (1955), 92–97
'Adolphe Appia et l'art scénique', *La Nación*, April 1928
Corradini, Enrico, 'Una lettera ad Adolfo Appia', 1924
Cosima Wagner's Diaries, edited by Martin Gregor-Dellin and Dietrich Mack, translated by Geoffrey Skelton, 2 vols, London: Collins, 1978–80
Couturier, Marie-Alain, *Sacred Art*, translated by Granger Ryan, Austin: University of Texas Press, 1989
Craig, Edward Gordon, *Fourteen Notes*, Seattle: University of Washington Book Store, 1931
Craig, Gordon, *On the Art of the Theatre*, London: Heinemann, 1911
Darcy, Warren, '"Everything That Is, Ends!": The Genesis and Meaning of the Erda Episode in "Das Rheingold",' *Musical Times* 129, no 1747 (September 1988), 443–47
Das Bayreuther Festspielbuch, edited by Bayreuth Festspielleitung, Bayreuth: Wagner-Buchhandlung Georg Niehrenheim, 1951
De Michelis, Marco, *Heinrich Tessenow 1876–1950: Das architektonische Gesamtwerk*, Milan: Electa, 1991
'L'Institut Jaques-Dalcroze à Hellerau', in *Adolphe Appia ou le renouveau de l'esthétique théâtrale*, 21–47, Lausanne: Éditions Payot, 1992
De Michelis, Marco, and Vicki Bilenker, 'Modernity and Reform: Heinrich Tessenow and the Institut Dalcroze at Hellerau', *Perspecta* 26: Theatre, Theatricality and Architecture (1990), 143–70
Della Portella, Ivana, ed, *The Appian Way from its Foundation to the Middle Ages*, Verona: Arsenale Editrice, 2004
Dent, Alan, ed, *Bernard Shaw and Mrs Patrick Campbell: Their Correspondence*, London: Victor Gollancz, 1952
'Die Bildungsanstalt Dalcroze in Hellerau bei Dresden', *Blätter für Architektur und Kunsthandwerk* 26, no 5 (May 1913), 17–20
Doepler, Carl Emil, *A Memoir of Bayreuth: 1876*, translated by Peter Cook, London: Staples St Albans, 1979
Doglio, Mazzocchi, *Il teatro simbolista in Francia (1890–1896)*, Rome: Edizioni Abete, 1978

Dohrn, Wolf, 'Die Aufgabe der Bildungsanstalt Jaques-Dalcroze', in *Der Rhythmus: Ein Jahrbuch*, vol 1, 2–19, Jena: Eugen Diederichs, 1911
Dreier, Martin, *Adolphe Appia (1862–1928): Zwanzig Faksimilies aus seinem bühnenbildnerischen Entwurfswerk*, Bern: Stiftung Schweizerische Theatersammlung, 1993
Dubreuil, Jean, *The Practice of Perspective*, translated by Ephraim Chambers, 4th ed, London: John Bowles, 1765
Dufour, Alfred, 'Musique: La musique et la mise en scène', *Journal de Genève*, 3 July 1899
Dutoit-Carlier, Claire-Lise, 'Jaques-Dalcroze, créateur de la rythmique', in *Émile Jaques-Dalcroze: L'homme, le compositeur, le créateur de la rythmique*, 305–412, Neuchâtel: Editions de la Baconnière, 1965
Eidenbenz, Céline, 'Hypnosis at the Parthenon: Magdeleine G, photographed by Fred Boissonnas', *Études photographiques* 28 (November 2011), 200–04
'Ein ehrwürdiges Stück Tuch: Dr Appias Armbinde', *Du: kulturelle Monatsschrift* 2, no 8 (1942), 3
Elcott, Noam, 'Spaceless Play: Oskar Schlemmer's Dance Against Enlightenment', in *Artificial Darkness: An Obscure History of Modern Art and Media*, 165–228, Chicago: University of Chicago Press, 2016
Etlin, Richard A, 'Le Corbusier, Choisy, and French Hellenism: The Search for a New Architecture', *Art Bulletin* 69, no 2 (June 1987), 264–78
Euripides, *Iphigenia at Aulis*, translated by W S Merwin and George E Dimock, Oxford: Oxford University Press, 1978
Iphigenia among the Taurians, translated by Anne Carson, Chicago: University of Chicago Press, 2014
Feudel, Elfride, 'Schule der Rhythmischen Erziehung', in *Hellerau leuchtete: Zeitzeugenberichte und Erinnerungen*, 154–70, Dresden: Verlag der Kunst, 2007
Feye, Carlheinz, and Jürgen Nottmeyer, eds, *Friedrich Gilly und die Privatgesellschaft junger Architekten*, Berlin: Willmuth Arenhövel, 1987.
Fiehler, Karl, in *Quellen und Dokumente zur Geschichte von 'Mein Kampf', 1924–1945*, Stuttgart: Franz Steiner, 2016
Fischer, Theodor, 'Was ich bauen möchte', *Hohe Warte* 3 (1906), 326–28
Forman, James, *Nazism*, New York: F Watts, 1978
Forner, Sean, 'War Commemoration and the Republic in Crisis: Weimar Germany and the Neue Wache', *Central European History* 35, no 4 (2002), 513–49
Forster, Kurt, "Only Things That Stir the Imagination', in *Karl Friedrich Schinkel: The Drama of Architecture*, edited by John Zukowsky, 18–35, Berlin: Wasmuth, 1994
Frampton, Kenneth, *Modern Architecture: A Critical History*, New York: Rizzoli, 1981
Frenzel, Andreas, 'Daß das Reichsehrenmal eine würdige Stätte finde bei Höxter', *Westfälische Zeitschrift* 150 (2000), 367–89
Friedrich Gilly: Essays on Architecture 1796–1799, translated by David Britt, Santa Monica: Getty Centre for the History of Art and the Humanities, 1994
Fröbe, Turit, *Die Inszenierung eines Mythos: Le Corbusier und die Akropolis*, Basel: Birkhäuser, 2017
Fuchs, Georg, *Der Tanz*. Stuttgart: von Streker & Schröder, 1906.
Die Schaubühne der Zukunft, Berlin: Schuster & Loeffler, 1905
Gargiani, Roberto, and Anna Rosellini, *Le Corbusier Béton Brut and Ineffable Space, 1940–1965: Surface, Materials and Psychophysiology of Vision*, Lausanne: EPFL Press, 2011
Geissler, F A, '*Die Dalcroze-Schulfeste in Hellerau*', *Die Musik: Illustrierte Halbmonatsschrift* 11, no 4 (1912), 154–57
Giedeon, Sigfried, *The Eternal Present: A Contribution on Constancy and Change*, New York: Pantheon, 1962
Giertz, Gernot, *Kultus ohne Götter: Emile Jacques-Dalcroze und Adolphe Appia: Der Versuch einer Theaterreform auf der Grundlage der Rhythmischen Gymnastik*, Munich: Kitzinger, 1975
Girardin, Daniel, 'Frédéric Boissonnas: Between Tradition and Modernity', *History of Photography* 22, no 3 (2015), 281–83
Goethe, Johann Wolfgang von, *Faust: Eine Tragödie*, Tübingen: Cotta, 1808
Faust: Part One, translated by Philip Wane, London: Penguin, 1949
Goethes Faust erster und zweiter Teil, Leipzig: Alfred Kröner Verlag, undated
Italienische Reise, vol 1, Leipzig: Insel, 1913
Goléa, Antoine, *Entretiens avec Wieland Wagner*, Paris: Pierre Belfond, 1967
Gradenwitz, Alfred, 'The "Telephot", A Novel Apparatus for Photographing at Great Distances', *Scientific American* 88, no 26 (June 1903), 406
Grave, Johannes, *Der 'Ideale Kunstkörper': Johann Wolfgang von Goethe als Sammler von Druckgraphiken und Zeichnungen*, Göttingen: Vandenhoeck & Ruprecht, 2006
Grayson, Cecil, 'L B Alberti's "Costruzione Legittima",' *Italian Studies* 19, no 1 (1964), 14–27
Gresleri, Giuliano, *Viaggio in Oriente: Charles Edouard Jeanneret fotografo e scrittore*, Venice: Marsilio, 1984
Grillparzer, Franz, *Des Meeres und der Liebe Wellen*, F B Wallishausser: Vienna, 1840
Grimm, Jacob, *Deutsche Mythologie*, Göttingen: Dieterich, 1835
Gropius, Walter, *Bauhausbücher 12: Bauhausbauten Dessau*, Munich: Albert Langen, 1930
Programm und Manifest des Staatlichen Bauhauses, Weimar, 1919
Gubler, Jacques, 'Des pieds nus gravissant un escalier', in *Adolphe Appia ou le renouveau de l'esthétique théâtrale: Dessins et esquisses de décors*, edited by Jörg Zutter, 93–108, Lausanne: Éditions Payot, 1992
Günzel, Stephan, ed, *Texte zur Theorie des Raums*, Stuttgart: Reclam, 2013
Haenel, Erich, 'Die Gartenstadt Hellerau', *Dekorative Kunst, illustrierte Zeitschrift für angewandte Kunst* 14, no 7 (April 1911), 297–346
Hamann, Brigitte, *Hitler's Vienna: A Dictator's Apprenticeship*, New York: Oxford University Press, 1999
Winifred Wagner oder Hitlers Bayreuth, Munich: Piper, 2002
Winifred Wagner: A Life at the Heart of Hitler's Bayreuth, translated by Alan Bance, London: Granta, 2005
Hartford, Robert, *Bayreuth, The Early Years: An Account of the Early Decades of the Wagner Festival as Seen by the Celebrated Visitors & Participants*, London: V Gollancz, 1980

Hays, K Michael, 'Not Architecture but Evidence that It Exists: A Note on Lauretta Vinciarelli's Watercolors', *Assemblage* 38 (April 1999), 48–57
'Tessenow's Architecture as National Allegory: Critique of Capitalism or Protofascism?' *Assemblage* 8 (February 1989), 104–23
Heidegger, Martin, 'Bauen Wohnen Denken', in *Mensch und Raum: Das Darmstädter Gespräch 1951*, edited by Ulrich Conrads and Peter Neitzke, 88–102, Braunschweig: Vieweg, 1991
Hellwag, Fritz, 'Der Deutsche Werkbund und seine Ausstellung Köln 1914', *Kunstgewerbeblatt* 3 (1915), 41–54.
Heuss, Theodor, 'Werkbund Beginn', in *Hellerau leuchtete: Zeitzeugenberichte und Erinnerungen*, edited by Erhardt Heinold and Günther Großer, 25–34, Dresden: Verlag der Kunst, 2007
Hitler, Adolf, *Mein Kampf: Eine kritische Edition*, edited by Christian Hartmann, Thomas Vordermayer, Othmar Plöckinger, Roman Töppel and Edith Raim, Munich: Institut für Zeitgeschichte, 2016
Monologe im Führer-Hauptquartier, 1941–1944: Die Aufzeichnungen Heinrich Heims, edited by Werner Jochmann, Hamburg: Albrecht Knaus, 1980
Sämtliche Aufzeichnungen: 1905–1924, Stuttgart: Deutsche Verlags-Anstalt, 1980
Hodgson, James, 'The Theory of Perspective', in *The Practice of Perspective: Or, An Easy Method of Representing Natural Objects According to the Rules of Art*, translated by Ephraim Chambers, i–xvi, London: John Bowles, 1765
Hoffmann, Josef, *Festgabe zur Neuinszenierung des 'Ring des Nibelungen' in Bayreuth*, 1896
Homer, *The Odyssey*, translated by Robert Fagles, London: Penguin, 2006
Howard, Ebenezer, 'Der erste Eindruck', in *Hellerau leuchtete: Zeitzeugenberichte und Erinnerungen*, edited by Erhardt Heinold and Günther Großer, 229–30, Dresden: Verlag der Kunst, 2007
Garden Cities of To-morrow, London: Swan Sonnenschein, 1898, translated by Maria Wallroth-Unterlip, Jena: Eugen Diederichs, 1907
'Leserbrief', *Dresdner Anzeige*, September 1912
Humbert, Georges, 'Littérature wagnérienne, 1894–1895, Adolphe Appia, La mise en scène du drame Wagnérien', *Gazette musical de la Suisse romande*, May 1895, 155
Ibsen, Henrik, *Little Eyolf*, translated by William Archer, *The Collected Works of Henrik Ibsen*, vol 11, London: William Heinemann, 1907
In My Mind's Eye: Edward Gordon Craig and Hamlet: An Exhibition of Prints & Books, Mainly from the Personal Archives of Gordon Craig and His Family from the Collection of Jason Buzas, London: Sophie Schneideman Rare Books, 2009
Ingham, Ethel, 'Lessons at Hellerau', in *The Eurhythmics of Jaques-Dalcroze*, 48–54, London: Constable, 1912
International Exhibition of Theatre Art, New York: Museum of Modern Art, 1934
Isaacs, Reginald R *Walter Gropius: An Illustrated Biography of the Creator of the Bauhaus*, Boston: Bullfinch Press, 1991
Walter Gropius: Der Mensch und sein Werk, vol 1, Berlin: Gebr. Mann, 1983
Iuliano, Marco, 'Lucien Hervé and Le Corbusier: Pair or Peers?', *Journal of Architecture* 21, no 7 (2016), 1100–26
Jaenicke, Dieter, and Ralph Lindner, eds, *Rekonstruktion der Zukunft: Raum, Licht, Bewegung, Utopie*, Leipzig: Spector, 2017
'Jahresbericht der Bildungsanstalt Jaques-Dalcroze für das Unterrichtsjahr 1910/11', in *Der Rhythmus: Ein Jahrbuch*, vol 1, 65–81, Jena: Eugen Diederichs, 1911
Jameux, Dominique, 'Wieland Wagner et le nouveau Bayreuth', *Musical* 8: Opéra et mise en scène (January 1989), 101–17
Jamin, Philip, 'Les châteaux vaudois: le château de Glérolles', *Le conteur vaudois: journal de la Suisse romande* 54, no 32 (1916), 2
Jaques-Dalcroze, Émile, 'Address to the Dresden Teachers' Association: May 28, 1912', in *The Eurhythmics of Jaques-Dalcroze*, 27, London: Constable, 1912
Eurhythmics, Art and Education, translated by Frederick Rothwell, London: Chatto and Windus, 1930
'From the Lectures of Émile Jaques-Dalcroze: Leipzig, December 10, 1911', in *The Eurhythmics of Jaques-Dalcroze*, 26–27, London: Constable, 1912
'L'Education par le rythme', *Le Rhythme*, 1909, 63–70
La Rythmique, Lausanne: Jobin, 1916
'Rhythm and Gesture in Music Drama and Criticism', in *Rhythm, Music and Education*, translated by Harald Rubinstein, 149–74, London: Chatto and Windus, 1921
'Rhythm as a Factor in Education', in *The Eurhythmics of Jaques-Dalcroze*, edited by Michael Ernest Sadler, 4–11, Boston: Small Maynard, 1915
Rhythm, Music and Education, translated by Harald Rubinstein, London: Chatto and Windus, 1921
'Was die Rhythmische Gymnastik Ihnen gibt und was sie von Ihnen fordert', in *Der Rhythmus: Ein Jahrbuch*, vol 1, 32–56, Jena: Eugen Diederichs, 1911
Jaumann, Anton, 'Vom künstlerischen Nachwuchs', *Innendekoration* 21, no 7 (July 1910), 268–73
Jeanneret, Albert, 'La Rythmique 1', *L'Esprit nouveau*, no 2 (1920), 183–89
'La Rythmique 2', *L'Esprit nouveau*, no 3 (1920), 331–38
Jeanneret, Charles-Édouard, Amédee Ozenfant and Paul Dermée, 'L'Esprit nouveau', *L'Esprit nouveau*, no 1 (1920), 3–5
Joe, Jeonwong, and Sander Gilman, eds, *Wagner and Cinema*, Indianapolis: Indiana University Press, 2010
Jones, Emma Letizia, 'The Wanderer', AA *Files* 72 (2016), 152–60
Kabus, Petra, *Innenansichten: Zwei norwegische Schülerinnen der Bildungsanstalt Jaques-Dalcroze in Hellerau*, Dresden: Deutscher Werkbund Sachsen, 2009
Kafka, Franz, *Tagebücher 1910–1923*, edited by Max Brod, Frankfurt am Main: Fischer, 1951

Kapsamer, Ingrid, *Wieland Wagner: Wegbereiter und Weltwirkung*, Vienna: Styria, 2010
Kaster, Robert, *The Appian Way: Ghost Road, Queen of Roads*, Chicago: University of Chicago Press, 2012
Kelly, Thomas, *First Nights at the Opera*, New Haven: Yale University Press, 2004
Kitao, Timothy, 'Prejudice in Perspective: A Study of Vignola's Perspective Treatise', *Art Bulletin* 44, no 3 (September 1962), 173–94
Koerner, Joseph Leo, *Caspar David Friedrich and the Subject of Landscape*, London: Reaktion Books, 1990
Kracauer, Siegfried, *History: The Last Things Before the Last*, New York: Oxford University Press, 1969
'Tessenow baut das Berliner Ehrenmal', *Frankfurter Zeitung*, 22 July 1930
'Zur Einweihung des Berliner Ehrenmals', *Frankfurter Zeitung*, 18 June 1931
Krauter, Anne, 'Die Schriften Paul Scheerbarts und der Lichtdom von Albert Speer: "Das grosse Licht",' PhD thesis, University of Heidelberg, 1997
Krier, Léon, Robert A M Stern and Albert Speer, *Albert Speer Architecture 1932–1942*, Brussels: Archives d'Architecture Moderne, 1985
Kubizek, August, *Adolf Hitler, mein Jugendfreund*, Graz: Leopold Stocker, 1953
Kuschnig, Claire, 'Beleuchtungs-konzept von Alexander von Salzmann', in *Rekonstruktion der Zukunft: Raum, Licht, Bewegung, Utopie*, edited by Dieter Jaenicke and Ralph Lindner, 103–07, Leipzig: Spector, 2017
Le Corbusier, 'Architecture II: The Illusion of the Plan', in *Toward an Architecture*, translated by John Goodman, 213–30, Los Angeles: Getty Research Institute, 2007
Carnet 3: Voyage d'Orient, New York: Rizzoli, 1988
Le Corbusier correspondance: Lettres à la famille, vol 1, *1900–1925*, Paris: Infolio, 2011
Étude sur le mouvement d'art décoratif en Allemagne, La Chaux-de-Fonds: École de l'Art, 1912
Journey to the East, translated by Ivan Žaknić, Cambridge, MA: MIT Press, 2007
'Le Couvent Sainte-Marie de la Tourette construit par Le Corbusier', *L'Art sacré* 14, nos 7–8 (March 1960), 5
Modulor 2: Let the User Speak Next, translated by Peter de Francia and Anna Bostock, London: Faber and Faber, 1958
New World of Space, New York: Reynal & Hitchcock, 1948
Le Corbusier et Pierre Jeanneret: Œuvre complète de 1929–1934, edited by Willy Boesiger, Basel: Birkhäuser, 1935
Le Corbusier: Œuvre complète de 1946–1952, edited by Willy Boesiger, Basel: Birkhäuser, 1953
Le Corbusier: Œuvre complète de 1952–1957, edited by Willy Boesiger, Basel: Birkhäuser, 1957
Precisions on the Present State of Architecture and City, translated by Edith Schreiber Aujame, Cambridge, MA: MIT Press, 1991
Ronchamp: Les carnets de la recherche patiente, translated by Jacqueline Cullen, Stuttgart: Gerd Hatje, 1957
Textes et dessins pour Ronchamp, Paris: Forces Vives, 1965
Texts and Sketches for Ronchamp, Ronchamp: Association œuvre de Notre-Dame du Haut, 1982
The Nursery Schools, translated by Eleanor Levieux, New York: Orion, 1968
Une maison, un palais, Paris: G Crès, 1928
Une petite maison, 1923, Zurich: Girsberger, 1954
Vers une Architecture, Paris: G Crès, 1923
Le Corbusier and Pierre Jeanneret, *The Complete Architectural Works*, vol 1, *1910–1929*, London: Thames & Hudson, 1964
Le Corbusier-Saugnier, 'Architecture III: Pure création de l'esprit', *L'Esprit nouveau*, no 16 (1922), 1903–20
'Trois rappels à MM Les Architectes', *L'Esprit nouveau*, no 1 (1920), 91–96
'Vers une architecture', *L'Esprit nouveau*, no 18 (1923)
Leatherbarrow, David, and Richard Wesley, 'Alone-Together Naturally', in *Three Cultural Ecologies*, 115–48, New York: Routledge, 2018
Lehner, Frederick, 'Goethes Faust auf der Bühne', *German Quarterly* 25, no 2 (March 1952), 95–102
Libeskind, Daniel, 'Die Zukunft aus der Vergangenheit rekonstruieren' [keynote lecture], Festspielhaus Hellerau, October 2017
Loach, Judi, 'Architecture, Science and Purity', in *Being Modern: The Cultural Impact of Science in the Early Twentieth Century*, 207–44, London: UCL Press, 2018
Loeffler, Peter, *Oskar Wälterlin: Ein Profil*, Basel: Birkhäuser, 1979
Loehr, Maja, 'Der Wiener Maler Josef Hoffmann als Mitgestalter der ersten Bayreuther Festspiele', *Theater einst und jetzt 1* (1947), 4–12
Loos, Adolf, 'Ornament et Crime', *L'Esprit nouveau*, no 2 (1920), 159–68
Lorenz, Karl, 'Der Untergang Helleraus 1914: Bericht aus Genf zum 60, Jahrestag des "Genfer Protestes",' in *Rhythmik in der Erziehung*, Seelze-Velber: Kallmeyer, 1974
Loriga, Sabina, 'The Role of the Individual in History: Biographical and Historical Writing in the Nineteenth and Twentieth Century', in *Theoretical Discussions of Biography: Approaches from History, Microhistory, and Life Writing*, edited by Binne de Haan and Hans Renders, 113–41, New York: Edwin Mellen Press, 2013
Magee, Brian, *The Tristan Chord: Wagner and Philosophy*, New York: Metropolitan Books, 2002
Magnin, Émile, *L'Art et l'hypnose: Interprétation plastique d'oeuvres littéraires et musicales*, Geneva: Atar, 1906
Malfroy, Sylvain, 'Der Aussenraum ist immer ein Innenraum', *Werk, Bauen + Wohnen* 81, no 6 (1994), 36–41
Mallgrave, Harry Francis, *Gottfried Semper: Architect of the Nineteenth Century*, New Haven: Yale University Press, 1996
Mann, Thomas, 'The Making of "The Magic Mountain",' *The Atlantic*, January 1953, 41–45
Melis, Paolo, 'Il "cadavere squisito" di Le Corbusier: Pierre Jeanneret e Charles Beistegui', *Controspazio* 9, no 3 (1977), 36–37
Mendelssohn, Peter de, *Hellerau: Mein unverlierbares Europa*, Dresden: Hellerau Verlag, 1993
Merbach, Paul Alfred, 'Modern German Theatre Art', In *International Exhibition of Theatre Art*, 29–32, New York: Museum of Modern Art, 1934

Mies van der Rohe, Ludwig, 'A Chapel', *Arts and Architecture* 70, no 1 (January 1953), 18–19

Milhaud, Darius, *Notes Without Music*, New York: Alfred A Knopf, 1953

Milius, John, and Francis Ford Coppola, *Apocalypse Now Redux: An Original Screenplay*, New York: Miramax Books, 2001

Mink, Louis, 'Narrative Form as a Cognitive Instrument', in *The Writing of History: Literary Form and Historical Understanding*, edited by Robert Canary and Henry Kozicki, 143–44, Madison: University of Wisconsin Press, 1978

Minor, Ryan, 'Wagner's Last Chorus: Consecrating Space and Spectatorship in "Parsifal",' *Cambridge Opera Journal* 17, no 1 (March 2005), 1–36

Moholy, Lucia, *Marginal Notes*, Krefeld: Scherpe, 1972

'Switzerland', *Burlington Magazine* 104, no 717 (December 1962), 556–67

Moholy-Nagy, Lászlo, 'Theater, Zirkus, Varieté', in *Bauhausbücher 4: Die Bühne im Bauhaus*, edited by Walter Gropius and L Moholy-Nagy, 45–56, Munich: Albert Langen, 1924

Moreck, Curt, 'Bühnenbilder von Emil Pirchan', *Innen-Dekoration* 31, no 4 (April 1920), 133–36

Mösl, Kristina, and Philipp Demandt, eds, *Der Mönch ist zurück: Die Restaurierung von Caspar David Friedrichs Mönch am Meer und Abtei im Eichwald*, Berlin: Staatliche Museen zu Berlin – Nationalgalerie, 2016

Muthesius, Hermann, *Landhaus und Garten: Beispiel neuzeitlicher Landhäuser nebst Grundrissen, Innenräumen und Gärten*, 2nd ed, Munich: Bruckmann, 1910

Nabokov, Vladimir, *Despair*. London: John Long, 1937

'Nachrichten über den Neubau des Instituts und die Unterrichtskurse 1911/12', in *Der Rhythmus: Ein Jahrbuch*, vol 1, 89–94, Jena: Eugen Diederichs, 1911

'Das Haus', in *Der Rhythmus, Ein Jahrbuch*, vol 2, 2–13, Jena: Eugen Diederichs, 1912

Naumann, Friedrich, 'Trauerrede zum Gedächtnis von Wolf Dohrn', in *Hellerau leuchtete: Zeitzeugenberichte und Erinnerungen*, 321–34, Dresden: Verlag der Kunst, 2007

Naumburg, Margaret, 'The Dalcroze Idea and What It Means', *The Outlook*, 17 January 1914, 127–58

Neumeyer, Fritz, 'Mies's First Project: Revisiting the Atmosphere at Klösterli', in *Mies in Berlin*, edited by Barry Bergdoll and Terence Riley, 309–17, New York: Museum of Modern Art, 2001

Newman, Ernst, *The Life of Richard Wagner*, 4 vols, New York: Alfred Knopf, 1933–47

Niemann, Gottfried, *Richard Wagner und Arnold Böcklin, oder über das Wesen von Landschaft und Musik*, Leipzig: J Zeitler, 1904

Nietzsche, Friedrich, *Der Fall Wagner: Ein Musikanten-Problem*, Leipzig: C G Naumann, 1888

'Richard Wagner in Bayreuth', in *Nietzsche Werke*, vol 4, edited by Giorgio Colli and Mazzino Montinari, Berlin: De Gruyter, 1967

Why I Am So Clever, translated by R J Hollingdale, London: Penguin, 2016

Obrist, Hans Ulrich, *Lucien Hervé*, Paris: Manuella, 2011

Odier, Henri, 'Essai d'analyse psychologique du mécanisme du langage dans la compréhension', PhD thesis, Université de Berne, 1904

Oechslin, Werner, 'Les Cinq Points d'une Architecture Nouvelle', translated by Wilfried Wang, *Assemblage* 4 (October 1987), 82–93

Ojetti, Ugo, 'Calvino alla Scala', *L'Avanti*, December 1923

Parr, Martin, and Gerry Badger, *The Photobook: A History*, vol 1, London: Phaidon, 2004

Pauly, Danièle, *Le Corbusier: The Chapel at Ronchamp*, translated by Sarah Parsons, Basel: Birkhäuser, 2008

Pausch, Oskar, 'Der Besuch Alfred Rollers bei Adolf Hitler 1934: Ein verschollenes Dokument', ÖZG 2, no 2 (2012), 237–44

Perrottet, Suzanne, 'Dalcroze' Lieblingschülerin erinnert sich', in *Hellerau leuchtete: Zeitzeugenberichte und Erinnerungen*, edited by Erhardt Heinold and Günther Großer, 141–53, Dresden: Verlag der Kunst, 2007

Petit, Jean, *Le Corbusier lui-même*, Geneva: Panoramas Forces Vives, 1970

Le livre de Ronchamp, Paris: Les Cahiers Forces Vives, 1961

Un couvent de Le Corbusier, Paris: Forces Vives, 1961

Pfäfflin, Anna Marie, 'Bühnenbild und inszenierter Raum: Zum Konzept des Theatralischen im Werk von Karl Friedrich Schinkel', *Jahrbuch der Berliner-Museen* 56 (2014), 111–21

Piranesi, Giovanni Battista, *Le antichità romane*, vol 2, Rome: Angelo Rotili, 1756.

Pishioneri, Albert F, *Me, Mom and WWII*, Bloomington: AuthorHouse, 2008

Plahte Tschudi, Victor, 'Goethe in the Hall and His Journeys in Printed Rome', *Architectural Histories* 3, no 1 (2015), 1–17

Piranesi and the Modern Age, Cambridge, MA: MIT Press, 2022

Plöckinger, Othmar, *Geschichte eines Buches: Adolf Hitlers Mein Kampf 1922–1945*, Munich: Oldenbourg, 2011

Pointon, Marcia, 'Casts, Imprints and the Deathliness of Things: Artifacts at the Edge', *Art Bulletin* 96, no 2 (June 2014), 170–95

Pope-Hennessy, John, *Adolphe Appia*, London: V&A Museum, 1970

Posener, Julius, and Kristin Feireiss, *Hans Poelzig: Reflections on His Life and Work*, Cambridge, MA: MIT Press, 1992

Potié, Philipe, *Le Corbusier: Le Couvent Sainte-Marie de la Tourette*, Basel: Birkhäuser, 2001

Procaccini, Alfonso, 'Alberti and the "Framing" of Perspective', *Journal of Aesthetics and Art Criticism* 40, no 1 (1981), 29–39

'Protestation contre le bombardement de Reims', *L'image de la guerre* 1, no 2 (1914)

Rapp, Franz, 'Das deutsche Bühnenbild unserer Zeit', *Die Form: Monatsschrift für gestaltende Arbeit* 1, no 3 (1922), 7–14

Rauscher, Ulrich, 'Hellerau' *Die Schaubühne* 9, no 42 (1913), 1003–06

Rehorst, Carl, ed, *Offizieller Katalog der Deutschen Werkbund-Ausstellung: Cöln 1914, Mai-Oktober*, Cologne: Rudolf Mosse, 1914

Reichlin, Bruno, 'My Father Lived One Year in This House, The Scenery Fascinated Him', in *Le Corbusier: An Atlas of Modern Landscapes*, edited by Jean-Louis Cohen, 64–71, New York: Museum of Modern Art, 2012

Reif, Adelbert, *Albert Speer: Kontroversen um ein deutsches Phänomen*, Munich: Bernard & Graefe, 1978

Renan, Ernest, *Prière sur l'Acropole*, Paris: Édouard Pelletan, 1899
'Als der 'Appia Ring' Zersprang', *National Zeitung*, 18 November 1961, 26
Ricoeur, Paul, 'Narrative Time', *Critical Inquiry* 7, no 1 (1980), 169–90
Time and Narrative, translated by Kathleen McLaughlin and David Pellauer, Chicago: University of Chicago Press, 1984
Riehl, Alois, 'Bemerkungen zum Problem der Form in der Dichtkunst', *Vierteljahrsschrift für wissenschaftliche Philosophie* 21 (1897), 283–306
Robbers, Lutz, '1912 – Hellerau as Spielraum', in *Participation in Art and Architecture*, edited by Martino Stierli and Mechtild Widrich, 197–226, London: I B Tauris, 2015
'Modern Architecture in the Age of Cinema: Mies van der Rohe and the Moving Image', PhD thesis, Princeton University, 2012
Ross, Alex, *Wagnerism: Art and Politics in the Shadow of Music*, London: 4th Estate, 2021
Rouché, Jacques, *L'Art théâtral moderne*, Paris: Edouard Cornély, 1910
Roussou, Matei, 'L'exposition internationale de theatre d'Amsterdam', *Le Monde illustré*, 18 March 1922, 193–94
Saddy, Pierre, 'Le Corbusier chez les riches: l'appartement Charles de Beistegui', *Architecture, mouvement, continuité*, 49 (1979), 57–70
'Le Corbusier e l'Arlecchino', *Rassegna* 3 (July 1980), 25–32
Saddy, Pierre, and Claude Malécot, eds, *Le Corbusier: Le passé à réaction poétique*, Paris: Caisse nationale des Monuments historiques et des Sites/Ministère de la Culture et de la Communication, 1988
Sadler, Michael Ernest, *The Eurhythmics of Jaques-Dalcroze*, Boston: Small Maynard, 1915
Salzmann, Alexander von, 'Licht, Belichtung und Beleuchtung', in *Claudel-Programmbuch*, 88–91, Hellerau: Hellerau Verlag, 1913
Säuberlich, Hartmut, 'Richard Wagner und die Probleme des Bühnenbildes seiner Werke im 19. Jahrhundert', PhD thesis, University of Kiel, 1966
Sauser, Ernest, 'Le Téléphot', *Revue suisse de photographie* 18 (1906), 269–72
Sbriglio, Jacques, *L'Unité d'habitation de Marseille*, Basel: Birkhäuser, 2004
Le Corbusier & Lucien Hervé: A Dialogue Between Architect and Photographer, Los Angeles: Getty Publications, 2011
Schäfer, Walter Erich, *Wieland Wagner: Persönlichkeit und Leistung*, Tübingen: Wunderlich, 1970
Scheffler, Karl, 'Das Ehrenmal', *Kunst und Künstler* 29, no 10 (1931), 399
'Das Haus', in *Der Rhythmus, Ein Jahrbuch*, vol 2, 2–13, Jena: Eugen Diederichs, 1913
Die fetten und die mageren Jahre, Munich: P List, 1946
'Heinrich Tessenow', *Kunst und Künstler* 11, no 1 (1913), 41–53.
Scheltema, Marie Adama van, 'Charakterbild des Meisters', in *Hellerau leuchtete: Zeitzeugenberichte und Erinnerungen*, edited by Erhardt Heinold and Günther Großer, 123–40, Dresden: Verlag der Kunst, 2007
Schiller, Friedrich, 'Der Taucher', in *Musen-Almanach für das Jahr 1798*, 119–30, Tübingen: J G Cotta, 1798
'Über die ästhetische Erziehung des Menschen in einer Reyhe von Briefen', *Die Horen* 1 (1795), Letter 9
'Über die ästhetische Erziehung des Menschen in einer Reyhe von Briefen', *Die Horen* 6 (1795), Letter 22
Schlemmer, Oskar, 'Bühne', *Bauhaus: Zeitschrift für Bau und Gestaltung* 1, no 3 (July 1927)
'Mensch und Kunstfigur', in *Bauhausbücher 4: Die Bühne im Bauhaus*, edited by Walter Gropius and L Moholy-Nagy, 7–24, Munich: Albert Langen, 1924
Schlemmer, Tut, *The Letters and Diaries of Oskar Schlemmer, Selected and Edited by Tut Schlemmer*, translated by Krishna Winton, Evanston, Illinois: Northwestern University Press, 1972
Schlosser, Heinrich, 'Die Zürcher Theaterkunstausstellung', *Das Werk: Architektur und Kunst* 1, no 3 (1914), 13–16
Schmidt, Karl, 'Die Gründung von Hellerau', in *Hellerau leuchtete: Zeitzeugenberichte und Erinnerungen*, edited by Erhardt Heinold and Günther Großer, 17–24, Dresden: Verlag der Kunst, 2007
Schnack, Friedrich, 'Mein Hellerauer Zeit war zu Ende', in *Hellerau leuchtete: Zeitzeugenberichte und Erinnerungen*, 415–24, Dresden: Verlag der Kunst, 2007
Schuldenfrei, Robin, 'Images in Exile: Lucia Moholy's Bauhaus Negatives and the Construction of the Bauhaus Legacy', *History of Photography* 37, no 2 (May 2013), 182–203
Schulz, Eberhard, 'Albert Speers Gefängnisbuch', in *Albert Speer: Kontroversen um ein deutsches Phänomen*, edited by Adelbert Reif, 473–79, Königsberg: Bernard & Graefe, 1978
Schulze, Franz, *Mies van der Rohe: A Critical Biography*, Chicago: Chicago University Press, 1985
Schuré, Édouard, 'Le drame musical et l'œuvre de Monsieur Richard Wagner', *Revue des Deux Mondes* 80, no 4 (April 1869), 948–91
Schwarz, Rudolf, *Kirchenbau: Welt vor der Schwelle*, Heidelberg: F H Kerle, 1960
The Church Incarnate: The Sacred Function of Christian Architecture, translated by Cynthia Harris, Chicago: Henry Regnery, 1958
Von der Bebauung der Erde, Salzburg: Verlag Anton Pustet, 1949
Seligman, Albert Franz, 'Josef Hoffmann und Richard Wagner', *Neue Freie Presse, Wien*, 4 October 1906
Semper, Gottfried, *Die Vier Elemente der Baukunst*, Braunschweig: Friedrich Vieweg und Sohn, 1851
Sereny, Gitta, *Albert Speer: His Battle with Truth*, London: Macmillan, 1995
Serlio, Sebastiano, *Sebastiano Serlio: On Architecture, Books I–V of 'Tutte l'opere d'architettura et Prospetiva'*, vol 1, translated by Vaughan Hart and Peter Hicks, New Haven: Yale University Press, 1996
Shakespeare, William, 'Macbeth', in *Four Tragedies*, 841–951, London: Penguin, 1994
Shakespeare, William, *Hamlet*, London: Penguin Classics, 1980
Shaw, George Bernard, *The Quintessence of Ibsenism*, London: Walter Scott, 1891
Siefert, Rebecca, 'Lauretta Vinciarelli Illuminated', *AA Files* 75 (2017), 71–85

Simonsen, Lee, 'The Designer and the Theatre', in *International Exhibition of Theatre Art*, 11–21, New York: Museum of Modern Art, 1934

Sinclair, Upton, 'Music Made Visible', in *World's End*, 11–24, London: T Werner Laurie, 1948

Skelton, Geoffrey, *Wieland Wagner: The Positive Sceptic*, London: Gollancz, 1971

Sonntag, Nina, *Raumtheater: Adolphe Appias theaterästhetische Konzeption in Hellerau*, Essen: Klartext, 2011

Speer, Albert, *Erinnerungen*, Frankfurt am Main: Ullstein, 1969

Neue deutsche Baukunst, Berlin: Volk und Reich, 1941

Spandauer Tagebücher, Berlin: Ullstein, 2005

Stadler, Edmund, 'Adolphe Appia and Richard Wagner', in *Adolphe Appia*, edited by John Pope-Hennessy, London: V&A Museum, 1970

'Jaques-Dalcroze et Adolphe Appia', in *Émile Jaques-Dalcroze: L'homme, le compositeur, le créateur de la rythmique*, 413–59, Neuchâtel: Editions de la Baconnière, 1965

Statius, Publius Papinius, *Silvae*, edited and translated by D R Shackleton Bailey, Loeb Classical Library 206, Cambridge, MA: Harvard University Press, 2015

Steffan, Beat, *Emil Pirchan: Universal Artist*, Wädenswil: NIMBUS, Kunst und Bücher, 2018

Stölzl, Christoph, *Die Neue Wache Unter den Linden: Ein Deutsches Denkmal im Wandel der Geschichte*, Berlin: Koehler & Amelang, 1993

Stonehouse, Roger, *Colin St John Wilson*, London: Black Dog, 2007

Storck, Karl, *E Jaques-Dalcroze: Seine Stellung und Aufgabe in unserer Zeit*, Stuttgart: Greiner und Pfeiffer, 1912

Strobel, Otto, ed, *Königsbriefe: König Ludwig II und Richard Wagner – Briefwechsel*, vol 3, Karlsruhe: G Braun, 1936

Sturm, Hermann, *Alltag & Kult: Gottfried Semper, Richard Wagner, Friedrich Theodor Vischer, Gottfried Keller*, Basel: Birkhäuser, 2003

'Sur les toits de Paris: Le jardin enchanté de Monsieur Charles de Beistegui', photographs by George Buffotot, *Vogue* (France), October 1932, 54–55

Syberberg, Hans-Jürgen, director, *Winifred Wagner und die Geschichte des Hauses Wahnfried, 1914–1975*, Bayerischer Rundfunk, 1975

Tafuri, Manfredo, 'The City in the Work of Le Corbusier', in *Le Corbusier*, edited by H Allen Brooks, 203–18, Princeton: Princeton University Press, 1987

The Sphere and the Labyrinth: Avant-Gardes and Architecture from Piranesi to the 1970s, Cambridge, MA: MIT Press, 1987

Tallon, Mary Elizabeth, 'Appia's Theatre at Hellerau', *Theatre Journal* 36, no 4 (December 1984), 495–504

Tesch, Sebastian, *Albert Speer (1905–1981)*, Vienna: Böhlau, 2016

International Exhibition of Theatre Art, New York: Museum of Modern Art, 1934

The Le Corbusier Archive, vol 8, *Appartement de Beistegui, Cité Univérsitaire–Pavillon Suisse, Ville Radieuse, and Other Buildings and Projects, 1930*, edited by H Allen Brooks, New York: Garland and Fondation Le Corbusier, 1982

The Le Corbusier Archive, vol 20, *Ronchamp, Maison Jaoul, and Other Buildings and Projects, 1951–1952*, edited by H Allen Brooks, New York: Garland and Fondation Le Corbusier, 1983

The Mies van der Rohe Archive: Illustrated Catalogue of the Mies van der Rohe Drawings in the Museum of Modern Art, vol 5, *Robert F Carr Memorial of Saint Savior, S R Crown Hall and Other Buildings and Projects*, edited by Arthur Drexler, New York: Garland Publishing, 1986

Thomas, Helen, 'Rudolf Schwarz and Another Kind of Modernism', *AA Files* 73 (2016), 163–82

Trahndorf, Eusebius, *Ästhetik, oder Lehre von der Weltanschauung und Kunst*, Berlin: Maurer, 1827

Trimmingham, Melissa, *The Theatre of the Bauhaus: The Modern and Postmodern Stage of Oskar Schlemmer*, New York: Routledge, 2011

Van Vechten, Carl, 'Adolphe Appia and Gordon Craig', *Forum* 17, no 10 (1915), 483–87

'Adolphe Appia and Gordon Craig', in *Music After the Great War, and Other Studies*, 159–68, New York: G Schirmer, 1915

Van Wyck, Jessica Davis, 'Designing Hamlet with Appia', *Theatre Arts Monthly* 9, no 1 (January 1925), 17–19

'Working With Appia', *Theatre Arts Monthly* 8, no 12 (December 1924), 815–18

Vazsonyi, Nicholas, 'Reading Right from Left: Hans Mayer and Postwar Wagner Reception', *Opera Quarterly* 30, no 2 (2014), 228–45

Veinstein, André, 'Redécouvrons Adolphe Appia', *Cahiers de la Compagnie Madeleine Renaud - Jean-Louis Barrault* 3, no 10 (1955)

Vidler, Anthony, 'Beistegui Apartment, or Horizons Deferred', in *Le Corbusier: An Atlas of Modern Landscapes*, edited by Jean-Louis Cohen, 274–79, New York: Museum of Modern Art, 2013

Vogel, Carl, 'Die letzte Krankheit Goethes, beschrieben und nebst einigen andern Bemerkungen über denselben', *Journal der practischen Heilkunde* 76 (1833), 17

Volbach, Walther R, *Adolphe Appia: Prophet of the Modern Theatre*, Middletown: Wesleyan University Press, 1968

'Adolphe Appia und Houston Stewart Chamberlain', *Die Musikforschung* 18, no 4 (October/December 1965), 379–89

'Appia's Productions and Contemporary Reaction', *Educational Theatre Journal* 13, no 1 (March 1961), 1–10

'Jacques Copeau, Appia's Finest Disciple', *Educational Theatre Journal* 17, no 3 (October 1965), 206–14

'Time and Space on the Stage', *Educational Theatre Journal* 19, no 2 (May 1967), 134–41

Vuillermoz, Émile, *La Musique des images*, in *L'art cinématographique*, 39–66, Paris: Felix Alcan, 1927

Wagner, Cosima, *Das zweite Leben: Briefe und Aufzeichnungen 1883–1930*, edited by Dietrich Mack, Munich: R Piper, 1980

Wagner, Richard, 'A Communication to My Friends', in *Collected Prose Works*, vol 1, *The Artwork of the Future and Other Works*, translated by William Ashton Ellis, New York: Broude Bros, 1966

Bayreuther Briefe Richard Wagners, 1871–1883, edited by Carl Friedrich Glasenapp, Berlin: Schuster & Loeffler, 1907

Das Bühnenfestspielhaus zu Bayreuth nebst einem Berichte über die Grundsteinlegung desselben, Mit sechs architectonischen Plänen, Leipzig: E W Fritzsch, 1873

Das Kunstwerk der Zukunft, Leipzig: Otto Wigand, 1850

Das Rheingold: Vollstandiger Klavierauszug von Karl Klindworth, Mainz: Schott, 1861

Das Rheingold, Vorspiel zu der Trilogie: Der Ring des Nibelungen von Richard Wagner, Mainz: Schott's Söhne, 1876

Die Kunst und die Revolution, Leipzig: Otto Wigand, 1849

Die Walküre, Erster Tag aus der Trilogie: Der Ring des Nibelungen von Richard Wagner, Mainz: Schott's Söhne, 1876

Götterdämmerung, Dritter Tag aus der Trilogie: Der Ring des Nibelungen von Richard Wagner, Mainz: Schott's Söhne, 1876

Lohengrin, translated by Amanda Holden, London: John Calder, 1993

My Life, edited by Mary Whittall, translated by Andrew Gray, Cambridge: Cambridge University Press, 1983

Oper und Drama, Leipzig: J J Weber, 1851

Parsifal: Ein Bühnenweihfestspiel, Mainz: Schott's Söhne, 1877

'Religion und Kunst (1880)', in *Sämtliche Schriften und Dichtungen*, vol 10, 211–53, Leipzig: Breitkopf & Härtel, 1911

Selected Letters of Richard Wagner, translated by Stewart Spencer and Barry Millington, London: Dent, 1987

Siegfried, Zweiter Tag aus der Trilogie: Der Ring des Nibelungen von Richard Wagner, Mainz: Schott's Söhne, 1876

Twilight of the Gods: The Essential Wagner Collection: Six Track Sampler, Deutsche Grammophon, 1998, compact disc

'Über die Ouvertüre (1841)', in *Sämtliche Schriften und Dichtungen*, vol 1, 194–206, Leipzig: Breitkopf & Härtel, 1911

Wagner, Wieland, 'Denkmalschutz für Wagner?' *Österreichische Musikzeitschrift* 13, no 9 (September 1958), 357–61

'Überlieferung und Neugestaltung', *Maske und Kothurn* 1, nos 3–4 (1955), 214–18

Wälterlin, Oskar, 'Adolphe Appia und die Inszenierung von Wagners "Ring",' in *Bekenntnis zum Theater*, 12–26, Zurich: Opprecht, 1955

Werfel, Franz, 'Die Bühne von Hellerau', *Die neue Rundschau* 25 (November 1913), 1623–24

White, Hayden, 'The Question of Narrative in Contemporary Historical Theory', *History and Theory* 23, no 1 (February 1984), 1–33

Wieland Wagner inszeniert Richard Wagner, Constance: Rosgarten, 1960

Wijdeveld, Hendrik, ed, 'Internationale Theater Tentoonstellung Amsterdam 1922', *Wendingen* 4, nos 9–10 (1921)

Wilczek, Ida, 'Die Festspieltage in Bayreuth', *Wissen und Leben* 4 (1909), 141–44

Winckelmann, Robert, *Der Genfer Protest und J-D Ausschuss zur Gründung eine Vereins zur Erhaltung der Methode J-D in Deutschland, Die Tatsachen über die Lostrennung der Bildungsanstalt von ihrem bisherigen Leiter J-D*, Berlin, 1914

Wolkonsky, Serge, 'Адольф Аппиа' (Adolphe Appia), Аполлон, литературный альманах *(Apollo: A Literary Almanac)* 6 (1912), 25–31

'Die Wende in meinem Leben', in *Hellerau leuchtete*, edited by Erhardt Heinold and Günther Großer, 198–212, Dresden: Verlag der Kunst, 2007

'Meine Erinnerungen', in *In Memoriam Hellerau*, edited by E Feudel, Freiburg im Breisgau: Rombach, 1960

Wolzogen, Hans von, 'Literarische Anzeigen: Adolphe Appia, La Mise-en-scène du drame wagnérien', *Bayreuther Blätter* 18, nos 4–5 (1895)

Woolf, Virginia, 'Impressions at Bayreuth', in *The Essays of Virginia Woolf*, vol 1, *1904–1912*, edited by Andrew McNellie and Stuart N Clarke, 288–93, New York: Harcourt Brace, 1967

Wyss, Beat, and Denise Bratton, 'Ragnarök of Illusion: Richard Wagner's 'Mystical Abyss' at Bayreuth', *October* 54 (1990), 57–78

Xenakis, Iannis, 'The Monastery of La Tourette', in *Le Corbusier*, edited by H Allen Brooks, 143–47, Princeton: Princeton University Press, 1987

Yates, Douglas, *Franz Grillparzer: A Critical Biography*, Oxford: B Blackwell, 1946

'Grillparzer's Hero and Shakespeare's Juliet', *Modern Language Review* 21, no 4 (October 1926), 419–25

Zadow, Mario, *Karl Friedrich Schinkel: Ein Sohn der Spätaufklärung*, Stuttgart: Axel Menges, 2001

Zelger, Franz, *Arnold Böcklin: Die Toteninsel: Selbstheroisierung und Abgesang der abendländischen Kultur*, Frankfurt am Main: Fischer, 1991

Zemka, Sue, 'Wagner's Opera of Redemption: 'Parsifal' at Bayreuth', *Criticism* 27, no 3 (1985), 263–82

Zinsstag, Adolf, 'Die Prostitution eines Kunstwerkes am Basler Stadttheater', *Rundschau Bürgerzeitung*, 6 February 1925

'Kunstfeindliches aus Basel', *Rundschau Bürgerzeitung*, 9 April 1925

'Via Appia', *Rundschau Bürgerzeitung*, 27 February 1925

'Zur neu-Inszenierung des Nibelungenringes', *Rundschau Bürgerzeitung*, 23 January 1925

Zuckerman, Elliot, *The First Hundred Years of Wagner's Tristan*, New York: Columbia University Press, 1964

Zutter, Jörg, 'La musique rendue visible', in *Adolphe Appia ou le renouveau de l'esthétique théâtrale: dessins et esquisses de décors*, edited by Jörg Zutter, 109–22, Lausanne: Éditions Payot, 1992, *Ludwig II und Richard Wagner – Briefwechsel*, vol 3, Karlsruhe: G Braun, 1936

Index

Image Credits

Copyright holders and sources are listed below. Every effort has been made to trace copyright holders and to obtain permission for the use of copyrighted material.

Ross Anderson *pp 372, 410–11*
Adolphe Appia, *L'Œuvre d'art vivant*, 1921 *pp 242, 243*
Adolphe Appia and Jessica Van Wyck, 'Six Designs for Hamlet', 1925 *pp 278, 279, 280, 282, 283, 284–85*
Bibliothèque de Genève, Centre d'iconographie *pp 21, 22 (above), 22 (below), 44, 45, 46, 120, 123, 125, 128, 129, 130, 131, 132, 133, 134–35, 142, 145, 180 (above), 180 (below), 181 (above), 181 (below), 192 (above), 192 (below), 193 (above), 193 (below), 194–95, 196, 203 (above), 203 (below), 209, 211, 212–13, 215 (above), 215 (below), 218, 220–21, 222–23, 225, 226, 307, 349 (below), 351, 436*
Bibliothèque nationale de France *pp 98–99*
© Bildarchiv Foto Marburg *pp 197, 337*
© bpk / Staatliche Museen zu Berlin, Kunstbibliothek *p 335*
© bpk / Staatliche Museen zu Berlin, Kunstbibliothek / Dietmar Katz *pp 161, 162*
Edward H Castens, ed, *The Story of the 446th Bomb Group*, 1946 *p 352*
Chicago History Museum, Hedrich-Blessing Collection *p 357*
© Columbia University, Rare Book and Manuscript Library *pp 270, 271*
© Deutsche Fotothek *p 179*
© Deutsche Fotothek / Fritz Eschen *p 114 (below)*
© Deutsche Fotothek / Li Naewiger *p 116 (above)*
© Deutsche Fotothek / Martin Würker *p 24 (below)*
© Deutsche Fotothek / Messbildstelle Dresden *p 336*
© Deutsche Fotothek / Walter Möbius *pp 24 (above), 48*
Deutsche Grammophon Gesellschaft mbH *p 348*
Deutsches Theatermuseum, Munich *pp 72–73, 150–51, 254, 255, 256–57*
Drawing Matter *p 334*
EPFL, Lausanne, Archives de la construction Moderne, Fonds Alberto Sartoris *p 165*
ETH Zürich Library *p 20 (above)*
ETH Zürich Library / Swissair Photo AG *p 169*
© Lyonel Feininger, VG Bild-Kunst/ Copyright Agency 2024 / Beinecke Rare Book and Manuscript Library, Yale University, New Haven *p 234*
© Fondation Le Corbusier, ADAGP / Copyright Agency 2024 *pp 217, 245*
© Fondation Le Corbusier, ADAGP / Copyright Agency 2024 / © J Paul Getty Trust / Lucien Hervé *pp 364, 365, 368, 369, 370–71*
© Fondation Le Corbusier, ADAGP / Copyright Agency 2024 / Marius Gravot *p 333*
Walter Gropius and L Moholy-Nagy, eds, *Bauhausbücher 4: Die Bühne im Bauhaus*, 1924 *p 236*
Harvard Art Museums, Cambridge Mass *pp 13 (detail), 14–15*
Harvard Art Museums, Cambridge Mass, Busch-Reisinger Museum, Gift of Herbert Bayer *p 237*
Émile Jaques-Dalcroze, La Rythmique, 1916 *p 124*
Albert Jeanneret, 'La Rythmique 1', 1920 *p 239*
© KHM-Museumsverband, Theatermuseum, Vienna *pp 41, 340*
Le Corbusier-Saugnier, 'Architecture III: Pure création de l'esprit', 1922 *pp 241 (above), 241 (below)*
Curt Moreck, 'Bühnenbilder von Emil Pirchan,' 1920 *pp 316, 317*
© Musée d'Art et d'Histoire, Ville de Genève *pp 159 (above), 159 (below), 170–71, 175, 176–77, 182–83, 184, 186 (above), 186 (below), 187 (above), 187 (below), 205, 248, 249, 258, 259, 288–89, 302, 303, 304–05, 310–11*
Museum für angewandte Kunst, Vienna *p 376*
Museum of Modern Art, New York / Scala, Florence *p 331*
National Library of Norway, Oslo *p 119*
Nationalarchiv der Richard-Wagner-Stiftung, Bayreuth *pp 32, 35, 36, 39*
Nationalarchiv der Richard-Wagner-Stiftung, Bayreuth, Zustiftung Wieland Wagner *pp 344, 345, 346–47, 349 (above), 382–83*
Österreichisches Nationalbibliothek, Vienna *pp 23, 308, 309, 342, 343*
Private Collection *pp 27, 31, 42, 96, 97 (above), 97 (centre), 97 (below), 109, 114 (above), 115, 117, 143, 188, 189, 214, 232–33, 252, 326, 358–59, 360, 361, 363, 366, 367, 384, 390, 396, 402, 407, 409, 428–29*
Pro Helvetia *p 378*
Reed College Archives *p 379*
© Albert Renger-Patzsch/Copyright Agency 2024 / Canadian Centre for Architecture, Montréal *p 354*
Arthur Seidl, 'Die hellerauer Schulfeste und die 'Bildungsanstalt Jaques-Dalcroze', 1912 *pp 208 (above), 208 (centre), 208 (below)*
Swiss Archive of the Performing Arts, Bern *pp 20 (below), 43, 47 (above), 47 (below), 51, 54–55, 56, 57, 58, 59 (above), 59 (below), 60–61, 68, 69, 70, 74 (above), 75 (above), 75 (below), 76–77, 86 (above), 86 (below), 87 (above), 87 (below), 88 (above left), 88 (above right), 88 (below left), 88 (below right), 89, 102, 103, 104–05, 110, 111, 113, 136–37, 141 (above), 141 (below), 148–49, 152–53, 154, 155 (above), 155 (centre), 155 (below), 156, 157, 166–67, 172, 173, 174, 185, 191, 198, 199, 200–01, 204, 206–07, 230, 231, 238, 250, 251, 260, 261 (above), 261 (below), 264–65, 266 (above), 266 (below), 267, 268, 269, 272 (above left), 272 (centre left), 272 (below left), 272 (above right), 272 (centre right), 272 (below right) 273, 274, 275 (above left), 275 (centre left), 275 (below left), 275 (above right), 275 (centre right), 275 (below right), 290 (above left), 290 (centre left), 290 (below left), 290 (above right), 290 (centre right), 290 (below right), 291 (above left), 291 (centre left), 291 (below left), 291 (above right), 291 (centre right), 291 (below right), 292–93, 294, 295, 296–97, 298, 299, 312–13, 314 (above), 314 (below), 315 (above), 315 (below), 318–19, 320 (above left), 320 (centre left), 320 (below left), 320 (above right), 320 (centre right), 320 (below right), 321 (above left), 321 (centre left), 321 (below left), 321 (above right), 321 (centre right), 321 (below right), 322 (above), 322 (centre), 322 (below), 323*
Swiss National Library, Bern, Prints and Drawings, Poster Collection *p 377*
Teatro all Scala, Milan *pp 253 (above), 253 (centre), 253 (below)*
Technische Universität Berlin, Architekturmuseum *pp 25, 26 (above), 26 (below), 38, 92, 93, 94–95, 100, 101, 338–39*
Theaterwissenschaftliche Sammlung, Universität zu Köln *pp 85, 262–63*

Universitätsarchiv der TU Darmstadt, Otto-Bartning-Archiv *p 353*
Serge Wolkonsky, 'Адольф Аппиа (Adolphe Appia)', 1912 *p 146*
Yale University, New Haven, Beinecke Rare Book and Manuscript Library *pp 63, 64, 65, 79, 80, 81*
Yale University, New Haven, Beinecke Rare Book and Manuscript Library, Donald Oenslager Collection of Adolphe Appia *pp 49, 71, 74 (below)*
Yale University, New Haven, Beinecke Rare Book and Manuscript Library, Walther Volbach Collection on Adolphe Appia *pp 16, 19, 324, 328*
Yale University, New Haven, Irvin S Gilmore Music Library *p 40*
Zürcher Hochschule der Künste *p 229*

cover image
Adolphe Appia, *Iphigenia at Aulis*, Act 3, Scene 2, 48.3 × 63.3 cm, 1926.

appendix images
Adolphe Appia (1862–1928): Zwanzig Faksimilies aus seinem bühnenbildnerischen Entwurfswerk, 1993; steps rising up to the twin columns that mark the termination of the Via Appia in Brindisi.

VOTA

Acknowledgements

This book was 25 years in the making and as the pages accrued so too did my debts of gratitude. These begin with Peter Carl, who not only introduced me to Adolphe Appia's drawings but helped shape my understanding of the broader conditions of modernity within which they reside. And it was Peter who encouraged me to approach Thomas Weaver with a proposition for an essay on Appia for *AA Files*. Tom said yes, marking the beginning of our decade-long collaboration. It has been a pleasure to work with an editor of Tom's nous, knowledge, experience and enthusiasm, and I thank him wholeheartedly. Over the years Tom has cultivated a talented and committed team, including text editor Pamela Johnston, who refined and elevated my writing, and book designer Mathias Clottu, who both captured Appia's aesthetic and delivered his own beautifully assured design. Mathias was most ably supported in his studio by Valérian Charmasson, and I thank him sincerely too.

Several colleagues in Sydney and abroad reviewed and gave insightful comment on drafts of the manuscript, while others provided less tangible but equally valuable support during the years I was writing it. Thanks to: Justine Anderson, Deborah Barnstone, Jason Dibbs, Robyn Dowling, Hannes Frykholm, Kate Goodwin, Tom Heneghan, Maren Koehler, Catherine Lassen, Andrew Leach, Kevin Liu, Cameron Logan, Jasper Ludewig, Matthew Mindrup, Rizal Muslimin, Daniel Ryan, Héctor Solari, Maximilian Sternberg, Lee Stickells, Thomas Strombeg and Michael Tawa. Sean Akahane-Bryen deserves special mention, having contributed in multiple substantial ways to the realisation of this book in the twin domains of word and image. I am very grateful to him both for the expert assistance he provided and the calm and infallible manner with which he did so.

Numerous institutions granted me generous access to materials in their collections, and I extend my thanks to the host of gracious staff who first of all welcomed me into their archives and then ensured my research was able to proceed smoothly from half a world away during the challenging times of the global pandemic: Simona Generelli at the Swiss Archive of Performing Arts in Bern; Christian Rumelin at the Musée d'art et d'histoire de Genève; Eloi Contesse at the Centre d'iconographie de la Bibliothèque de Genève; Isabelle Godineau at the Fondation Le Corbusier in Paris; Moira Fitzgerald at the Beinecke Rare Book and Manuscript Library at Yale University in New Haven; and Theodor Böll at the Kunstbibliothek in Berlin.

I am deeply appreciative for the financial support provided by various organisations and individuals, including the Ernst Göhner Stiftung, Elise Jaffe, The Leonard A Lauder Research Center for Modern Art at the Metropolitan Museum of Art, and The University of Sydney.

On a personal note, I would like to express heartfelt thanks to my dear friends and family for their unwavering love and support. My friendships with Chris L Smith in Sydney and Sören Chun in Berlin are two that are especially dear to me. I am profoundly grateful to my parents Colin and Narelle Anderson, and to my brother Peter and sister Katrina, for their lifelong love and encouragement. Finally, I would like to thank Almut Weiler Anderson for all the years we shared together, and above all for our boundless daughter Hannah, to whom this book is dedicated.

A Note on the Type

The main body of this book is set in Lexicon No 2, designed by Dutch typographer Bram de Does for the *Van Dale Groot woordenboek van de Nederlandse taal*, the most commonly used dictionary of the Dutch language. Its publisher had originally looked to use an earlier de Does typeface – Trinité – but the unusually small, 7pt size of the printed type led de Does to suggest that he develop a new letter face specifically for the dictionary. Ultimately, two versions of Lexicon were produced, No 1 – the dictionary version – which because of its printed size has very small ascenders, and No 2, which has more regular proportions and which was released by The Enschedé Font Foundry in 1995. Like Trinité, Lexicon shows the influence of Renaissance typography and the calligraphic flourishes of broad-nibbed pens, as much as it reflects the perfectionism of its designer, a man who once insisted that a book of his design be printed using paper made according to his own recipe.

The display face used for the book's cover, section dividers and initial caps is set in LL Heymland, a revival of Antiqua, a rather eccentric decorative typeface designed in 1922 by Rudolf Koch and then heavily promoted by the Klingspor foundry throughout the 1930s. Koch seems to be something of a kindred spirit to Adolphe Appia, devout in both his faith and loyalty to his trade, and more than a little idiosyncratic – his love of the English arts and crafts once prompted him to declare that 'I feel such a closeness to William Morris that I have always had the feeling that he cannot be an Englishman, he must be a German'. The story goes that an unsigned, undated study of Antiqua was found by Ukrainian type designer Yevgeniy Anfalov among the archival papers of legendary Soviet graphic artist Solomon Telingater, who with Rodchenko, Eisenstein and Lissitzky had helped found the October group. Prompted by this discovery, Anfalov developed a revival which he named after the Yiddish word for 'homeland' (*Sovetish Heymland* was also a celebrated literary magazine designed by Telingater and published in 1961), and which stripped Koch's original design of those elements he deemed superfluous, while still maintaining its obvious quirkiness.—*Thomas Weaver*

The Appian Way: Adolphe Appia and the Scenography of Modern Architecture
Ross Anderson

Edited by Thomas Weaver

Text editing: Pamela Johnston
Proofreading: Colette Forder
Design: Studio Mathias Clottu
Image processing: Marjeta Morinc
Print: Gugler, Austria

Park Books AG
Niederdorfstrasse 54
8001 Zurich
Switzerland
www.park-books.com
T +41 44 262 16 62
E info@park-books.com

Product Safety
Responsible person pursuant to EU Regulation 2023/988 (GPSR):
GVA Gemeinsame Verlagsauslaieferung Göttingen GmbH & Co KG
Post Box 2021
37010 Göttingen
Germany
T +49 551 384 200 0
E info@gva-verlage.de

Park Books is supported by the Federal Office of Culture with a general subsidy for the years 2021–2025.

ISBN 978-3-03860-405-1